HOW CIVIC ACTION WORKS

PRINCETON STUDIES IN CULTURAL SOCIOLOGY
Paul J. DiMaggio, Michèle Lamont,
Robert J. Wuthnow, and Viviana A. Zelizer,
Series Editors

For a full list of titles in the series, go to https://press.princeton.edu/series/princeton-studies-in-cultural-sociology.

How Civic Action Works

FIGHTING FOR HOUSING
IN LOS ANGELES

PAUL LICHTERMAN

PRINCETON UNIVERSITY PRESS

PRINCETON & OXFORD

Published by Princeton University Press
41 William Street, Princeton, New Jersey 08540
6 Oxford Street, Woodstock, Oxfordshire OX20 1TR

press.princeton.edu

Library of Congress Control Number: 2020944358
ISBN 9780691212333
ISBN (pbk.) 9780691177519
ISBN (e-book) 9780691200040

British Library Cataloging-in-Publication Data is available

Editorial: Meagan Levinson and Jacqueline Delaney
Production Editorial: Karen Carter
Jacket/Cover Design: Karl Spurzem
Production: Erin Suydam
Publicity: Kate Hensley and Kathryn Stevens
Copyeditor: Cindy Milstein

This book has been composed in Arno

Printed on acid-free paper. ∞

Printed in the United States of America

10 9 8 7 6 5 4 3 2 1

CONTENTS

ACKNOWLEDGMENTS

A LONG-RUNNING project with a lot of moving parts encounters a lot of contingencies. I am thankful that people from the world of LA housing advocacy met me at these forks in the road with openness, kindness, and good humor. I regret that I will not be able to thank everyone for everything here. If it were not for several extraordinarily helpful people, this would have been a different and thinner book. I am deeply grateful to Francis for welcoming me to several of the sites in this study and helping me understand how a broad-based campaign for affordable housing works. His organizer's savvy enlightened and inspired me. I heartily thank Ethan, too, for taking a chance and inviting me to an antidisplacement campaign. Theresa's thoughtful hospitality knew no bounds, and she never seemed to tire of that guy she kept seeing at different meetings around town. Participants in the three coalitions and four campaigns were graciously inclusive, honored me with their insights and wit, never asked why I was still there, and gave the lie to easy folk wisdom about how superficial and rootless Angelenos are.

Some of the empirical exploring and conceptual questioning that became this book was nurtured early on in conversations with members of two collaborations supported by the National Science Foundation. Thanks to Chris Weare, Juliet Musso, Ann Crigler, Nina Eliasoph, and Nicole Esparza. Many thanks to the National Science Foundation for support of this work (grants SES-0719760 and SES-1024478). Ethnographic research really does benefit, immensely, from paid course release for the fieldwork. Support from the Spencer Foundation allowed me to try out ideas about the different ways people attach to and learn from civic organizations. I am grateful as well to the Robert Wood Johnson Foundation for supporting my initial research on the rhetoric of housing advocacy. Housing problems can indeed be health problems too.

How great to have previewed various parts of this work for such attentive audiences at the University of California at Davis, Boston University, University of Paris VIII, University of Notre Dame, Universität Erfurt, École des Hautes Études en Sciences Sociales, Center for American Political Studies at Harvard University, Center for Cultural Sociology at Yale University, University of California at Irvine, University of Pennsylvania, Tulane University,

University of California at Los Angeles, University of Tampere, University of Chicago, Forschungskolleg Humanwissenschaften, Institute for Social Research at Goethe-Universität Frankfurt am Main, University of Milano-Bicocca, and University of Trento. Thanks to everyone who shared their wisdom, good humor, cautionary tales, and more on these sorties and sojourns, including John Hall, Robert Fishman, Michele Lamont, Evan Schofer, Jeff Alexander, Richard Swedberg, Melissa Wilde, Mimi Schippers (who reminded me that I don't need to tell readers everything in chapter 1), Stephen Ostertag, Stefan Bargheer, Kevan Harris, Aliza Luft, John Martin, Lis Clemens, Kimberly Hoang, Kristen Schilts, Terry Clark, Omar McRoberts, Mario Diani, Daniel Cefaï, Édouard Gardella, Erwan Lemener, Danny Trom, Violaine Roussel, Jörg Rupke, Mathieu Berger, and Julien Charles, who also made time for bike adventures on slag heaps. Thanks to Eric Doidy for adventuring with me into the thickets of cross-national ethnographic comparison. Laurent Thévenot generously shared seasoned perspective as I sought out points of convergence between French pragmatism and the more strictly US version, and once treated me to a suspiciously sanguineous appetizer, the name of which he wouldn't say. I still am pondering marvelous conversations with Ferdinand Sutterlüty, and grateful he hosted me for a summer of thinking and writing in 2019 at the Forschungskolleg Humanwissenschaften in Bad Homburg. I am delighted to have learned from and chuckled with Till van Rahden, Keti Gurchiani (whose work reminds me that field insights won't always stay put in my categories), Felix Stielen, Christian Sperneac-Wolfer, Yael Peled, Orit Bashkin, Sanjay Reddy, my other fellow Fellows, and administrator Beate Sutterlüty at the FKH, and look forward to much more conversation.

Thanks also to audiences at the annual American Sociological Association conferences in 2013, 2014, 2016, and 2018 for thoughts on this work. The *American Journal of Sociology*'s Causal Thinking and Ethnographic Research conference in 2012, the Pragmatism and Sociology conference in 2015, and a follow-up conference, Sociology and Pragmatism: Renewing the Conversation, offered wonderfully generative forums for trying out some conceptual story lines that are woven into this book. I'm grateful, too, to editors and reviewers at the *American Journal of Sociology*, *Sociological Theory*, and *Social Science and Medicine* for comments that improved arguments I continued and expanded here.

Over the years I have shared intellectual gambits, raw guesses, or raw drafts from this study with Mabel Berezin, Sebastiano Citroni, Andreas Glaeser, Isaac Reed, David Smilde, Lyn Spillman, and Rhys Williams. I'm lucky to have learned from and with colleagues, coauthors, and friends who join in intellectual commitments bigger than any of us. I'm grateful to Nina Eliasoph for weaving with me a rich fabric of living, writing, and pondering together. She shares the civic action idea with me and shared sparkling insights that enriched other themes in this book. Thanks and warm hugs to Leo, who came with me on fieldwork excursions, and Olivia, whose own civic action is endlessly inspiring.

This project continued beyond the lives of some people who inspired it. I hope the book's themes, in their own key, honor the legacy of Robert Bellah, one of my teachers. I hope they honor the memory of my parents, Harold Lichterman and Edith Bloch Lichterman, who worked hard to do good. My mother, a refugee, was the first to show me that civic freedoms are worth close attention.

Many thanks to graduate research collaborators who carried out indispensable tasks and helped grow this project. Early on, Brady Potts helped me explore the discursive parameters of homelessness, and took piercingly sharp field notes. Brad Nabors and Kyunghwan Lee also assisted me during shorter sojourns with the project. Kushan Dasgupta coded documents perceptively, followed winding trails to the facts historical, technical, and descriptive that this book needed, and best of all, coauthored papers with me from this research. In the final stages, Minwoo Jung's research assistance expanded my knowledge of urban development. Thanks to the Advancing Scholarship in the Humanities and Social Sciences grant program at the University of Southern California for two small grants, and Pew Charitable Trusts and USC's Center for Religion and Civic Culture for a grant to support exploratory work early on. You would not be reading this if it were not for Meagan Levinson at Princeton University Press. She saw potential in the project, and shepherded the book toward publication, along with a wonderful team. I greatly appreciate as well the two manuscript reviews who helped me think more sharply and discover more of what I wanted to say.

HOW CIVIC ACTION WORKS

Introduction

Making Problems

Social advocates turn conditions into social *problems*. They craft compelling claims about the problems, and build campaigns to solve them. It is hard work with uncertain prospects. How do social advocates make the claims and sustain the relationships of collective problem solving? Those became the central questions of this study.[1]

The best way to answer them was to follow the action, making lots of comparisons along the way. I spent four years observing and participating alongside social advocates working on housing problems in Los Angeles. My observations gave me close-up views of four campaigns, three coalitions—two in depth—and twelve organizations. The advocates pressed for more affordable housing, fought gentrification, and promoted the kinds of urban development that could benefit low-income residents. Some of them pointed out health, environmental, and safety problems as part of their fight for housing. I followed some of the advocates to different organizations and settings; I followed some dissenters in one of the coalitions to a competing coalition. I observed several organizations and projects that publicized homelessness or served homeless people to better understand what made "homelessness" and "housing" into such separate issues for a lot of advocates. And I took on work stints at the office of an affordable housing developer to see how they planned and financed, built, and leased the housing that advocates fought for. I compared campaigns, coalitions, organizational settings, claims about housing, and claims about homelessness. To contextualize the ethnographic findings, the study draws in evidence from hundreds of documents, and dozens of hours of audio- and videotaped city hall deliberation.

Many studies already investigate the rhetoric and organizing techniques that empower social problem solving. Claims making and relationship

1

building became my central focus because LA housing advocates carried out these big tasks in such perplexing ways. Let's listen in.

Puzzling over Claims Making: Why Isn't Imitation Flattering? Why Isn't Housing about Compassion?

Housing advocates and I were at a town hall meeting in a working-class neighborhood of weathered bungalows and stucco box apartments with a good view of the hillside Hollywood sign. Solicitous city planning department staff and chirpy interns greeted people who gave their Saturday morning to learn more about what "affordable housing" is, and why Los Angeles needs more of it. Attendees perused booths with display boards documenting housing conditions in the city. The planning department's associate director was telling an informally gathered audience at one poster display that the vast majority of housing built in Los Angeles was affordable only to people who earned more than $135,000 a year. The posters conveyed the same reality with graphs and charts. I had tagged along with two campaign organizers from Housing Justice (HJ), a broad coalition of nonprofit, affordable housing developers, tenant organizations, and labor groups—one of the two main coalitions in this study. The coalition was pushing a proposal for a citywide affordable housing mandate. The campaign organizers smirked at the display boards and sounded suspicious of the whole affair.

Why weren't they happy that a city administrator was using exactly the same language and signal statistic that HJ circulars used to document the dearth of housing opportunities for low- and moderate-income people? Why was this not a satisfying sign that municipal agencies endorsed the coalition's way of framing Los Angeles' housing problems? Isn't that what activists would want?

Meanwhile, advocates with Inquilinos del Sur de Los Angeles / Tenants of South Los Angeles (ISLA), the other coalition, were warily monitoring some new construction projects in the working-class, largely Latinx neighborhoods south of downtown. ISLA's way of relating to claims making was not so easy to understand either. It brought tenant groups, community development organizations, and nonprofit health providers together to challenge new real estate developments that were hastening the exit of lower-income people of color from those neighborhoods. Surveys by ISLA staff documented what residents already had been saying: many longtime neighbors were moving out as rents went up. The area was becoming more appealing to wealthier and whiter tenants. A similar dynamic was happening in surrounding neighborhoods, where a recently repackaged downtown scene of upscale apartments, chic lofts, nightlife, and shopping was enticing affluent professionals to make their homes alongside the financial towers corralled just east of the Harbor Freeway.[2]

One plan to erect a massive, luxury apartment on a block with a hospital, in a largely lower-income neighborhood, had agitated ISLA activists for months. Suddenly, though, they set aside the central focus of their antigentrification campaign, gathered allies, and learned what they could from sympathetic city officials in private meetings after an ISLA activist heard a bulldozer demolishing part of the medical facility that some local parents depended on for specialized pediatric care. Alarmed ISLA advocates and residents lined up inside the theatrically ornate city hall chamber where the city planning commission held its hearings, each filling the allotted two minutes of individual speaker time with reasons why commissioners should reject the proposed upscale complex and protect the hospital. Most appealed to fairness and opportunity. Almost none called the plans for the huge apartment complex and shrunken hospital a failure of compassion, and precious few said the development would diminish their quality of life.

ISLA staff had already made it clear that they cared about their constituents as people trying to live decent lives. They lamented the flight of longtime local residents to cheaper housing far away. One said that when she heard the bulldozer start in on the clinic, it felt like a punch to the stomach. Another led a consciousness-raising tour of the neighborhood, pointing to ample evidence that city planning routines had led to inhospitable uses of local space—a freeway right next to a house and a gas station next to a century-old church. So why didn't languages of caring or quality of life enter more into the appeals ISLA advocates and their constituents made at city hall?

Puzzling over Relationship Building: Why Can't We Stand (with) Our Allies?

The ethnographer found relationship building no less puzzling. Tenant advocates and nonprofit housing developers had crowded onto city hall's steps one early spring day. It was the long-planned kickoff rally for the HJ coalition's campaign to promote affordable housing legislation. Camera shots captured tenant advocates braving the LA noonday sun, clutching colorful banners with brash messages; they stood just behind a row of dark-suited nonprofit housing developers and religious leaders. After the rally, tenant advocates complained bitterly that what really took bravery was the group photo session with the affordable housing developers—their *allies*. A HJ staff person got an earful and spent precious phone time talking the tenant advocates down. This was the campaign's long-awaited public launch, a chance to perform broad-based enthusiasm for better housing policies. Why were the advocates so bitter about the photo opportunity? As the campaign intensified, so did rancor between different factions of the coalition. The lines of division were not so obvious.

Proponents of extremely low-income and precariously housed people stood on *both* sides, but the tension was unmistakable.

Why was it so hard for these allies to fashion a collaborative modus vivendi, even if only long enough for city council to vote on a housing mandate? It turns out that coalition leaders were hardly strangers to one another. Some organizations in the coalition had been working off and on for over eight years toward the goal of affordable housing legislation. If passed, the mandate would cover far more renters than current mandates in any of the other 170 US cities with similar municipal ordinances in 2008. This would be a historic victory with national reverberations. The activists had so much shared experience and struggle, and so much to win. To paraphrase the now-famous Angeleno whose police beating precipitated riots in 1992: Why couldn't they just get along?

To solve puzzles like these, this book offers a cultural and action-focused sociological approach. Following the action closely, I show how symbolic categories of a larger culture empower and limit the strategic claims that advocates and their opponents can make. I demonstrate that when advocates organize meetings, public events, or entire campaigns, they do so in line with culturally patterned ways of coordinating relationships. In this way, we can explain perplexing scenarios like the ones I just pictured and more. Beyond the case of housing advocacy in Los Angeles, this approach gives us a more accurate and ultimately useful view of how social advocates take on two fundamental tasks of collective, social problem solving. These tasks go together for advocates, and pair closely in scholarly thinking as well.

A lot of research has conceived of social advocacy groups as savvy operators carrying out these tasks strategically. This book shows that as advocates strategize, they are embedded in cultural and social contexts every step of the way. These contexts shape advocates' notions of what counts as savvy—and in which situations—what counts as a win, and how to get there. Solving social problems, in other words, depends a lot on *how* advocates pursue the solutions, not just what their solutions are. There are distinct ways to be strategic, with different trade-offs. My arguments depend on a different conceptual box from the one sociologists most often use to understand social advocacy. It will help to introduce that box informally here before unpacking it systematically in chapter 1.

Another Box

There are lots of questions to ask about social advocacy, and different ways to study it. Over the past forty years, many studies have considered social advocates to think and act rather like businesspeople: they make investments in rhetoric and people, taking risks for a goal that lies waiting in an uncertain future. They want to influence bystanders and institutional authorities to "buy" their message. They start new relationships efficiently and try to hold onto them, somewhat as businesses want to develop a market for their product and entice loyal shoppers. Of course the commercial metaphors are not perfect; for social advocates, the point of the "sales" and "marketing" is to win resources, power, or honor for some constituency, not primarily for their own private gain. Still, thinking in metaphors from the world of entrepreneurialism, these studies have taught us a lot about why social movements emerge, why they succeed or fail, and why some recruit members more effectively than others. The entrepreneur image captures some memorable scenarios from my time among housing advocates.

While useful for important questions, the entrepreneur image limits what we can know about the everyday world of social advocacy. It invites us to imagine advocates and advocacy groups as striving in constant, uniform pursuit of a win. It sounds safe enough to assume that advocates want to win, and I would not argue otherwise. The point is that when this image deeply informs our research questions, it becomes easy to assume that the very meaning of "working toward a goal" is obvious and unremarkable. We do not say much about where advocates' ideas about goals come from. We don't ask what holding a goal means to advocates. And we underplay questions about how activists know when they have succeeded. That is why I found it more useful to make this a study of collective, social problem solving instead of highlighting entrepreneurial actors and social movement organizations. I use a different terminology, with a long history in social thought.

When people work together, voluntarily, to address problems they think should matter to others, they are engaging in *civic action*.[3] There are different ways to do civic action. Civic action may or may not be contentious; that is part of what actors decide as they figure out how to address problems. Civic action may or may not address government, and may take up issues that are local, national, or global. Participants are relatively free to decide how to coordinate their collective effort rather than assuming their action is mandated or completely scripted by preexisting institutional rules and roles. Participants are the ones who decide what counts as "improving," and for whom. Civic action is not necessarily prodemocracy, prosocial, or virtuous. Participants in civic action act in relation to some shared understanding of "society," no matter how expansive or restrictive. Put simply, civic action happens when citizens work together to steer society, identifying problems and collaborating on solving them.[4]

Developing claims and sustaining relationships are central civic tasks that come with seemingly inevitable surprises as well as teachable moments. Social philosopher John Dewey wrote that when people work collectively on social problems, they discover things about the social world and respond to unpredicted contingencies as the action unfolds. They do not simply execute plans made in advance. Dewey's ideas about collective action and the conduct of social research will inform arguments throughout this book. Thinking alongside Dewey in light of contemporary developments in sociology, I will argue that there are powerful, cultural contexts that *pattern* the unfolding action of social problem solving, conditioning what social advocates can say and do together.

This book shows how civic action works. Practical as well as sociologically valuable insights await when we view social movements, nonprofit organizations, and volunteering projects from the standpoint of civic action. Welcome to the bigger box.

———

Appreciating the bigger box's benefits will be easier if we first address two potential challenges to this whole project. To some specialist readers, it may sound as if I am simply rediscovering the massive body of research on civic engagement and the nonprofit sector. While I will draw on important insights from that research tradition, this study is different. Many prominent studies of civic engagement measure an individual's beliefs, orientations, or social resources, and treat these as the impetus for acts we conventionally consider "civic," like voting, joining a volunteer group, or contacting elected officials.[5] With the focus I have introduced here, in contrast, "civic" refers to ongoing, collective action, not internal beliefs, individual attitudes, or resources, nor single acts that emerge from individual beliefs and attitudes. Of course, the beliefs and attitudes are part of action. But "civic action" spotlights *patterns of collective action* over time. It is a different conceptual box.

Civic action does not map so closely onto ideas about a civic "sector" either. Distinctions between market, state, and a "third"—or "nonprofit" or "civic"—sector are common in sociological views of public life, but assumptions about a sector get in the way of practical differences that matter in a study of civic action.[6] The idea of sectoral distinctions echoes US folk notions of a sharp line dividing everyday people and governmental agents. This understanding distorts US historical and current realities. Chapter 9 shows that nonprofit professionals who build affordable housing are in some ways much more like outsourced governmental actors than civic ones. The sectoral metaphor is even less adept at capturing the long-standing institutional realities of many other societies.[7] The various sectoral tags—"nonprofit," "voluntary," or "third"—each refer to a different collection of organizations, and each overlaps only partly with the arena of ordinary people's collective, problem-solving efforts.[8]

Even if we restrict our notion of a civic sector to collective, grassroots problem solving, we still have to bear the risky assumptions that go with talk of a sector. Many studies implicitly, if not explicitly, hold that a civic sector hosts and promotes "democratic skills," or sacrificial, citizenly commitments that other sectors do not readily host.[9]

As the world of housing advocacy in Los Angeles demonstrates vividly, however, different kinds of civic action promote and depend on different kinds of skills. They prize different virtues. The differences matter a lot to advocates, but they fade when we imagine a sector defined by generic virtues and skills, or aggregate "social capital" that other sectors supposedly lack.[10] It is more il-luminating to follow action we can define as civic, whether or not we find that action to be virtuous, prosocial, or democratic. We do not have to think that all kinds of collective problem solving are laudable. We need a concept that can accommodate lots of differences—political, cultural, social, and national.

A second, stronger objection is that the groups in this book that fight for more affordable housing will sound quite a lot like social movement partici-pants as we know them from other studies. Social movements are made up of collective actors, often organizations, that challenge governmental or other institutional powers.[11] The housing advocates in this study pressured munici-pal legislators and property-owning entities for more affordable housing, so why not just say this is a study of social movement organizations? If I want to focus more on culture and everyday action, why don't I just make this a study of social movement culture and action? Why bother introducing a new, less familiar sounding conceptual box?

Housing advocates were doing the kinds of things social movements do sometimes. But I wanted to understand closely *how* housing advocates do their work. The social movement "box" is useful for a variety of questions, but would have ended up leaving out important parts of the "how," and distorting or else excluding some of the relevant actors too.

To start with, how did social advocates set off the "social movement" part of their organization from other parts, and how did they negotiate the parts? The sponsor of the HJ coalition, for example, was the Western Housing As-sociation (WHA), a trade association of nonprofit housing developers, non-profit social service agencies, and several banks—not the usual image of a social movement organization. The trade association hired community orga-nizers who would *create* a temporary, local social movement from among labor unions, community organizations, and churches to pressure municipal leaders. The category of civic action obviated the need to classify which, if any, activi-ties I was studying belonged to a social movement organization.

The bigger box opened up room for following advocacy beyond what usu-ally counts as part of a social movement. Following the action occasionally led me to advocates acting like political lobbyists or consultants at city hall, or once in a while, like business partners—more literally than what the entrepreneurial model of action says metaphorically. Sometimes these advocates were from the same organizations that held feisty rallies and packed city hall meetings with loud supporters. With a broad focus on civic action, we may ask how and why advocates address problems in diverse ways, whether or not they are part of an identifiable social movement, and whether or not their strategies and tactics look like what we think social movements do.

To be fair, social movement scholarship does portray activists inside as well as outside powerful institutions.[12] Movement activists, classically understood as outsiders, sometimes participate in governance, advise elected officials and state agencies, or partner with businesses. Studies of these processes frequently invoke some notion of hybridity, institutional tension, or professional or personal ambivalence. These signal that activists are crossing lines since most of the time, they do not intend to become governing agents or institutional elites themselves, or adjuncts to corporations and bureaucracies in the greater scheme of things.[13] If our goal is to explain outcomes of social movements, then it may be fine to count hybrid activists who "wear two hats" as part of a social movement, if we can agree on some criteria for counting. But I needed more tools for exploring how and when advocates crossed institutional lines and juggled different kinds of action. Working with blanket categories that locate actors as either inside or outside a social movement would have chopped away some of the tangle of relationships that make up social advocacy.

The civic action framework's bigger box also helped me pay attention to a wider set of actors. Social movement scholarship already views movement organizations in "multiorganizational fields" where allies and adversaries contend with each other, and where media, the state, and larger publics play important roles too.[14] This is a helpful move. With the notion of civic action, we may also discover relations between social movement actors and other collective problem solvers, beyond the allies, adversaries, or bystanders that theorists have already identified.[15] For example, to understand LA housing advocates' public arguments, or their "claims," it turned out to be useful to compare what they asserted with what interest or volunteer group members maintained. I wanted to understand, for instance, why ISLA coalition advocates devalued environmentalist-sounding, quality-of-life arguments about urban development when they were fighting tenant displacement. Why couldn't they argue for environmentally sustainable housing opportunities for low-income people? I discovered it was not that they didn't care about the environment, safety, or even neighborhood aesthetics; they brought these up on their own in some settings. To grasp the pattern, it helped to understand that these advocates made their claims in relation to the arguments that representatives from neighborhood and business improvement associations made. These interest groups counted as civic actors too, but conceiving of them as part of a social movement or countermovement, with the imagery and assumptions that accompany those terms, would be a conceptually forced fit. Something similar happened with HJ advocates, who spent time at coordinating committee meetings grimly envisioning what neighborhood association members might say about affordable housing at city hall or on their own local turf. Housing advocates' claims formed in relation to and ricocheted off those of a variety of groups, not all of which were organized primarily to challenge one or more big institutions, as social movement groups are.[16]

The bigger box also helped me find out why advocates' goals made sense to them. Why did it *make sense* to HJ advocates to mount a citywide campaign for a housing ordinance instead of some other, less legislation-centered campaign to begin with? By the same token, why did it make more sense to advocates in the ISLA coalition to fight for a clutch of local neighborhoods, and why were ISLA advocates cool to HJ's efforts on a citywide campaign that could have benefited them greatly? These questions are different from asking what makes advocates win or lose a given campaign. They require a different kind of inquiry into goals, outcomes, and the meaning of success, which I explain more in chapter 6.

There is at least one other reason to go with the bigger box. Focusing intently on forms of action and less on the entrepreneurial actor relieved me of the temptation to ignore an inconvenient reality. Among LA housing advocates, it was not always clear *who*—which organization or coalition—was the actor in a situation. Maybe the problem was me; I just was not observing the right things. Yet experienced antigentrification activists in one coalition I studied puzzled aloud during a long coalition meeting about who they were, organizationally. They misidentified one of their own leaders along the way, making me realize how practical this existential-sounding problem could be. I was confused too. Moreover, in one of the coalitions, I noticed the same advocates identifying themselves with different organizations depending on the setting and audience. Different organizational identities cued different understandings of trust and loyalty. The civic action box can accommodate the differences rather than trying to make them disappear by inserting an ever-present collective actor into the story. Focusing intently on capacities or outcomes of individual or collective *actors* would have obscured the interesting ambiguity regarding who is the actor, thus mischaracterizing some of the action.

Turning to the bigger box helped me address questions that bedevil advocates as much as they intrigue researchers. In the case of LA housing advocates, why did people who agreed on basic issues have such a hard time working together? Why were seemingly interrelated issues—housing and environmental sustainability, say—harder for some advocates to combine in their work than housing and health? Why was homelessness not more commonly treated as a housing issue? This book will show that we can address these questions, at once practical and scholarly, when we pay more attention to cultural contexts than the entrepreneurial actor model leads us to do. We need to zoom in on cultural patterns of everyday group action, and we need to zoom out to cultural parameters that limit what advocates can say about social problems, where, and to whom.

For scholars, this call for a bigger box is also an invitation to a bigger community of inquiry. We usually identify ourselves with smaller disciplinary boxes dedicated to social movement research, or civic engagement studies or scholarship on nonprofit organizations, but recently, researchers have been helping bring a larger scholarly community into being.[17] Students of Latin American political activism have been developing terms of inquiry that sidestep the popular tendency to call the polite kinds of people's action "civic," and label the contentious kinds as "social movement" or "activist."[18] These scholars point out that "civic" does not always enhance people power, as neo-Tocquevillians would imagine. But neither does it always mean a charade of grassroots participation that only legitimates state or corporate power, as critical writers sometimes suppose. Western European scholars show us the value of research that spans academic niches devoted to social movements, civic engagement, interest groups, or the construction of social problems.[19] It is not a new idea that the sociology of both public problems and social movements share common themes. Sociologist Herbert Blumer (1969) argued long ago that people figure out which conditions are problems through collective action; Dewey (1927) wrote the classic account of that process forty years earlier.[20] Yet social problems and social movements have tended to remain separate topics for social scientists. The concept of civic action contributes to an interdisciplinary community-building project that would connect the dots for a bigger picture of collective problem solving, whether contentious or not, elite driven or widely participatory.

US social movement scholars have been finding empirical uses for the "civic" box too. They use it to categorize the many public projects that "blend" social movement–style contention with volunteer service and community education efforts that scholars do not usually highlight when writing about social movements. Having combed through thirty years of publicized events in Chicago, one prominent study found that the great majority of those events included "community" and nonpolitical activity as well as the claims making we typically expect to hear from social movement activists.[21] These events were community festivals, charity promotions, educational or ethnic solidarity events, or municipal hearings where people aired grievances. Relatively few of the events included the activity most typically associated with social movements: protest.[22]

The bigger box is likely to be equally good at picking up public advocacy–related events in Los Angeles. One of my housing coalitions organized street fairs with speakers who educated and advocated against gentrification alongside aerobics trainers as well as health promoters staffing informational tables, ready to teach passersby how to brush their teeth. Another coalition packed mayor-sponsored "town hall" meetings to speak up for affordable housing. For some purposes including my own, it is better to distinguish different lines of collective action than to lean on sometimes-unreliable distinctions between what is or isn't part of a social movement—all the more since a clear, consensual definition of that category has eluded researchers.[23]

Collective, social problem solving is this book's object of investigation. Housing advocacy in Los Angeles was a good, if challenging, site for following civic action.

1

A New Sociology of Civic Action

HOW DO ADVOCATES for social change act? Cultural stories give us familiar answers. They march down the street, chanting, fists aloft. They risk arrest, jail time, and occasionally even life itself. They scale high-rise office buildings and unfurl banners with cheeky messages; they snarl traffic. Scholarly accounts show us the flashy, risk-taking aspects of advocacy too. They add, though, that advocates spend much of their time writing position papers, raising money, enduring meetings, or running educational workshops—like the ones that taught local residents in ISLA how to think critically about the work of down-town city planners. All these activities fit within the usual definition of a social movement: collective action that challenges institutional authorities to redistribute resources, remake policy, or bestow social recognition.[1] In the last several decades, studies of both the showier and more backstage kinds of movement activity share something else that may seem simply like common sense, but should not.

Problems with a Prominent Approach to Social Advocacy

The Entrepreneurial Actor

Researchers often assume that social advocates are goal-oriented operatives. Yet the scenarios in the introduction could suggest that housing advocates in Los Angeles were sometimes confused, petty, even incompetent. We would expect leading advocates to use easily accessible reasoning, like appeals to compassion, for people who need housing and health care. Leaders with widely appealing rationales should entice more people to join the cause. We would expect advocates to be happy when the powers that be see the problems the same way they do. And we would expect that advocates want to keep relationships with their allies strong and positive so that they keep working together to achieve whatever participants consider success. There is power in relationships as well as rationales.

Studies that rest on assumptions like these imagine the social advocate as what I will call an *entrepreneurial actor*. They think of actors, individual or collective, who take initiative proactively, using their skills to launch collective efforts, convince people to join up, and take risks to win their ends. In this view, social advocates are like savvy business entrepreneurs.

More and less explicit notions of the entrepreneurial actor animate many studies of social movement activity. In fact, the term "social movement entrepreneur" helped destigmatize collective action participants in the eyes of social scientists a half century ago.[2] Previously, scholars had imagined the participants as not patient or reflective enough to translate personal grievances into calmly stated claims, and communicate those through the normal channels.[3] The image of the entrepreneur seizing opportunities to turn grievances into powerful campaigns dignified extrainstitutional, collective action as rational and political, not just a collective behavioral meltdown.[4] As sociologists Patricia Ewick and Marc Steinberg (2019, 22–23) argue, the predominant view of social advocates in contemporary research is that of actors who carry out preplanned strategies that drive consistently toward preplanned goals. They execute plans instrumentally in hopes of (uncertain) success, taking the kinds of risks entrepreneurs take.

Some social movement studies depart markedly from the entrepreneurial actor model, and I have benefited greatly from their insights.[5] Some conceptual statements open up room for social advocates whose moral understandings as well as emotional or self-expressive motives matter alongside entrepreneurial ones.[6] And to be clear, not all studies that lean on the entrepreneurial model do so exclusively or say so explicitly. The model, I am arguing, is often an implicit intellectual sensibility, or a way of wording research questions, even in works that aim to challenge that model. The image of the striving entrepreneur *is* in some ways useful for our thinking—and decades of research bear that out. Still, it is good to be critically aware of this imagery whether or not we are academics. It limits our imagination for what advocates do. The more we rely on that image and the vocabulary that goes with it, the harder it is to break away and ask other important questions.

Recently, some scholarship argues for broadening beyond the focus on material and political grievances along with governmental targets that has characterized a lot of research on social movements. Social movements challenge cultural as well as economic or political hierarchies; they want to change our ideas of what women are suited to do, what a family should be like, and what counts as a good life—as ends in themselves. These challenges may be "instrumental" and "expressive" at the same time, not simply either rational or irrational.[7] Important institutional challenges come into view that we otherwise miss or dismiss when we think of these kinds of social movement goals. We see that powerful cultural contexts set the stage for some social movement activity. This valuable scholarly move multiplies the kinds of targets we can recognize and kinds of challengers—LGBTQ advocates, for example—we can study as social movement actors. It puts more emphasis on the question of what strategies develop, and somewhat less on what current political opportunities activists can exploit.

These moves go as far as the gravitational pull of the entrepreneurial model allows. They broaden our horizons helpfully, while leaving unaddressed the question of what counts as a strategy and goal.[8] Undisturbed is the entrepreneurial actor who carries out preplanned strategies, whether instrumental or expressive, toward preplanned goals, whether those involve change in corporate, legislative, or cultural institutions.

The same observation applies to important writings since the 1980s that focus closely on the cultural and emotional dimensions of social movements. Many scholars have explored the collective identities, emotional tones, culture-building strategies, rhetorical frames, and stories that animate social movement activity.[9] On the one hand, these writings show that social movements thrive as their participants develop a new sense of who they are, where they are from, and what they are fighting for.[10] Activists speak, write, and sometimes sing in striking idioms and images; they feel; and they aspire to a more moral social order. This newer work calls into question the whole idea that being strategic means being coolly calculating and unemotional. Yet alongside these helpful developments, important conceptual agenda-setting statements have continued to assume social movement leaders are a particular kind of strategic actor: the savvy entrepreneur.[11] "Strategic" means getting new participants to do what movement activists want them to do, as social movement scholar James Jasper (2006) refreshingly puts it. In this view, then, advocates *strategize with* striking idioms and images, feelings, and moral aspirations in pursuit of preplanned goals.

The problem is that we need room to imagine different *ways of relating to* intentions and goals, deciding what counts as a goal, and what counts as winning. Rather than look for universal principles and dilemmas of strategic action, in other words, we can learn what being goal oriented *means* in different settings. I learned in LA housing circles that advocates with different understandings of strategy—not simply more or less efficient strategies— encountered quite different dilemmas. We need a bigger conceptual box to apprehend different ways of getting others to do what actors want them to do.

Prominent social movement scholarship has gone another direction. It fits out the entrepreneurial actor with an ultimately psychological notion of "skill."[12] Here again is the strategic actor who is a first mover, albeit one constrained by one or more hierarchical social fields, using special skill to conceive plans, meet goals, advance in the field, or create new fields. Situations and opportunities may vary, but in that picture, skill is a generic quality. In this study, in contrast, being "skilled" involved different ways of coordinating action in different social contexts. The entrepreneurial actor model is not necessarily "wrong" in relation to my own findings. It would be *right* to suppose that housing advocates in Los Angeles craft claims and try to sustain relationships strategically. Advocates certainly did try to get others to do what they wanted them to do. The question is how they did that. The image of entrepreneur does little to highlight capacities and sensibilities that mattered to LA housing advocates, and ought to matter to researchers.

ENTREPRENEURIAL CLAIMS MAKING: THE MISSING "HOW"

In the last thirty years, our understanding of political claims making has become closely associated with research on framing. A "frame" is a mixed package of messages that social movement actors hope will resonate with a targeted audience.[13] Advocates hope the frame will convince by-standers to become supporters; that aspiration to success is built into the notion of framing in social movements research. In the most prominent statements, framing is the work of innovative, strategic leaders aiming to "sell" a message. This top-down understanding of how ideas generate collective action travels some distance from the framing perspective's original statement, which presented framing more as an ongoing, collective, sense-making activity.[14] The strategic framing perspective became popular in the study of social movements because it could complement an already well-established "instrumentalist" approach to collective action.[15] That is, it adopted the entrepreneurial actor model.[16] Framing studies have tended to see symbols and meanings as pliable media for movement actors' strategies.

HJ advocates certainly orchestrated the framing of their campaign message. In position papers and flyers, and on city hall's steps, leaders consistently referred to housing conditions in Los Angeles as a "crisis."[17] The solution to the crisis was a "three-point plan" of action that, as one campaign leader told me, the campaign crafted to appeal to a varied set of potential supporters, such as housing developers, tenant associations, and labor groups.

If the point of framing is to produce a winning message, puzzles still remain. Why were the HJ advocates I accompanied to the town hall meeting not happier to hear city planning officials echoing and promoting the activists' preferred frames? Why didn't ISLA advocates frame their opposition to the large apartment complex in the compassion terms that many people would find less threatening than more political-sounding appeals?[18] Why did they downplay appeals to quality of life when the city officials they wanted to convince talked in these terms frequently at public hearings?

Skilled actor theorists would find the answer back inside the actor. ISLA leaders applied their skills, sized up the local environment, thought through the different potential pitches, and decided that opportunity and justice language would be more successful than appeals to caring or quality of life, given the array of actors in the field. Skill is a "blend of pre-existing rules, resources, and social skills [*sic*]."[19] A sympathetically critical response might point out that this is an abstract, broad-brushstroke answer to the puzzle; a crispier response might also note that the definition of skill is circular. In any event, we need to know more about the complicated skills that direct advocates to act compassionately with their constituents while not *talking* that way in public forums.[20]

ENTREPRENEURIAL RELATIONSHIP BUILDING: AGAIN, THE MISSING "HOW"

The entrepreneurial actor model understands social advocates' work of sustaining relationships in two ways. In one of those, building relationships with new participants is a matter of telling motivational stories to entice new members. The relationships are the successful outcome of rhetorical devices that mobilize individuals.[21] But what about the qualities or textures of the relationships themselves? What do the relationships mean? Studies of social networks focus on the relationships as facts in themselves, not only outcomes. These studies point out that people are more likely to attend meetings or join protests when they know other participants.[22] Similarly, when organizational leaders want to recruit other organizations to a coalition, they start with leaders they know already.[23] Preexisting relationships build movements, in other words, and in these studies, the logic is entrepreneurial: advocates read the social environment, size up the possibilities, and gravitate toward preexisting relationships because it is easier to secure commitment from people you know. As social movement scholar Mario Diani points out, alliance building is risky, calling on activists to step into the fray of competing agendas and potential mistrust, hoping to create new bridges of solidarity between organizations.[24]

It makes sense to begin with people who are familiar from previous campaigns. That is one way for overworked, time-starved advocates to surmount the challenges of organizing people. And that is part of the reason that a former HJ campaign convener invited some people into the coalition at the outset.[25] In studies of social movement networking, there is also an underlying assumption, seemingly unremarkable, that savvy activists *will* work at sustaining relationships because it is in their collective interest. *They want to succeed.* Yet at a special event put on by the HJ coalition for its supporters, an experienced advocate launched a sharp staccato of critical, probably rehearsed questions, wrecking the cheery harmony that was supposed to have been the theme song of this "unity meeting."

That is why I ask again, What do relationships *themselves* mean to advocates? Studies find that advocates need to appeal to potential participants' sense of personhood before the familiarity between advocate and potential participant becomes an effective attraction.[26] So an entrepreneurial advocate can command "numbers" (social ties) by offering potential participants an interesting collective identity—something they get to *be* if they join up.[27] But relationships mean more than the collective identities participants honor together, if any. The opening puzzles suggest that there are not only varied identities that advocates might use to entice recruits but also different ways to build relationships, about which advocates may be less self-conscious. There are different notions of what counts as a *good* or *appropriate* relationship, quite apart from the identity—feminist, green, queer, Christian, or Angeleno—that may accompany the relationship.[28] The fact that a relationship exists or not—what network studies traditionally examines—does not tell us a lot about what it means. In short, to understand how advocates make claims, or build and sustain relationships, we need to ask more about what skilled actors know or assume, whether they fully realize it or not.

More Skilled Than We Might Guess: The Entrepreneurs' Cultural Know-how

The advocates I came to know in LA housing circles were skilled, in both the sociological and conventional sense of the word. That does not explain, though, how they defined what was a good rhetorical appeal, good relationship-building practice, or good strategy. Cultural parameters guided them.

In both the ISLA and HJ coalitions, advocates knew to stick to a limited range of claims from what was theoretically a much larger universe. When ISLA advocates, for example, argued repeatedly that tearing down half a hospital to build luxury apartments in a working-class neighborhood was a matter of fairness and opportunity, and rarely said it was a matter of compassion or quality of life, the pattern was too well defined to be an accident. Patterned, cultural know-how constrained their framing strategies.

It was the same with relationships. In both the ISLA and HJ coalitions, advocates built and sustained social ties according to implicit understandings of a good or adequate relationship. The executive director of the HJ campaign and his assistants did act entrepreneurially in building a core membership along with a longer roster of paper endorsements big as well as diverse enough to pressure city council successfully. Yet there is much more to it than that. HJ leaders assumed specific things about coalition relationships. They should not be all encompassing, and shouldn't have to be an organization's primary public attachment. They should be open to a great variety of members—homeless service nonprofits, labor unions, a Catholic-centered community organizing outfit, and more. That all may sound like "the right way to win an ambitious affordable housing mandate in a big, diverse city." But the ISLA coalition pursued a much more explicitly race-conscious, highly selective strategy of relationship building. Leaders of both coalitions got others to do what they wanted them to do sometimes. One was not "more" strategic than the other in any absolute sense. They relied on different ways of coordinating action to get what they wanted.

That is why the tenant advocates took such offense at the colorful rally photos. And that is why the tenant leader disrupted the unity meeting. She was signaling her refusal to go along with a model of coalition building that assumed loyalty meant suppressing criticisms of police actions downtown in order to get along with coalition partners for short-term gain. The adversarial tenant leader and her surprised coalition colleagues all were "being strategic" on the basis of different cultural know-how.

Some research influenced by the entrepreneurial actor model has been moving toward the same conclusions about culture. Researchers increasingly have contended that framing studies oversimplify the meaning-making work that advocates and publics do to interpret messages in light of a larger symbolic environment.[29] Some are also concerned, rightly, that if we focus a lot on cultural context, we might underestimate advocates' creative rhetorical work.[30] We can conceptualize claims making as embedded, not imprisoned, in a cultural context. A parallel move toward appreciating cultural context is afoot in studies of social advocates' relationship building. While studies based on the entrepreneurial model view relationships in terms of the frequency or density of network ties, Doug McAdam (2003, 284–85) offers a helpful reminder that "ties" are relationships, implying they can have different qualities.[31] We know that civic relationships can do different things; for example, they may be largely instrumental exchanges, or more personal or identity-driven partnerships.[32] This study takes a still more qualitative view with its focus on often-implicit understandings of what a good relationship is. The mechanical and pecuniary metaphors—networks and social capital—that we frequently use to talk about political ties can obscure these meanings.[33]

One response to these critiques is to conclude that we need to study the culture of social movements more, or make fewer or softer assumptions about how entrepreneurial advocates really are. That is what some recent studies do, and they inform the arguments in this book. But those moves by themselves still would leave in place the implicit idea that there *is* a unitary, collective actor—often, the social movement organization—that we can point to. That leads to a last puzzle we need to confront.

Who Is the Actor?

In the entrepreneurial model as well as common sense, a person or group is basically the same wherever we find them or it. And we frequently treat whole organizations like individual speakers or actors. An organization does things, we say. Or we use the action of one person, maybe a group representative at a coalition meeting, to stand in for "what the organization is doing." I have written this way sometimes to convey things about ISLA and HJ, or their organizational participants, without getting caught up in sprawling locutions. For instance, "ISLA spoke out against the upscale residential complex" and "Housing Justice fought for more affordable housing." The typical language of research on social advocacy encourages us to imagine entrepreneurial actors are acting continuously on behalf of a definite organization, speaking on "its" behalf.[34] This reification of an organization or coalition is indispensable sometimes; advocates have the same habit.

Yet it was not so easy to tell who or what I was studying, and whether or not it should be considered part of a social movement. Scenes from the two housing coalitions will help make this puzzle more vivid so that it is easier to see why I want to move some of the spotlights away from actors and toward action.

My early field notes on ISLA-initiated activism used a vague name for what I was studying. They were titled "the Balboa projects." I could not figure out what else to call it—or them. For over a year, I had been observing and participating alongside a shifting coalition of tenant activists, community development advocates, and labor advocates. These people were trying to reverse a frightening disappearance of affordable apartments in their South LA neighborhoods, especially near Balboa Boulevard. They considered these neighborhoods an irreplaceable home for residents who sadly, anxiously, were watching their neighbors being displaced by tenants who could pay rents that kept going up. After a year, I was still calling it/them the Balboa projects because it was not clear which or how many organizations were or should be under study. I kept assuming the subject would come apparent if I just kept observing.

Listening in at a May 2009 meeting, I considered a succession of answers—none of them adequate. Early in the meeting it seemed easy; I decided I was studying a coalition, Balboa Communities for Economic Development (BCED). Yet as meeting facilitator Ethan implied, no one really knew which organizational representatives were empowered to vote on BCED's steering committee. The coalition also needed a new board of directors to satisfy terms of a new grant from a Catholic philanthropy. Legally, the BCED coalition did not even exist then. The newly funded board would oversee a campaign of BCED, named ISLA. As Ethan put it, "ISLA *is* the major campaign of BCED." ISLA was going to promote affordable housing construction in BCED's neighborhoods south of downtown by organizing local residents at monthly meetings, and pressuring big developers and officials at the Department of City Planning. Maybe I was really studying the ISLA campaign.

But what was ISLA? It had no well-defined organizational structure. This meeting's leading participants, who also attended ISLA campaign meetings regularly, fell into a more seemingly solid and much smaller category. They were staff people with three of the organizations active in the ISLA coalition, one of which evolved out of one of the other two. So maybe I was really studying an alliance of three active organizations. Yet that would not answer the question either. These staff people each wore more than one organizational "hat." At this meeting, one of the activists had to tell us which of his hats was facing forward, so to speak. It was hard to keep up and easy to get bogged down in a thunderstorm of acronyms, as in this exchange:[35]

> Victor: "I'm here as CGTC [Common Ground/Tierra Común]—I'm on the SLACE [South Los Angeles Communities for Equity] board, but—a lot of the stuff [work on the ISLA campaign] has been inside SLACE. . . . SLACE has to rethink its work."

> Marina, a longtime resident and activist, complained, "I've never been clear on BCED, SLACE."

> Ethan responded that SLACE has been the "fiscal sponsor" for BCED, but that it may be time to move outside SLACE with the ISLA campaign. He saw this as "a positive thing, an opportunity for growth."

> Monica and Marina both said here that they were not sure on how SLACE and BCED related to each other anyway. Marina said that she felt "mixed up," and "it's good to be under SLACE's umbrella, but it would be good to know who I am!" Later she referred to Victor as "from SLACE—"

> Victor, cutting in to correct: "—Common Ground."

> Marina, a little exasperated: "Common Ground, SLACE, so many branches!"

I was at least as confused as Marina.

There was one identity, though, that everyone at this meeting and every other BCED, ISLA, SLACE, or CGTC meeting I had attended agreed on. All talked routinely on behalf of "the community." Upscale residential development threatened to displace the community. The community needed to

fight for more affordable housing. The community was not against development; it was against displacement of the community. Maybe I was studying
activism by the community!

But who was the community? On the one hand, ISLA spoke for the community and its perilously shrinking supply of low-rent housing. ISLA staff and
neighborhood residents had been tracking the exit of working-class people of
color from the neighborhoods around us. They came up with statistics that
neither property developers nor city officials disputed. Yet as Ethan and Victor
noted, the next ISLA campaign coordinator needed to get "buy-in" for the
campaign from "the community." So the community did not necessarily support the community's campaign.

This discussion about choosing a new campaign coordinator drove home
how unclear it was who could speak for the community and was really a
member of it. This new coordinator might emerge from the annual stream
of young interns coming to work temporary positions in Los Angeles' advocacy organizations—people from Public Ally, say, who were passionate about
their work and "not necessarily from our neighborhood," as Victor put it.[36]
That is how he himself had come to be involved in SLACE; he stayed on after
the end of his internship. In other words, some advocates from *outside* the
community embraced strident advocacy on behalf of the community, while
some longtime, local residents balked. What would it mean, then, to say I was
studying an effort of the community? In short, identifying the collective actors
was surprisingly difficult.

It is fair to ask if I had simply caught these activists in transition. Maybe at
the moment, the Balboa projects lacked the budget to afford an established
identity and stable organizational flowchart. Maybe I simply had rediscovered
the endearing or annoying quirks of progressive activism on a shoestring—a
side note to the story of big organizations and big budgets that researchers tell
about the contemporary US advocacy world.[37]

Comparisons made the skeptical objection unconvincing. The bigger, more
professional, much more powerful, and better-funded regional housing coalition
I was studying posed *similar puzzles* regarding who exactly the acting subject
was. It also introduced even more complexity. Beginning in 2007, the HJ coalition orchestrated a campaign to pressure governmental agents for new mandates
for affordable housing construction in its region. An office staff of six people
coordinated the coalition, and this office also called itself HJ. Those staff people
were paid by the Western Housing Association (WHA), an association that held
educational workshops and lobbied on behalf of members—who included affordable housing developers, community advocates, governmental agencies,
and some banks. In short, the WHA sponsored the HJ coalition along with HJ
office staff. In all, actors who identified with "Housing Justice" actually were

spread across three separate organizations: the coalition that called itself HJ, the small staff organization that also called itself HJ, and the WHA. That means I may have been studying a social movement group, public interest organization, or professional association.

Multiply affiliated advocates are hardly news, but again it was hard to say who exactly I was studying at any one time. I could have treated HJ staff as members of a single organization called HJ, or members of WHA, the organization that paid their salaries. To complicate matters further, during the ritual introductory go-arounds, the same staff person would not necessarily identify as coming from the same organization every time. What was the note-taking ethnographer supposed to do with that? Several people attending HJ coalition meetings identified sometimes as "WHA staff" and other times as "Housing Justice." Which group(s) was/were the object of study?

The immediate point is that it is not always so obvious whether or not there is a single identifiable, collective actor. It is not so clear either if that actor is a social movement organization, especially when collaborators in the organization or coalition include professional associations and interest groups that do not carry on contentious, social movement–style action, as we just saw with HJ. Once we stop taking for granted that there is a unitary, collective actor and look more closely at patterns of *action*, we may need to move beyond the social movement or social movement organization as a conceptual "container" for a study. And at the same time, we may need to understand how the same actors, even entrepreneurial ones, act differently in different settings even within the same organization.

The civic action lens helps us zoom *out* beyond social movement organizations to other sites where collective, social problem solving is happening. It helps us zoom *in* to powerfully different settings of the same organization, where different forms of action may be in play. To "see" civic action, we need a different way of looking from the more usual focus on groups, organizations, and individuals: *actors* who do things. We need concepts that focus us instead on different *kinds of doing together*, which may cut across actors, organizations, or even entire institutional spheres. The bigger box of the civic action approach comes with that conceptual vocabulary.

What to Look for and Where to Look When We Study Civic Action

The Concept of Civic Action

Civic action is flexibly organized, collective, social problem solving. Participants are coordinating action to improve some condition of common life that they think should matter to members of a larger imagined society, however they envision it.[38] They organize themselves voluntarily rather than understanding themselves as strictly subject to preexisting, externally enforced rules and roles.[39] In contrast to the traditional entrepreneur who is subject to the basic rules of market exchange and aims consistently toward the goal of making money, civic actors by definition have more flexibility in accomplishing their ends. Their ends may change, and their sense of who they are collectively may change too. The *metaphor* of the entrepreneur, while useful for some questions, makes it difficult to apprehend these qualities and consequences of action.

Wide swaths of action in groupings we call social movement organizations, volunteer groups, community service networks, or nonprofit goods and service providers can go in the bigger box of civic action. Each of these groupings pursues collective problem solving. Using the bigger box, we can compare the benefits and liabilities of these different efforts. We can contrast their consequences for problems and the people who live with those problems instead of treating them as fundamentally different, each accessible only in a distinct disciplinary vocabulary. Comparative thinking here is all the more important because a lot of organizations that address social problems host several of these kinds of activity at once, even if sometimes emphasizing one and then another.

Not everything that social movement, volunteer groups, and nonprofit organizations do is civic action, and that makes for crucial comparisons as well. When action is highly scripted by institutionalized routines that actors violate at their legal or immediately financial peril, then we are not talking about *flexibly organized*, voluntarily chosen action anymore. Agents of social change or social improvement are not all necessarily doing civic action all the time. Some do it intermittently, as chapter 9 shows in the case of affordable housing developers who follow governmental rules and regulations in order to win grants that keep them funded. Theirs will be an example of "hybrid" civic action. Of course, even members of grassroots activist groups risk violating powerful norms of appropriateness if they signal that they are not hip to a group's ideology or its way of identifying itself. But that is a different kind of peril from violating institutional routines that carry the weight of legal sanction or determine the conditions for making money. Representatives in the US Congress certainly can be advocates for new lines of policy that change how institutions work, improve common life, and matter to society at large, but they pursue that advocacy in their capacity as legislators sworn to the US Constitution, and bound to a host of strictures regarding how congressional committees and government work. They are "institutional activists," and we can consider them interesting and important for sure without treating their action as civic.[40] Why should we aim to be careful in designating what is or is not civic action? Is this just a niche theoretical concern?

Civic action is, to the contrary, a central concern in over two centuries of Western social thought. Probably the most well-known articulation is Alexis de Tocqueville's vision, part description and part hope, of civil and political associations in which US citizens learned to work together on public issues as opposed to waiting for governing elites to act for them. Émile Durkheim's notion of public-spirited occupational assemblies, developing the interests and capacities of different kinds of workers for a greater social good, is not drastically different. In early twentieth-century US pragmatist thought we find visions of inquisitive, self-organizing, grassroots publics that steer the course of a socially diverse, industrial society rather than standing by to let impersonal mechanisms—the market's invisible hand or state's gloved fist—do that work alone. Pragmatist writings deeply influence this study's questions and methods. The German critical theory tradition rearticulated a similar vision of a public whose social power rests on people's regard for collective deliberation and social obligation, instead of money or administrative power. This diverse, long-standing theoretical conversation treats flexible, problem-solving action as a collective reality in itself, apart from the tactics, values, ideologies, or personal qualities that accompany it.[41]

Contemporary social science circles have rediscovered collective problem solving as a subject to study and debate. Starting in the late 1990s, researchers argued over the news that citizen associations in the United States were in a steep, twenty-five-year-long decline.[42] Calls for "civic renewal" echoed among public-minded social scientists, and spread to television talk shows and the book talk circuit. On the hope that renewal was possible, social researchers published upbeat case studies of people collaborating to regenerate local economies, or make cities more environmentally sustainable or sociable.[43] Often these pictured the kinds of efforts people usually call volunteering or community service, not social movement activity. Some critics doubted aloud that local problem solving could possibly address national economic inequality or institute new social safety nets with seemingly apolitical, local action.[44]

Beyond the celebratory or skeptical takes on civic renewal, there are useful comparative studies. Among those, Xavier de Souza Briggs's (2008) research on equitable redevelopment in six cities around the world shares with my study a pragmatist language and focus on collective problem solving. Briggs's study features the "civic capacity" that cities, or their leaders, manifest when they assemble coalitions of advocates, elected officials, and ordinary residents to solve major social problems. Dilemmas of accountability, and trade-offs between grassroots empowerment and efficiency—getting the problem solved—test that capacity. I address some parallel themes, but with a different approach and different goals. Briggs's engaging case studies are built mostly on secondary or journalistic accounts, official documents, and interviews with main players about agendas, strategies, and relationships after the fact. My research accessed agendas, strategies, and relationships as they were happening by following the action ethnographically.[45]

Follow the Action, Not Just the Actor

ISLA and HJ coalition members said and did puzzling things, but not randomly. Even if they did not always "know who they were" organizationally, as Marina put it in the previous chapter, they kept making claims and relating to each other in patterned ways. That is one big reason to look for patterns of action, instead of focusing so much on attributes of collective actors. Of course, actors individual and collective populate this study. There won't be any edgy writing experiments here that try to represent action without subjects acting. The point is just to put more emphasis on how collective action unfolds. That is what I mean by "follow the action."

My approach starts with insights from John Dewey and other twentieth-century American pragmatists.[46] These writers share the simple idea that action is meaningful, and neither wholly predictable nor random. Action ranges across an arc of human responses from customary habit to highly reflective deliberation and planning. People act, individually and collectively, in response to problems in living. In this book, we observe problem solving in two senses: we watch advocates treating housing conditions as problems, and at the same time, observe them working on the day-to-day problems of creating collective action—the work of putting claims into words and building relationships. As Dewey viewed it, action is not a matter of one-off acts that either solve or fail to solve a problem. Actors respond to problems with chains of action, interpretation, and more action. Actors are not simply "reacting" to each other like billiard balls. They are constantly trying out ideas about what the other's action means, and what their own action means as they act. We all are experimenters. As we experiment, we sometimes reinterpret ourselves too; others' perceptions become a part of who we *are*. Throughout this book, we will follow chains of everyday action.

This may sound like an invitation to focus only on "small" things. What about "big" things like changing housing policy or shifting the debate about what makes people homeless? When we look and listen closely, we find social, cultural, and institutional power, "big" processes, inscribed in civic action. I *do* mean to turn our attention to patterns of interaction, and sociologists often call that a focus on the "micro" level of social life—but observing the patterns closely, we see those bigger powers in motion, shaping the action that is entangled with them as I describe below. Where exactly do we look?

Civic Action Unfolds in Scenes

Civic action happens *someplace*, whether real or virtual, highly institutional-ized or highly informal. A still-underappreciated insight from interactionist Erving Goffman (1961, [1974] 1986) is central. Different settings can elicit different modes of action and interaction even from the same people. Studies already picture how this insight on situated action can apply in advocacy or volunteer settings.[47] Sociologist Ann Mische's study of Brazilian political activ-ists gives us especially striking examples. In one group, an activist might have been pondering their moral role in Brazil's turbulent transition to democracy, while in another, they were the coolly rational strategist getting the most out of a coalition, and in yet another, a practical problem fixer. Activists deftly avoided modes of argument in one setting that they cultivated in another. It was just as important to know about the setting as to know which actor was speaking.

"Setting" is a good, catchall term, but to make useful distinctions, it helps to conceive of settings in terms of *scene*. A scene is a "strip of action" in which the actors implicitly agree about "what we are doing here" and what it means to interact.[48] A scene may be bounded by physical setting or cued by physical or temporal qualities of the setting, like participants' clothing, leather-bound volumes on a bookshelf, a pause between events, or a change of speakers or activities that constitute different scenes within one physical setting.[49] The scene will be a central unit of observation throughout this study.

Sometimes people are working together on social problems in only some scenes of a large organization. We will focus mainly on scenes of *civic* action. Our look at affordable housing development will compare and distinguish civic from noncivic action in order to clarify what is or isn't "civic," and why that matters concretely—and politically. But mostly, we want to know how advocates make claims and build relationships, not how staff balance the books and rent conference rooms. The Western Housing Association offers a good illustration. Some of its paid staff were administrators, while a few were organizers and conveners for the HJ coali-tion. Broadly, they all contributed something to the cause of affordable housing, but we already saw what troubles brew if we treat a whole organization as a single actor. We will concentrate on scenes of civic action instead of following "an organ-ization." The same actors change how they interact when the scene changes. Dif-ferent scenes follow different patterns of action.[50] Those patterns of action are *style*.

Scenes Run on Different Styles of Interaction

Styles are mostly taken-for-granted, shared expectations about how to do things together, and how to relate to each other and participate.[51] Since much of our focus will be on civic action in scenes, we will follow *scene style*. We can recognize something like style operating in our own lives whether or not we are social advocates. When we work with others, sometimes we assume that "we" are professionals expecting to collaborate on the basis of our expertise. Other times we assume that "we" are individuals with unique stories who expect each other to share our feelings, or perhaps "we" are loyal members of an oppressed group expecting each other to challenge the oppressor and affirm our commonality. The hypothetical "we" in each of these examples may even be the same people, but acting in a different style. Each of these turns out to be a style of collective problem solving too.

To make it easier to identify and compare styles of action, two dimensions are particularly valuable. A style enacts participants' collective, implicit sense of "who we are" in relation to social reference points in the wider world. That is the "map" dimension of style. And a style enacts participants' collective, implicit sense of "what kinds of mutual responsibility bond us to one another." That is the "bonds" dimension of style.[52] A style is a collection of implicit social maps and bonds. While advocates in this study tended to prefer one style over others, they knew how to perform more than one. At several points, they argued over or quickly switched the style in play. Research views style as enduring over repeated gatherings in a similar setting rather than made up from scratch, gathering by gathering.

Style has a powerful effect on social problem-solving efforts. That is why it is so valuable to follow styled action closely instead of contenting ourselves with saying that an organization, or sector of organizations, follows this or that strategy for success. A distinct style cultivates distinct notions of good leadership and understandings of success. Styles induce different rhythms of time and collective effort. In each style, actors also privilege different "speech norms"—or preferred genres of speech and emotional expression.

How do we recognize a style? A style is a pattern, a routine way of doing things together, so one of the best ways to identify one is to watch what happens when a problem threatens the collective routine. Social advocates, like everyone else, inevitably—and quite frequently—run up against challenges to their routine way of doing things. We will see lot of examples of advocates dealing with challenges to routine ways of sustaining relationships or making claims. Those challenges clue us in to patterns—style—that actors were taking for granted, and maybe the researcher took for granted too. I will call these challenges, after Dewey ([1925] 1958, 61), *tests*. Often advocates responded to these tests with more of the same style—sometimes making it explicit and defending it. Following the responses to tests helped me identify styles of action.[53]

TWO SCENE STYLES: COMMUNITY OF INTEREST
AND COMMUNITY OF IDENTITY

This study looks in depth at the workings of two scene styles, and briefly introduces several others later on. Scene styles are not specific to one city, region, or social background. Each of the two here have been observed in big metropolitan areas and small cities, in the Midwest, and on the East and West Coasts of the United States. Participants in either may identify as people of color or white, and professional or working class. Both of the main styles are common in US advocacy circles.[54]

Acting as a *community of interest*, participants treat each other as loyal partners pursuing a specific goal limited to an issue for which they share concern. They assume good members coordinate themselves around an interest in an issue, not a population or community. Participants collaborate with those who share the focal interest. When acting as a community of interest, advocates aspire to accumulate the support of an increasingly general constituency. They create expanding circles of interest in and attention to the issue, with different levels of commitment, rather than expecting tight, mutual identification among participants. Communities of interest often form for relatively short-term campaigns.

In a setting styled as a *community of identity*, in contrast, participants assume they should coordinate themselves as fellow members of a community resisting ongoing threats from the powers that be. The community may identify itself ethnically, racially, geographically, or politically, or through a combination of these. Participants understand themselves as protecting the moral and/or geographic survival of the community and its authenticity. They maintain relatively high boundaries, collaborating selectively versus imagining their issues should appeal to an indefinitely expanding general audience. Supporters must *identify* closely with them. Participants assume good members are long-term ones who remain involved with the community beyond a single campaign or goal, and maintain tight solidarity and "speak with one voice."

Action unfolds, and we follow it as the actors interpret, act, and interpret some more. And yet there are recognizable patterns to the action—patterns we can discover especially when tests illuminate their workings. There is no necessary contradiction between focusing on unfolding action and looking for cultural patterns. Dewey thought the same: while we experiment our way through life, acting and interpreting and setting and resetting goals, these actions happen only in a tissue of cultural, sometimes institutionalized meanings that help organize experience.[55]

ENTANGLED IN SOCIAL CONTEXTS:
EACH STYLE INCORPORATES A DILEMMA FROM
THE SURROUNDING WORLD

It may sound as if communities of interest or identity are self-sustaining little cultural worlds. But style is not a purely "micro" phenomenon even though participants enact it in specific scenes. Actors always are "entangled" in surrounding realities *as* they are coordinating action, as Dewey (1922; [1925] 1958) would put it.[56] Style is not a kind of subculture that develops autonomously, easy to separate from its surroundings. Neither is it strictly determined by the social position of the advocates or the people they advocate for.[57] Across the two main coalitions in this study, social advocates worked in both styles on behalf of housing for low-income people of color. How, then, does style relate to the surrounding realities?

Sustaining a community of interest or identity can puzzle or challenge advocates in different ways. I discovered that styles jell *in relation* to different kinds of pushback from the wider world. From some distance, social scientists talk of "external," structural, or institutional realities that are pushing back on the actors whether or not they recognize the realities the way a sociologist does. As they keep coordinating their action, actors interpret and respond to the pushback with recurrent, unavoidable choices. That is why it makes sense to think of action as being styled—a pattern in the motion. These recurrent choices become part of keeping that style going as long as the larger realities are not changing. If the same advocates switch styles, they switch one set of choices entangled in one thicket of pushback for another set of choices and pushback. These fraught choices that become incorporated in a style are what I call a *dilemma*. I discovered a central dilemma in each of the two main styles in this study.[58]

When actors act as a community of interest, the central dilemma is a choice between dealing intently with the power brokers who can secure the shared interest or else expanding the political voice of the community pressuring the power brokers.[59] As a community of interest, actors may do either. Borrowing terms that advocates themselves used, I call this the *dilemma of insider versus outsider strategies*. In the first option, advocates act as political insiders, negotiating with powerful institutional incumbents. In the second, advocates act as political outsiders, attracting more participants to the cause so as to make their demands that much more impressive and compelling. Communities of interest do both to some degree. Promoting participation runs the risk of inviting in people who don't like and even challenge the style in play. Yet if participants deal only with power brokers and do not cultivate at least the appearance of breadth of support, the community looks small as well as unrepresentative of the people. That is the dilemma.

This dilemma emerges because the institutionalized reality of representative governance both elicits and pressures a strongly insider-focused strategy. Representatives make policy decisions in a political system that recognizes interest groups, so a group that advocates its interest insistently to representatives is hardly surprising.[60] What it is doing seems institutionally mandated. Representative governance also privileges majority wills, so claims about an interest risk looking less significant and widespread, and therefore less publicly legitimate to powerful gatekeepers, if only a narrow range of people promote them. That is one reason that advocates for narrow, frequently elite or corporate interests try to make those interests appear popular by organizing local citizen support groups. Think of the ones that promote luxury residential developments or speak up in support of a new big-box store in their neighborhood. Advocates and public relations professionals obscure ties between narrow interests and the "grassroots" support campaigns they sponsor.[61]

The dilemma of insider versus outsider strategies did not just result from HJ coalition peculiarities. We will see in chapter 5 that when ISLA coalition advocates formed a short-term community of interest to win concessions from a big residential developer, the same dilemma emerged. ISLA advocates suddenly acted like insiders. Instead of galvanizing neighborhood residents and upping the volume, they encouraged residents to accept a deal they negotiated with the developer—who was until then the target of indignant ire. Softening participants' critical voices, they temporarily risked weakening the collective commitment to ISLA in order to get a deal done with an unavoidable gatekeeper. They secured residents' support partly by reaffirming their commitment to the people of the community, promising a visibility action (a protest) if the deal failed.

A different kind of pushback induces the central dilemma of a community of identity. I call this one the *dilemma of acting "from" versus "for" the community*. Strategies *from* the community are devised or approved directly by people considered the community's most authentic members. Strategies *for* the community come from people with a more distanced, less deeply authentic, if supportive, relation to the community.

Strategies from the community comport the most closely with advocates' and constituents' vision of a shared identity that needs protecting. Yet these strategies bump up against the external realities of social, political, and cultural inequality in the United States. In lower-income neighborhoods of color such as the ones ISLA worked with in South Los Angeles, many residents lack the time, specialized skills, or sense of entitlement to craft claims and build relationships to protect the community.[62] As urban sociologist Robert Sampson

(1999) has pointed out, even self-identified local communities, keen on building their own capacities, probably will need resources that come from outside
the community, though through no fault of their own.

Put compactly, multiple hazards resulting from institutionalized race and
class inequality push back on community-oriented advocates like those in
ISLA. It becomes more necessary for them to depend on strategies *for* the
community. College-educated, articulately English-speaking ISLA staff who
did not all grow up or do not currently live in ISLA's target neighborhoods
acted "for" the community at crucial points. This is what ISLA advocates did
when they used a leader's connections to university urban planning programs
to access free professional-level assistance with research and documentation.
Acting "for" the community, ISLA leaders imparted to local residents the cultural know-how to read planning documents critically and understand planning policies at a "people's planning school." Participants also learned to conduct surveys of neighborhood conditions. The information they gathered
formed the centerpiece of one of the most beloved of ISLA-sponsored events:
a public education and speak-out assembly held with city planning officials
and a city council member.

Strategies "for" the community worked well sometimes, but staff agonized
over them. ISLA staff spoke frequently and assiduously *as* community members, especially at city hall hearings, projecting that they were *from* the community. During my fieldwork, strategies from the community were the moral
default. They were the standard against which some boundary-policing ISLA
staff tested the strategies for the community that well-meaning outsiders
sometimes devised. In chapter 4, we see how the test fails when students from
a distant college come to ISLA bearing valuable research and professional
skills along with (understandable) cluelessness about the preferred style of
action.

A style, then, is a patterned accommodation with particular, surrounding
structural or institutional realities that impinge regularly on actors' collective efforts. Those realities might be the uequally distributed availability of
spokespeople who can sound articulate in the dominant idioms or the capacity of a group to project a popular will larger than the group. When
participants have frustrating experiences or doubt their choices as they are
working collectively, they have several alternatives. They can maintain the
style of action and shift to the other horn of the dilemma. Or they can re-
coordinate themselves and act in a different style altogether, transforming
their form of togetherness and inviting a new dilemma that goes with that
different style.[63] Or else they may split into factions, or disband and stop
working together at all.

Instead of following patterns of action, studies of social movements often make the organization the consistent, unitary actor in a study. The researcher pieces together what an organization did through retrospective accounts from interviews with activists, newspaper accounts, or both. The goal is to see which strategies or organizations win or lose. My approach is closer to that of sociologist Kathleen Blee's painstaking research on emerging, grassroots activist groups in Pittsburgh. Blee (2012, 14; 2013) looked at "sequences of action and interpretation" more than "the organization," following actors as they interpret each other's responses and create a pathway as they narrow their sense of acceptable options for the group as a whole.[64] I too follow collective interpretations, but find these embedded in scenes of action. Civic action becomes meaningful to actors and their audiences in scenes. Now we just need the term for one other cultural context.

Civic Action Unfolds in Discursive Fields

Advocates usually gravitate to culturally appropriate ways of putting claims about social problems into words. The concept of *discursive field* is a powerful tool that helps us understand why some claims about social problems are culturally appropriate, while others just as logical and grammatical on paper are not. A discursive field is like a territory of problem solving, where advocates and their opponents all implicitly agree to talk about the problem at hand using the same basic symbolic categories—even if the actors speak differently on other turf. As cultural sociologists Robert Wuthnow (1989, 13, 555) and Lyn Spillman (1995, 140) put it succinctly, in a discursive field, claims makers craft claims about social problems by using the same "fundamental categories" that set the "limits of discussion." That way, even competitors and adversaries *understand* each other's arguments though they often do not agree. They do agree that they are competing over the same thing.[65] In the case of our housing advocates, they were competing over how to articulate housing problems and organize people to act collectively on those problems. Advocates and their opponents constructed claims and counterclaims about housing problems from mostly the same symbolic building blocks.

Discursive fields develop their own symbolic weight on participants' imaginations. It is hard to craft claims without the symbolic building blocks the field provides when you are in the fray, talking to, competing with, and fighting against other advocates. Newer participants get cultivated from listening to the established conversation and noticing reactions to their occasional "mistakes." Advocates settle relatively soon on rhetorical conventions, just as they settle on a limited number of organizational strategies and goals, while others brought up early in a group's history drop out of consideration.[66] They may contest those conventions too, but that means they have indeed noticed them. The field with its categories and conventions develops a verbal life of its own. Sociologists say the field develops "relative autonomy"—its own influence on claims makers.[67] That means that when advocates are speaking, arguing, and pondering, their claims are not necessarily simple reflections of their social position—be they tenant, property owner, racially subordinated person, or majority-culture person.

Now we can preview the main arguments, and see how those depart from what the entrepreneurial actor model would suppose.

The Central Arguments

Actors Are Socially Embedded and Culturally Cultivated

Shifting some of the analytic weight from actors to *action* does not remove actors from the story. It puts the spotlight more on the power of contexts that shape action and less on the power of strategic actors to shape contexts. The entrepreneurial actor creates the contexts in which they and others then act. Using verbal and interpersonal *skill*, the actor sizes up situations and wields meanings strategically, producing a context of identities, stories, and rhetorical appeals that will win over others, and therefore meet the actor's goals. In Neil Fligstein and Doug McAdam's (2012, 34–56) account, entrepreneurial actors deploy their skills ultimately in efforts to gain a positive sense of self through the satisfaction of accomplishing collective projects.

The civic action approach proposes, in contrast, that action is more contextual to begin with, and more deeply relational.[68] To interact, actors have to have a sense of who each other are socially while in that scene. Those perceptions shape the action, constraining as well as enabling what the strategic actor can say and do.[69] Actors don't *use* scenes so much as they are *embedded* in scenes with different styles. This hardly makes them helpless dupes. Yet it will be important to recognize that even the leading actors who clue others to the appropriate style are subject to that style's limits. They cannot dismantle the dilemmas that are part of a style.[70] Further, actors are *cultivated* by the big symbolic categories of a discursive field.

The master finding of this study is that there are different ways to be strategic or skilled, with remarkably different practical consequences. There is not simply more and less strategic action. Rather than assume skill is one, general quality, the civic action approach finds different patterns of claims making and relationship building that count as skilled in different contexts. Two contexts, the *style* of a scene and the *discursive field* in which scene participants speak, shape civic action. The book develops three arguments about these cultural contexts.

Styles Shape Actors' Strategies and Goals

The way we often see it, collective action starts when individuals who have the same interests come together to work for a shared goal. Their shared goal motivates them to act. They strategize and pick a style of action that helps them achieve their goal effectively. This study takes a different perspective. It understands actors' strategies and goals as products of relationships, not just reflections of ideas or interests people first carry around in our heads—much as, yes, people have ideas and interests.

Different styles of relationship, pictured in chapters 3 and 4, strongly influenced the LA housing advocates' strategies and notions of "success." In one style of relationship, advocates collaborated as loose, part-time partners with one, narrowly defined interest in common. They thought it made sense to try different alliances or work with different gatekeepers; whatever might win was worth trying. In this context, a short-term campaign could seem sensible and worth doing. For advocates with a different style of relationship who acted as loyal comrades sharing an emotionally resonant identity threatened by powerful outsiders, it made sense to ally mainly with others who identified with the same, imperiled identity. It made sense to envision long-term struggle alongside those allies because short-term "wins" were unlikely to change long-lasting social subordination. Goals that made sense to that first collective could seem relatively trivial to the second; goals that sounded appropriate to the second could sound impractical or rigid to the first. These two different styles of relationship could even coexist in the same coalition or organization, in different scenes, as chapter 5 shows. The combination might endure through creative compartmentalizations or tense standoffs. That is why it is good to follow styled action, not simply "an organization that does things."

Studies from the entrepreneurial actor perspective, in contrast, argue that entrepreneurial actors create strategies and goals in relation to the political opportunities they perceive. Chapter 6 discusses this further, pointing out that these studies say less about why advocates want the ends they want to begin with, and how long they imagine working together to meet them. These are crucial parts of the "how" story. My point is not that political opportunities don't matter; they just don't explain, by themselves, what counts as "strategic" or "successful" to advocates. Illustrations from the two coalitions show that through different styles of relationship, social advocates create different strategic arcs. The same goals come to have different significance and relations to "success" on those different arcs.

Discursive Fields Shape Actors' Claims

LA housing advocates made claims about social problems guided by assumptions about the culturally appropriate ways to put problems into words in a particular setting. By listening to housing and homelessness advocates make claims about housing problems in different settings, I discovered that advocates crafted claims from a relatively few symbolic categories. In public forums like city council chambers, they drew on even fewer categories—fair opportunity and quality of life, mainly—than when they talked about these problems in informal conversations or smaller forums, when occasionally language implying compassion or social structural change came into play. There was a cultural funneling process at work in the larger public settings of the campaigns and projects I studied; some symbolic appeals largely dropped out.

The entrepreneurial actor model primes us to suppose something different. We would assume that advocates use more kinds of rationales in big public forums than smaller, informal ones because they select whichever rationales they think would best convince powerful authorities or win over larger constituencies. We might guess they would manage the risk of alienating listeners, and losing, by selecting their rationales or frames instrumentally as well as being flexible, aiming for the listener. Advocates certainly did engage in strategic framing sometimes, but that happened *within* the parameters of a discursive field and its main categories. Sometimes that meant advocates actually shied away from the symbolic categories that powerful decision makers favored.

Styles Shape Discursive Fields

Shared style informs what advocates can say or else avoid saying for fear of sounding inappropriate or challenging group togetherness. As advocates are making claims, and downplaying or rejecting other claims, they hear each other—and new participants hear them. As the public debate continues, advocates are giving off and picking up signals that some claims are fully legitimate, some are marginal but OK, some are appropriate only in certain spaces, and some should be beyond the bounds. In this way, styled interaction generates boundaries for a discursive field.

When I say that style "informs" what advocates can say, I mean two things. One is that style selects some symbolic categories over others. The other is that different scene styles induce advocates to fashion rather different-sounding, specific claims from even the same symbolic category. For instance, acting as a community of interest, housing advocates turned the category of "fair opportunity" into the specific claim that Angelenos who work in Los

TABLE 1.1 Two Conceptual Approaches to Social Advocacy

	Entrepreneurial actor approach	Civic action approach
Conception of an actor	Actors are always already existing. They are back loaded with skills and motives.	Actors are products of interaction. They are socially embedded and culturally cultivated.
Conception of how collective action transpires	Skilled entrepreneurs drive action.	Action (including a leader's action) is patterned by shared styles in scenes.
Relation between actor and claims	Entrepreneurs use or innovate meanings to create claims. Claims may vary depending on the entrepreneur's perceptions of the audience.	Discursive fields and scene styles together shape actors' claims in specific scenes. The same actor may make different claims depending on the scene.
Relation between actor and relationships	*Univalent* Actors use or create identities to mobilize others for collective action. Relationships are resources for strategies.	*Multivalent* Different scene styles cultivate different meanings of relationship and different ways of coordinating strategies.
Relation between actor, action, and outcomes	Actors with goals initiate action; the outcomes succeed or fail the goals.	Actors following styled lines of action produce goals of varying significance; outcomes emerge on different timelines of success.
Central research questions	Which actors succeed or fail in meeting their goals? Which combination of factors produce which outcomes? "Who wins and why?"	How do collective goals develop? Why are some claims more legitimate than others? What counts as success? "Who can say and do what, and with whom?"

Angeles should be able to live in Los Angeles. That claim projected an interest of LA residents in general. Acting as a community of identity, however, advocates turned that same basic category of fair opportunity into the somewhat different claim that a *specific, underserved community* ought to be able to afford living in its rightful home.

The entrepreneurial actor model would lead us to think something different. We would suppose that claims depend not so much on claimants' own style of togetherness but instead on advocates' perception of what will appeal to the leaders and bystanders they want to convince. Wouldn't advocates create claims with a keen eye for the city officials and landlords who control advocates' access to solutions? Perceptions of these external actors matter. But even as advocates are framing issues strategically, their relation to fellow advocates shapes what they claim publicly about social problems. This pattern became even easier to see when I followed the same advocates to a different scene with a different style of action.

In short, *previous research has tended to overestimate how much claims making is about appealing strategically to others and underestimate how much it is about maintaining the solidarity of the claimants.*

———

Following the action with the conceptual tools of scene style and discursive field, the civic action approach grasps some fundamental *hows* of social advocacy that we miss if we start with skilled, strategic actors. Table 1.1 summarizes the difference in emphasis and different research questions we ask with each approach. The next chapter introduces broader contexts for the campaigns and organizations I studied. It discusses the research methods I used to follow them. Appendix I goes into more detail about the reasons I chose the coalitions and organizations in this study, and how they worked as comparison cases. Appendix II reflects on my own practice as ethnographer and the kinds of relationships I negotiated in the field.

2

Placing and Studying the Action

What Makes Housing Unaffordable:
Contexts Near and Far

Fighting for housing is just one instance of civic action. We will understand better how challenging this instance is if we know what kind of problem housing might be from a sociological point of view. Advocates across the coalitions and organizations in this study talked about housing "affordability" as one of their primary concerns, and often the biggest one. When they said housing in Los Angeles was unaffordable and there was a "housing crisis," they usually meant housing was too expensive for many ordinary Angelenos or frequently unavailable at an affordable price.[1] Using the same language of affordability, it makes sense to ask about the big picture. Is housing unaffordability usually temporary or chronic? Does it result from deep, institutional processes or contingencies relatively easy to alter? Does it affect only particular kinds of people or places? It makes sense to ask about this study's locale too. What might make housing conditions and problems in Los Angeles distinctive, or characteristic of life in the United States, or global, or maybe all three? Here is a brief sketch of crucial contexts that affect the affordability of housing and make it potentially a problem. Following that, I describe the sites of problem solving I studied, and methods I used to access them.

National and Global Contexts for Housing Affordability

Housing is a commodity as well as *home*. Or as urban political economy scholars John Logan and Harvey Molotch (1987) have pointed out, it has exchange value as well as its use value as shelter and locus of personal security. In a capitalist economy, housing is a salable good, like other goods. As a commodity, housing can generate wealth. It does so directly for property owners, and indirectly for local governments, big employers and retailers, and cultural and other institutions that all benefit financially from the higher taxes and fees,

larger workforces, bigger consumer markets, and more sales that more housing, and more expensive housing, can generate.

Put simply, large property owners, local political leaders, and other institutional managers all stand to gain from treating the city and its housing as a
"growth machine" that turns increasingly intensive development into higher
rents and other forms of income for those elites.[2] Under these conditions,
those elites often become boosters for the idea that growth is good for a city
in general. A central role of municipal political and community leaders in
this vision of the city is to assiduously cultivate relations with investors,
national and international corporate employers, and property developers to
produce a good business climate for more growth. In the past several decades, these "public-private partnerships" have switched urban growth machines into high gear, increasingly steering urban development in cities large
and small.[3]

One particularly visible kind of wealth generation happens through the
investment, architectural restoration, and urban redevelopment that scholars
and critics call gentrification. As urban scholar Sharon Zukin (1995, especially
23–24) explains it, "gentrification" is a synthesis of financial investment and
cultural creation. In residential neighborhoods, gentrification generally ends
up displacing lower-income or working-class residents with more affluent
ones who can afford the rents plus property taxes that new or refurbished
housing incurs.[4] In commercial areas, it produces social spaces that generate
wealth for investors and entrepreneurs by appealing to shoppers who want to
be the kind of person who buys shoes or drinks coffee in a renovated factory
warehouse with carefully exposed brick walls, not a big-box discount store or
donut chain. Whether residential or commercial, gentrification enlists lifestyle
preferences in the ongoing process of generating wealth from the city. Gentrification is far bigger than any one city or region. It has become a powerful,
global strategy for redeveloping cities and growing wealth, creating a steady,
sometimes precipitous rise in real estate prices and rents in cities across the
globe. In some ways, then, the shape of recent urban development over the
past several decades in Los Angeles parallels that of New York City, Tokyo, Rio
de Janeiro, and Mumbai.[5]

Some people benefit far more than others from the exchange value of housing, whether or not a given real estate investment or sale is an instance of
gentrification. In his sweeping view of the contemporary city, theorist David
Harvey (1989) has argued that municipal leaders' cultivation of partnerships
with property developers often ends up increasing impoverishment while ex-
acerbating income and wealth inequalities. For tenants who use housing as
home rather than as an object of profitable exchange, life becomes increasingly
uncertain the more that real estate prices increase and property owners hold

out for higher-rent-paying tenants, or else redevelop a residential building altogether.

Redevelopment and gentrification have frequently reinforced or exacerbated race-based as well as social class inequalities. Studies tell us that people's preferences for neighborhoods sort out in a racial hierarchy. Survey respondents have favored white neighbors the most, African American neighbors the least, and Asian and Hispanic neighbors somewhere in the middle—reflecting the prevalent US order of prejudice toward racial minority people and neighborhoods.[6] The biases are institutionalized, not just an individual choice, as minority applicants face lower chances of getting mortgage loans approved and higher chances of being rejected in gentrified neighborhoods than elsewhere.[7] In all, gentrification ends up being strongly associated with race-based exclusionary practices in banking and the housing market.

These sociological views converge on a stark, simple point. Civic action for affordable housing confronts a deeply institutionalized problem. Increasingly unaffordable housing has become endemic to property development in many urban areas over the last several decades. It is hardly an LA story only. In cities across the world, local leaders increasingly and routinely cultivate collaborations as well as pursue policies that perhaps unintentionally, make affordable housing less available. In the United States, African American and Latinx residents frequently suffer disproportionately from those institutionalized relationships. Unaffordability is not simply a sad aggregate of private misfortunes, or temporary effect of economic hard times or local governmental screwups.

Housing advocates have developed a variety of collective efforts to slow, freeze, or even reverse unaffordability. These include municipal regulations, grassroots mobilizations against gentrification, citizen planning projects, and land trusts in which local residents own and develop property in common. LA housing advocates in this study pursued all these avenues to some extent. Studies document that efforts toward more affordable housing in New York, Brooklyn, San Francisco, Caracas, London, Berlin, Istanbul, and other locales have relied on one or more of these strategies too.[8] How, if at all, was Los Angeles different?

Los Angeles as a Place to Study Housing Advocacy

In some ways, Los Angeles was an atypical place to follow housing advocacy. At the same time, the city's housing and property development trends roughly paralleled those of many other big cities. When I started out, Los Angeles had become a city of distinctions prideful and dubious. It was the most culturally diverse city in the United States, and over a third of Los Angeles County residents were foreign born. It was a city of highly class-segregated locales, and greater income inequality than that of the state or nation as a whole.[9] It was also the "homeless capital of America," as a video produced by one of my co-alitions trumpeted sourly; it had more homeless people per capita than New York City or other large urban centers. Los Angeles was also geographically distinctive. The modern, industrial city as charted by early Chicago school sociologists has a coinciding geographic, political, and financial center; think Manhattan in New York. In contrast, Los Angeles in the eyes of its own "Los Angeles school" of urban geographers is a "young, sprawling, suburban, cen-terless, multinucleated" place.[10] Educated opinion and snide commentary from the East tended to agree; a bunch of neighborhoods in search of a city is one way I heard it put.

It was also a city of renters. At the start of this study, only 38 percent of LA residents were homeowners, 20 percent lower than the national proportion. That is partly because while the LA metropolitan area continued to be the number one manufacturing region in the country, the proportion of higher-paid and generally unionized jobs to lower-wage jobs had fallen precipitously. More of the workers in manufacturing were sewing pants and fewer were building airplanes.[11] In all, Los Angeles was home to a relatively large popula-tion of low-wage workers, many recently arrived in the United States. Though plenty of Los Angeles County residents including Angelenos inside the city limits defaulted on mortgages during the Great Recession of 2008, advocates had been talking of the housing crisis for years before that, particularly with tenants in mind. The groups I studied certainly did not exhaust housing advo-cacy in Los Angeles at the time, but they appeared to make surprisingly few, if any, significant changes in organizing strategies on account of the recession.

The longer-term "crisis" is a big clue to what makes Los Angeles like other contemporary metropolises after all. Though it started later than other big cities, Los Angeles kicked its own "growth machine" into high gear and used it to power downtown redevelopment.[12] By the 1980s and 1990s, it was gener-ating a new high-rise skyline downtown, museums, hotels, restaurants, the-aters, and sports and shopping centers, displacing former residents.[13] As else-where, ambitious developers and private investment partnered with city officials to market Los Angeles as a destination for tourists and shoppers, and make downtown a home for affluent professionals and artists. Loft living came to Los Angeles. The nonpoor resident population of downtown started grow-ing for the first time in several decades. The features of growth machine–style development described above were easily visible to a visitor or ethnographer. A new city ordinance put in place several years before this study aided de-velopers that wanted to turn historic buildings—pillared banks and marble-sided corporate headquarters—into new and generally upscale housing.[14] One could draw a line on a map from downtown southward several miles and label it with new cultural institutions, restaurants, and entertainment com-plexes; an intensively developed city center was emerging, and so was the disproportionate displacement of Latinx and African American residents from areas surrounding the largest developments.[15]

So it is not necessarily surprising that unaffordability could resonate as a problem when advocates pitched it to tenants, especially in central Los Angeles, but other city districts too. It resonated with important labor and religious leaders. Rents were rising faster than incomes, and as the HJ coalition liked to point out, many ordinary Angelenos—cooks, janitors, social workers, and high school teachers—would not be able to afford average rents on a single salary; homeownership similarly was out of reach for the typical nurse, firefighter, urban planner, or film editor. Developers were not building primarily for them. In 2007, developers built less than a third of the housing units needed for residents classified as having "very low income," less than half needed for those who fell into the "low-income" category, and less than a tenth of what moderate-income people needed. They built almost double the documented need for residents with above-moderate incomes.[16] The "multinucleated" city hosted a number of gentrification hot spots, including the city center, and displacement hot spots mapped onto them closely.[17] Redevelopment and displacement were evident in several neighborhoods of South Los Angeles where this study's advocates did their organizing, and numerous others in Los Angeles during this study.[18]

The fact that some city council members *also* were ready to consider unaffordability a severe problem, not simply an unavoidable trade-off of prosperity, is a clue to another, more distinctive condition. At the new millennium, urban scholars were starting to argue that while Los Angeles' growth machine had spurred lots of development, local economic and political elites' growth consensus had weakened and fragmented, despite the continuing influence of business and real estate developers at city hall.[19] Alongside growth had come world-renowned freeway traffic, air pollution, and homelessness as well as the disappearance of public places. One urban scholar has argued that it is for lack of a stronger, progrowth consensus that large-scale urban development projects often contend with opposing views on the use of the city's space.

Since 2000, big developers and local tenant advocacy groups have contended over large entertainment or residential developments, for example. Tenant groups have increased their leverage with a new device: the community benefits agreement (CBA). These are contracts through which a developer promises goods, such as local hiring or affordable units inside a new apartment complex, intended for a local constituency impacted by a new development.[20] During this study, the ISLA coalition secured a CBA for these and other benefits in exchange for ceasing public criticism of a developer, and was working toward securing another. The CBA suggests a world of urban development in which coalitions of low-income and often minority tenants potentially have new power, and also difficult new trade-offs, as we will see.

The LA context, in short, offered some special potentials and challenges for housing advocates as well as for a study of civic action on housing. Without a rigidly hegemonic growth coalition, housing advocates stood a significant chance of winning some of their aims.[21] And winning had the potential to improve life for a large proportion of people in many parts of the city. The strong Latin American and other immigrant presence along with an established African American community offered housing advocates a potential diversity of cultural vocabularies to integrate into their work. Regarding this study, that diversity would be a good test for concepts from cultural sociology, style and discursive field, which suppose that certain meaningful, powerful patterns of action exist even *across* different ethnic, national, and linguistic idioms and social locations. The comparison of African American with Latinx-centered housing advocacy later in the book is one sign that the concepts pass the test. Distinct cultural idioms and unequal social locations of course mattered. Styles of action and discursive fields happen only through them, but are not reducible to or direct reflections of them.

The campaigns I studied represent a range of organizing and claims-making strategies, any of which might make good sense given the contexts sketched here. If the economic and political forces of an intensive, high-speed growth machine are (at least) citywide or regional, then campaigning for a citywide affordable housing mandate as HJ did could be a reasonable response. If gentrification proceeds by block or project, especially in hot spots as it did in Los Angeles, then campaigning around particular developments with discrete developer targets could make sense too. A differently designed study with many more comparisons might begin to determine which set of strategies is the most feasible or successful for which given conditions.

I aimed to do something else. Advocates do not simply calculate which strategies are the most feasible or likely to succeed under given conditions, and then choose them. But even if they *did*, knowing that a strategy is an intentional, maximizing response to external conditions—whether that includes municipal politics, developer hegemony, the pressure of other advocacy groups, or all three—does not tell us *how* that strategy produces outcomes or what it means to the strategists. Instead of weighing in on "which strategy is better," I point out the dilemmas and trade-offs of different kinds of action, all of which could be found in each campaign I studied.

Civic Action on Housing in Los Angeles

In this study's approach, chains of action create coalitions along with their member organizations and campaigns. We can highlight the action without ignoring that advocates as well as researchers usually talk about coalitions, organizations, and campaigns as acting entities in themselves. Approaching a large theme such as housing advocacy through multiple entry points opens a study to comparisons we need if we are going to understand how the theme plays out in action.[22] I thought of coalitions and organizations as potential entry points to diverse kinds of civic action rather than as objects of study in themselves, or simply representatives of neighborhood-centered versus city-wide strategies. My docket of coalitions and organizations to study expanded as a conceptual agenda about civic action, claims making, and relationship building crystallized.

The study settled on three sets of collective efforts on housing. I begin the discussion of each set with a sketch of the relevant conditions that informed that set of advocacy efforts at the start of this study late in 2007 and over the next four years. After each sketch of conditions comes a description of the campaigns or organizational efforts that addressed those conditions as problems during my research. There were four campaigns, pursued by three coalitions, and a total of twelve organizations and projects observed in some way in this study.[23] After introducing the campaigns, coalitions, and organizations, I lay out the methods I used to study them.

Acting for Citywide Affordable Housing Mandates

Conditions: Unaffordable Housing in Los Angeles

Los Angeles was an inordinately expensive place to call home for many Angelenos during the decade leading up to my study's start. Construction of city-subsidized, below-market-rate housing dropped by half during the 1990s while the city gained 300,000 residents.[24] The median home price in Los Angeles County in 1998, already a relatively high $183,000, had climbed to $440,000 by 2005, and the proportion of first-time home-buying households able to afford that median price had dwindled to 14 percent.[25] Between 1998 and 2005, the Los Angeles–Long Beach area weighed in as the fifth least affordable metropolitan area in the nation, and the city lost over 9,000 rent-controlled units either to demolition or condominium conversion. The affordable units built tended strongly to cluster in lower-income areas of the city, while the eight *least* affordable neighborhoods saw the construction of 10,000 units of market-rate housing, but only 225 units of affordable housing.[26]

Plenty of Angelenos suffered the housing that they did manage to find. In 2002, one in seven apartments were considered substandard, and a third of all apartments counted as "overcrowded"—and this by a criterion that counted the kitchen as a "bedroom" for one inhabitant.[27] By 2004, 18 percent of households in Los Angeles experienced "severe overcrowding"—meaning 1.5 people per room, *including* living rooms, kitchens, and dining rooms as well as bedrooms.[28] The dismal statistics became palpably tragic in late 2000, when a slum apartment building in a working-class Latinx neighborhood collapsed, killing the father of 2 small children and injuring 35 other residents.

These are the conditions that advocates were calling a "crisis" years before the mortgage default epidemic that accompanied the Great Recession of 2008. The HJ campaign I studied was one of three separate but related efforts publicizing the crisis of insufficient affordable housing during the decade before my study. A shifting coalition of advocacy groups calling itself HJ orchestrated each of the three campaigns as a fight for municipal policy solutions. Initiated by the Western Housing Association (WHA) in 1998, the first iteration of the HJ coalition centered labor, religious, and tenant organizations, other nonprofits, and a few banks on one specific goal—a $100 million trust fund to support affordable housing construction. The former WHA director described the kinds of relationships I would find nearly a decade later in a later incarnation of the HJ coalition that I studied: a diverse community of interest whose member organizations each apportioned a small part of their staff time to strategy meetings, meetings with city council members, and public events in support of HJ's single, delimited goal. The city council approved the trust fund in early 2002.

The second HJ campaign, in contrast, did not meet its self-stated aim of an "inclusionary zoning" ordinance. The ordinance, introduced by a city council member in 2004, would mandate housing developments with five or more units to offer a percentage of those units below ordinary market rates in exchange for incentives. Rhetorical appeals and lines of opposition familiar from the HJ case in this study seemed to play out in the second campaign. The cardinal of the local archdiocese championed the ordinance for balancing "private initiative and social justice," while a less supportive city council person declared, "My focus is to maintain quality of life in a community." Real estate developers warned city council members that without a "balancing measure" of incentives for them, inclusionary zoning would make developments, and therefore land, only more expensive. Neighborhood councils went on record opposing the ordinance for threatening to bring "oversize housing projects" and raise "quality-of-life issues" by overburdening roads, schools, and parks. The mayor and at least one powerful council member said neighborhood council opposition informed their own opinions. The mayor also argued the ordinance would diminish business opportunities. Fair opportunity and quality-of-life appeals along with the antagonism of the local neighborhood councils would all replay in the third HJ campaign, which I studied intensively. Moves toward an inclusionary zoning ordinance stalled in 2005 and never came to a full vote in the city council.[29]

The Mixed-Income Housing Ordinance Campaign of the HJ Coalition

In 2006, housing advocates began reassembling an HJ coalition for the third time, and trying out policy positions and slogans, in another bid to institute citywide policies to produce more affordable housing. When the new campaign for a mixed-income housing ordinance (MIHO) went public at a rally in March 2008, 35 percent of working households were paying more than half their income on housing—a rate over 50 percent higher than the average for major metropolitan areas.[30] The newly (re)constituted HJ coalition included nonprofit housing developers, tenants' associations, community advocacy groups, and labor leaders. Coalition members converged on a three-point program that demanded permanent funding for the already-established housing trust fund, protection against the demolition or conversion of existing low-rent apartments, and most centrally, a fixed quota of affordable units in any new development above a certain size. Representatives from eighteen different organizations attended coordinating committee meetings during the time of my observation from September 2008 to September 2009, though individual organizations' levels of involvement waxed and waned. The coalition secured roughly a hundred organizational endorsements, from community groups, tenant associations, nonprofits, governing agencies, and organizations less central to construction of or advocacy for affordable housing, such as the YMCA. The coalition successfully convinced a number of city council members to sign a pledge supporting the three-point plan. As scenarios in chapter 3 depict in much more detail, the campaign gained momentum, commitments from council members, and at least general support from the mayor, but also was hampered by a bitter internal division before running into a legal roadblock. HJ's campaign dissipated in 2010.

This HJ coalition was tense from the start. Two leading advocacy organizations in South Los Angeles, Los Angeles People's Organization (LAPO) and Southside for Equitable Development (SED) (see table 2.2), were one-time coordinating committee members. They chose to "endorse" rather than work more closely with HJ coalition leaders either prior to or during the most active period of coalition building and pressuring, which corresponded to the early period of this study. They first formed a "subset" of the HJ coalition that would focus on preserving housing for the lowest-income residents.

Tensions increased, and LAPO and several other organizations that had also participated on the HJ coordinating committee began forming what became the new, separate, Housing Rights Now (HRN) coalition.

The Housing Preservation Campaign of the HRN Coalition

The HRN coalition went public early in 2010. It included five, onetime organizational members of HJ coalition's coordinating committee. The HRN and HJ coalitions both included organizations representing low-income and racially diverse constituencies. HRN, however, made economic and racial exclusion much more salient—albeit indirectly by means of talk about "the community." Given that salience, I add these social descriptors for the HRN organizations: two were mostly Latinx, working-class tenant organizations; one was a multiracial, lower-income tenant organization in another part of town; another was LAPO, with a plurality of African American members; and SED, an organization centered in South Los Angeles, had a mostly Latinx, blue-collar, or underemployed membership. One of those organizations continued to collaborate with the HJ coalition too, while the other four distanced themselves from HJ's leadership and remained paper endorsers only. LAPO plays an especially important comparative role in the study. HRN was still jelling as a coalition and developing housing preservation strategies during my short time observing alongside it. Coalition leaders orchestrated a four-hour "town hall" meeting at which hundreds of tenant members of HRN organizations came to alert a city council person to tenant living conditions in southern and eastern LA neighborhoods.

Acting to Curb Residential Displacement South of Downtown

Conditions: Residential Redevelopment and Displacement

During the same decade that housing became increasingly unaffordable and overcrowded for nonaffluent Angelenos in the city at large, particular pressures were transforming two neighborhoods south of downtown. In the late 1990s, a neighborhood adjacent to Balboa Boulevard was swept up in a larger plan to reimagine downtown and adjacent neighborhoods southward as a destination of choice for shoppers, culture tourists, nighttime revelers, and hip loft dwellers. Emblematic of the challenge to the top-down rebranding of this area was the finding from a study commissioned by a local museum that patrons "liked going to the museum once they were there but did not like having to be in the neighborhood." The particular Balboa Boulevard neighborhood germane to this study, a heavily working-class and Latinx enclave of modest bungalows, the occasional Victorian, dingy strip malls, and freeway underpasses, acquired a new skyline, and its footprint changed dramatically during my research. Several massive apartment buildings shot up, and construction began on a shopping and housing complex. Architecturally derived from Spanish mission, Italian, or Gothic styles, the developments brought an assertively ornamented presence to the neighborhood. Commercial developers and an expanding college sited their residential and commercial projects in the area.[31]

To local housing advocates, throughout this study's duration, these developments together portended massive residential displacement for working-class tenants of color. Research by as well as the daily experiences of staff and members of SED, a locally leading housing and economic advocacy organization mentioned above, suggest the apprehension was realistic. SED's own studies indicated that by the early 2000s, as much as half of the housing formerly occupied by longer-term residents in neighborhoods near Balboa Boulevard had shifted to "student-occupied" units. Tenants told SED staff that landlords were harassing them, trying to evict or scare them away to then rent their units at higher rates to students. The same staff reported hearing from local churches that congregations had shrunk by as much as half in a short time, presumably because former attendees were deserting a neighborhood they could no longer afford. These housing and antigentrification advocates along with labor and community development groups had participated in the Balboa Equitable Development Coalition, which several years earlier won commitments from the developer of an entertainment complex to make affordable housing construction and employment opportunities part of the development package. Similar kinds of CBAs would eventually become the material centerpiece of two campaigns I studied.

The Antidisplacement Campaign of the ISLA Coalition

The Balboa coalition was coasting toward semidormancy by early 2008 when one of its organizational leaders proposed a new campaign to slow, if not reverse, the displacement of many tenants who had long resided in the area. That winter, some organizational staff and core participants from the old Balboa coalition attended a daylong workshop that kicked off this new campaign. In the following months, their organizations reconvened and renamed the coalition Inquilinos del Sur de Los Angeles (ISLA), which now would exist largely to propel this campaign. The next year the campaign focused intensively on a nearby neighborhood centered on Draper Boulevard, where advocates' door-to-door surveying revealed similar displacement trends during roughly the same period.[32]

Staff employed by several tenant and community development organizations apportioned part of their time for ISLA's leadership of the campaign. Slowly at first, they assembled a coalition and pursued a multipronged effort. Field organizer staff worked at publicizing the campaign to local storefront businesses, churches, and ambivalently, college students. Field organizers and resident leaders from the impacted neighborhoods attended, monitored, and gave testimony at public hearings mandated by the city planning commission to update urban planning protocols for the relevant neighborhoods, and assess new development plans. There were local door-knocking and public education efforts too. The campaign acquired a "planning mobile"—a cross between a trailer and boat—that passersby could board and view proposed neighborhood plans inside. In its third year, the campaign became increasingly issue focused, especially on affordable housing and local job development, attracting more organizational allies. The campaign hatched a half-year-long project of grassroots planning workshops and research on Draper neighborhood residents' needs and visions. The project produced "alternative" development plans drawn up by urban planning students from a distant college, informed by data from ISLA's research team. Contacts with property development officials at a local college, intermittent and often frustrating for many months, intensified, ultimately producing a CBA for affordable housing construction and local hiring, among other goods, in 2012.

The most frequently attending local residents at antidisplacement campaign activities were blue-collar or underemployed, low- to moderate-income Latinx people. Many, if not most, spoke Spanish comfortably or as a first language, and many spoke English. Meetings often happened with speakers alternating Spanish and English, or occasionally, in Spanish almost entirely. Usually staff were on hand to translate Spanish-language presentations and comments to English for larger meetings where a significant number of English-only speakers might be present. Occasionally the reverse also happened. Roughly half the main staff spoke Spanish as well as English at campaign events. The organizational staff who did the bulk of campaign planning and led meetings were college educated and ethnically and racially diverse; one campaign organizer identified as African American, and two organizers identified as white—one of those was Spanish speaking, and two identified as Latina or Latino; and the overall visioning of the campaign was initiated by two directors, one Latina and one white, from one of ISLA's core organizations.

The Manchester Apartments Campaign of the ISLA Coalition

In the middle of its long-term antidisplacement campaign, ISLA ran an intensive, five-month campaign pressing for alternative building plans for the Manchester, a high-rent apartment complex whose development would require demolishing part of a hospital site. ISLA member organizations had monitored the development for over two years and were busy with their larger antidisplacement campaign when the Manchester's threat materialized suddenly, and a bulldozer began making room for the new apartment complex. Hurriedly, ISLA organized local residents, planned with allies, and attended public hearings, just as construction leveled part of the hospital. Advocates and residents demanded that the city planning commission withhold approval until the builder agreed to alter building plans, offer some affordable units, and support a community medical clinic. Within a few months, ISLA won a revised plan for the Manchester, and a CBA that provided for a quota of reduced-rent apartments and a low-cost medical clinic inside the Manchester development.

The ISLA organizations supplying most of the personnel and local resident participants in the Manchester campaign were SED, the CGTC land trust, a community development corporation that also trained health educators for ISLA's neighborhoods, and a labor development nonprofit. The most heavily participating staff were the same as those orchestrating the antidisplacement campaign.

Action on Homelessness

Conditions: Homelessness in Los Angeles

During the first year of my study, the city of Los Angeles estimated the number of homeless people at around seventy-four thousand. While the amount dropped to the high forty thousands by the end of my study, the city retained its title as "homeless capital of the United States." Commuters driving past small "pocket parks" or through freeway underpasses could glimpse people braving the multiple assaults of unhoused existence in makeshift assemblies of circular tents—little pop-up carnivals of survival. Pedestrians in some parts of town regularly encountered sun-beaten people clothed in matted layers, soliciting spare change. That was especially true in commercial districts without the security workers, incongruously cheery looking in their turquoise or purple polo shirts, that local businesses contracted with to roust "panhandlers." On metro lines in the central city, solicitors were a familiar presence— like the woman who ambled down the aisle soliciting in a piercing soprano voice, jiggling coins in a white Styrofoam cup within millimeters of noses and eyeglasses. Homelessness was figuratively as well as literally in the face of many Angelenos. Some of the same contexts that made housing unaffordable—an urban "growth machine" set on high speed with the accompanying racialized gentrification and loss of higher-paying manufacturing jobs—contributed to increased homelessness at the start of this study and a disproportionately African American homeless population in the center city. I examined several differently styled organizational responses to homelessness.

Organizations and Projects Addressing Homelessness

I did not study long campaigns of homeless advocacy. As an issue that was potentially separate from housing, homelessness served mainly as a point of comparison. The study included homelessness-focused groups to try out ideas about how discursive fields work. Instead of coalition campaigns, I chose a range of field sites where I might hear actors treating homelessness or homeless people as a problem, whether alongside or apart from the problem of unaffordable housing. I aimed to tap different approaches to homelessness, from in-your-face protest to charitable volunteering, to professional service delivery. Two of these sites were organizations that also participated in campaigns orchestrated by HJ or ISLA coalitions, so their engagement across "housing" and "homelessness" offered valuable comparative angles. Other sites concentrated exclusively on serving homeless people, or educating or advocating on their behalf.

Coalitions as Sites for Observing Campaigns

Apart from the relatively brief look at collective efforts on homelessness, the study's principle subject matter is *campaigns*, not coalitions. The organizational realities of the coalitions themselves—their membership, structure, and history—are important mainly to the extent they come out in the action I followed. Important details on the coalitions were sketched above. Most of the coalition participants came from already-existing organizations devoted to housing, homelessness, urban development, and related issues. I chose scenes from those organizations, or else leading representatives of those organizations acting in other scenes, for ethnographic focus. That helped build my arguments and test out alternative accounts.

Table 2.1 summarizes the campaigns. The table also names organizations participating in those campaigns that I chose for participant observation. Table 2.2 offers brief descriptive sketches of these coalition organizations and others that addressed homelessness specifically and were not involved in coalition campaigns. These thumbnail treatments are offered in the spirit of

TABLE 2.1 Sites of Campaign Action

Campaign	Coalition	Scene styles observed in the coalition	Main topics of claims	Participant observation of sites or with staff from these organizations + *Member of multiple coalitions* **H** *Significant engagement with homelessness issues or homeless people*
Citywide affordable housing campaign (MIHO)	Housing Justice (HJ)	Community of interest; community of identity; hybrid civic action; noncivic action	Affordable housing	Housing Justice staff organization Western Housing Association **H** Stop Homelessness and Poverty-LA +**H** Los Angeles People's Organization +**H** Caring Embrace of the Homeless and Poor Housing Solutions for Los Angeles
Housing preservation campaign—breakaway from MIHO campaign	Housing Rights Now (HRN)	Community of identity	Affordable housing	+**H** Los Angeles People's Organization +Southside for Equitable Development
Manchester campaign	ISLA	Community of identity; community of interest	Affordable housing; health	+Southside for Equitable Development +Common Ground/Tierra Común
Antidisplacement campaign	ISLA	Community of identity; community of interest	Affordable housing; to lesser extent, urban development	+Common Ground/Tierra Común +**H** Caring Embrace of the Homeless and Poor +Southside for Equitable Development

TABLE 2.2 Sketches of Housing and Homelessness Organizations Represented in the Study

Organization	Description	Sites/people observed
Housing Justice Staff Organization (HJ staff)	Staff group of six people who coordinated the HJ coalition. Included a field organizer, intern, coalition director, and publicist.	Five office work shifts Two field organizers at monthly HJ coalition meetings and rallies; two staff at a LAPO rally and at three CE meetings
Western Housing Association (WHA)	Regional association of several dozen nonprofit housing developers, advocates, government agencies, and banks. Sponsored HJ coalition. Held conferences and workshops, and lobbied for affordable housing.	Two daylong WHA conferences One staff member at monthly HJ coalition meetings and at office work shifts
Stop Homelessness and Poverty-LA (SHAPLA)	Small grassroots advocacy organization that monitored policy making on homelessness. Sponsored grassroots organizing committee. Representative attended some HJ coalition meetings.	Three meetings of grassroots organizing committee One "tent city" protest at city hall One staff person at HomeWalk event
Los Angeles People's Organization (LAPO)	Downtown grassroots organization that advocated with low-income tenants and homeless people for housing and civil rights as well as protection from evictions. Sponsored housing committee, which organized protests of landlords and testified at city hall hearings on tenant issues. Sponsored monthly general meetings for area residents. Dropped out of HJ coalition.	Nineteen housing committee meetings Four general meetings Four protest march/rallies Three hearings at city hall Director at one HJ coalition meeting Staff and members at HJ rally Staff and members at HRN workshop, and at speak-out with city official Staff and members at four city hall hearings
Caring Embrace of the Homeless and Poor (CE)	Small grassroots alliance of religious congregational leaders and advocates concerned with homelessness in South Los Angeles neighborhoods. Sponsored the Nails Project public education campaign on homelessness for LA congregations. Peripherally involved in HJ coalition.	Twenty monthly meetings and three performances Two convocations on homelessness with religious congregations Director at ISLA general and strategy meetings Director at one HJ coalition meeting

Continued on next page

TABLE 2.2 (*continued*)

Organization	Description	Sites/people observed
Housing Solutions for Los Angeles (HSLA)	Nonprofit organization of six staff and interns that developed affordable housing projects in Los Angeles. Belonged to HJ coalition but did not send representatives to meetings during this study.	Office work shifts (average of three hours a week) for four months—main office and satellite office Community liaison at two local resident meetings, five neighborhood booster association meetings, and ISLA coalition's kickoff meeting
Southside for Equitable Development (SED)	Grassroots organization advocating affordable housing and health care access for low-income tenants in South Los Angeles. Maintained leading role in ISLA coalition's antidisplacement and Manchester campaigns.	Directors, organizing staff, and members at ISLA general and strategy meetings and four public workshops on redevelopment, over four years Three participatory urban planning workshops Directors, organizing staff and members at four city hall hearings Staff person and members at HRN workshop and at speak-out with city official
Common Ground/ Tierra Común (CGTC)	Grassroots organization whose members owned land in common in South Los Angeles. Provided staff prominent in ISLA's Manchester and antidisplacement campaigns. Led implementation of community benefits agreement with Manchester developer.	Twelve general member meetings and neighborhood celebrations Director, staff and members at many ISLA general and strategy meetings over four years Director and staff at Manchester CBA implementation committee meetings
The Way Home (TWH)— Outreach	Volunteer ride-along program with TWH outreach workers who invite homeless people to shelter and personal rehabilitation program.	Ten ride-alongs (four hours each) Two tours of a TWH shelter One volunteer training
The Way Home (TWH)—Faith Brings Us Home	Short-lived network designed to involve religious congregations in collaborative, service, advocacy, or home-building efforts for homeless people.	Two luncheon workshops Staff member at a HomeWalk event
HomeWalk	Annual five-kilometer fundraising walk with speaker program, organized by United Way charity organization to raise funds and increase awareness of housing solutions to homelessness.	Two HomeWalk fundraising walks

orienting you to the collective actors and issues treated in the study, not to provide exhaustive descriptions, which would not be relevant for the kinds of arguments this book will make.

How I Studied the Action

Participant Observation

If we want to follow the action, participant observation is the royal route. Starting in November 2007 and continuing through August 2012, I attended, observed, and sometimes participated in a variety of sites related to the MIHO, antidisplacement, and Manchester campaigns, and homeless service and advocacy organizations. During periods of funded, partial release from teaching obligations and over the summer, I attended as many as four sites a week.[33] During normal teaching semesters, I attended roughly one site every week or two.[34]

I spent roughly two years with the HJ coalition's MIHO campaign sites. This included the monthly campaign coordinating committee meetings for ten months, several rallies and public education or "town hall" events, several workshops for tenants, and four two- to three-hour stints of office work in the HJ staff office. I observed two annual conferences put on by the professional association WHA, and three city hall hearings on a MIHO.

I spent four years with ISLA's antidisplacement campaign and Manchester campaign sites. These included general monthly meetings over several years' time, semimonthly strategy sessions, and a half-dozen rallies and marches—usually downtown. During this time I also observed two town hall events dedicated to redevelopment plans in ISLA neighborhoods, and observed and assisted with note taking at three morning-long presentation and focus group breakout events that ISLA staff orchestrated to elicit local residents' opinions about the redevelopment of Draper Boulevard. A research team met semiweekly to analyze focus group and survey data produced from these events, and I participated in three of those meetings as well as two long sessions during which student urban planners presented their findings and plans for the neighborhood. I also observed three city hall hearings related to the Manchester campaign, and three Balboa neighborhood visioning and citizen planning meetings orchestrated by the Community Redevelopment Agency (CRA), a state-sponsored body which apportioned developer fees to urban redevelopment projects all over California.

Over three months I watched as HRN started generating a housing preservation campaign, beginning with a daylong retreat, then a rally on city hall's steps, and a raucous three-hour "town hall" meeting at which participants told a city council member about smelly, unsafe, roach-infested apartments that rented for far too much money. In all I followed HJ, ISLA, and HRN advocates to over a dozen meetings and hearings at city hall, at which city council, city planning commission, or council committees dedicated to housing or land use heard testimonies from advocates and local residents, and made decisions about affordable housing legislation, the Manchester apartments development plan, and proposed rent control ordinances.

As members of multiple coalitions, LAPO and Caring Embrace (CE) each played especially pivotal roles. Over two years' time, I attended monthly meetings of CE and two of its breakfast summits. I attended five LAPO general meetings, two fundraising galas, and roughly eleven months of LAPO monthly housing committee meetings and phone canvasing sessions. I accompanied LAPO advocates and residents to three city hall meetings, one protest march to a city council member's house (he was not home), and several other downtown protest march/rally events—one attended by a huge, green, papier-mâché dragon I will never forget.

Sites of service and advocacy for homeless people played important comparative roles, mainly for chapter 8. A research assistant and I logged a total of fourteen field visits with projects run by The Way Home (TWH), a large nonprofit organization serving homeless Angelenos, between winter 2007 and spring 2009. Ten of these visits were to accompany TWH staff doing outreach work shifts, traveling in TWH's little white trucks in search of homeless people to invite back to shelters. I also participated in one informal and one formal tour of TWH's signature shelter facility, and had two conversational meetings with the volunteer coordinator and one with the executive director. TWH's short-lived Faith Brings Us Home project for religious congregations had two quarterly lunch presentations and one training for volunteers participating in Los Angeles' annual homeless census; I observed and participated alongside all these, and a research assistant participated in a census of homeless people. I participated in and observed two annual HomeWalk five-kilometer walk-athons. I caught three meetings of the grassroots organizing committee of Stop Homelessness and Poverty–LA (SHAPLA), and visited a tent city protest orchestrated by SHAPLA, set up on the lawn outside city hall, before the organization dissipated.

Finally, to understand how civic action played into affordable housing development, I spent on average three hours a week for four months with nonprofit housing developer Housing Solutions for Los Angeles (HSLA). I worked as a pro bono grant writer, office tasker, and office assistant at the real estate management company that contracted with HSLA to administer leases for tenants in one of its new apartment complexes. I was surprised and delighted that HSLA staff were not only willing but happy to introduce me to the grant writing that funded their enterprise. They welcomed me also to the community-relations-building work they—especially the community liaison—did to maintain a high public reputation as well as assist tenants with food and educational needs beyond housing.

With each new site, I first introduced my goals as a mostly observing, sometimes volunteering participant to staff connected with the campaigns, then to a large initial meeting of each coalition.[35] I introduced myself subsequently to unfamiliar participants. Following well-established practice, field notes began with jottings in all settings researched and were later expanded to complete notes.[36]

One of the central goals of participant observation research was to figure out how actors were styling their action. I needed to see, too, how actors made claims about housing and other problems they saw as adjacent. And ultimately I would want to try out the idea that style shaped the way advocates articulated claims about problems. That is why the scenes of action that get the most attention in the study were coordinating committee and other meetings that determined strategies, rallies and protest marches, "town hall" assemblies of Angelenos and their municipal leaders, and city council hearings. These were scenes in which advocates decided how to word claims and build relationships, and where they sustained the ordinary working relationships that keep aloft a shared imagination of "the organization." To identify scene style and switches in style between scenes, I coded and compared field notes over time and between different scenes of observation.[37] I established the existence of a relatively stable, dominant scene style in scenes of each of the campaigns and other organizations from observations of interactions that transpired prior to interactions that I mined for evidence of a style's influence on claims making, recruiting, or coalition building. The point here was to avoid the circular reasoning that would result from using the same ethnographic evidence to establish the existence of a style and also portray its influence on subsequent interaction.[38]

Archival Research

Empirical arguments about claims making and styles of relationship can be held to different standards of exhaustiveness. The analyst of style needs to be content with relatively consistent, in-person observation over time, unless the analyst videotapes meetings—an option that social convention along with some advocates' wariness of trickery made nearly unthinkable.[39] Given the definition of style, the observer can be fairly sure that the style of a routine scene will not frequently change much, though civic actors do occasionally switch styles and hive off new scenes, as we will see.[40]

Opportunities for studying claims making are different. Actors along with their devices and hosting institutions record claims, in legal depositions, flyers, PowerPoint presentations, and videotaped meetings at city hall. An actor's claims often did not change much from one public hearing or staff meeting to the next. Still, it was possible to track claims more exhaustively than through participant observation either alone or with occasional assistance. So while I kept track of claims about housing, homelessness, health, the environment, and related issues in field notes, I also summoned the most exhaustive, and sometimes the only available, archival evidence on two central and contrasting campaigns in this study: HJ coalition's 2½-year campaign for citywide affordable housing mandates, and ISLA's briefer campaign to alter development plans for the massive, Manchester apartment complex.

ISLA and HJ staff as well as the city of Los Angeles supplied archival data sources. Both ISLA's and HJ's managing organizations (SED for ISLA, and HJ staff for HJ) provided access to files containing fact sheets, talking points, meeting summaries, and letters to officials, sometimes including different drafts of each. This produced 327 documents for ISLA and 156 documents for HJ. These documents may not represent the affordable housing and Manchester campaigns exhaustively, but staff confirmed that no other comprehensive source existed for reconstructing the campaigns. The LA city clerk's office offered access to the video or audio recordings for meetings held at city hall involving each campaign. For the Manchester campaign, there were three meetings with the city planning commission. Separate from the commissioners, sixty-nine civic actors, including ISLA advocates and the opposing side, spoke publicly at these meetings—some multiple times. For the HJ campaign, a city council subcommittee discussed an affordable housing ordinance during two meetings. At those meetings, fifty-five civic actors spoke publicly, including HJ advocates along with opposing actors representing commercial and building trades outfits. These audio and video recordings of city hall proceedings, along with ISLA and HJ files on their respective campaigns, constituted the body of archival data for analysis.

3

Solving Problems by Fighting
for an Interest

Isn't This Just Good Strategy?

It was late September 2008. Two Wall Street financial giants had just declared bankruptcy. Many people in the United States were defaulting on their mortgages as the Great Recession deepened. In Los Angeles, housing advocates decried a housing crisis that they said had been worsening for years already. The HJ coalition's campaign for a citywide affordable housing ordinance was picking up steam, and advocates at the monthly coordinating committee meeting agreed that the previous week's housing summit had been a success. The summit dramatized support, especially by labor groups, for a MIHO, and the mayor had spoken, seeming to endorse the citywide ordinance.[1] The summit's first speaker, from a community organizing outfit, summed up the story line:

> "It's all over the news, we're in an economic disaster in our country, but on top of that in the city of Los Angeles we have a housing crisis that we need to get out of. So today, as we've seen, we're here to learn about how the housing crisis is affecting all of us and what we must do together to make the changes needed. We need a housing market that will work for all of us, for all economic levels. Today we are representing Los Angeles with over 100 people from the community . . . community groups, labor unions, renters, faith groups, housing developers, city officials. We are here together as Housing Justice."

The next speaker, a financial manager, told us her clients had been calling all week to ask if they should take their money out of Merrill Lynch and find new home insurance brokers. She mused that even someone like her, with a middle-class job servicing the investments of actors, producers, and directors, could barely afford to live in the city. Paid twice a month, she turned her first check straight over to her landlord for her one-bedroom apartment, where she and her daughter slept on a single queen-size bed.

Going on record in support of HJ's initiative would serve the mayor's own ends as well as the coalition's. He could use the summit performance to portray himself as an ally of tenants in a city where most residents were tenants. And that was just fine with coalition leaders, as long as all could agree in public on the value of a MIHO. "Let us help you help us" is how one of the community organizers on the coordinating committee described the relation.

A *community of interest* formed the dominant scene style at the coalition's coordinating committee meetings and public rallies. Participants collaborated around a limited, shared interest in affordable housing: a proposed MIHO requiring the city to protect existing, low-cost rentals from being converted to condominiums or office spaces; mandate some below-market-rate apartments in large, residential developments; and create an enduring trust fund to support affordable housing construction. My notes on how advocates talked about the summit's positive points at the next coordinating committee meeting give us a good sense of how people string together meaning and action in a community of interest:

> León, a new representative from a Latinx tenant's group, started a go-around of comments. "Good turnout."
>
> Robert, a former housing agency director and the group's strategy sage, joined in: "It got good media—go on the web! Councilman Yates was not great but OK, the mayor was great. The room looked good, crowded. . . . I went to a fundraiser for the mayor and he made a big deal out of it."
>
> Octavia, a housing policy specialist, said that "the stories were really good—the guy who works for the city [of Los Angeles] but lives in Long Beach—that really drove it home."
>
> Community organizer Keith added that it was good for the coalition to have the president of the local labor federation there—"just to coalesce. . . . It was good for the coalition—good for press, but also to coalesce."
>
> Robert reminded everyone that "it was all about the mayor" and that "he was setting us up for a compromise."

None of the commentary was about how the well-covered event might somehow empower the maids, janitors, and cooks in the audience. No one said it was an opportunity for working people to give voice to their difficult circumstances while powerful people in the room were forced to listen. One of the primary goods, for HJ advocates, was that it created an image that would get a lot of press play. It projected that the interest in a MIHO was a *general* interest, a broad-based one, that evidently was circulating to a satisfyingly diverse audience.

At this debriefing session, members put into words the implicit expectations participants share when they are collaborating as a community of interest. As for their relation to the larger world, they were, first of all, competing and fighting for something. They expected resistance and tough compromises, and so needed stories that could "drive it home" and allies to help them push back. They hoped a relatively broad diversity of people would identify publicly with their cause; even a man who lived outside sprawling Los Angeles, in Long Beach, could speak on behalf of HJ, as Octavia observed. And a simple, short story of a miserable commute could be quite enough to make the audience comprehend HJ's interest in more affordable housing; communities of interest do not make appeals to systematic, ideological visions of social change even if some participants affirm those in other scenes. Their cause is not just for a distinctive geographic or cultural niche defined against other niches, so it is important to project popularity. A crowded room matters.

And participants expected to depend on each other in particular ways too. They did not expect to identify at the start with the same issues or bounded locale. They stretched their interdependence across geographic, social, and cultural distances. Keith's remark about "coalescing" makes sense in this light. Coming as they did from separate organizations with their own interests to pursue beyond this particular fight, coalition partners sometimes just needed to be together—though togetherness here happened for perhaps ninety minutes at the most.

A lot of this sounds like what many people would imagine about a group that is "being strategic" and seems unremarkable. Who would not want good publicity for an issue they think the public should care about? Who would *not* want a more—rather than less—general audience? Common sense aside, solving problems by creating and fighting for an *interest* is not just logical, not just human nature. The community of interest has a distinct history in US political life.[2] Other collective action on housing problems in Los Angeles was strategic in different ways. A contrast is useful. During the ISLA coalition's antidisplacement campaign, as chapter 4 will show in detail, advocates focused on a much more distinctively self-identified "community," not the *general* public of one city, or even the general public associated with one racial or ethnic category, social class, or neighborhood. Being "used" by powerful, sometime allies was not simply an inevitable feature of social advocacy but instead a moral affront. ISLA advocates' favorite event with city officials was one at which local residents got to "speak truth to power" and empower themselves in the process. There was no discernible journalist presence at that event, and no one said they wished otherwise.

A community of interest is not intrinsically more strategic or effective than other forms of collective problem solving. The HJ and ISLA coalitions both experienced victories and disappointments. When it was time to end the field research, ISLA participants had won more of what they *said* they wanted than did the more conventionally strategic-sounding HJ coalition. The term "strategy" itself is confusing, having acquired a thick lacquer of academic, sometimes politicized, and moralized uses. For now, its conventional meaning serves well. Before elaborating her widely known, academic meaning of the term, sociologist Ann Swidler (1986, 277) puts the conventional meaning succinctly: a strategy is a "plan consciously devised to attain a goal." This is how advocates themselves typically use the term too. While different housing advocates in Los Angeles all wanted more affordable housing, they devised differently timed, differently pitched plans to secure it. Followed closely, a community of interest turns out to be a particular, sometimes exhilarating, and sometimes frustrating *way* to be strategic—a way of working toward a kind of goal.

This chapter shows how fighting for an interest works as a strategy of collective problem solving. It describes what that strategy sounds and feels like, and the central dilemma it produces for participants. We look closely at everyday tests: points at which participants in a community of interest are faced with challenges and potential alternatives to their usual style of action. The activists' responses to these tests show concretely what kinds of decisions, arguments, and avoidances perpetuate a community of interest.

The HJ campaign strategy, in the simple sense of the word, changed twice during my fieldwork. A year into the study, coalition members admitted that many Angelenos knew little about their campaign. One leader pointed out to me that even her housemate did not know what HJ did. How could it represent a general interest if most locals did not know about it? So coalition leaders invested more time in an "outsider" strategy to complement the predominant "insider" strategy that looks like what political interest groups and lobbyists do. Chapter 6 will show how coalition leaders began exploring a legal strategy too. In larger or smaller ways, at least some HJ advocates experienced these and other developments as a test of their way of doing things. Each of these episodes might have driven HJ participants to readjust how they work together. They could have made themselves a different kind of organization.[3]

But they did not. HJ coalition actors' predominant *style* remained consistent, even as their particular strategies changed or oscillated between one side of this style's distinctive dilemma and the other. That is why it makes sense to talk about style as a cultural reality in itself that participants quite often sustain even under pressure. HJ's outsider strategy was a *community of interest's* outsider strategy, and that failed to please dissenters, for whom acting like an "outsider" should look and sound different. Style mattered practically for how the HJ coalition responded to external shocks and opportunities and how it reached out to potential supporters.

Following the Style

A community of interest defines itself in terms of problems in the social and political or natural world that participants make into objects of concerted action. Participants call themselves "housing activists," "human rights activists," or "supporters" of a particular political candidate. Etymologically, "interest" denotes a shared *thing* that exists *between* people or groups that may otherwise differ. By contrast, a community of identity defines itself as a collective that shares social and cultural similarities, and faces problems that threaten the collectivity's well-being. Participants make themselves, for example, into activists on behalf of the low-income "community" of color of South Central Los Angeles or people who identify strongly with a suburban neighborhood in the San Fernando Valley, not "housing activists" or "transportation activists."

To be clear, both styles are methods of solving problems. Both depend on participants' willingness to talk and feel with abstractions, such as "housing" or "the community." One is not more abstract than the other in any objective sense. But to a lot of US readers, a community of interest will sound more abstract and less personal—people who identify with "an issue out there"— while a community of identity sounds more authentic and personally connected, and that is how some participants in this study articulated it. Communities of interest imagine an arena full of other groups or individuals with interests in a variety of problems, and more or less power to realize their interests. Communities of identity imagine an arena full of other groups or individuals who inhabit and affirm identities (designated by neighborhood, ethnicity, race, religion, or a combination of these, for instance), with more or less power to ally with or subjugate those groups.

Style is a particular dimension of collective action, not a catchall term for everything that collective actors do together. Advocacy groups gravitate toward some collective identities as opposed to others, or may care relatively little about identifying collectively at all. They may tell their stories with some narrative devices versus others and articulate claims with some "frames" rather than others. Style inflects and sets parameters on the collective identities, narratives, or frames on which US social movement research quite often focuses; these are not simply "part of" or strictly determined by a style. Scene style is not a substitute term for these other concepts; it has its own analytic work to do.[4]

The HJ coalition scenes of greatest interest were those in which leading members haggled over which rhetorical appeals would work best for a MIHO, and how best to strengthen and expand the relations of the coalition. That is why observations from HJ's coordinating committee meetings and organized, public assemblies figure large in the study. Other scenes of coalition-related activity, like the HJ staff office, were important for the coalition of course, and are relevant for my particular questions in a more limited way.

Scene style—how participants coordinate themselves in a scene—can be a vague-sounding quality. To review from chapter 1, when participants coordinate themselves as a community of interest, they act in relation to a distinctive *map*, or sense of "who we are in relation to a wider world." And they sustain distinctive *bonds*, or ongoing expectations about "what obligates us to each other." This chapter looks more closely at these two dimensions playing out in HJ's MIHO campaign. It concludes by exploring the forms of talk and emotional expression tagged with the concept of "speech norms," a third dimension of style.[5]

A Map for a Quest

In the simplest terms, a community of interest solves problems by generalizing the base of support for the interest. It aims to win over gatekeepers and some ambivalent actors, while competing and conflicting with more adversarial actors.[6] It would be hard to deduce this mode of relating to the wider world of housing actors and issues if we go only by statements on paper. An internal coalition memo summarized the "Housing Justice agenda" as winning more affordable and mixed-income housing, and described the "opposition agenda" as "profits and control, free market/nonintervention [and] NIMBYism/anti-growth/classist/racist." While no doubt a sincere statement of participants' social perspective, documents like this make for an incomplete and misleading guide to action. The document by itself would be no help whatsoever in distinguishing loyal participants in the HJ coalition from those who broke away bitterly. HJ participants did not publicly score commercial real estate development for socially heedless profiteering, but we would not guess that from the memo either.

That is why discerning actors' implicit map in everyday interaction is worth the time. We look and listen for how participants perceive and categorize actors in their world of action—*as they are acting*, not in summary statements after the fact. "Map" and "bonds" are interpretative concepts that help us grasp meanings in everyday action. Those are the meanings we follow in this chapter, and sometimes they challenge both common sense and scholarly theories of collective action.

OVERVIEW: CONCENTRIC CIRCLES, CONFLICT, AND
COMPETITION IN A ZONE OF ASPIRATION

To use a pictorial metaphor, a community of interest aims to expand across widening concentric circles of mostly dotted lines. Dotted, rather than sharp or firm lines, represent the potential to ally at least temporarily with supporters or endorsers of the interest (rings close to the center), win over or neutralize other actors and especially gatekeepers such as political officials (somewhat more distant, middle rings), and hold off the hard opposition (distant rings, separated with firmer lines). The middle rings are the "zone of aspiration" where actors in a community of interest focus a lot of energy; imagine them highlighted to represent that effort.

The distant rings were the terrain of developers. When HJ representatives said "developers," they usually meant large property entrepreneurs who develop massive complexes of apartments that rent at market rate. They meant *for-profit* developers. Nonprofit organizations that apply for grants to build housing to rent at below the market rates—the affordable housing developers—were members of HJ. I never heard nonprofit developers called simply "developers," and never heard them pitched as adversaries, although some participants in the HJ coalition viewed the nonprofit developers skeptically or with indifference. "Developers," on the other hand, were the threat—though HJ leaders recognized that a few for-profit developers supported affordable housing construction, as we will see.

During 2008 and a year into HJ's campaign, coordinating committee members started worrying that their main champion in the mayor's office was not pushing hard enough for the MIHO. Members considered other avenues, and first among them in the conversation was a new initiative against "developers." Quentin (a community organizer) suggested the coalition could "bring out the hypocrisy" of developers who have said they can't afford the MIHO yet have done it in other cities. Another strategy was to "put some developers on the defensive" instead of targeting council members who were in fact working to pass the MIHO. A new community organizer in the room seconded the idea to embarrass developers. Other members piled on. Imagining a media campaign, one said, "You say you can't afford this, but you do it in other cities!" Another added, "Tie it to the foreclosure crisis." Another remarked that it was better to "tie it to developers who got big beautiful developments no one can buy!" Committee members went on envisioning a media-worthy protest action at some strategically chosen developer's new construction site.

"Developers" represented a broad category of property owners, managers, and their spokespersons. Members rarely named particular developers, even the one who became a landmark of entitlement by suing a council district over its affordable housing policy and winning. Committee members repeatedly associated "developer" with Dora Tisch, not actually a real estate developer, but longtime president of a downtown neighborhood association as well as tireless advocate for high-end residential developments and their affluent residents. Léon, the new Latinx tenant organization representative, asked who she was. "She's the bad guy," deadpanned another activist. "The wicked witch," others said, half serious. HJ participants mapped their opposition in terms of perceived *interests*, not occupation or residence.

Though "developers" usually earned HJ participants' scorn, even for-profit developers *could* be allies—just across a dotted line on the map. At least one nonprofit housing developer had moved into for-profit real estate development and continued to develop affordable housing too. HJ craftily placed him on the speakers' lineup for the coalition's big kickoff rally in order to demonstrate that even a market rate developer was saying affordable housing is a good idea. The point is that in a community of interest, only a few actors are *categorically* rejected as potential supporters. Experience may ratify, though, that some categories of actor are little worth trying to make into allies. The dotted lines become more solid for the outermost rings of the map.

A leap beyond the "we" of MIHO campaign leaders and endorsers lands us in the highlighted zone of aspiration. City council people figured large here. The coalition needed nine city council votes to pass the MIHO. Throughout the campaign, meeting participants heard detailed reports, month after month, on the state of play with city council members. Some supported the proposal more unambiguously than others; several, coalition leaders assumed, either opposed the proposed ordinance or were likely enough to do so that competing for their favor was not worth the work. HJ coalition leaders would try to push those few most firmly in the supportive camp toward an even stronger position. Coalition leader Mary told coordinating committee members that the office staff person for one such city council member said of her boss, "He [just] wants something passed," to which policy virtuoso Robert responded, "Talk to the council member. He's more progressive than his staff." Powerful city council member Hernandez was more ambiguous on the MIHO, and became the subject of far more second-guessing and hand-wringing at committee meetings. His assistant told an HJ leader that the proposed ordinance would force developers to sacrifice too much and put too much time into accommodating a complicated system of quotas of affordable apartments for different income levels. Committee members would not take the assistant's skepticism for an answer.

Robert: "That's bullshit."

Community organizer: "Get a memo from a developer . . . saying 'this can work!'"

Terry: "Do any of the council members want to push what WE want and lobby the ranks?"

Mary: "That's the challenge."

Mary's comment summarizes the larger gambit for HJ in the competition zone. Coalition leaders pitched much of their effort toward convincing the actors they mapped as most able to secure their interest in the MIHO. They concentrated heavily on the most important gatekeepers: city council members. Terry, as we will see shortly, viewed the action on a different map.

Hernandez remained a magnet for frustration and intrigue throughout months of coordinating committee meetings. For example, Mary reported at one meeting that he would not meet with HJ leaders again before a major city council hearing. Field notes recorded the dismay:

> For the next fifteen minutes they agonized aloud, sort of like jilted lovers: What does it *mean* that Hernandez won't meet with them until Nov. 19? Does it mean he'll vote against a MIHO? Where is the relationship at now?? After all that relating, for months.

It was kind of like a junior faculty member trying to divine senior members' votes on a tenure case.

> Mary said that Hernandez "cares about—neighborhood council people, housing advocates, developers. . . . That's what makes this so hard for him." He wants to care about everybody.

> Carol: "The coordinating committee is disappointed. Is that where the relationship is at?" Hernandez's staff person said her boss had talked to HJ a lot in the past—the implication being that he's already shown he cares. No one said this was comforting.

HJ's relationship with city council members such as Hernandez follows the traditional story line of relations between civic and governmental sectors. Grassroots advocates organize and then petition governing officials. Officials for their part follow the much less flexible script of their institutional sector; that is what makes them governing versus civic actors. They must at least appear to listen impartially to a variety of voices from the electorate without committing themselves permanently or exclusively to any one interest.

DOTTED LINE BETWEEN CIVIC AND STATE TOO

When we follow the action instead of assigning all the actors to a sector, we realize that this traditional understanding of civic and governmental "sectors" sometimes fails to capture what we are seeing.[7] HJ's concentric circles of relative competition and allyhood did not closely map onto a distinction between civic and state sectors. It turns out that governmental officials can participate, at least to some extent, in the civic action of a community of interest—a reality that initially perplexed the sociologist far more than the HJ staff people I asked about it; they seemed to take it for granted.

HJ leaders included a city housing agency director, Joyce Jackson, inside their circle of close partners. For several months, coordinating committee members had informal conversations with Jackson about policy figures. How high a percentage of new apartments per development should a MIHO mandate for below-market rents? How many of these apartments should developers set aside for different income brackets of tenant? How low should the income brackets go? At one local forum on housing policy, held toward the start of the MIHO campaign, Jackson narrated a slideshow that used *exactly* the same statistical comparison HJ leaders used, pointing out that during a recent year, developers had built less than 1 percent of the homes needed for residents in the $48,000–$78,000 income range. Jackson said, "We tried before . . . in an earlier campaign, and got so close to a city council vote." Strikingly, Jackson said "we," mapping herself onto an earlier HJ campaign. Working for an administration moderately and inconsistently on record in support of the general idea of a MIHO, Jackson suggested figures and brackets that did not always match HJ leaders' aspirations. At committee meetings, leaders occasionally said or implied that Jackson would not mind if HJ promoted even bigger quotas of affordable housing than she could push for herself. Heard from the HJ participants' point of view, it sounded like a dance of expectations with a partner who probably had others on her dance card too—a tricky game of political competition, all the more because Jackson wanted at least some of what HJ leaders said they wanted.

EXPANDING CIRCLES

Communities of interest want to attract nearly anyone to support or at least tolerate the shared interest. What they see on their map is a diversity of other *interest groups*, be they developers, ethnic populations, diverse occupational categories such as "laborer" or "commuter," or religious constituencies. On this map, these groups have an interest that defines their togetherness, and varying degrees of ability to realize their interest against others' interests, but even some groups perceived as cultivating conflicting interests may be worth trying to convince. A community of interest projects onto its shared map an indefinitely expanding constituency that can share the interest that community is fighting for even if constituents' other interests differ. In this way, a community of interest has universalistic aspirations, even if its universe is one city, as in the case of HJ, or one neighborhood or social category. Communities of interest want relatively diverse supporters within the region or category, but they don't expect supporters to identify closely or deeply with the community. Communities of *identity*, in contrast, expect participants to share a categorical, social identity or a tight synthesis of identities. Would-be participants from outside that kind of community do extra verbal work signaling their crossover to solidarity with the community.

The HJ coalition's efforts to solicit support letters are a good illustration of how a community of interest gathers supporters to project the breadth of an expanding constituency. From its beginning, HJ envisioned itself as a coalition of diverse social and occupational categories—particularly labor, tenant, and religious groups—which converged on an interest in affordable housing. HJ staff or committee members wrote template letters that could be revised, then signed, by leaders whose endorsements could project the broad appeal of this interest in a socially and culturally diverse city. During my fieldwork, campaign coordinators strategically timed the release of these letters to coincide with the city council's schedule of deliberations on housing policy. One letter represented "African American civic and religious leaders in Los Angeles," signed by people who included with the signatures their positions as directors of social service or community advocacy organizations—not necessarily ones specifically African American oriented, or members of labor union locals or pastors of churches. Another letter spoke on behalf of "civic, business, labor and religious leaders within the Latino community." Signatories identified themselves along similar lines as the African American leaders: they were Latino but not necessarily leaders of Latino-specific groups. Another letter's endorsers spoke "as concerned members of the Los Angeles community and as Jews." The signatories all were rabbis in the region. Each letter explained why African Americans, Latinos, or Jews could have particular reasons for sharing the *general* interest in affordable housing, not a specific interest in housing for their racial or ethnic category. This strategy projects generality. Taken together, the letters would project support for the MIHO spread across a substantial swatch of the LA electorate. The fact that these three categories of signatories—civic leaders who happen to be African American, Latinx, or a rabbi—are not parallel representatives of group identities only strengthens my argument that what mattered about the groupings is that they signified a broad general interest, not a specifically located one.

Universality was an aspiration, not a finished accomplishment. For HJ, LA neighborhood councils occupied the outer reaches of the zone of competition, and some even occupied the rings of adversaries. The prospect of their support for HJ was enticing and frustrating at the same time. In the early 2000s, when LA voters approved a system of neighborhood councils, these were supposed to have been a means to engage residents more in municipal governance and make city hall more responsive to them. Neighborhood councils got an official voice in annual city budget planning and advance notice of important city council decisions. Though bearing only a consultative, not directive, influence in city governance, the councils had become a regular forum for council candidates and proponents of new policies to seek support, or legitimacy. In an infamously disorienting sprawl of a metropolis, with a messy, multilayered congeries of governing agencies and committees to match, the councils could seem like stable wellsprings of public opinion, no matter how much or little they actually represented neighborhood publics. The nearly one hundred local councils shared no single political valence, style, or reputation; political points of contention at one council could shift unpredictably depending on who happened to have the time to join council leadership or attend meetings in a given year.

Conversation at one meeting near the height of the MIHO campaign in early 2009 illustrates the situation. Carol brought up the possibility of making headway with neighborhood council opinion leaders. She herself waffled on whether or not it was worth the investment. Carol said that "neighborhood councils are negative: they don't like the city" and "they don't like the mayor either. . . . I've been out there on mixed income [advocating for a MIHO] and treated really bad. And people said, 'No one spit on you. That wasn't so bad!'" Still, Carol suggested the idea of getting "resolutions from neighborhood councils" supporting the MIHO. Terry asked what would happen if word got around about HJ's initiative and other neighborhood councils start passing resolutions *against* the ordinance. That would be the risk, Carol replied, and reversing herself, she added flatly that "we've decided we don't have the resources to engage at this level," and concluded that they would have to be careful and strategic in how they approached neighborhood councils at all.

The next month's meeting was spent preparing for a big hearing on affordable housing at city hall. Committee members carefully selected a collection of union leaders, affordable housing developers, and low-income tenants to pitch different appeals for the MIHO to a powerful municipal committee. Now what kinds of "community members" should speak?

Member: "Should we get a neighborhood council man?"

Another member: "Get a [neighborhood] council member—a stereotypical one!"

Westside community organizer: "A stereotypical one won't say what we want!"

Laughs all around the table.

Half winking at their stereotype, coordinating committee members expressed the same skepticism as they did the previous month. In this conversation, coalition leader Mary from HJ's sponsor, the affordable developers' association, proposed to get assurance from neighborhood council people that they would not actively wreck the coalition's efforts: "We want neighborhood council people to say 'I and a hundred other people sign on' to say they are *not opposed* [emphasis added] to mixed-income housing." Later, as committee members talked about whether or not to orchestrate a grassroots mobilization for the MIHO, the dreaded topic came up again.

Tommy: "I think it's [grassroots effort] worth it because one of the largest sources of opposition is neighborhood councils."

Jorge: "It's going to take a lot of work."

Mary: "No question, it's going to take a lot of work."

HJ coalition participants had good reason to perceive neighborhood councils as a political thornbush. The previous "Housing Justice" campaign for a citywide housing ordinance had heard neighborhood council spokespeople make the same kinds of arguments at city hall—ones that we will see in more detail in chapter 7: affordable housing would mean more density, slower traffic, and a perilous drain on the urban infrastructure's ability to keep water, sewage, and automobile traffic all moving expeditiously in the right directions. Considering their relative power, it is not obvious why the councils provoked more dark humor, foreboding, and irony than even big, for-profit developers. It makes sense, though, if we suppose that a community of interest *expected* for-profit developers to be the enemy. Neighborhood councils, on the other hand, stood on a more ambiguous territory: the jungle zone of aspiration for advocates who wanted to spread the word about the MIHO as broadly as possible.

A TEST OF THE MAP

Terry annoyed HJ leaders. She represented SHAPLA, an advocacy group for homeless and extremely low-income people. After one of the angst-airing sessions about where "the relationship" was at with council member Hernandez, Terry asked, "Where do the community groups fit into all this?" Lisa said flatly, "They do the pushing." Terry countered just as declaratively: "We need a community strategy." Ordinary people needed to drive HJ strategies, not just provide the protest labor. At a string of coordinating committee meetings, Terry argued similarly that HJ's plans relied too much on an "insider strategy" of attending to city council members, municipal agency staff, and interest group leaders who could pressure them on the coalition's behalf. Terry insisted the coalition attend more to everyday supporters—a "grassroots mobilization," as she put it, from political outsiders. She repeatedly called Mary and Carol's strategy "playing politics." Terry did not reject their focus on powerful insiders out of hand but instead argued for bringing in outsider voices whether or not those voices represented groups with a reputation for clout.

For her part, Mary spoke from the map that features groups that carry interests and different amounts of influence on gatekeepers that could satisfy those interests. On HJ's dominant map, housing advocates needed to focus most on actors perceived as having the most control over the possibility of affordable housing. That was the zone of aspiration. On that map, tenant and local community groups were important but less highlighted than the zone of aspiration. In contrast, for Terry, these groups were the prized source of authentic, popular will.

The difference had concrete, strategic significance: Mary said at the next month's meeting, as members decided who should address a big city hall event, "I'd rather have a housing person speak" [a professional housing advocate], and "not a community person if that person is going to say something crazy. . . . I want to have confidence that they'll be good, not be crazy." She assumed that pressuring city council members with professional-sounding appeals rather than rough-edged authenticity was a surer route to success. Carol agreed.

Terry preferred addressing housing problems as a community of identity. Her repeated appeals to a "community" strategy only riled up Carol and Mary. Testing but not derailing the dominant style of action on the committee, Terry earned other members' ire. Carol told Terry dismissively at one meeting, "You're still learning." Terry was not alone in preferring a community of identity, and the issue will come up later, explosively, but the point for now is that the community of interest passed her test of it; it remained the way to play. The last meeting at which I saw Terry, she no longer contested the focus on power brokers and insiders. As the coalition ramped up in winter 2009, she was no longer attending the coordinating committee's meetings.

Bonds in a Community of Interest

HJ advocates depended on coalition participants' loyalty for the duration of the MIHO campaign, not necessarily longer. HJ leaders made it clear that members were free to pursue other interests as long as doing so did not threaten the shared interest that focused HJ's group solidarity. The indefinitely expanding circle of allies, supporters, and sometime supporters would treat their support of each other as a means to a well-defined, short-term end: winning the MIHO campaign at city hall. "Let us help you help us," as Keith had described the coalition's relation to the mayor, was not heedless self-interest but rather a special kind of togetherness.

INTEREST GROUP LOYALTY

HJ advocates' solidarity around a group interest already had struck me during my first field visit. In fall 2007, nonprofit housing developers and tenant advocates from South Los Angeles in the not-yet-public HJ coalition attended a workshop on how to submit community development plans to a California state agency. Affordable developers and tenant advocates were evidently the main attendees. They asked repeatedly how to document their claims that South Los Angeles needed more housing for low-income people. The official quickly got hip to who was in the room, going out of his way to affirm their presence, saying that time spent participating in what could seem like a boring planning process was "on the money," offering a real "opportunity" to win more housing.

Yet one attendee from a neighborhood council was treating the session much more as an informational forum than a source of practical tools. When she asked questions—and she asked a lot of them—other attendees' faces crinkled. She asked if New York City had similar statutes. She asked what supportive housing is. When the official said that market rate and affordable apartment developments should look equally appealing when you drive by them, she blurted out, "You need to call a barracuda a barracuda." The affordable developer next to me gave me an "I can't believe that person is here" look and then said sotto voce, "I'm turning this way"—physically rotating in her molded plastic seat away from the neighborhood council woman. I gathered that most attendees depended on each other to demonstrate for the state agency official their common interest in affordable housing developments. Face time with a Sacramento official really was not the scene for questioning the virtues of affordable developments. The curious neighborhood council member with the demeaning fish metaphor was testing the interest group solidarity in the room whether she meant to or not.

Interest group bonds carried HJ into its fully public phase next spring and passed a bigger test several months after the coalition's kickoff rally. Coalition member LAPO, whose organizers used in-your-face tactics on behalf of low-income tenants and homeless people, staged a protest march through the downtown streets. Marchers bearing papier-mâché pigs' heads on sticks demanded that police discontinue their new policing routines. They said police slowed their cruisers to a crawl near Pershing Square when they spotted people layered in grimy T-shirts and sweatshirts (evidently homeless) pushing shopping carts down the sidewalk. Police were giving out literally thousands of tickets for jaywalking. The organization's leaders considered all this gratuitous, illegal intimidation. A chance encounter with an HJ staffer on the way to the rally revealed to me HJ's distanced relation to this event: asked if other HJ participants were there too, the staff person responded that she came only "as me," not representing the coalition. The protest had become a small problem for the coalition. "HJ couldn't endorse it, but encouraged members to go," she said, elaborating that the coordinating committee decided it could not officially endorse an event if individual organizations had reservations. Some city leaders liked the downtown policing initiative; protesting it might alienate them and complicate efforts to secure some council votes for the MIHO.

The problem and HJ's response illustrate how bonds work in a community of interest. The protest addressed policing practices, a contentious issue *outside* a community of interest bonded in relation to a proposed MIHO. Loyalty to that interest compelled abstention from the protest. But that strained other loyalties that some HJ actors maintained with a low-income community whose members endured invasive policing as well as a lack of adequate housing. Participants in a community of interest have to sustain loyalty amid the other, sometimes competing or conflicting interests they represent. Low-income tenants of color and middle-class professional housing developers stretch over multiple forms of social distance when they converge on a shared interest in housing. In this game of coalition gymnastics, it is easy to sprain a muscle of the coalition body. Recall the controversial photo op at HJ's kickoff rally. Literally, physical proximity compromised social distance that the activists insisted on honoring, like the distance between the housing advocate and the woman who saw barracudas where others saw homes. Protecting this kind of interdependence while respecting multiple kinds of distance would require distinctive leadership skills.

LEADERSHIP IN A COMMUNITY OF INTEREST: SKILLS OF FINESSING, COMPARTMENTALIZING, AND SATISFICING

Leadership in social advocacy is the site par excellence for the entrepreneurial actor of social movement scholarship. In that line of thinking, leaders by definition have social skill. Skill is the ability to read people and mobilize them to pursue given ends in a given social environment, paraphrasing Fligstein and McAdam (2012). But *how*? Settings with different styles elicit and depend on *different* kinds of leadership, not simply strong or weak leaders, or more or less skill. It is not a stretch to say that from the civic action perspective, a leader is one who is good at helping keep the right style in play in the right scenes while advancing the organization toward its agenda setter's goals.

When HJ participants were acting as a community of interest, leaders were orchestrating the action by finessing and compartmentalizing, and as we see later, satisficing. Compartmentalizing meant deftly switching scenes and scene styles to maintain the community along with its interest. When HJ coalition leaders decided the coalition could not publicly endorse a protest against police practices, and encouraged members to go as individuals if they wanted to, they were *compartmentalizing* competing issues to protect the coalition's shared interest. During one of my participant observer stints with the HJ staff organization, in WHA's office suite, I found it hard to get some coalition leaders on my phone list to commit to the coalition campaign's big kickoff rally. Coalition convener Francis advised me to say I was calling from HJ, which sounded "activist," not from WHA, which sounded less activist and might just draw a blank. Francis was teaching me to compartmentalize HJ and WHA identities. When Francis braved testy phone calls from activists who thought that photos of the kickoff rally positioned them merely as eager adjuncts to professional power, he reaffirmed space for their distinctness within the coalition; he *finessed* the momentarily smudged separateness. Francis was a skilled leader in his employer's eyes. When his initial contract ran out, WHA offered to renew it.

Speaking effectively to the coalition's different constituencies on their own turf was one important part of the job. Several months earlier, when Francis spoke at a gathering of local clergy worried about homelessness, he worked with the familiar terms of the audience he was addressing, much as he also wanted his audience to expand their perspective. He told them, "Our response, traditionally, in many religious communities has been immediate service. But we need to broaden our imagination to think about what we can do to end homelessness." Francis never identified as a religious person in any settings of this study, but he allied himself with the congregational world by observing "our" response to homelessness. Yet he did not criticize a coworker who made a face when he told her that one of HJ's allies *really was* religious. Finessing and compartmentalizing, not strident self-expression, were the leadership skills that helped socially distant others keep coordinating themselves as a community of interest.

Francis's nuanced relation to the housing summit with the mayor, pictured at the start, illustrates other kinds of compartmentalizing. While we were cleaning up the meeting hall after the summit, Francis told me his misgivings about how much the mayor would push for a MIHO. It bothered him that the mayor favored a policy geared primarily to middle-class professionals, teachers, or public servants who had a hard time finding affordable apartments in the city. Francis worried at least as much about janitors, one of whom had spoken at the summit, and were in the same predicament but with far fewer resources. The mayor had said he wanted to see housing built in subway and bus corridors—the "transit-oriented developments" that city planners were proposing as a way to entice Angelenos out of their car-centered lifestyles. Yet HJ proposals insisted that affordable housing be built all over the city, not just near transit lines and in low-income neighborhoods. That is what "mixed-income" housing meant. To keep orchestrating the community of interest, Francis needed to compartmentalize some of his own differences of opinion at the same time he remained openly mindful of the distances between constituencies represented in HJ coalition meetings.

Take, for instance, the distances between the mayor's skilled professionals, blue-collar workers in community organizer Quentin's bailiwick, and extremely low-income and homeless people on whose behalf Terry fought. Francis said that Quentin "was in a weird position because [his organization] is basically people from south LA," a lot of whom have low incomes, but Quentin acted fearful of endangering the MIHO initiative—even if one passed that ended up doing relatively little for his low-income constituency. Quentin was a voice of caution on the coordinating committee, Francis implied. I observed that Quentin had said at the last meeting that he didn't want the summit to necessarily feature "the lowest of the low" and "I wondered if Terry chafed at that." Francis smiled and nodded, but didn't say anything.

On the other hand, Francis reasoned aloud, Quentin's organization had been working on affordable housing for eight years. He needed a "win" for his organization; it would want something after all that time. He contrasted it with LAPO, whose representative had recently dropped out of the coordinating committee because, as Francis put it, "they thought to themselves, 'Why should we put up with this' when their own needs weren't getting addressed."

> Francis observed, "They don't get a lot of things passed, but they get what they want."

A good leader had to understand that coalition members converged on a common interest from different social vantage points, different ideas about political compromise, buffeted by different organizational pressures. The leader had to imagine other representatives' compartments.

Compartmentalizing and finessing became even trickier when differences strained participants' ability to keep working together at all. This was the biggest kind of test for bonds in a community of interest, and the biggest test of Francis's leadership skills. A few months later, Francis let me in on some of the strains that made some time traveling abroad seem more appealing than keeping his convener position with HJ. My field notes reflect that:

Francis described himself as having been the go-between with Carol or Mary, on one side, and groups representing largely low-income tenants, the "community groups," on the other. Francis said he had to make decisions when to tell Carol about these groups' dissatisfactions and when to protect her. He pondered aloud for a minute if maybe he should have told Carol more often that these people were upset. All the same, he said, "I don't want to shoot down Housing Justice either."

This time, when HJ's sponsor, WHA, offered to renew Francis's contract, he passed up the offer. He reappears later in this study, working at LAPO. Francis was not the only one to depart from HJ as members' disagreement over style fragmented the coalition.

ANOTHER TEST OF BONDS AND AN
UNIMPEACHABLE RESPONSE

Representatives of several tenant and community organizations who disrupted a coordinating committee meeting later jelled into a new coalition, HRN, viewed in chapter 5. The new coalition made preservation of existing low-cost housing—SROs and relatively cheap, old apartment buildings—its main demand.[8] "Preservation" had been part of HJ's three-point plan, but in the eyes of HRN leaders, it received too little of the HJ coalition's energies. Having diminished HJ's organizing capacity and its reputation with at least some tenant advocates, HRN was a competitor as well as a loyalty test for other HJ organizations. The representative from one of HJ's longtime member organizations, Beach City Tenant Union (BCTU), was starting to work with HRN. When not so subtly quizzed about this new relationship, the BCTU representative parried the question of loyalty and reaffirmed coalition bonds in a way that Carol, though hurt and suspicious, had to accept given the dominant style of the coalition.

At an HJ coordinating committee meeting a couple of months after HRN went public, Carol fished for a way to get Beach City's representative to talk about his involvement.

Carol asked Chuck, "You have a meeting with Joyce Jackson?"

Chuck, sort of surprised: "I don't—think so."

Carol: "She mentioned it to me—she's meeting with you and LAPO."

Mention of LAPO was a red flag since its representative had withdrawn the organization from the committee. Mary changed the subject. It came up again fifteen minutes later.

Carol said, "There is a new group consisting of SED and LAPO," and looking at Chuck, said, "I don't know if you are part of it."

Chuck: "I don't know—I have to find out what it is."

Carol explained it as a "campaign on preservation."

Chuck asked, "It is outside MIHO?"

Carol nodded yes.

Chuck now spoke up for making preservation a bigger part of the HJ's overall policy platform. His way of putting the pitch, and Quentin's response to it, says a lot about how participants in a community of interest maintain expectations about bonds even during disagreements. Chuck said, "Our goal, BCTU's goal, is we want the mixed-income policy that HLA has supported, plus a replacement [preservation] policy. That's why we're here at this table." Chuck affirmed, in other words, that his organization's interests did intersect with the central concern of HJ's community of interest. Quentin, the community organizer, questioned whether or not preservation of extremely low-income housing concerned enough people citywide the way the rest of HJ's platform could; in effect, he was asking if it could be generalizable for a community of interest. Carol implied that Chuck's proposal was too complicated for policy makers, let alone nonspecialists.

Chuck's reply sustained the norms of a community of interest:

Chuck: "I don't see what's wrong with pushing for the people you are working for. . . . My people are getting killed (losing their homes)."

Quentin reasoned that "we have the same goals over all," but different strategies for meeting them. And as for preservation, "really that may be a different campaign."

Chuck affirmed the group's shared interest that brought him to the table to begin with. "Pushing for the people you are working for" is just what participants in a community of interest do—as long as they support the collective. Quentin in effect was suggesting that Chuck may need to *compartmentalize* preservation as a "different campaign" from the MIHO campaign that HJ was pursuing. Yet he also suggested gently that Carol tweak HJ's current policy proposal with the preservation issue in mind. Carol agreed. Taking the last word in the discussion, Chuck again affirmed the community of interest:

Chuck: "Just so you know, we're sticking with the coalition, I just want to make that clear. We're gonna fight like hell for preservation. But at the end—[we stay in the coalition]."

While Chuck was going to push his organization's big issue, he did *not* imply, as LAPO representatives had months before, that the big issue was a nonnegotiable priority that mattered more than HJ's survival. His organization would maintain HJ's solidarity based on a shared interest, without asking HJ to guarantee support for other interests BCTU wanted to pursue.

In the spirit of a community of interest, Chuck's organization ended up following Quentin's advice about compartmentalizing too. When I saw him at competitor coalition HRN's daylong kickoff event, he told me straightforwardly that "we're working in both coalitions." BCTU had two compartments for housing advocacy. Months later, BCTU was still a loyal member of HJ, and Chuck was working hard alongside other representatives to find new ways to fight for a MIHO even after new developments had made the fight even more challenging.

The Central Dilemma: Insider or Outsider Strategy?

A community of interest aims to project the will of a large constituency with some internal diversity. At the same time, HJ coalition leaders spent a lot of time courting municipal leaders and agonizing over the hot-then-cold reception from some council members' offices. They tried to induce powerful gatekeepers in the zone of aspiration to support them in securing the interest. Time and effort spent on cultivating governmental insiders was less time and effort available for broadening and firing up the "community" that shared the interest. Coordinating committee members recognized that the "grass roots" that Terry spoke up for was an important part of the community of interest too. As the MIHO campaign revved into high gear, leading coordinating committee members talked more about getting "ordinary people" into the campaign. That sounds like what Terry had promoted, and at first, I thought it was, but it wasn't. The difference matters for understanding how style shapes strategies. Figuring it out pushed me toward one of this study's central findings: that different styles came with different dilemmas. Sometimes these were on display at the same meeting. HJ leaders' increasing attention to grassroots participation followed a community of interest's logic, not the style of grassroots participation Terry had in mind.

In HJ discussions, ordinary people mattered primarily as a means of impressing policy gatekeepers such as council member Hernandez and the mayor. They mattered secondarily as subjects of empowerment and activation. If ordinary people expressing their voices could symbolize *general* support among Angelenos for a MIHO, then that was a good thing. Committee members considered a batch of strategies to project an image of generalized will, in tandem with the effort to cultivate and sustain favor from insiders. Balancing the voice of the people, especially angry ones, with the favor of council members or mayoral staff was a big dilemma for the community of interest.

In November 2008, Mary started to promote a vision of how to mobilize public opinion: HJ needed to collect stories of personal housing hardship that were fit for the coalition newsletter and press releases. The idea was that readers would identify with a personal storyteller as a general person. When ISLA advocates use the same storytelling strategy in the next chapter, in contrast, the idea is that storytellers would emphasize the hardship of a particular, low-income community, not people in general. HJ's goal was to release twelve stories over ninety days. HJ facilitator Francis proposed weekly message packages, each with a presentation of someone's story and picture of the storyteller.

Carol said, "It's a strategy used in Sacramento a lot around budget time."

A low-income people's advocate made a pitch to "get ordinary people involved—especially people who don't look like they are totally organized by us."

Another member pitched in that people "organized by us" don't look like "ordinary Joes."

For these HJ participants, stories from ordinary Joes served a messaging function, and a means to an end as much as a good in itself. They would project the popularity of the MIHO initiative. Trotting out a music metaphor, a new community organizer on HJ's coordinating committee argued HJ's insider strategy would not work unless the coalition also got the public excited about the MIHO: "It's like Hall and Oates! You can't have one without the other."

A community of interest is entangled with the institutional reality of interest group politicking: with a strategy that pushes an interest, advocates learn from experience that they have to develop a formidable constituency allied on that interest. That helps make sense of Mary's comment earlier that council member Hernandez cared about neighborhood councils, housing advocates, and developers—groups that brought different interests to the question of affordable housing mandates. Gatekeepers would be hearing from a variety of self-organized interest groups, including developers and property owners who had far more money to publicize their own story about the general interest. One way to rise above the cacophony of competing interests and siren song of propertied opposition to regulations would be to portray the interest in affordable housing as everyone's interest—the stratagem Carol said advocates used in Sacramento to sway legislators voting on the state budget.

A few months later, the focus on grassroots voice became more urgent. Mary said that sympathetic people in the mayor's office were getting

outmaneuvered. Some around the table now proposed actions to publicly embarrass local developers or generate thousands of phone calls from constituents to their city council members' offices. A phone-calling and postcard-
writing campaign did emerge in spring 2009, along with a plan for HJ
supporters to attend one of a half-dozen "town halls," in far-flung districts
across the city, scheduled by the mayor's office. The mayor's housing policy
staff had planned these meetings to promote the potential benefits of affordable housing construction, and neutralize some taxpayers' and suburbanites'
skepticism. An informational flyer from HJ put it this way: "Come tell the city
of Los Angeles that too many ordinary people—schoolteachers, security officers, hotel workers—cannot find housing that they can afford. Los Angeles
needs mixed-income housing so community members from all walks of life
can find affordable homes in Los Angeles." This was a new focus on grassroots
participation carefully paired with the ongoing need to cultivate city officials.
It could have been a deft way to bridge the dilemma of insider versus outsider
strategy that, as chapter 1 described, is endemic to the community of interest
style.

Rather than finesse the dilemma, this turn to the grass roots widened the
gap. It revealed the divisive potential of the central dilemma at its worst. Broadening participation beyond civic leaders, pastors, housing specialists, and city
hall officials was supposed to produce the image of a diverse, widespread constituency for affordable housing. At a town hall in South Los Angeles, grassroots voices resisted going along with HJ leaders' "let us help you help us"
strategy.[9] They risked alienating city officials. Many of the "ordinary Joes" at
the Hillside district's town hall, people HJ encouraged to go, cheered on different arguments from the HJ-approved ones the flyer nudged them to make.
As a supporter of HJ told me shortly after this town hall, coalition leaders had
wanted people to come and *support* the mayor's initiative for more affordable
housing. The mayor and his housing department were to some extent allies, if
not easily tractable ones—a loose part of HJ's community of interest. In effect,
the idea was for ordinary Hillside residents to come and speak as political sur-
rogates for the mayor—the ultimate insider—to pressure more skeptical city
and interest group leaders. That is not what happened.

Mayoral staff set and tried to control the agenda for the meeting. The focal
presentation made the main points of the mayor's housing plan for Los Angeles available online. The presenter entreated the audience, "We need your
input. If you want to read the plan, it's a little bit long and boring [chuckles
from the audience]." Another staff person bid the attendees to join breakout
groups to "get more information." No one seemed interested in small-group
talk. He left time for questions, but no one raised a hand. He repeated the first
staffer's offer: "Now we want to hear from you." But attendees already

supported more affordable housing; that was not the issue. They were not looking for more information, and apparently were not interested in projecting themselves as a de facto mayor's bloc either.

Instead of performing comity in hopes of being rewarded with a good deal from the mayor's office, they challenged the terms of the forum itself. It started when a staffer from the mayor's office asked audience members, How small did a residential project need to be to earn an exemption from proposed mandates for low-rent apartments in every new apartment complex? The choices were fifty, twenty, or ten apartment units. Now, woman-about-town and gadfly Cleo, familiar from other forums, launched into a rant: "Personally, I think *none* should be exempted. Period! No exemption! We have to cover everybody. We have to build for everybody!" Suddenly the nonprofessionals in the room were beginning to engage. A call-and-response rhythm ensued, with rejoinders of "yeah" and "mm-hmm." "No exemptions!" Cleo urged. "We build 'em all! We're taxpayers, we deserve 'em all!" Later she took the floor again, challenging the mayor's office to "just have some balls" and quit letting for-profit developers off the hook.

Next, the staffer asked attendees what messages about affordable housing would "be the most powerful," and "resonate with the media and opinion leaders." Francine, an ISLA coalition leader we meet in the next chapter, used rhetoric that HJ's coordinating committee had rejected months earlier as too strident for any general appeal: "Housing is a fundamental human right. . . . The overproduction of housing for the sector of society who can afford to live anywhere is a *scandal*." She challenged the mayor's emphasis on building moderate-income apartments near transit lines. "Transportation access should not be limited to the middle class and the workforce. [So] I would take a human rights frame." The staffer interjected with a different idea about what message would appeal broadly. He said volunteering to participate in the annual count of homeless people in Los Angeles and telling "a story of what you experienced—that would be a powerful message." It was an odd non sequitur, but whatever the staffer may have intended privately, it sounded like he was trying to soften Francine's harsh social critique with an anodyne, consensual appeal to the pathos of homelessness.

The clash of purposes had become obvious. Mayor's office staff, just like HJ leaders, had imagined the town hall as an opportunity for attendees to perform a shared interest and join forces with the mayor's office to *promote the mayor's vision*, and help staff figure out how to appeal to skeptics. Vocal attendees, on the other hand, saw it as a chance to speak truth to power right now, and tease the mayor's representatives with the suggestion that their boss had been an impediment as much as an ally. Several HJ coordinating committee members at the meeting tried to re-center the mayoral staff's agenda rather than connect rhetorically with the more popular sentiment in the room. When the staffer had a hard time getting takers on his bid to imagine the opposition's arguments on affordable housing, Carol piped in with one about economies of scale—clarifying, first, that she supported as much affordable housing as possible. And later, just after Francine's appeal to "housing as a human right," Quentin from the HJ coordinating committee proposed a framing much closer to that in HJ's pamplets and flyers. He said the affordable housing mandate would benefit "the people that keep this city moving . . . janitors, night watchmen, bus drivers."

In short, HJ's "outsider" strategy defined ordinary people in relation to the political process that shapes a community of interest and its possibilities. That means outsiders would assist HJ advocates' strategy of massaging and pressuring insiders to make a good deal. That is a different strategy from one in which outsiders voice their needs and *confront* instituted leaders, including the mayor. Both arguably have their value, but it is the first one that comports with a community of interest.

When we rejoin the coalition in chapter 6, HJ advocates are recalibrating as the MIHO's chances of passage diminish. They consider new insider strategies as well as briefly mention outsider strategies. During my remaining time with HJ, they planned only for the first kind. Dilemmas are *built into* styles of problem solving. They endure and can be managed differently, but they do not simply resolve. Advocates oscillate between them as they hit up against what observers at a distance call social or institutional realities. I discovered that a community of identity endures a different dilemma, though with a similar oscillating dynamic, as participants' style confronts them with different, salient social realities.

Talking and Feeling in a Community of Interest

Orchestrating Excitement on a Short Timeline

Many of us are familiar with a campaign for an interest—whether it is a campaign for elected office or a legislative initiative pushed by advocates like HJ coalition members. As spectators, we often are skeptical about the "hoopla" of a campaign the way we are skeptical about advertising, two-for-one deals, or anything else that is trying to get something from us. But as participants, we may get swept up in the rightness of our cause and the energy of the moment, and stop thinking of ourselves as being "in a campaign" at all. Exploring style means stepping into the space between skeptical distance and immersion, discovering norms of speech and emotional expression that are distinctive to different styles as well as part of what makes style a powerful shaper of strategies and outcomes.[10] As sociologist Erika Summers Effler (2010) pictures in marvelous detail, people working for a cause may frequently live out emotional rhythms that are as palpable and effective a part of collective life as group beliefs or statements of principle.[11]

During my 2 years with HJ's MIHO campaign, participants talked strategies, numbers, and policies, but they also spoke about and planned for feelings. They aspired to a nearly universal audience by orchestrating excitement and argument. It showed in the timing of events. Though coalition participants already had been meeting with supporting groups for months and documenting housing needs for a state agency, HJ leaders held off on announcing the coalition publicly. HJ leaders carefully timed the March 2008 kickoff rally to project broad-based enthusiasm for a MIHO at a point when they imagined they would be ready to spotlight the coalition's breadth at public events and on letterheads.

At a meeting later that year, coordinating committee members planned a ninety-day crescendo, timed to begin with a particularly important joint meeting of planning and housing subcommittees of city council. Members talked of maintaining a "drumbeat" for the campaign. They imagined a public and set of elected leaders all jarred by a succession of emotional appeals. WHA staffer and HJ leader Mary said it was important to continue pushing on all fronts and "keep up the drumbeat of the personal crisis [of unaffordable housing]." Committee members saw themselves as pressing city council members and a wider public into the committee's own short-term timeline. They wanted to spread *feelings* of urgency. HJ leaders knew that plenty of tenants in Los Angeles had been living difficult stories—displacement to far-flung, cheaper suburbs with lengthy commutes—for a long time, and had already invited a few to represent many tenants' plight by speaking at the kickoff rally. HJ's MIHO campaign was at this point officially eight months old, but committee members imagined *now* was the time to collect and distribute those stories systematically to heighten the tension.

Mary mentioned an advocacy outfit that had generated pressure that induced some city council members to sign HJ's three-point housing plan. I had watched one version of this pressure tactic unfold already a year earlier. To secure a city council member's endorsement, community organizers packed a church in South Los Angeles with three hundred supporters, projecting a popular will. The council member signed a big poster display of HJ's three-point plan set up at the front of the sanctuary. People stood up in the pews to cheer, giving the council member the chance, in turn, to project herself as the friend of an entire low-income, largely Latinx community that those attendees would represent in the news.[12] It need not impugn the sincerity of attendees or council member to observe that HJ leaders and their community organizer allies orchestrated the excitement.

HJ actors made space for enthusiasm in *compartments* of time and space. They not only chose particular weeks or months for generating the "drumbeat" but also included different-feeling displays of support even within one event. Compartmentalizing excitement and righteous indignation was one of the most important speech norms.

At HJ's kickoff rally, for example, tenants' rights advocates used a call-and-response format to criticize landlords for victimizing low-income people. At the speaker's mention of an injustice, the audience chanted, "That's not fair!" The speakers were angry, and the tenant group members bused in for the rally matched the tone with righteous indignation. Then the scene changed when an affordable housing developer in a suit promoted HJ's housing policy platform, affirming that people of different backgrounds should live together, and what's more, affordable housing never lost anyone any money. Attendees listened attentively, without any call and response. It was this careful partitioning of speech genres and emotional outbursts for the consumption of others that dissenter Terry had violated, and in two ways. She had criticized how the coalition itself operated at a meeting designed to bracket differences and project warm unity to the audience of endorsers in the room, and had "used drama," as Carol put it, bringing *to the coordinating committee* the kind of hectoring critique that HJ welcomed to carefully defined speaker slots at a public rally.

It would be wrong to say that HJ participants were cold and calculating manipulators with none of their own feelings in the game. It would be wrong, too, to suppose that they did not feel and move with the emotions they tried to generate for a larger public. For HJ advocates, the MIHO campaign produced crescendos of anxiety, then diminuendos of relief, as the kickoff rally illustrates.

At 8:00 a.m. on March 5, on city hall's steps, Francis realized he had forgotten to bring a microphone. Nervously he finger-punched numbers on his cell phone, calling for someone who could deliver one. Happily someone came. Five minutes later there was another minicrisis: Where was that electric plug on the south lawn? Setting up the speakers and duct-taping the wiring to the steps, Francis glanced across the plaza, still largely empty around 8:40, observing, "This is the part that makes me nervous. . . . Will they come? It's kind of like holding a college party." I joked that he should have brought a keg. But he clearly felt pressed to succeed in terms of numbers. I asked if there was something else I could do. "You can just convince me that this is going to work out." A bit later, I hugged Gabriela, HJ's chief organizer, congratulating her on a rousing, well-attended event. Earlier, she looked to be on the verge of tears as Pastor Sean, the first speaker, began describing Los Angeles' housing crisis.

The sound volume was too low for an outdoor rally. Cheerier now, Gabriela said, "Now we can get back to work." Francis replied, "I haven't thought about March 6 in such a long time that . . ." I said he should take the rest of the day off. He joked that he'd do that and go get drunk. When HJ actors got back to work at coordinating committee meetings, they engaged a different kind of communication with a different emotional tone.

Being a Player

Before attending coordinating committee meetings, I had heard they could be contentious, which not everyone thought was a good thing. My experience over the first few meetings confirmed the reputation, but I noticed there was at least one set of conversational qualities that experienced participants all seemed to expect. Members talked like "players," strategic operators in a high-stakes game, people in the know who relied on each other to understand verbal shorthand in lieu of complete explanations of people, places, or policies. It took me several meetings to figure out who some of the other players in the LA housing arena were that they referred to by first name only. As the months went on, new participants cycling onto the committee sometimes would ask for explanations of basic, occasionally important details, but neither they nor experienced members ever suggested that the committee should offer intro-ductory background or spot tutorials more systematically. Longtime commit-tee members seemed not in the least burdened by fears of appearing nonin-clusive, nonaffirming of individuals, or nonempowering—fears that have spooked many US grassroots movement groups and exercised some advocates in this study too.

Committee meetings unfolded in a fast-paced, nervous buzz of abbreviated thoughts and unspecified references. Longtime attendees never asked for ad-ditional explanation. Notes from my first meeting recorded some of my out-of-the-loop feeling, apparently shared by another newcomer, Terry the dis-senter from SHAPLA—whom I quickly learned could be counted on to ask questions, forthrightly, when puzzled.

> There have been meetings with "Joyce," who appears to be a kind of sup-porter of mixed-income housing, but is in the position of presenting it to others; that is what I gather at any rate . . .

> Carol said that there would be "pushback" (didn't say from whom) on sev-eral items, including not wanting to set aside 30 percent. She also said that "the pushback will be voluntary versus mandatory."

> Terry asked what Carol meant by mandatory.

Carol said it meant "the percent that would have to be a certain level (of income in relation to average monthly income—always abbreviated in these discussions as AMI [area median income]).

***

Ken from Southland Organized for Change said we "need to make sure our coalition members are talking about it."

Someone then asked if the mixed-income housing issue would be at the WHA conference next week.

Francis said he would "talk to our honorary committee" about it.

Terry: "What are they talking about?"

Carol looked amused or puzzled and said, "This!" In other words, there should be talk about the MIHO campaign.

***

Now there was a little discussion of the mayor's press conference.

Ken said that "a woman is going to come who drives eighteen miles to work."

Carol, jokingly: "The 'real' person."

A new participant needed to be quick on the uptake, or else familiar with an affordable housing policy argot of set-asides and AMI. The reasonably informed newcomer who had spent a little time in Los Angeles would probably get it easily enough that pushback came from large property developers, but it might take longer to pick up on committee in-jokes and understand the self-deprecatory irony with which they were delivered. Experienced activists like Carol could wink at the activist's need to bring "real people" onstage who convincingly represent widespread hardship in unrehearsed-sounding cadences. Advocates relied as well on others around the table to hear the friendly humor in scare quotes and not take it as demeaning to the speaker in question.

Participants needed to keep up and catch up. At other meetings, new participants sometimes asked about someone or something unfamiliar: "Who is Dora Tisch?" Or in response to conversation about yet more office meetings with city council members, participants asked questions like, "Is there an overall purpose to meeting? Is it to get them to sign on?" or "Is there anyone who could say, 'This Housing Justice stuff is the pits'?" On hearing about new strategy options late in the campaign, a well-respected staffer with a regional labor federation commented that he would need to "explain to my leadership, to my folks," a lot of technical details. "It's all confusing," he said.

A crucial speech norm, then, for coordinating committee meetings was that expert players "play" at expert speed. That rhythm of conversation can facilitate decisions on the cascade of technical and tactical issues that HJ's campaign negotiated on its short timeline—such as how large a development should have to be before a MIHO applies to it, or which city council people are best to talk to, and when, with what questions and demands. That rhythm would offer few openings, however, to participants who want space to enhance their capacity to participate or learn how to communicate the MIHO campaign to their own organizations, or build more solidary relationships among committee members or the organizations they represent. No wonder Keith said at the labor housing summit, pictured at the start of this chapter, that it was good partly just to give HJ coalition members the chance "to coalesce."

What the Entrepreneurial Model Misses

Seen from some distance, HJ's coordinating committee and other communities of interest look like what many people imagine with the word "strategic." This reflects historical and cultural developments in the United States, not natural or logical ones. It does make sense that skilled entrepreneurs would focus their energy on one interest for the sake of an efficient campaign with fewer fault lines of difference—or does it? Some research shows it can be at least as efficient to combine issues, picking up more support in the process.[13] It does make sense to pursue a campaign in a short span instead of subjecting it to a longer timeline's unpredictable risks—or does it? What if substantial and lasting change may take more than one political season?

The entrepreneurial actor model imagines advocates who organize relationships skillfully and efficiently to make the collectivity more effective. Yet there are different and even opposed ways to meet these standards. It depends on *how* advocates practice "efficiency," "skill," and "effectiveness." Participants in a community of interest act skillfully and strategically in particular, patterned ways. One of those patterns was an action dilemma that HJ advocates could not easily opt out of; they could choose one horn or the other.

Strategies are embedded in social and cultural contexts. Scene style turns generic, scholarly abstractions such as "social skill" into the freighted relationships and difficult decisions that constitute collective action. If to be strategic is to be good at getting other people to do what you want them to do, as social movement scholar James Jasper put it, style inflects what advocates recognize and affirm as "being strategic" to begin with. Within the HJ coordinating committee and other collective efforts that have worked as a community of interest, I would argue that "skilled" leadership means compartmentalizing and finessing differences.[14] Skilled leadership is less centrally about drawing out new participants or finding ways to incorporate political education into general meetings, but historically these goals have been important to some advocates' notions of being strategic. For a community of interest, strengthening the collectivity means expanding relationships into potentially adversarial terrain—even the dreaded land of neighborhood councils. It means conducting a boundary-spanning kind of coalition building that is distinct from what we see in the next chapter's version of strategic, collective action. And being "effective" means devising strategies for a win in the short term.

The idea of the entrepreneurial actor by itself makes it difficult to imagine actors embedded in, not only manipulators of, emotional relationships. In theoretical statements, the entrepreneurial actor quite often comes off as a calculating risk taker or a savvy bargainer. This is someone who "finds a usable collective identity" to attract other people.[15] It is easier to picture this kind of entrepreneur as someone who uses drama to manipulate others' feelings than someone who also rises and falls in the rhythm. Yet if people like Francis and Gabriela had not felt the urgency of the kickoff rally themselves, they would not have responded so viscerally when, momentarily, the event seemed to them at risk of faltering. Advocacy on the timeline of a relatively short campaign elicits jolts of uncaged emotion; that is part of collective problem solving—for advocates as well as constituents—when the strategy develops in a community of interest. It is not just an add-on.

Entrepreneurial advocacy took a particular shape in the HJ coalition—one that scholars find active in plenty of other contemporary advocacy efforts. It is absent or secondary in plenty of contemporary efforts too. We could still ask if the HJ coordinating committee simply was responding to contingencies peculiar to the case at hand. The mayor happened to be up for reelection soon; maybe that is why they needed the short timeline if they were going to accomplish anything at all. Maybe HJ staff made the coordinating committee into a single-interest, short-term, campaign-focused effort mainly because, as advocates sponsored by nonprofit housing developers that needed to keep getting contracts, staff had little choice but to do their sponsors' bidding. In other words, maybe what I am calling a community of interest is less a cultural shaper than a set of choices shaped by other things. Comparison sites described in chapter 5 show that other social advocates with quite different contingencies also acted like a community of interest in some scenes on occasion. When they did so, their implicit notions of a good relationship, good decisions, or survivable trade-offs became similar to those of the HJ coordinating committee. Before pursuing those comparisons, we need to see how else advocates might style their action as they turn housing conditions into problems.

4

Solving Problems by Protecting
an Identity

Another Way of Being Strategic

In early winter 2009, activists at the ISLA monthly general meeting pondered their next moves in the battle against residential displacement in South Los Angeles. While no longer as smooth running as in previous decades, the city's growth machine was churning out new, upscale apartments in neighborhoods south of downtown. In some areas, a growing population of professional and student residents was driving up rents and driving out low-income tenants. Ethan, ISLA's witty and energetic lead staff person, told us the city planning department was letting for-profit builders construct bigger, denser (more profitable) buildings than normally allowed in a neighborhood south of downtown in exchange for including some lower-rent units in their plans. And that reminded him:

> Ethan: "Just so you know, there is a conflict going on with housing advocates—there's a mixed-income ordinance [being considered]....
> Housing Justice is working on it, and SED and LAPO and others have said that you need to replace [low-rent units with other low-rent units] so there's not a loss of them."

> Woman from California Nurses Association: "You need a coalition for that."

> Ethan: "Right—that's all of LA, whatever happens with LA, we are talking about this very specific area, [a] specific plan where there's high displacement."

One of the participants read aloud from the city planning department's website on her laptop. It said that new development in the Balboa area should embody the spirit of "the new urbanism." Half-muffled, cynical chuckles broke out around the table. One member asked, "What's the new urbanism?" One of ISLA's core members, grad student Mabel, answered that it's "not like Manhattan, but Brooklyn. . . . People can walk, it's pretty." Another participant asked, "Does it talk about mixed income?" Mabel said that was the problem.

> Mabel: "The 'pretty' part gets kept and the mixed income part gets removed."

> Ethan: "When we snicker, it's because they leave out the people who aren't there . . . When we had people envision what a city should be like, a lot of what people drew is the new urbanism. It's not a mystery that people want that—but our question is who can afford it!"

Participants at this meeting sounded committed to the same cause that drove the HJ campaign, now in high gear. As the attendee from the nursing association put it, and Ethan had agreed, "you need a coalition" to push a new housing policy effectively, particularly a policy that for-profit developers would likely oppose. HJ was just that coalition. Mixed-income housing in walkable, livable neighborhoods was exactly what HJ leaders and campaign newsletters said the coalition was working to institute citywide. Yet Ethan referred to HJ's citywide MIHO campaign as a distant happening, a quick mention on the way to other topics, not something for ISLA's neighborhoods.

Why wasn't HJ's campaign more significant to Ethan? It was going to force progressive policies that would meet some of ISLA's own goals. A public interest attorney assisting both HJ and ISLA had told me a couple of months before this meeting that the same "large principle" connected both campaigns, and— in a telling, if simple, observation—"the pushback will be the same" for both. What's more, throughout the fall, Ethan had been worrying eloquently aloud that ISLA lacked the staff to orchestrate a big campaign against displacement in the neighborhoods of South Los Angeles. Staff had lots of other things to do: run the weekly tenant assistance clinic, educate about the health hazards typical in low-income people's homes, monitor properties where landlords were especially resistant to dealing with those hazards. Networking with HJ's citywide campaign could have produced some of the goods ISLA wanted, making more of precious staff time, or perhaps using less of it. Given the same principle and foes, building more relationships between the two coalitions should have seemed like a logical move for a skilled, entrepreneurial facilitator like Ethan.

Participants in the two campaigns were not unaware of one another. ISLA members had attended the training workshop about the state's six-year plan, where HJ leader Carol taught activists how to locate good sites for building affordable housing. Ethan and Francis of HJ knew who each other were too; Francis had attended ISLA's first, large public meeting with municipal leaders

a half year ago. Yet two months earlier, when I pointed out to the public interest attorney that ISLA leaders had scheduled a meeting about the rezoning
effort on the same day that HJ planned a meeting about housing in South Los
Angeles, the attorney looked surprised and said he would ask Ethan to follow
up with Francis. Apparently the two efforts just did not coordinate. More time
spent in ISLA scenes finally helped me figure out why not.

The answer turns on style. When they are acting as a community of interest,
advocates try to generalize the appeal of an issue across a wide swath of
society—"all of LA," as Ethan put it. A community of *identity*, on the other
hand, constructs a problem as a shared threat to the community's socially and
culturally distinct identity that community members aim to protect. Compromises and broad alliances diminish that quest. Both are styles of problem solving. Participants in both kinds of action get people to do things with goals in
mind. Both are strategic, in other words, but in different ways. It is the community of interest, not identity, that usually comes to mind when we use the
word "strategic."

This chapter follows the action in scenes from the earlier phase of ISLA's
antidisplacement campaign. I discovered that when advocates style themselves as a community of identity, they give themselves a distinctive dilemma.
Their style of action, with its emphasis on a distinct, subordinated community,
entangles them with different social realities from the ones immediately salient
to a community of interest. The central dilemma for a community of identity
is to balance strategies that are *from* the people most central to "the community" and those crafted by advocates *for* the community.

The community of identity is a cultural reality of its own, with its own influence on how activists make claims and build relationships around claims. It generates distinct ways of talking and feeling. To anticipate a common assumption,
a community of identity is not simply a necessity for US activists of color; some
activists of color in the HJ coalition preferred to act as a community of interest.
It is not specific to Latinx activism. The chapter ends with scenes from LAPO, a
predominantly African American group that pursued housing and civil rights
issues in the same style of interaction. Style is a reality—a pattern of interaction
we can see playing out similarly across and within different organizations, across
issues and social categories of the participants.

Identity Politics and Community Empowerment?: Beyond an Unsatisfying Debate

The community of identity is not just another name for "identity politics,"
which often ends up being a fuzzy, moving target of criticism. To many commentators, identity politics is an escape from (properly political) strategy

rather than a kind of strategy, a collective quest for honor as opposed to a collective struggle for material or political resources. These dichotomies, along with blanket assumptions about personal motives and collective goals, would get in the way of understanding a community of identity as a form of problem solving. Discussing them briefly will help clear the way for my different approach.

Fifty years ago, US observers puzzled over a kind of collective action they considered only ambiguously political. They heard young protesters sounding emotional and moralizing rather than strategic in the sense that observers understood that term: instrumentally organized for impact on policy makers and focused on material grievances. They called it "expressive politics."[1] In some of these accounts, instrumental or "strategic" and expressive currents drove separate trajectories of collective action, while other observers figured collective action always included both.[2] In nearly all these accounts, though, expressive politics results from morally and emotionally laden personal motives that drive activists to act.

In the succeeding decades, feminist and moral philosophers rethought the instrumental/expressive dichotomy. Rather than unchained personal motives, they saw collective bids for social honor. In this view, suppressed social categories need recognition—legitimate collective identities—before demands for resources and rights or inclusion in the political community can be heard from the people who identify with those categories.[3] Social philosophy made way for the "identity politics" of women, racial, ethnic, and sexual minority groups as a political end, not simply a misplaced, private gripe. The enhanced theoretical attention to group identities in politics did not make "identity politics" a more precise category—so all the more reason we should not consider "identity politics" and "community of identity" interchangeable even if both share certain themes.

For instance, theorists called identity politics "the politics of recognition."[4] But what was the HJ coalition's community of *interest* trying to do with its drumbeat and crowded rooms if not generate recognition? Of course, what the coalition wanted recognized—a general will for affordable housing—was a carefully orchestrated construction, not a representation of some preexisting objective reality. Yet proponents of identity politics would be the first to say they are not just representing but actively constructing an (affirming, appropriate) identity too. To be fair, there is a heritage in social theory and philosophy that elaborates on the kind of "recognition" that socially subordinated groups seek, helping us distinguish it from the recognition that housing advocates want to direct to a policy proposal and its constituency.[5] That is the point, however; the terms of discussion about "identity politics" often have been too imprecise or abstract to help us study what people *do* collectively.

Not all US observers accepted the valorization of group identities in politics either. Some charged that identity politics distracted people from progressive political action or divided the nation into enclaves of identity consciousness.[6] This critique from the 1990s recirculated widely among academics and journalists while I wrote this book.[7] In one view, a "pseudopolitics" of identity, born in the 1960s' student New Left, had grown up, taken up residence in US universities, and trained two generations of college students to think that politics is about me and not we, about selves and not citizens.[8] Writer Mark Lilla rendered identity as *motive* and also (pseudo)political *end*, bringing us back full circle to the dichotomies of a half century before.

Even studies that do consider identity as a *strategy* carry along the worn baggage of a fifty-year-old debate. In one account, colorfully expressive identity politics emerges as a strategic response that lesbian and gay activists make when they see their opportunities for political gain blocked.[9] When you can't win, you bide your time, celebrate difference, and build internal group solidarity. This view partly revalorizes what others have condemned about identity politics without really disturbing the old preference for instrumentality; sometimes even expressiveness is instrumental, goes the thinking.

Other research reverses the arrows of culpability, and social advocates are *objects* rather than subjects of an identity strategy, but the role of group identity is still suspect. City planners and commercial developers elicit "community" voices at public hearings. These forums hold out a deceptive promise of communal empowerment without ceding any real decision-making authority.[10] Advocates get to speak up forcefully as "the community," similar to how advocates in this chapter do. They become unwitting pawns of a strategy that municipal officials and developers use to make them feel recognized. In this community empowerment scenario, local advocates are victims of something similar to Lilla's pseudopolitics.[11] Whether or not top-down, or government- or nonprofit-sponsored, community participation forums end up disempowering participants is an important empirical question on its own, but it is different from the ones here.[12]

I ask how protecting community works as a strategy for addressing collective problems. Those problems themselves are not about low collective self-esteem, insufficient group solidarity, or lack of opportunities for other kinds of political action; they were mostly about housing. A community of identity denotes a way of organizing collective action instead of a motive or the end of action. It is a collective strategy with virtues, drawbacks, and trade-offs of its own, whether it guides Latinx neighborhood activists, African American civil rights proponents, white college students in solidarity with low-income tenants of color, or professional advocates paid to organize particular constituencies.

A Community of Identity

Mapping: Sharp Political and Moral Boundaries,
Fuzzy Geographic Ones

The community of identity style jelled early in ISLA's history as the dominant way of orchestrating general meetings, public rallies, and a lot of the earlier strategy sessions. In these scenes, throughout my 3½ years following ISLA's antidisplacement and Manchester campaigns, ISLA participants spoke relentlessly and often exclusively as members or supporters of "the community."[13] Rather than positioning their sense of "we" within dotted-line, concentric circles as HJ coalition participants did, ISLA participants imagined a sharp boundary around a unitary "we"—the community and close allies—protected from a powerful "they" ringed around them. The community protects itself, and extract rights or benefits to redress some of the harm *they* cause.

At ISLA's initial meeting, a retreat held to envision the antidisplacement campaign, speakers and videos projected a social "map" like this, with the community and confirmed, local ally groups in the center. Outside the center were some ambivalent and uninformed outsiders, and then looming threats— abstract forces like gentrification, and specific actors like property owners, developers, or simply "all these elites," as one leader put it. Rather than orient to a zone of competition and aspiration in a middle ring, on this map actors orient to a side, inside or outside the circle, as in, Which side are you on? A slideshow followed by a succession of speakers described the threat of gentrification to the neighborhoods of the community. One speaker, a health aide, explained she grew up in "this neighborhood," but "I had to move because there's no affordable housing. . . . I am in Pleasant Valley, but *this* is my home, this is where I work, my parents live here." She teared up, and someone kindly brought her a tissue and rubbed her back.

Learning the right map meant, above all, expressing identification with the community. Most participants picked up on that pretty quickly. I noticed that many attendees at the retreat who, going by appearances, were unlikely to identify as low-income tenants of color, narrated themselves into solidarity with the community during a long go-around of introductions that followed a slideshow on gentrification in South Los Angeles.

> Mabel, the white grad student with purple hair, told us she identified with her Latino, nonstudent neighbors. They had "babies, and chickens and parties and—real people!" She said it wasn't a good experience to just be around "people eighteen to twenty for four years."

> A white man training to be a pastor said, "I'm tired of just walking through the neighborhood without knowing much about it."

Ethan said, "I live in Balboa Heights [a newer residential complex near downtown], and that development could not have happened without displacing many people and it's a great example of what NOT to do." He said he wanted to do something to change that. ISLA activist Marina, seated behind me, muttered cynically, "So are you going to move out?"

A fresh-faced student said that he lived in the neighborhood north of the college and he was afraid that the slideshow was going to show his house because he probably displaced people who used to live there. So he figured he needed to take the responsibility to do something.

The speakers all expressed a wish to make up for their social distance from the community and justify their physical proximity to it. They narrated themselves as tenants or students who regretfully displaced community members, or suspected their own lives to be less authentic than those of community members. A community of identity is, literally, one in which membership depends strongly on participants either *identifying* themselves as members of the same community, or else allying or taking sides with the community as outsiders. The pull of identification or allyhood could be compelling.

Sharply bound in political and moral terms, the community was not strictly a geographic entity. Early in the antidisplacement campaign, an ISLA ally tipped off coalition leaders that a company hired to redraft the city's master planning document for ISLA's neighborhoods had been speaking to homeowners in a small, tree-lined, fastidiously maintained enclave of Victorian houses, wealthier and whiter than the other neighborhoods in which ISLA worked. Theresa, a church leader active with ISLA, charged that progentrification planners were finding congenial informants to "make up a whole new community." In other words, they had a different vision of the community from ISLA's, grounded in the same locale.

Not only did the designation "the community" apply to some people more than others within a given geographic area, but the term itself blurred boundaries that a city planner would see distinctly. Ethan and other members decided that two geographically distinct neighborhoods, about three miles apart, would host block parties to spread the word about ISLA toward the start of the antidisplacement effort. Ethan himself said he was not familiar with one of them. The Juniper neighborhood was home to largely Latinx residents in a dense collection of duplexes, small apartment clusters, and an occasional Victorian, bounded by a park and major expressway. The other, Lincoln, was predominantly Latinx and African American, and less densely built, with old bungalows and cutoff streets—some of them brutally bereft of trees in the glaring summer sun—and bisected by a wide thoroughfare lined with stucco apartments along with an occasional *panadería* or dollar store with handwritten signs. It would be hard to say Juniper and Lincoln inhabited the same community if that word meant an urban locale in which people call each other neighbors, or a socially or aesthetically distinct, contiguous enclave bounded by natural or manufactured features, such as seasides, hills, bridges, and expressways. I noticed that community rarely mapped onto something materially, geographically distinct, and rarely, if ever, did ISLA advocates ask each other to be that specific.

I risked being a pest or looking clueless, and felt like both when the opportunity came up to pitch the question informally at the Lincoln street fair. ISLA leader Francine told me she set up one of her programs "in this community":

Paul: "So you mean right here in Lincoln area?

Francine said it was centered here and in Juniper, and recited two zip codes.

Paul: "Do you know how far east this neighborhood goes?"

Francine said she did not know, and asked Thalia, another ISLA leader and longtime South Los Angeles activist from the CGTC land trust.

Thalia: "I really don't know."

Paul: "So people don't have a sense that the neighborhood is some specific area . . ."

Thalia: "It's not that they don't have a sense of place," she said quickly, maybe to fend off any implication (unintended by me) that local residents didn't belong there. Thalia continued that the neighborhood did not have real specific boundaries. "For some work that [CGTC] is doing, it is Lincoln Avenue and Vista." I had the feeling by now that my curiosity sounded somehow critical of the community.

Paul: "The reason I ask is I used to live in the Bay Area, and in San Francisco, people would say 'the Fillmore' and they meant a very specific area that ended on a specific street." Thalia said this wasn't like that. "We decided to have the fair at Lincoln and Meridian Avenues, and it's 'the Lincoln and Meridian street fair.'"

Paul: "But people wouldn't necessarily say 'I live in the Lincoln and Meridian Street area.'"

Thalia: "People say they live in South LA, or South Central LA."

As Francine and Thalia both implied, few, if any, residents would have identified firm outer boundaries of their social enclave with zip codes or streets.

Following the action and settings, I learned that the community encompassed relatively low-income or working-class tenants of color, mostly but not necessarily Latinx, in a locale whose imagined geographic boundaries shifted depending on the issue at hand—a building impacting a half-square-mile neighborhood hugged by a freeway, or a shopping center development that might directly impact traffic patterns, rental opportunities, and circuits of social intercourse within a three- or five-mile radius.

MAPPING A COMMUNITY OF IDENTITY FOR LOW-INCOME PEOPLE OF COLOR

The objective contours of urban development and gentrification, the "social" as distinct from symbolic boundaries, were heavily racialized in South Los Angeles, as the discussion in chapter 2 noted.[14] That makes it reasonable to think that a community of racial identity emerges naturally from residents' experiences and grievances. Still, experiences do not translate directly into styles of collective action. Some of HJ's organizations were advocating primarily on behalf of constituencies of color, but did not choose to organize themselves as communities of identity. The community projected onto a community of identity's map, in other words, is a social construction. That does not mean that ISLA's community was not real in the lives of ISLA participants, or not real in its consequences. Neither do I mean to imply that ISLA's participants were exaggerating the toll that displacement took on themselves or their neighbors. The point is only that strategies for orchestrating collective problem solving are not simply natural or logical. They are cultural, even for people who would seem to have little "distance from necessity."[15]

When social advocates say they are fighting on behalf of the community, they are making normative as well as descriptive claims. The claim intends to compel potential participants. The appeal goes like this: if local residents have a decent sense of commitment to people socially similar to them in important ways, they will recognize themselves in our claims about the community; they will recognize who their people are. Communities of interest make claims to compel potential participants too. HJ leaders' talk of a "broad-ranging coalition" was supposed to urge diverse groups to embrace claims about a general interest—and pressure city hall to act as if a broad and general citizenry was demanding the right decision. ISLA's advocacy campaigns on behalf of the community were similar to other battles over urban development and environmental hazards in that they sometimes projected a community more socially homogeneous than the actual neighborhoods in which advocates worked.[16] This relation between community as diverse population and symbolic construction became particularly clear when advocates put their projection of community to the test.

At an early ISLA meeting, for example, longtime local resident and ISLA participant Marina said that "a lot of the community is not as aware as we are . . . of the past, the history." Being fully "aware" meant recognizing danger-ous agents of unwanted neighborhood change. Among these, Marina and others included commercial developers and a local college with building plans that members thought would lead to more displacement. Members pointed out that some low-income tenants did not want to criticize the local college, though, because they liked the college-sponsored programs for local kids. To Marina, college-sponsored youth programming was a sugarcoated pill for the neighborhood: "They say 'here's a candy'—then they kick your ass!" Ethan did not disagree, but cautioned that when it comes to the possibility of dis-placement by people, especially students, who could pay higher rents, "a homeowner doesn't feel the same as someone else." Marina agreed that home-owners might appreciate the boost in property values that could accompany higher rents. Ethan added, however, that "there *are* homeowners who don't want the whole block taken over," and coalition leader Victor finished the thought: "We have to find them."

It is exactly that enticing opportunity as well as tension lurking in the gap between ISLA participants' vision of the community and the diversity of views held by the local population that would generate crucial tests for ISLA. Who exactly, then, was outside the community that Ethan, Marina, Theresa, and others projected?

The entities on the other side of "we" in ISLA were not so different from those that the HJ coalition contended with: property developers and their allies. ISLA advocates understood and lived the contestation differently, though, with different terms, imagery, and emotions. While even some prop-erty developers could be at least short-term allies in the HJ coalition, ISLA advocates understood their opposition in more categorical terms, in more boldly contrasting shades corresponding to more clearly demarcated "we" and "they."

The categorical approach to opponents emerged in comments from the director of one of ISLA's bigger member organizations. Making informal chat over bagels and coffee at the start of the kickoff meeting for the antidisplace-ment campaign, the director told me how much fun it would be to go to public hearings on development in South Los Angeles and yell at big developers, "Liar, liar, pants on fire!" He did not make fine distinctions. "Athletic center, the college, it's the same—it's all these elites!" The director, long experienced with urban issues, most likely saw distinctions between various property-owning entities in South Los Angeles. I gathered what mattered more in this conversation was the performance of categorical opposition, instructing a newcomer in the style that oriented the action here. Advocates needed to remember which side they were on.

Participants at ISLA meetings did in fact see more than an undifferentiated property-owning elite on the other side of a thick line of opposition. At the follow-up after a big town hall meeting with city planners, for example, a labor organizer suggested that ISLA's emerging antidisplacement campaign should spotlight a variety of property developers' roles in unwanted neighborhood change and not focus as much on the college as participants sometimes did. Ethan took a poll, and everyone agreed, including outspoken Marina: "Developers have been taking properties away for a long time; the college doesn't have anything to do with [them]." And at ISLA's kickoff meeting, the leader who had castigated "all these elites" told a student attendee who sounded contrite about his small business landlord, "He's not the real enemy, like Residential Management Professionals [the owner of many apartments in the area]." The point is that ISLA's map made different kinds of opposition visible—but they were all an opposition, not competitors with whom one might make occasional deals.

City planning officials looked different on the map of a community of identity than they did to ISLA's coordinating committee too. Rather than potential subjects of dealmaking in the zone of aspiration, they were more often objects of skeptical monitoring and pointed social critique. Only rarely were they admitted as allies of the community. At the kickoff for the antidisplacement campaign, participants asked, "Who is the main target?" and one answered that "the city is letting all this happen." City officials were not the heaviest opposition, but ISLA advocates mapped most of them over the line separating adversaries from allies—as passive and sometimes active enablers.

Bonds: Commitment That Is Residential, Political, and Moral

ISLA's favorite slogan, reproduced on window signs dotting the neighborhoods, aptly conveyed the bonds in this community of identity: "Proud member of this community for ___ years." Residents filled in the blank; the higher the number, the greater the moral weight. While the physical or geographic boundaries of community were fuzzy, community members' perceptions of each other's *rootedness in* a community were unambiguous enough for a numerical measure. Local residents testifying at city hall frequently started their two-minute public comment statements by announcing their local longevity. This simple affirmation is a clue that ties in a community of identity differ from those in a community of interest. In ISLA's community of identity, community took on layers of residential, political, and moral as well as demographic meanings simultaneously.

First, the community projected in these claims of membership encompassed members' life experience as a whole. Bonds were commitments of a large piece of self to a local people whose well-being was a source of pride. Ties sustained by a community of interest, by contrast, bid loyalty to a stance on an issue but not to a morally potent sense of peoplehood. That is not to say that ISLA participants necessarily talked or even thought about ISLA or the community all day long as they went about their lives. I mean that members who were considered good or appropriate participants in ISLA expected each other to act loyally to a people and community of fate. HJ participants advocated a political platform—citywide policies they thought would be good for Los Angeles in general—but did not give special moral or political significance to Angelenos as "a people," or socially and culturally distinct community. While ISLA participants, like HJ ones, enacted their sense of loyalty mainly in campaign scenes—at meetings, the occasional protest, and hearings at city hall—they *pictured* that loyalty more as a feature of a whole, locally situated life, not the relatively small, if energetically sustained, segment of life devoted to fighting one public issue.

Political campaigns come and go, but lives, and the neighborhoods that host them, grow and regenerate over long periods. It is not surprising, then, that for ISLA participants, good bonds were long-term ones. ISLA participants would applaud for the speaker at city hall who affirmed being a "proud member" of the (residential) community over many years, signaling authentic belonging. Good members of ISLA's community did not simply fight a particular battle with a property developer, win or lose and then go home, but rather identified and affirmed their place in an ongoing chain of events—the history of their community. A display panel that ISLA staff created to tell the story of one battle over local redevelopment put it this way: "The remedy lies not just with. policy makers or landlords. The deepest healing occurs when our communities tell their stories, organize, build power, and struggle."

Physical, residential displacement was at the same time a symbolic blow to the bonds of community. At the Juniper neighborhood block party, for example, a big sign instructed partygoers how to memorialize displaced neighbors and small businesses. They could write down the names of neighbors and businesses, the number of years either of those had spent in the community, and a story about them on a paper facsimile of a brick, and tape it up alongside other paper bricks to form a memorial wall. I copied inscriptions verbatim from typical bricks, including these two:

Maria-Susanna

>   deslojada por alto costo de renta (evicted by high rent)
>   renta antes 400 (rent before: 400)
>   renta ahora 1,400 (rent now: 1,400)

Lupe Hernandez

> Lived in [zip code] for thirty-one years. Left my neighborhood due to high cost [of] rents that were targeted to students. I have been displaced by people who don't believe that the working class should live here.

Telegraphically mournful like gravestone inscriptions, the stories communicated that longtime community bonds had moral as well as purely residential, physical significance.

Bonds are not simply a matter of what people say about social ties after the fact but what meanings shape people's ongoing relationships too. I have been using what ISLA participants were saying as a window on normative expectations about how to jell as the community. We get a sense of how ISLA advocates *acted* on their understanding of bonds by observing scenes in which actors are affirming loyalty under pressure. Loyalty for HJ coordinating committee members meant compartmentalizing issues and refusing to endorse a protest if doing so risked alienating partners willing to commit to the coalition's focal issue. Loyalty was different at ISLA general meetings and public events, directed to the community, not the issue.

The single action that earned the most praise during my entire time with ISLA was the Somos la Comunidad (we are the community) event. ISLA members presented findings from their research on local neighborhoods, and themselves as the voice of a unified, self-protecting community challenging city officials to hear their complaints, questions, and demands. Nine months later, ISLA leaders were still talking about the event because community members "spoke truth to power." They acted as a mutually dependent, steadfast collective facing potential threat; they enacted bonds expected in a community of identity. This kind of unity came off clearly in one of the speaker's opening comments:

> "I'm an active member of this community and I've lived in LA nineteen years and in this community six years. . . . I want to get power and money for the working people. . . . The two people sitting here who have the power [referring to two city planning officials seated, facing the audience] . . . I'd like to ask you to put yourself in our shoes."

Participants related to one city council member attending the event differently from other officials, identifying him as "one of us" and therefore dependable.

> Neighborhood resident: "I know you're our people, and you're here when we need you. I've lived in this community thirty-three years, and seven years in Juniper." She referenced some figures showing that before 1998, 3 percent of the housing was for "college" people, but now, ten years later, the figure was 32 percent. "This is unfair, and we have to work together."

The council member did not disappoint. He responded to residents' entreaties by identifying himself with the community:

> "I'm anxious ... because I know what we are going through as a community. I've been working in this community fifteen years. . . . My parents were immigrants so [I feel the problems too]. . . . We don't have good coordination. . . . At community meetings we need to have the community present. . . . I'm your voice, but I'm one of fifteen. . . . I tried to push inclusionary housing seven years ago . . . but none of the council members were supportive."

The council member was an ally who took a side.

Taking sides was what one did in order to participate in the community's bonds. When the leader of a community development corporation in ISLA saw me at the Juniper block party, *immediately* she handed me a red construction paper brick and said I should write down any stories of displacement I knew. The displacement stories I knew were only secondhand. I knew personally of displacement elsewhere in town. Would that be good? Francine equivocated: "Maybe." Later, embarrassed, I figured out the lesson that bonds of solidarity committed members to the community—ISLA neighborhoods—not to concern for a housing *issue* in the abstract.

LEADERSHIP IN A COMMUNITY OF IDENTITY: SKILLS OF SOLIDARITY BUILDING AND BOUNDARY DEFENDING

Ethan, the leading researcher and organizer for ISLA's antidisplacement campaign, had a knack for integrating members' needs and insights into conversation at meetings. Making people feel valued was one way to get participants to do what the coalition needed them to do. That made him an especially skilled facilitator—as was Francis of HJ—but the entrepreneurial actor model's notion of "skill" would not easily distinguish the two. While Francis was skilled at compartmentalizing and bridging, Ethan was skilled at tireless solidarity building and agile boundary defending.

At a meeting called to discuss a new financial sponsorship for ISLA and new campaign that might produce a "win" for ISLA, participants laid out their assumptions about what makes a good leader. Given this double context, ISLA members might have emphasized how important it was for a leader to be detail and numbers oriented. Or they could have spoken up for a leader with strategic savvy—someone good at figuring out how to frame some local issue for an ISLA campaign.

Uniformly, participants gravitated toward something else: a spirited communicator who could keep people emotionally committed. Longtime participant Opal said that the people involved in a new campaign need to have an "emotional" commitment because "it's about our people." Ethan wrote "spirit and communication" on paper posted on an easel in front of the room. Ron said he thought Victor could be a good coordinator for ISLA.

Victor demurred: "Spirit and communication aren't me: I'm not always smiling."

Ethan mugged a toothy grin.

Victor: "Ethan has the morale that has helped bring us to the table."

Both Francis and Ethan were articulate and sharply observant, and masters of understated irony. But neither Francis nor anyone else in the HJ scenes I observed ever implied that his job depended on being a personable and rousing manager of people. Francis pointed out to me how much his difficult job depended on seeing HJ participants as embodiments of abstractions—constituencies with interests and varying amounts of influence, not people in need of minding and cultivating.

Ethan lived up to the job description. He cheered, figuratively speaking, when others might have shrugged or else skulked away. For example, Ethan and core members observed not infrequently that ISLA participants did not like going to monthly general or planning meetings. About five minutes after the starting time at one of these, pulling chairs into a small row, Ethan said in a quiet newscaster's voice to no one in particular, "We're going to have a very, very, very, very low turnout." He proceeded to facilitate a meeting-cum-slideshow in his usual, articulate, voluble way. With Ethan, publicly visible emotions ranged from neutral up and out to righteously indignant, or joyful, on behalf of the community and ISLA. Once he literally jumped out of his seat, excited to tell us about a breakthrough in negotiations with a big developer, lassoing bits of his story into separate phrases as a Spanish translator tried to keep up.

Participants at another ISLA general meeting had planned a neighborhood dinner party at core member Marina's house, intended to get some pastors from the many local churches interested in fighting displacement. We had spent at least fifteen minutes discussing congregations to tap, puzzling over how to entice African American congregations and storefront churches. The goal was a relaxed, conversational evening, but one with some payoff for organizing efforts. Ethan recounted for me after the party that Marina made a marvelous dinner, and had said people really just need to be together and have a good time, and "you build from that." "She is right," he averred. It turned out that the only clergy member who attended was an already-committed pastor. The dinner did little, if anything, to create new contacts for ISLA. Ethan described it cheerily.

Ethan was a solicitous guardian of ISLA's community. Protecting boundaries, he treated meeting participants to cheeky humor and ironic quips, reminding us where we were on the map of a proud, embattled community. For a good leader in ISLA, protecting the boundaries could matter more than winning supporters. He told us at one meeting, with the casual pride of someone who knows what's what, that he would pass up an invitation to speak about displacement at WHA's annual conference. After all, "the answer is obvious and doesn't need a long presentation! You just stop gentrification."

The Central Dilemma: From or for the Community?

Frustration and Lack of Resources Switches the Strategy, Not the Style

Campaigns take money and staff time, as social movements scholars have long argued.[17] Someone needed to plan and lead meetings, run committees, orchestrate outreach events like the two street fairs, attend meetings at city hall, keep antennae sharply attuned to backroom and front-stage decision making, and apply for grants to keep the organization going. That someone was Ethan. But Ethan managed other projects for his organization too, and even an energetic orchestrator might have a hard time keeping up and keeping others up too.

By September, Ethan had reached his limits. He opened the monthly meeting by observing that "a lot of our vision has been tied up in a large group of people coming to consensus around our vision of the neighborhood." The trouble was, Ethan said, it was not clear ISLA had the resources and staff time to make that happen. Over the past half year, Ethan noted, ISLA had managed to "shift the frame" with some local college officials, who now recognized that the displacement of longtime residents was a problem. ISLA had "cultivated community leaders"—people who had attended grassroots planning workshops put on by SED and gone on neighborhood walks, and then reported their findings at the Somos la Comunidad event. Staff person Eduardo agreed, adding that "there are at least thirty trained people available, so that we could stick a microphone in their faces and they know what to say. I'd rather have a hundred folks like that than a thousand who are there for some other reason." Yet these positive developments put only more pressure on Ethan. "We don't have a lot of dedicated staff time. . . . I don't feel like I can be effective," he said.

With that homely statement, ISLA leaders commenced legitimating to themselves a twist on the community of identity's basic strategy. They would speak more forthrightly *for* the community without worrying whether or not every ISLA statement was directly *from* the community, produced or vetted by neighborhood residents. Waiting for a large group of local residents to come to consensus would only lose the coalition precious time building an authoritative public presence. Organizers would not know how to describe ISLA's positions to potential new partners.

Still the risk was that too much staff-initiated speaking *for* the community would threaten ISLA's claim to be *from* the community, the authentic voice. Clearly the change sat uneasily with people in the room. Pastor Chuck worded his way awkwardly toward this new strategic stance:

> "We have to give up the notion of being a grassroots organization; what matters is that others don't know who we are. . . . [So] ISLA is grass roots, but not grass roots in the usual sense. . . . Maybe we're not all going out [seeking consensus from neighbors], but ISLA becomes more visible, and builds that database for people who want to be involved."

Participants could have gone door knocking, a classic activist means to discovering grassroots opinion, but that would take precious staff time. If ISLA leaders could rest their legitimacy more on staff members along with people like those thirty already-available community leaders who knew what to say in front of a microphone, then they could still run meetings as a community of identity without violating the basic boundary between authentic insiders and suspect outsiders.

ISLA members actually had been speaking *for* the community from the coalition's earliest meetings. Otherwise it would not have made sense for Victor to say that ISLA needed to "find" people who agreed with ISLA's stance, and "aware" enough not to take the college's bait while their asses were getting kicked, in Marina's pungent metaphor. If staff people could be trusted to speak authentically for the community, they could build the coalition faster while having something more solid to which they could invite ally groups and with which they could reciprocate when it came time. Participants in other, similarly oriented campaigns could become authentic members of ISLA's community of identity even if they did not go to face-to-face meetings with neighborhood residents. Or as Ethan put it, "That can be our grass roots," but "not in the usual sense," in Pastor Chuck's ambiguous locution.

Speaking authentically *for* the community was, in short, a strategy to empower the staff. Ethan complained, "We have this idea we can't say anything without the community vetting it. We have to be willing to put it on paper! . . . This idea that we won't put forward anything without the community—at this point it is holding us back." Francine agreed: "We had this idea about starting at zero [each time we talk to the community, and] we don't have to be going back to 'what do you want.' Theresa reasoned similarly that "at some point we have to say we've created a process that is legitimate, and we have to go with it."

The defensive rationalizing, the tortured locutions, a grass roots that is not quite grass roots: Why was this so difficult and angst provoking? If local resident voices were so indispensable to ISLA's legitimacy, then why not simply wait for local residents who cared about the community to present themselves? Maybe staff actually were less servants of the community than they were agents of their own ambition; now was their chance to take over the effort forthrightly. But even if that were the case, the fact is that they did not do that previously and did defer to community voices for the long nine months of the campaign. Another possibility is that few residents cared that much about what ISLA leaders claimed they cared about. Research by residents and leaders of SED, a leading organization in ISLA, showed an overwhelming pattern of displacement of longtime former residents by recently arriving, higher-rent-paying tenants on some neighborhood blocks. Some local residents did speak up at meetings and street fairs about their fears of being priced out along with their desire to stay. ISLA leaders insisted these residents gave voice to what many of their more timid neighbors felt.

A more plausible reason for all the angst is that hard, persistent social and cultural realities confront people who just as persistently act as a community of identity in neighborhoods like ISLA's. ISLA leaders themselves had said as much. It was an "accomplishment" that local residents had been "trained" and now knew what to say if someone stuck a microphone in their faces, as Eduardo explained it. Staff must have thought residents could benefit from being "trained" to read urban planning documents or give testimony, or scarce staff time would have gone to other things. Middle-class, native English speakers may teach *themselves* how to read technical reports and speak forthrightly to officials at public hearings.[18] Scenarios from the world of community organizing, on the other hand, show that residents fighting for a safer environment, more responsive schools, and public services in lower-income neighborhoods of color benefit from tutelage that compensates the multiple disadvantages of marginalized social backgrounds, including the lack of a sense of being entitled to speak publicly at all.[19]

A community of interest may take root in the same social circumstances, but participants do not center their action on a shared, authentic identity that makes "for" versus "from" into a tension. That style of action does not entangle participants so thickly in the constraints of ill-distributed capacities, as long as someone (perhaps professional staff) is able to propel a campaign on behalf of others. A community of identity that draws its authentic members from lower-income neighborhoods of color risks the awkward position of needing special outsiders who can make themselves (nearly) legitimate, like Ethan.

The move toward a more staff-led strategy was not a change in style. The community remained the privileged "we" on the map, the arbiter of legitimate participation, its identity strictly bounded and protected from others who were unacceptable as partners, or would need to show some degree of conversion to become trusted members of the community of identity. The strongly and explicitly staff-led strategy did not last either.

Nine months later at a monthly meeting, ISLA participants looked over their accomplishments and reversed course. They headed again for less staff-led action and more action from the community. Ethan, Mabel, and Victor were pondering the disappointing juncture they found themselves at. A friendly contact at the city planning department had told Ethan not to wait for the department's new neighborhood planning process to call out, much less reverse, the displacement of longtime residents. Budget cutting had severely shrunk the department's staff. A labor ally at the meeting summed up the mood: "We need a win." Ethan's contact suggested that ISLA develop a "people's plan." ISLA research staff had guessed that Draper Boulevard would be the next zone of contention over the displacement of low-income tenants. Just to the south of the college, Draper was a thoroughfare of bodegas, nail salons, *panaderías*, and the occasional real estate office set up for students moving into a neighborhood increasingly catering to them with apartments cut into formerly single-family Victorians and bungalows. The friendly planner urged that a truly professional-quality, urban development plan produced by ISLA could influence planners and city council members.

Ethan warmed to the idea. He sketched a campaign within a campaign, a participatory planning project codirected by community leaders. Local residents would envision housing, shopping, and park space that would serve their needs. Ethan observed that "this is not the testimony model of getting people to be trained to speak for one or two minutes, but back to the original vision of [community] people leading it." Victor was excited; it was "something we can win." The labor activist agreed. It sounded like a return to the old strategy: a campaign *from* the community, though of course with staff tutelage. But that is not what happened. The project, Dreams for Draper, turned out to be one of the biggest tests of ISLA participants' ability to deal with their style's central dilemma. The style endured—yet we might say, at the cost of a project that had generated lots of effort, lots of participation, and little, if any, impact.

A Big Test of the Map and Bonds: The Dreams for Draper Project

Urban scholar Robert Sampson (1999, 2012) has argued that while a shared sense of collective responsibility can improve the quality of life in low-income neighborhoods, neighbors still need resources from outside in order to thrive.

That was the big test for ISLA supporters. How could a community of identity integrate outsiders with resources and expertise not widely available in neighborhoods like Juniper or Lincoln?

Outsiders came in the form of college students. Some were taking an urban planning sequence at a distant university, from a professor who knew a leading figure in ISLA member organization SED. Draper Boulevard would constitute their studio project. Students would gather information about their "client," as the professor put it, in the first quarter, and draw up final street plans during the second. Others from another university offered their data analysis skills. The person tapped to be the project coordinator of Dreams for Draper was an urban planning student too. In all, the project was an ambitious experiment in collaboration. Neighbors and local business proprietors would attend meetings, talk in focus groups, and fill out surveys on what was treasurable or deplorable about the Draper Boulevard neighborhood. Students would aim to summarize faithfully the dreams and frustrations expressed in focus groups, analyze survey responses, come up with rough plans for community comment, and then draft a series of final street plans. Local neighbors would give feedback on the draft plans; the students from the planning studio would rethink and redraft. Outsider students would in effect facilitate the Draper neighborhood talking to itself.

I too became a collaborator. I joined the Dreams for Draper research team as an additional "research ally," in project coordinator Beth's words. While studying the research scene, I advised on how to phrase questions as well as appreciate the differences between focus group and survey data as windows on public opinion. I learned that well-meaning outsiders posed a menace to a community of identity if they participated not simply as adjunct helpers but also bearers of expertise. Their participation threatened displacing the community with a different source of authoritative knowledge and different temporal rhythm—a different style.

These fundamental tensions were not immediately obvious. At the first research group meeting, coordinator Beth implied that our group's legitimacy flowed ultimately from the community's judgment, not from professional know-how; the scene style here would be the same as at general meetings. Two days earlier, ISLA activists had invited local residents to view a huge GPS map of Draper and adjacent streets, and mark off sites they would like to "keep," "improve," or get rid of with different-colored pushpins. Beth said the "facilitators" who would shepherd the whole project and explain it to neighborhood residents should "come from the neighborhood, and it's important they remain from the neighborhood." They were in the best position to interpret what "keep" or "improve" meant. Beth meant for community members to occupy the driver's seat; we, the adjuncts, needed to avoid giving a lot of backseat advice.

In hindsight, the collaboration challenged the boundaries and bonds that defined the ISLA community. Its logistics followed professional rhythms rather than the rhythms of a community of identity. Beth had the unenviable job of orchestrating the work of student urban planners and data analysts with a series of four meetings at which community members would generate the "data" by talking about their visions. Plying giant maps with color-coded push-pins and sticker dots, neighbors would critique tentative plans drafted in response to their ongoing visioning and sticker posting. The student planning studio's services needed to fit a two-quarter course schedule that comported with ordinary academic routines, but that did not give the students much chance to learn in depth about the Draper neighborhood. Their contacts with it were limited to several weekend visits the first quarter. While the community of identity measured the depth of commitment and belonging by time spent living in its neighborhoods, students needed to make the most of their little time. Beth's own contract ran six months. Victor articulated just this clash of timelines while the two of us scurried down Draper Boulevard one afternoon in search of students for whom I would translate as they administered surveys to Spanish-speaking passersby.

> Victor: "Community process and [students'] homework process are different." He said that arranging a timeline that works with "class assignments" isn't easy because "it takes time to get the opinion of the community."

Second, at crucial points, the collaboration depended on professional know-how conserved by outside experts—the students—not the community. They would have the last word on how and when to deploy technical skills that had made their presence valuable to ISLA to begin with. There were bound to be tensions for advocates and neighbors used to projecting a community that knows itself best. Those emerged at the next research meeting, in a politico-moral tug-of-war between Beth and a new community advocate, Enira, over who was really directing Dreams for Draper.

> Enira: "Will the students interact with community people?"

> Beth: "One of the things we are sensitive to is community-generated process, and they're [the students are] turning that process into language understood by the city. . . . It's a translation process in the end. . . . They have to remember who they're working for [the community]."

> Enira: "I would challenge you to teach them [students] how to translate their process *to* the community."

Beth, not missing a beat: "This is the challenge we're taking on as a group: 'tell us how to do it better.'"

Enira persisted calmly: "I understand the value of the students. But it is important to have community members DO the survey." Beth affirmed the comment and said that students could ask, "You want to come survey with us?"

Beth was working hard to meet the moral high ground of Enira's critique, but she did not offer to restructure the researcher-researched relationship into a transfer of expertise. Members of the community would have to go with a research partner's authority to represent the community.

Enira soon came back to her point, speaking evenly: "The students are doing the [research], but that's my problem. Community members should be doing it. . . . We should leave room and [grant] that community members will be autonomous, and we can support that autonomy."

Beth: "I respect this conversation."

Pressed by Enira, Beth finessed the discussion with a bit of solicitous managerialese, but did not alter the relationship.

Strikingly, Enira's boundary policing turned out to be work *for* the community since Enira herself was not *from* it. This was her second day on the job as an intern at one of ISLA's organizations. She was placed there on a ten-month contract by AmeriCorps. Though a newly arrived outsider in terms of the geographic locale, Enira gave a virtuoso performance of the style. She was easily, stridently an *insider* to the community of identity that ISLA projected. She knew as well as Ethan or Victor how to draw the map, tie the bonds, and work for the community appropriately.

Over the next six months, the student planners evidently tried to take on what they perceived as local neighbors' perspectives. At the end of their second quarter, the class presented a set of fourteen, professional-quality streetscape plans along with slides portraying local "issues" the students had discovered during their work to a panel of ISLA leaders and me. The presentations included references to "the community" with its distinct or vibrant "culture"—terms of recognition I had not heard when I accompanied some students five months earlier during one of their weekend visits. It came off as a hard-won vocabulary that the students still were learning. One presenter observed, speaking slowly and pausing at points, that "there is a unique—cultural—aura in this area through history." Another student presented a streetscape plan with statues and explained, "We created these [the statues], but ideally they would be created by the community to express their cultural values." A third said that commercial building facades "could have community-oriented design."

The director of CGTC land trust appreciated the students' work, adding it would be good to "think about the *political* work that it would take to make any of these happen." Beth gently criticized the presentations for not having "worked on the harder issues first," and done "aesthetics and streetscapes in the context of" other issues like affordable housing. Francine said politely that "leading with the streetscapes concerned me." The presentations gave little evidence that the student planners' "clients," community residents, were people who said they felt besieged by new developments, stalked by the fear of displacement, and indignant that local student neighbors got discount offers from local shops that did not offer the same enticements to longtime residents. Wanting to represent myself truthfully, I told an ISLA neighborhood organizer that "I don't live in the community, but these plans raise a lot of issues." She replied with the quietest hint of dismay, "Imagine if you *did* live in the community."

Despite earnest nods to the community of identity, the students had missed its basic features, especially its sharp, defensive boundary between community and outsiders. One well-intended slide on cultural preservation proposed that "because of student infringement," the area needed to "establish its distinct identity." The student who crafted the slide may have heard the stories I had heard about nighttime carousing and the student couple who had sex on the hood of a parked car. The proposed solution was an "event" where residents could come and tell their "cultural heritage stories. . . . The college can get together these people to establish a sense of place." But on ISLA's map, the college was not a partner so much as a *threat* to the community's continued sense of place.

Dreams for Draper had been an ambitious, exciting vision of collaboration. It depended on contractual relations with outside, professional, and preprofessional specialists with short-term timelines, and a grant. The project started with an expert-client relationship, grafted onto a community of identity in which authenticity (however earned) and the slowly accreted local knowledge of community members, not professional expertise, was the basis for authority. A clash of maps and timelines—a clash of style—generated tensions along the way and, sadly, eventuated in beautifully professional plans that misperceived the community.

How did a clash of style matter beyond palpably awkward interactions? The Dreams for Draper project was supposed to be the "win" that ISLA needed. It slipped off ISLA's docket of strategy altogether. I could find no evidence in ISLA files nor in my field notes of the project being mentioned at ISLA meetings more than two months after the students' presentations. It helps to compare with the Somos la Comunidad event, which was an exercise in grassroots planning too. Residents trained by ISLA presented simple pie charts, graphs, lists, and photos documenting the local urban geography. Their presentation was a far less elaborate report, with no executive summaries or professional-quality mock-ups of streetscapes. Over a year later, ISLA members still were remarking fondly on this "truth speaking to power" event. ISLA leaders understood it as a project of the community.

The Dreams for Draper collaboration failed the test of style, rather than style failing the test of collaboration. For better or worse, nothing of the months of collaborative effort, reams of surveys and focus group transcripts, pin-coded maps, or beautiful architectural plans would empower strategies in ISLA's next phase, viewed in the following chapter. It would be wrong to conclude that outside expertise and connections never can benefit a community of identity. It is fair to conclude that this project's awkward relation to the community left the project with an ambiguous reputation. It was neither *from* nor *for* community since it did not clearly bear the mark of ISLA's style.

Another Test: Students as Potential Allies

The presence of college students in some of ISLA's target neighborhoods resulted as another interesting test of the style. Allyhood in ISLA's general meetings and public event scenes required boundary work on the part of facilitators, leaders, and ordinary participants alike. It required some extra work on the part of students—outsiders—to adopt the dominant map and honor the community. A neighborhood tour put on by ISLA leaders for students offers a brief illustration.

Ethan explained before the tour that ISLA teaches community members they have a right to get involved in city planning. Mabel guided one of several walking groups, pointing out good and bad features of the cityscape. "There's a house by the freeway, kind of an odd place to live." She elaborated that when the freeway was built, people weren't able to say, "I don't want a freeway." She made a pitch for taking the bus to Eastview Park, "a really interesting, bustling Latino area." Few Angelenos would consider Eastview a likely destination for student newcomers. A student got a snapshot of a cathedral dome sharing the sight line with Porky's Burgers and Stop-for-Gas signs on the same block. The incongruities struck Mabel too: "An old cathedral next to a gas station—kinda funky. . . . There are some really cool local businesses. We don't want to lose those," she said, pointing to a taqueria across the street. In all, it would be hard to understand the tour as something other than an invitation to adopt a particular map, social as well as geographic.

At the end, each walking group made a short presentation. One walker praised a Central American–themed outdoor market space: "The food looked really good, pretty authentic." Another said he saw banners announcing "Collegiate Rentals Inc." wrapped across a refurbished apartment building and told us that marketing only to students is illegal. Ethan gave a wrap-up pitch, assuring the students that the college does a lot of wonderful things, and like a lot of other educational institutions, its real estate dealings are separated from the rest of its mission. He said they had now gotten to "find out what other students don't know" about the community and suggested they remain concerned.

Learning the style turned out to be the implicit curriculum of the tour groups. Students learned that routine city planning processes produced social inequities and aesthetic hazards unless the community was involved. Development was good if it signaled the community's ethnic identity, but not if it seemed to exclude nonstudent neighbors and drive up rents. Students learned to talk of "the community," like one man who asked where the community will get together and bond without more public spaces; I did not hear students speak of "the community" before the presentations. Light chat among the staff after the workshop confirmed my analysis of the "test." Mabel appreciated the man who had surmised aloud that there were not many banks in the neighborhood because banks did not trust the neighbors.

Talking and Feeling in a Community of Identity

Keeping the Community Central

ISLA meetings and events drew on a broader range of speech norms than HJ coordinating committees and workshops. Sometimes, like HJ staff at coordinating committee meetings, ISLA staff were "players" who talked fast and assumed everyone knew who's who in the local political scene. Much more than at HJ meetings, speech norms organizing ISLA's strategy sessions and monthly coalition meetings made language itself into a defensive battle site, not just a fast route to an end.

Obvious but worth emphasizing is the way "community" worked as a claim to turf at once geographic and moral. It obviated some potentially complex differences and lent gravitas to the action that actors attributed to it. Newcomers to ISLA activity like the participants at the daylong kickoff meeting worked at presenting themselves as aligned with the community. By the end of their engagement with ISLA, the urban planning students' presentations referred liberally, if awkwardly, to the community. The speech norms of ISLA did not just represent but also contributed to producing a community of identity. Distinctive speech practices marked out and policed the central boundary on the map. They wove the community's bonds, and aroused feelings of prideful separation and protectiveness.

Ironic GPS Sharpens the Central Boundary

Throughout my time in ISLA settings, at office meetings as well as much more public events, I heard participants joke ironically about who or what was on the community's side. I labeled one of their distinctive speech devices "ironic GPS." Participants used it to navigate aloud the perimeters of the community, momentarily reminding each other which was the good side. One of the participants at the meeting just after the Somos la Comunidad event, for example, remarked mischievously that she had seen a surprise guest from the college. "He came with his two babies," she said, pointing toward imaginary little heads at knee level, adding, "Well, not babies, but as buffers." Marina asked why he was there. Ethan observed, lightly, "A little bit of spying, if you ask me." The exchange clarified that the surprise guest came from the other side.

Ironic GPS could also affix moral and political coordinates to new subjects of conversation, saving everyone a more pedantic, deliberative exploration. At the meeting that opened this chapter, facilitator Ethan and others did not talk at length about the new urbanism. Instead, the conspiracy of snickers around the table gave a clue, which Ethan translated into a quick, instructive remark that mapped the topic cleanly:

> "When we snicker, it's because they leave out the people. . . . It's not a mystery that people want [the new urbanism]—but our question is who can afford it!"

Irony was not just extra show; often it helped constitute the map in ISLA scenes.

Ironic GPS signaled the safe territory and no-go zones for new participants who might need instruction. Sometimes the irony simply dug trenches around something or someone occupying a place on the other side of the line from the community. A slideshow introducing local property developer Lionel Quinn treated viewers to a feast of ironic bite. Some of the slides were phrased like an announcer's script on a late-night TV crime show: "Who is Lionel Quinn?" asked one. "Lawyer—and likes to go to court," answered the next slide. Another depicted one of Quinn's new developments, and the next slide taunted, "Show me the zoning!" Other times the irony reminded longtime participants of who they were and who the antagonists were. At a staff meeting one day, someone described watching an African American male duo walking down the street, hoping they would make it to their destination; she saw a police car cruising several blocks away. An ISLA leader cracked, "Of course racism doesn't affect policing."

Protective Rearticulation Guards the Central Boundary

Sometimes activists try to find familiar language for unfamiliar ideas. HJ activists, for instance, tried to articulate affordable housing mandates as a matter of offering more "choices" in the housing market. Sometimes instead, activists challenge commonsense terms of debate in order to post a figurative "hazard!" sign next to widely received ideas that the community disowns. In ordinary meeting conversation, ISLA advocates chose the latter rhetorical route much more frequently than did HJ advocates. They would protectively rearticulate a topic that might otherwise invite commonsense thinking that could harm or obscure the community. Protective rearticulation, like ironic GPS, was more than rhetorical flourish. It was a pattern that became predictable. It instantiated ISLA's central boundary on the map.

The topic of neighborhood safety elicited a lot of protective rearticulation. Victor said at an early meeting that the local college tended to blame the community for safety problems. "We want to be clear that our approach to safety is different." The self-identified African American activist continued:

"When I think of safety I think of driving. What street has less cops, so I don't get pulled over. That's 'safety' for me."

The topic was a risky boundary object, too easily associated with negative images of racial minority groups. It needed rearticulation. Even an indirect allusion to safety could elicit protective rearticulation. At one meeting, participants were talking about the day's news of assaults against students. The reports did not specify who had assaulted students, but ISLA leaders played out a preemptive, protective defense against faulty assumptions:

Victor: "How the community is portrayed in the conversation about safety—they don't even say if the [perpetrator] is a community member or not. . . . Not to downplay the crimes, but it's to—not to say the community is making victims at the school."

Theresa said it seemed like the policy was only to send out notice of "community-on-student crime, not student-on-student crime, which is a much bigger problem."

Victor said it's "important to get the community side into the conversation."

Eduardo: "FYI, the person they caught from the stabbing, they weren't even from the community."

Victor and Theresa feared that casual readers of crime stories would assume a parochial standpoint and take lower-income neighborhoods of color to be a safety threat. Participants at this meeting wanted to halt that fast train of mental projections and rearticulate the issue from the community's perspective.

Even environmental hazards might be subjects for protective rearticulation. The planning students from the Dreams for Draper project saw Rodriguez Auto Repair in the middle of a residential neighborhood. They retained it in one of their streetscape renovation sketches. ISLA leader Francine affirmed the repair shop "has a life in the community."

Spanish Language and Latinx Cultural Forms Tie the Bonds

ISLA staff meetings and steering meetings were not always so different from those in HJ. In-the-know "players" used acronyms, name-dropped, and did not often stop to let new participants in on who and what was being talked about. It is a telling difference between ISLA's community of identity and HJ's community of interest that ISLA also hosted parties for members and neighbors, and retreats for staff. HJ hosted committee meetings, staff leader meetings, and an occasional workshop on policy issues. Whether or not they are always thinking about their relation to the community, participants in a community of identity *represent* more of the personal self as involved in the action.

The self being elicited was Latinx identified or Latinx affirming, if rarely specified so explicitly. ISLA's daylong kickoff meeting, called a retreat, signaled the coalition's cultural coordinates from the start. Early in the day, a meeting facilitator put on salsa music, invited us to dance our way toward other participants and introduce ourselves, and when the music stopped, head for chairs. Then the sequence ran again, with fewer chairs, leaving whichever participants were stranded to introduce themselves to the whole group. Anyone minimally hip musically had to get it that this salsa-powered game of musical chairs was neither a cakewalk, waltz, nor rap. General meetings for members included food of similar provenance: frijoles, pollo con arroz, and tamales.

More than music and food, though, ISLA's commitment to bilingual meetings in a normatively monolingual society signaled a preferred basis for group bonds. On the one hand, bilingual meetings were a practical necessity for an advocacy coalition that wanted members and a good reputation in neighborhoods in which many first-generation immigrants spoke predominantly Spanish. Yet as sociolinguist John Gumperz (1982a, 1982b) helpfully observed a long time ago, to speak a language in a multilingual setting is to convey a social identity. The coalition's name, ISLA, itself said a lot, as a Spanish acronym created from Spanish words. General coalition meetings included English translation more frequently than Spanish translation. I heard ISLA leader Ethan say at least once that his own organizing work was hampered by his inability to speak Spanish, and in fact he took Spanish lessons during his time with ISLA. I never heard an ISLA leader or participant lament rudimentary English skills. Neighborhood residents who gave testimony at city hall in Spanish could count on an ISLA staff person to translate to council members. Language use and attributions of language capability to others worked as signals of insiderhood or outsiderhood. While staff sometimes asked "non-Latinx-appearing" people if we wanted English translation, several of the regularly attending members of the coalition, older Latina women, would encourage my Spanish-language participation. One could *belong* by speaking Spanish.

Feeling the Scene with Indignity and Pride

Leading participants sometimes sounded off in a particular emotional register that I rarely heard voiced at the HJ coordinating committee. At the earliest meetings, when ISLA members were discussing how to attract more participants who appreciated the community the way they did, an indignant tone rang out consistently.

> Marina: "They [the college] always are *saying* that they're good for the community."

> Ethan: "They keep saying this community is unstable, but the community of *students*—no matter how wonderful a lot of them are—is inherently unstable."

At a general meeting a year later, ISLA leaders were talking about how to create a positive vibe with the Dreams for Draper project. Members had said for months that they were not "against" the college or students but rather against displacement. Herb, a new participant and web designer volunteering his free hours to help publicize ISLA, had gotten other members talking about how to present ISLA's campaign positively. Members were on board with positive messaging, yet voiced indignation on behalf of the community all the same:

> ISLA organizer Hortencia now brought up that "there is a rumor that the college is buying Washington Park to develop on it."

> Mabel, interjecting indignantly: "That's the only park in the area! The next one is a mile away!"

Herb proposes: "We're educating the college and city hall about how to do fair development. . . . Remember, we said we weren't going to be strident."

Mabel agreed it's not good to criticize the college, but all the same, "we were working with them and then they did something behind our back."

To say only that ISLA participants coconstructed a sense of indignity would miss part of the dynamic. Indignation sometimes bids us to shore up what has been wounded: pride. Quite literally the displacement issue did just that in ISLA campaigns. Those window signs on houses announcing one's longevity in the neighborhood read "*proud* [emphasis added] resident of this community." Both sensibilities in the indignation/pride couplet helped instantiate community boundaries and made communal bonds a palpable, breathing reality.

In meeting conversation, the hurt of indignation usually came first. Pride was the normative response—one that ISLA participants saw as both emerging from and enhancing communal solidarity. The collective, emotional couplet was particularly clear at an early coalition meeting, at which Victor asked attendees to describe negative images they heard associated with the community and then say "what the community is really like."

Victor asked now what is "our essence. Not what everyone *says* it is, but our natural diversity, not the fake diversity." He himself pitched in that what was "real" about the community was the grassroots organizations that had put so much of their effort and reputation into it over the past twenty or thirty years.

A labor activist added "all that SED has done" with creating a Latin-themed business zone.

D: "This is not a resource-poor community but a resource-rich community."

While the HJ coalition orchestrated spurts of excitement on a relatively short timeline, ISLA's antidisplacement campaign sustained a continuous performance of indignity and pride. Certainly, HJ and ISLA activists alike signaled nervous excitement—talked more animatedly, listened more tensely, and organized their seating and coordinated their speakers much more tightly—when they were at city hall meetings. Activists in both coalitions were perfectly capable of darting sarcastic quips at perceived competitors and adversaries. The point here is that ISLA's community of identity and HJ's community of interest also reached into different, collective emotional registers. Each made distinctive claims on activists' feelings.

Communities of identity are easy to find in grassroots social movements and among some nonprofit advocacy groups in the United States.[20] Local resident activists in New York City, Chicago, Provincetown, and other locales have styled their challenges to gentrification this way. They maintain a sharp boundary between a neighborhood resident "we" and invasive, powerful "they," and define authentic membership in the community in terms of longevity.[21] They organize themselves in varied ethnic and racially based idioms of community and identity—feeling their bonds with different symbolic objects from the ones that Latinx-centered ISLA members shared. Scenes with a similar style of action may share different *idiocultures*, or different collections of cultural items—the stories, jokes, tastes in food, or honored language that we often think of when we say "subculture."[22] To suggest the diversity of idiocultures that may carry the same style, we need comparisons.

Here, then, is a brief look at scenes from LAPO, an organization that includes and advocates for low-income and homeless people in downtown Los Angeles. I did not observe LAPO's executive meetings, but saw that in the housing committee and monthly general meetings of LAPO, participants created a community of identity. It was broadly similar to what ISLA participants did together in their general and strategy meetings, but LAPO participants had their own collection of collective memories, cautionary tales and rage rituals.

Subcultural Variety in a Style

It is not quite 6:00 p.m., and we are at LAPO's monthly general meeting in the narrow commons room of headquarters downtown. The thirty, mostly African American participants are seated in metal folding chairs, facing a writing board. In the huge mural on the wall behind them, community empowerment slogans swirl amid a cityscape—Peter Max meets 1960s' street art. An African American facilitator is engaging the audience in a fight-back drama that I will see at other meetings. He asks if people know about the city police department's new approach to minor infractions. The facilitator asks, "Does it make our city safer?" A young woman in the back row says no, it brings abuse and genocide—a war on the poor.

The energizing discussion is part Socratic dialogue, part call and response, part afternoon TV talk show. The facilitator says the new policing approach started when "they decided to gentrify LA, put money in the area in order to get yuppies to come [downtown], . . . and get rid of poor folks . . . black and brown folks—and poor folks." He called it a conspiracy—one that has led to issuing thirteen thousand tickets, and five thousand of those for jaywalking, and otherwise harassing and intimidating his community. "We all would like to get some 'revitalization,'" but the revitalization downtown isn't with them in mind; it's "only for some people." The new policy has resulted in six beatings, and one person choked to death.

Facilitator, rhetorically: "Why??"

Attendee (who later turns out to be a white student supporter), ironically: "To make us safer."

Facilitator: "To move us out!" He asked how many people had been arrested, and roughly a quarter of the participants raise their hands. "How did you feel?"

Older man: "Like a caged animal."

A middle-aged woman said she felt "terrified and humiliated, but mostly terrified."

Another man: "The reason I'm ticked off is because I'm a pawn; the only reason I got arrested is I don't look like everyone else."

Woman sitting up front: "Like I'm not a citizen of Los Angeles, California."

We launch into some chants, and then watch some role-playing skits that the facilitator says will help prepare us for the phone calling and door knocking we will do to turn people out for a rally to oppose the new policing. In one skit, a woman tries to get a man interested in going to the rally:

Woman: "Are you a resident?"

Man: "Nah"

Woman: "Well, what corner do you live on?"

Man: "Fifth and San Fernando." Some people laugh.[23]

The woman tells him about the rally, and he playacts a blasé demeanor.

Man: "What's it about?"

Woman: "It's about getting rid of you!"

Then the man says, "Oh, we're talking about the police!" Then he seems to get more interested and wants to come.

The facilitator reminds us all to include the date, time, and address of the rally, noting that remembering these details is probably more of a challenge than giving the pitch because "we all got the rap inside of us, because we're all angry. . . . We're rallying against the abuse in our community."

In another role-play, a woman makes a pitch for the rally and describes LAPO as an organization that fights for "homeless rights." She says, "They are having a rally." The facilitator corrects her, "'They are having a rally.' THEY aren't doing anything. WE are having a rally."

Another facilitator tells us that "residents of this community" should meet before the rally at 9:30 a.m. at the park near San Fernando and "supporters" should meet at 10 a.m. at the office; it was important for "the residents to meet on our own." A guy seated next to me yells, "Power to the people!" The meeting is drawing to a close. We chant "fight back!" and belt out other chants lampooning city officials.

I chose this scenario, similar in tone to other general meetings I attended, because it shows some of the most typical idioms and images through which participants marked off and bonded their community. It also illustrates my claim that the same scene style can organize collective action on a variety of issues, not just affordable housing. Like ISLA participants, LAPO members defined themselves as a tightly bound, if geographically fuzzy, "downtown community" in perennial conflict with dominating, dishonoring outsiders. And like in ISLA scenes, the distinction between strategies "from" and "for" the community was important—though LAPO leaders finessed it by distinguishing "residents" and "supporters." Members performed tight, collective-oriented bonds, just like in ISLA; a sense of "we-ness" was an obligation. It was not a convergence of people on a shared interest but rather a community of shared fate and anger. Speech norms and emotional registers were in some important ways similar to those in ISLA. As the meeting scenario pictured, participants often would express indignity ("like a caged animal") and pride ("a citizen of Los Angeles" and "power to the people!"). One or two leading members sometimes did protective rearticulation, such as the facilitator who reminded the audience that urban "revitalization" sounds great yet is not really for everyone downtown, and one leader was a virtuoso of ironic GPS.

A brief look at LAPO suggests how the same style can live in quite different idiocultures. To someone familiar with grassroots activism in the United States, ISLA mixed the Spanish-language-affirming and Latinx-informed ethos of 1980s' Central America solidarity activists with a version of empowerment that many progressive activists learned from educator Paulo Freire's (1970) *Pedagogy of the Oppressed*.[24] LAPO scenes, in contrast, resonated with the cadences of black community struggle and a kind of charismatic leadership that some writers consider distinctively African American.[25]

A Map with a Central Boundary

In protests and routine general meetings like the one I pictured, LAPO participants projected a *map* of precariously housed, low-income tenants—the community—poised against money-hungry property owners, unresponsive city officials, and sometimes brutalizing police. A good illustration comes from a march and rally to protest the demolition of residential hotels where many low-income tenants lived. LAPO sponsored this boisterous, colorful protest, accompanied by a menacingly energetic drumbeat, down a main street. Hundreds of units in a small urban enclave had already become expensive condominiums or chic work spaces. Having reached the march's destination, a park near city hall, a speaker yelled into a bullhorn, "There is a lot of redevelopment here. Who's losing?" There were multiple responses from the crowd, like, "We are!" and "Tenants are!" A LAPO leader took the bullhorn and shouted, "Why don't we have an ordinance? Bureaucracy! City bullshit bureaucracy is holding it up!" She said we're the people that the bureaucracy is supposed to serve. "Today is just the beginning. We will be back next week. We'll be here every day until they serve *us*!"

Who, exactly, could count as part of the community? The formulation a LAPO director used frequently was that policies ought to be made by the people who will be most directly affected by them. On this principle of radical empowerment, LAPO participants learned to save full community membership for those low-income inhabitants evidently affected directly by the actions of property owners, police, or city officials in downtown Los Angeles.[26] Inside this circle, members projected the community as unitary in its grievances and moral determination. Or as the facilitator put it in the opening scenario, there was no "they" in LAPO, only a "we" who do not count on others to do things for us.

Traversing the Central Boundary: Limits to Conversion

Participation status was actually more complicated, though, in general and housing committee meeting scenes. Just as in ISLA, participants in these meetings might be either *from* the community in both the geographic and politico-moral sense, or staff people who worked either *from* or *for* the community, but usually spoke, acted, and were treated as *from* the community, or "supporters" beyond the community who stood in solidarity with it. Just as in ISLA scenes, LAPO general meeting and housing committee scenes encountered the dilemma of balancing efforts "for" and "from" the community. It became especially visible as members distinguished between supporters and the other two kinds of participation.

LAPO's decision-making formats marked off the different status of supporters. Recall how only the community residents officially voted on the Manchester agreement, not the ISLA staff, pro bono lawyer, or ethnographer. In parallel fashion, LAPO decision making recognized differences between community members and others not fully of the community. When it was time for participants at a general meeting to consider endorsing a new tenant bill of rights and protections, the director instructed, "It has to be low-income downtown residents who vote. Everyone else can support them after the fact." The distinction between community members and supporters played into protest strategies too, like in the protest against the new policing practices, where community residents would meet in a different location from "supporters."

The distinction mattered because risk taking was tied up with reputation and too easily misrecognized. Rather than projecting the image of a general interest as HJ tried to do, LAPO members' risk taking helped maintain LAPO's reputation for fearlessly giving voice to a distinct community. The meeting facilitator had implied this message might get diluted or lost if residents and supporters were together for the entire protest event, because police might feel free to victimize community residents after outside supporters had left the scene assuming everything was fine:

> "They get some numbers [at the march], but most of these folks will be gone after the rally. . . . Most of those people won't feel the handcuffs [from being arrested], 'so we're good' [supporters might assume]."

Better, in other words, if police target community members while a separate but nearby contingent of supporters was around to take in as well as spread the lesson that community members lived with perilous risk daily. The chance of brutality only heightened the dilemma. On the one hand, LAPO's cause benefited from bigger "numbers" with outsiders acting "for" the community, but the outsiders' mere presence complicated an urgent message about injustice faced by community insiders.

Supporters recognized the distinction between from and for too. Several times, I heard what sounded like statements of a kind of conversion from supporters, parallel to what ISLA leaders hoped some students would feel. One supporter, a white man who lived in a different neighborhood, got a special award to honor his countless unpaid hours assisting committee meetings, and doing research and administrative work. The gesture demonstrates that supporters could in fact be valued participants. Accepting the award, he said that "the community has taught me far more than I could ever teach you." I heard similar phrases when talking to white, college student interns at LAPO.

Given their way of associating community membership with authenticity and subjection to risks, it would be hard, though, to fully extend organizational kinship to outsiders in solidarity. A core member's backstage comment to me after a general meeting clued me in. She groused that a (relatively privileged) outsider volunteer could buy a bottle of wine anytime and would never really know what it is like to live in poverty, subject to police brutality in their downtown neighborhood. The community could include supporters who offered valuable free labor as well as moral support. But a community defined sharply by boundaries of authenticity and shared experience granted them a somewhat ambivalent status all the same.

Bonds of Risk and Implicitly Race more than Residence

There are a lot of ways to honor group bonds. While in ISLA scenes, longevity in the community was itself an honor, LAPO scenes celebrated special gifts of time and effort to the organization, as pictured above with the award ceremony. Leaders also cultivated and honored group bonds by acknowledging risks members took to defend the community.[27] At one general meeting, a leader taught the hierarchy of honors awaiting LAPO participants who stepped up a ladder of personal risk for the community. Attendance at two protest marches or rallies earned the participant a gray T-shirt. Arrest earned the participant a yellow T-shirt. Honored members never entirely left the community. Longtime, honored members who passed away were immortalized with a photo on a wall of the group office. General meetings would announce recent deaths among the membership. Braving risk could mean braving police intimidation or even physical violence—a relationship that is racialized not only through differential rates of arrest but also symbolically.

This was one of several ways in which racialized imagery informed members' notions of their bonds in LAPO scenes. The "we" implicitly was black or black-affirming.[28] It is important to say that in any of the scenes I ever was part of, LAPO was officially a multiracial organization. During my time attending meetings, LAPO staff members increasingly mentioned their valued partners from predominantly Latinx and other neighborhoods in the new HRN coalition. As the facilitator put it in the opening scenario, LAPO's leaders intended the organization to be the voice of a neighborhood including people who could be described as brown or poor people, not only Black people. The most common, racially distinct symbolism leaders and leading participants expressed, though, was *historically* African American. Several general meetings ended with a single chant: "All power to the people!" The facilitator in the opening scenario said it would not be hard to convince locals to join a LAPO event because "we all got the rap inside of us." During his two-minute public comment at a city hall meeting on rent control, one member observed that it was Black History Month, a good time to speak up for the just cause at hand. During my time in LAPO general meetings and the housing committee, I heard none of the solicitous English-to-Spanish translating that was de rigueur at many ISLA events; free dinners after monthly meetings did not feature tamales. It is also fair to say Spanish speakers or Latinx-identified people would have made up a relatively small minority of the participants. One did not need to identify as African American to be a member in good standing in LAPO. Being familiar with African American cultural and political idioms would likely have made participants feel more connected, though.

Bonding Cultivated by Tutelage

In the tightly bound "we" of LAPO scenes, good leaders were solidarity builders and boundary policers like in ISLA, and also tutors. In ISLA, members could sign up to attend the People's Planning School sponsored by member organization SED, learn conventional and critical perspectives on land use, and be invited to speak publicly—at the much-lauded Somos la Comunidad event, for example. Staff imagined that many, at least ideally, would be counted on to speak for the coalition if "someone sticks a microphone in front of them," as Eduardo had said. Staff aimed to empower participants in LAPO scenes too, yet in a different way. Teaching and learning were not for separate sessions as they were in ISLA.

A LAPO staffer and the student volunteer who ran housing committee meetings both took the liberty and responsibility to orchestrate these as something like classroom interaction. At one meeting, LAPO staffer Tony and members were talking about their upcoming visit to city council to speak out against a proposal to allow rents citywide to increase 5 percent:

> Tony wrote on the board: "8:00 a.m., meet at the office." Then he asked, "Does anyone know what we're doing? I'll go around. Start with Keith."
>
> Keith: "We want to push the review forward." Tony wrote this on the board.
>
> Tony: "Earnestine?"
>
> Earnestine: "It's delegation action day. [We will] demand things they have been putting off."
>
> Steve: "Em?"
>
> Em: "Public comment to the city council."

Tony had been writing what people said on the board, and Mary took it as an opportunity to agree or disagree with the answers so far.

Mary: "All of the above—and do delegation visits to three council members."

Loyal said "all of the above."

Tony told him he wasn't really answering the question.

Bert went next: "We've spent millions finding out what we know already."

Mary soon added, "We don't want them to just review . . ."

And Michael finished the sentence, "but act on it." Mary concurred.

Tony wanted to hear what people were going to comment specifically.

Bert: "I'm going to give them some hell. Try to wake them up!"

Tony: "Anything besides 'give 'em hell'?"

Bert said he would tell them that "we are the people who put you in those [official] seats . . . and we expect you to do your job."

Vern asked, "How many council members are there? Fifteen?"

Tony: "Fifteen."

Tutelage at the housing committee happened in a teacher-student relationship. Tony was an affectionately disciplined teacher. He occasionally tested participants' attentiveness, including mine, by calling on us. He took the liberty to say some answers were wrong, pushed and probed to get participants to say more, and once chided a member under his breath for excessive swagger. In other grassroots advocacy groups, tutelage happens through a leader who coaxes participants into more individualized expression.[29] The more "we" focused and unapologetically hierarchical tutelage at the housing committee was another instance of communal bonds in LAPO scenes.

We can recognize the same patterns of style across scenes with diverse rhetorical practices, shared stories, and historical allusions. Concentrating on scene style, though, means using the extra words necessary to tell readers something happened in a particular scene—a strategy session, for instance—rather than simply saying "ISLA did" something. That makes the account sound less like many studies, and less like journalistic writing or a novel, and more complicated. The next chapter shows the benefits of taking this longer narrative route.

5

Why Follow the Style, Not Just the Organization?

Scene Matters

Journalists, politicians, and sociologists often treat an organization like a single being. Doing what participants themselves do, we talk of a collective "it" that acts when its members are acting. For simplicity's sake, the previous two chapters matched each chapter's featured style to the coalition or organization in which that style predominated. If scene style matched up one to one with a coalition or organization, then following coalitions or organizations rather than scene styles would make good narrative sense. But the reality in ISLA and HJ coalitions was more complicated.

Different scenes of the *same* coalition may take on different styles. Put differently, a coalition is not just one "thing." The same coalition may take on different kinds of tests, trade-offs, and emotional sensibilities, in different scenes. This chapter shows how different scene styles inhabit different spaces of a coalition. Part of what we learn from following styled action instead of treating organizations as uniform actors is how distinctly patterned and emotionally powerful scene style can be. Even people accustomed to the dilemmas of one scene style suddenly become like different people when they act in a different style. We can see that when ISLA advocates, normally proud to defend the community against outside powers, justify a potential deal with a big real estate developer to community members—a scenario below. They switch styles. None of this is a statement on advocates' willingness to stick to principles. One takeaway is that individual advocates are, like the rest of us, more complicated and have more capacities than stock images would suggest. A look at shifts in style teaches more novel things too:

Following scene style gives us a new angle on what makes or breaks a coalition. Students of social advocacy have paid increasing attention to coalitions as the traditional model of the one-issue mass movement—for voting rights or against US military involvement in the Vietnam war, for instance—becomes increasingly distant from what much social advocacy work is like.[1] Advocacy organizations join coalitions to accomplish what they cannot do alone. Coalitions amass the power necessary to redirect local economic development, improve inner-city schooling, reform national military policy, strengthen reproductive rights, or remove existing reproductive rights, among other achievements.[2] The research record shows that tensions and tenuousness have threatened a great many advocacy coalitions, including labor-environmental alliances, civil rights campaigns, lesbian and gay coalitions, feminist networks, joint projects of peace and labor union groups, and cross-issue environmental partnerships.[3] Working together can be hard even when advocates from different organizations agree on what the problem is and what the solution should be.[4] In one compelling example, a coalition to oppose the construction of a federal biodefense laboratory in the Boston area, activists united in opposition to the lab but chafed at clashing modes of leadership. Each side mistrusted the other side's judgment. To keep collaborating, the Boston activists needed to finesse different styles of interaction in a tense division of labor. When strained coalitions manage to do that, they expand coalition members' capacities to attract different constituencies and stay cohesive enough to win some of their aims.

Not all coalitions endure the dissonance.[5] Disagreements over style can weaken a coalition. Sparks flew as a clash of styles rent two HJ coordinating committee meetings. After those episodes, the HJ coalition fractured as several HJ ally organizations withdrew their representatives and energies from the coalition's work. Field evidence will suggest that these decisions emerged from an ongoing commitment to a style of action—in this case, a community of identity. These former HJ coalition allies, including LAPO and SED staff who had withdrawn their organizations from the coalition earlier, initiated the HRN coalition. Acting predominantly as a community of identity, HRN pursued some of the same housing problems HJ's coordinating committee tackled as a community of interest.

This all gives style a big role in the story of how HJ fractured. The entrepreneurial actor model offers a more common explanation, which builds on the idea that advocates wield frames strategically to attract supporters and fend off opponents. A dispute over which frames to privilege might fracture a coalition. I argue that HJ advocates had a different kind of disagreement about framing from what the entrepreneurial model highlights. A close look at several dramatic HJ meetings shows that advocates' deeper clash was over what framing is for to begin with.

Multiple Styles in a Single Coalition
Style Switching in the HJ Coalition: Compartmentalization

It was my second day volunteering in the HJ staff office. I was phoning coalition members, urging them to attend the big kickoff rally. Embarrassed, I discovered I had been saying the wrong thing, telling members I was calling from WHA. A staffer let me in on that when it came to organizations on my list: "Some people don't even know we're part of WHA. WHA is for the [housing] developers; *these* organizations may not know." The first day, I had been phoning affordable housing developers, which would recognize WHA. Today, it was tenant groups, but it had not occurred to me to change my script. Staff organizer Francis agreed with the other staffer that it was better to say I was calling from "Housing Justice coalition." WHA sponsored the coalition, and paid Francis and the other staffer's salary, but tenant groups likely would not know or care about that, and I gathered that somehow, naming it would send the wrong signal.

The same organizational hat switching would happen later that year at coordinating committee meetings. Sometimes Mary said that "Western Housing Association" would bring ten people to a rally. Mary helped plan strategy for the HJ coalition, so I didn't understand why she was speaking for WHA, nor why she did that at city hall. In other settings, she would say she was from HJ. The office staffer's casual comment helped me figure it out. Naming an organizational affiliation was a way of priming the listener's *map*. Calling tenant group leaders on behalf of an activist-sounding entity might warm them up to the rally. They might imagine HJ as part of the community, on their side. A phone call from a distant-sounding professional organization might actually be a turnoff. Tenant groups lived in the world of grassroots activism, not the world of professional nonprofit affordable housing developers who belong to trade associations, and spend more time refreshing their funding streams and keeping their government contacts warm than allying with the community.[6] Organizational names could cue different maps and scene styles, and HJ staff members used their intuitive sense of the differences to present themselves effectively.[7] This applies not only to brief encounters but entire scenes styled for a particular audience too.

Early in the HJ coalition's public existence, coalition leaders occasionally departed from the usual style and orchestrated scenes for a community of identity. This means that sometimes, HJ participants acted like a different organization. This "other" version of HJ came with a different sense of how "we" relate to "them," a different kind of solidarity, and different kinds of speech and emotional tone. Rather than concentric circles of closeness to a zone of aspiration, participants would imagine housing advocacy as a battle between a localized community and outsiders trying to deceive or destroy it. Participants in those scenes counted on each other to identify strongly with the community in some depth and be rooted in it—implying long-term affinities that stretched far outside the meeting room, not the short-term bonds people activate at an interest group's campaign meetings. The communication—in conversation or video slides—was cheeky and angry, not wonky. In these spaces, HJ organizers welcomed the kind of communication that coordinating committee members found out of place when firebrand homelessness activist Terry brought it to their meetings.

Other observers of civic action up close also find that sometimes actors affiliated with one organization switch the style, creating a different kind of scene in the process. Scholars have long known that complex organizations may cobble different kinds of scenes in different settings of the organization, but the insight has only rarely made it to research on civic action.[8] In some organizations or coalitions, one style is clearly dominant in most scenes while another, subordinate style is found predictably in only certain scenes, perhaps cued by predictable signals—a socially distinctive speaker or topic of ritual denunciation.[9] Through experience with these situations, participants know the cues.[10]

HJ leaders carefully *compartmentalized* those scenes. At the end of the chapter we will see what happened when activists breached this interactional rule, acting as a community of identity at HJ coordinating committee meetings, outside the few compartments activists marked off for that style.[11] These incidents made it all the easier to recognize where in the organization and for how long HJ staff allowed or actively orchestrated scenes for a community of identity.

One place for people to act like a community of identity was in tenant workshops. HJ leaders hoped these would entice tenants to participate in a state-mandated planning exercise, identifying properties that might be good sites for affordable housing development. Just as in the case of the mayor's town hall meetings about housing, HJ activists wanted to intervene in a governmentally sponsored process. Only this time, they intervened as insurgents protecting and resisting rather than as allies of public officials setting the agenda.

At the workshop I attended, coordinating committee member Carol facilitated with roughly thirty, mostly Spanish-speaking tenants associated with LAPO, SED, and other tenant activist groups. It was the same sharp-witted and articulate Carol from chapter 3, but with a different persona. We started with a not-so-subtle bit of political education on slides, full of cues as to how audience members should think of themselves. The slides instructed that

58 percent of Angelenos were renters, and the annual median income of renters in South Los Angeles was a mere $22,000. As Carol summed it up, "We are a divided city." The slideshow confirmed that much more market-rate housing than affordable housing was being built in most neighborhoods. Carol concluded, "When we let the market build, it doesn't build what we need." In this context, the "we" was low-income, working-class people of neighborhoods in South Los Angeles—like people in the room. It was not the more usual, expansive we of HJ: teachers and accountants as well as laborers and service workers throughout the city. The we of this room, in contrast, was more like the antigentrification activists pictured in another slide who marched with a banner declaring "displacement-free zone."

The map and bonds shared in this scene were parallel to what I usually heard at ISLA meetings. Carol invited attendees to tell stories of what they were seeing with housing in their own neighborhoods. One said there was a lot of new housing construction in her neighborhood, but "only for people with high incomes, not for workers."[12] Another told of tenants who had made their apartment home for twenty years, paying $400 or $600 monthly, while newer tenants had to pay $1,100 or $1,500. Another asked, "What can the community do, not people with a lot of money?" Carol's cofacilitator, a staff person with HJ, urged attendees to participate in the planning exercise because it "gives some power to interject our needs."

A much larger meeting for activists citywide, also dedicated to the planning exercise, sounded similar. But here, compartmentalization worked inside the same physical setting, at the same meeting. Some segments of the meeting, cued by a change of speaker, delivered technical-sounding presentations for what speakers took to be a community of interest. Other segments, cued by invitations to be angry or tell stories, played for a community of identity. The two kinds of scene sat uneasily together, like two videos alternating, one on and the other off; this happened more frequently in ISLA scenes, as I will describe shortly. At the start, attendees told stories about greedy landlords. The audience learned that one landlord, who planned to convert cheap apartments to boutiques, told tenants to vacate within twenty-four hours, and pulled a gun on the ones who challenged his right to evict. The sense of shared threat and solidarity in suffering—a beleaguered community of identity—only hardened when a real estate developer in attendance spoke up.

Real estate developer: "You have a high number of renters, so probably they're not being pushed out; they're moving on with their lives."

Skeptical muttering reverberated around the room.

Legal aid activist, sharp and loud: "They're moving to the street!"

Tenant rights activist: "People who have lived generations in the same place are being pushed out of state."

Soon after the real estate developer's comment, the scene suddenly shifted to a community of interest: A housing law attorney opened an instructive slideshow about housing development, including "analysis of governmental constraints" along with "fees and exactions." A housing advocate asked a long question about how to "strengthen the Mello Act," to which the attorney responded with a riff about "the cost of the differential between creating units from scratch versus preservation." Some tenant activists were getting up to leave. We were now in the world of *housing* and the legislative maneuvers necessary to produce it, not the world of community suffering. The housing law attorney encouraged attendees to get involved in the planning exercise. One activist still there responded plaintively, "Participate *how*?"

The HJ coalition was a collection of scenes and agreements about what goes in which scene. Scenes might play out either of two different styles of action, orchestrated by leaders who helped keep one style dominant, especially in decision-making scenes, and the other sequestered in different spaces or segments of meetings. We would not necessarily predict how HJ participants would stay connected to the coalition simply by knowing "the coalition" sponsored an action or did outreach. We need to investigate the scene for the style in play.

Style Switching in the ISLA Coalition: Acting in and Watching Two "Movies" Simultaneously

In most ISLA scenes where I spent any time, participants acted as a community of identity. Then toward the end of ISLA's long antidisplacement campaign, ISLA activists carved out a community of interest inside the larger community of identity, as ISLA leaders slowly, haltingly, cultivated a platform of issues: affordable housing, local labor hiring, and small business preservation. When acting as a community of interest, ISLA advocates bonded and mapped themselves in relation to generic *issues* like "hiring." HJ leaders similarly had formulated a platform (the three-point plan) to realize their interest in the generic issue of "affordable housing." That was the focus of their bonding and mapping.

In ISLA, at first, each style corresponded to either strategy or community meetings. Increasingly in both kinds of meeting, participants switched between a community of interest and community of identity. Style switching could be cued by a conversation topic that suddenly called for a different kind of script, different imagined audience, and different emotional tone. Rather than a tightly orchestrated compartmentalization, it is more fitting to think of the relation between the two styles in ISLA as "alternating movies" of differing length, one nested inside the other.

THE ANTIDISPLACEMENT CAMPAIGN GROWS A COMMUNITY OF INTEREST

In January 2010, just before the undergraduate planning students presented their Dreams for Draper street plans, ISLA participants met for a strategy session to take stock of the antidisplacement campaign to date. Leaders from SED and another ally organization were there, and so were the project director, Beth, and outspoken intern, Enira, who argued so tenaciously for the community to control the Dreams for Draper project. Some of the conversation seesawed on the same dilemma I had been watching in play for many months: the tension between the staffing realities of a campaign that spoke sincerely *for* the community, and the aspiration that participants and campaign demands be *of* the community. Yet participants also said things I had never heard at a meeting before.

ISLA advocates were imagining themselves on a variegated map, not a simple battle zone with community on one side and "all these elites," in an ISLA leader's words, on the other. They talked of ISLA's constituency as potentially all eighty thousand residents in the neighborhood, not only the "aware" community members who would not settle for "candy" while getting their asses kicked, as Marina said a year earlier. The world was getting more complicated, and so was ISLA's menu of meetings. By September of that year, the coalition had started hosting special community meetings for whomever identified as the community. In these, the style was familiar, with talk about threats and resistance.

That month's strategy meeting did a different kind of group building, though. Starting with the same slides Hortencia used for the community meeting, staff invited labor and community development organizations in South Los Angeles to connect their organizational goals with a shared *interest* in ISLA's antidisplacement campaign. "How do you see the college's development affecting your work," a coalition leader asked, not, "How long have you been in the community?" a typical icebreaker to build solidarity at community meetings. The concluding slides presented the emerging ideas about a CBA that they might fight for. As the conversation unfolded, it became clear that the lead facilitator assumed participants identified with the community along with its needs and grievances. Still, she also invited participants to consider interests they might share in job programs, small business preservation, and other elements of a potential pact with the college—instead of emphasizing the identity they ought to share as the community fighting oppression.

This was an invitation to act like a community of interest, where participants might be something other than community members. This opened the conversation to new participants like Frank from a job training nonprofit; he was interested in a CBA that could include a promise by the developer to hire local residents. He was proud of his organization's training program. It served convicts and multiply marginalized people; it helped African Americans break into the hospitality industry, which had long discriminated against them. The biggest new departure of all was that participants at these strategy meetings talked about the local college as a potential *partner*. Longtime campaign leader and staffer Thalia said it is important to

> "work with the college to get this money [for job training] into neighborhoods for training programs. . . . So if we think of [the college] as not being conflictual—of course they don't *want* to put money into!—but . . . people inside [the college] could troubleshoot. So we think in terms of partnership and collaboration."

Even Victor suggested in the same vein that the college might play a supporting role. "It might take a role in educating small landlords" near its campus, because it may have its own frustrations with small-time proprietors who rent to some students. The web of shared interest was expanding in surprising new ways. It was a new movie.

Just after Victor spoke, Mabel brought up "the fence." Suddenly a different movie switched on—the story of a demeaned, subordinated community, with sympathetic victims and bad guys. Anyone in ISLA with a decent sense of ironic GPS would recognize the fence, literally and symbolically: a minimally decorative wrought iron barrier running alongside part of the nearby college. To neighbors, it symbolized the college's self-interested aloofness. Mention of the fence led to talk of policing. A new, African American ally from a community development corporation suggested that college police needed sensitivity training. For Thalia and others, the topic called up the more emotionally charged and categorical terms of battle familiar from the last chapter:

> Latina ISLA participant: "I saw some young boys of color walking down Balboa and I thought to myself, 'It's only a matter of time before—[they would be stopped by police]."
>
> Victor: "There's increasing harassment of our folks."
>
> Frank from the job training center hesitated; this didn't really sound like housing and land planning.
>
> SLACE director: "It's all part of pushing people out."

Frank said that "then you have to get the police on board" and talk to them about it.

Thalia replied, "I think that the college is the driver of the police."

Longer-term ISLA advocates still easily related to each other as a community of identity. Frank was much less used to that map. Thalia treated Frank's comment to protective rearticulation; it had inappropriately conjured up a search for shared interests with the police, when the scene of this "movie" was the battle against outside threats.

The point of following this meeting closely is to get a good look at how style switching worked. Particular topics could trigger the conversation and emotional register of a community of identity. But discussion focused increasingly on how to move the college to an agreement; this alternative movie ran for more minutes at some meetings. To that point, ISLA leaders had considered the college a frustrating partner. A sudden building demolition changed all that.

THE MANCHESTER APARTMENTS AND ANOTHER COMMUNITY OF INTEREST

A developer with a taste for imitation brick siding was planning a big apartment complex. Building the Manchester apartments to plan would require the partial demolition of a nearby hospital clinic. ISLA member organizations had monitored the development for over two years and were busy formulating demands for the antidisplacement campaign when the Manchester's threat to the hospital "came out of nowhere, and we *had* to fight it," said one of ISLA's community organizers. Hurriedly, ISLA staff organized local residents, planned with allies, and attended public hearings and backstage meetings with planning officials and city council members, just as a wrecking ball was leveling part of the hospital. Within a few months, ISLA and the developer agreed to a revised plan and a CBA—considered a "win-win" situation by both sides. The CBA including reduced-rent apartments and a low-cost medical clinic inside the development. ISLA celebrated a victory.

At the first discussion of the proposed Manchester project several years earlier, ISLA participants had spoken as a community of identity once again threatened by outside incursions. The upscale apartments would not be affordable to *us*, said meeting notes. Yet the first strategy session of the Manchester campaign started with a question just like the one that kicked off the new strategy meetings about a CBA with the college: "What makes *you* care about the Manchester project?" This question pointed us not to the community so much as to an issue, the Manchester development, that we might share from different vantage points as an *interest*. An electric workers' union representative said that the developer had "never used union-wage labor." A student from a university thirty miles away said he was concerned about "the human right to health care." Others spoke as worker advocates or health care professionals who wanted continued medical services in the neighborhood.

Each strategy meeting presented us with alternating movies. At the first, a staffer presented a slide about the Manchester development, calling the campaign a "struggle about preserving *community* resources." It was about defending the community of identity in other words. In the same key, the director of SED closed the meeting, saying that they "can't give away our land and rights without our input." At other points, however, attendees related to the Manchester development as a shared *interest*. A shared identity needed protection and defense, but a shared interest needed competitive advantage, deals, and compromises. Some were there more for the interest than the identity. When the facilitator at one meeting asked how many supporters they could roll out for hearings with the city planning department, Frank, from the job training and placement program, initially hesitated:

> Frank: "I can't—what's in it for them? There's no motivation." He said that usually he could easily load two buses with people, but probably not for this.

> The facilitator asked what about coming to support the bigger "alternative vision" of development in ISLA's neighborhoods.

> Frank: "I don't . . . bring people to shut down a project." He asked rhetorically, "You know what will happen if I bring people?" Answering his own question, he replied, "The developer would say, 'I'll hire you!'" to some of this man's job training graduates.

The "alternative vision" the facilitator referred to was the *overarching* commitment to the community. Participants needed to keep their bearings regarding two sets of map and bonds.[13] Frank wanted his job trainees to get their share of community benefits if the developer agreed to any—such as, for instance, a promise to hire neighborhood construction laborers. When Raimunda suggested that at the upcoming hearing, everyone could wear *big* square stickers announcing opposition to the development, Frank asked if his could be just "a nice square that you put here"—patting an imaginary lapel. He leaned over and told me sotto voce that it would be great to pack the hearing with protesting students, considering the developer's claim to be building student-oriented housing. He was not unsympathetic to community claims; he just did not want to alienate potential future employment contacts for his trainees.

After two months of strategy sessions, testimonies at city hall, and closed-door negotiations with the developer, ISLA coalition leaders and the developer had arrived at a CBA draft that included space for a community medical clinic, free rent for twenty years as compensation for shrinking the hospital, a quota of the Manchester's apartments rented below the market rate for the area, and a percentage of construction jobs allotted to local residents. ISLA staff hurriedly called a meeting to vet the agreement with the community, and leaders found themselves in an awkward new position.

TRADING DILEMMAS

Francis of HJ had led by finessing and satisficing, trying to keep diverse representatives focused on a shared interest. ISLA's Ethan led by building solidarity and defending boundaries. Now on the brink of a big agreement with the Manchester's developer, ISLA leaders Raimunda and Thalia led much more like Francis than Ethan for most of the meeting.

Seventeen Spanish-speaking residents of the immediate neighborhoods agreed to come on short notice, hear a presentation on the agreement from ISLA organizers, and take a vote. Residents asked pointed questions.[14] One speaker in her late forties wanted to know how much affordable housing would be built under the agreement. And how much of that would be accessible to people with low incomes? Thalia explained that state regulations would not allow apartments targeted to income brackets below $40,000. That was a problem for a family with four or five kids, the questioner observed. Another asked just how much affordable housing there would be. Neither she nor the first speaker looked completely pleased at the answer—5 percent of the units—but did not press the point. Thalia said summarily, "That is not going to change," then blurted a theatrical side comment in Spanish, venting her frustration with the situation. The first questioner had "heard people in the community say" they were worried that the new clinic would pass up low-income people or subject them to long waits. Raimunda responded that the nonprofit chosen to manage the clinic was "capable of running urgent care" and could be counted on.

Raimunda and Thalia were satisficing, promoting a compromise. Leaving the world of local communal solidarity, they were inviting residents along with them into a zone of aspiration, potentially sharing an interest with a for-profit real estate developer. Quite a dilemma—but this was not the usual predicament of choosing between being "from" and "for" the community. That dilemma rarely surfaced by the time Frank and other organizational leaders in South Los Angeles were attending strategy sessions. This was instead the characteristic problem of a community of interest: Should we put our energy into getting a good deal from power brokers or strengthen relations with a community of outsiders to the negotiation process who shared a strong interest in its outcome? Residents' skepticism tested that community's viability until Raimunda compartmentalized the deal from the dealmaker, clarifying that residents could affirm the deal but pass on the developer. They could *compartmentalize*—the same strategy HJ honored—and manage the sharper edge of tenant grievances.

On the second vote, seventeen hands went up, approving the agreement; a visiting filmmaker and I were not asked to weigh in. Community members had agreed to enter a community of interest with the developer, without surrendering their community of identity. They accepted the compartmentalization. As one of the seventeen put it, they supported the *deal*; that was different from endorsing the project. But what if the developer refused to commit to an agreement after all? "¡Las camisetas blancas!" the facilitator answered mischievously. ISLA members would turn out in white T-shirts (*camisetas blancas*) emblazoned with "proud member of this community." Deserting the possibility of a shared interest for now, they would return home to communal pride.

BACK TO THE ANTIDISPLACEMENT CAMPAIGN: NOW ISLA IS A PLAYER

The developer and ISLA representatives signed an agreement. Now ISLA was in the affordable housing management business. In effect, it was collaborating with the developer too. We will take a brief, closer look at this arrangement in chapter 9. ISLA had won a lot. Maybe the biggest thing it won was a bigger reputation. The next week, according to an ISLA leader, college staff contacted ISLA saying the college was now ready to negotiate a CBA of its own. ISLA leaders Thalia, Francine, and others credited this new initiative to the Manchester agreement. The college, they figured, was ready to respect ISLA as a player with a reputation, if not necessarily as the voice of an authentic community speaking truth to power.

Respect in a world of interests and bargaining had become ISLA leaders' goal over the previous year, though the coalition certainly did not start that way. Even before the college came calling, the strategy conversation had come to focus more on bargaining position, juggling the "insider game" with the "outsider game." Toward the end of the Manchester campaign, for example, ISLA leaders considered sending a letter to the college's development department, inviting a dialogue. As Frank put it, "Let them know we're here," and that "there are community resources that may be of use to [them]." Contrast the talk of one year earlier. Then, who said they wanted to *offer* resources to the college? Now, as Raimunda from SED observed, they could build on their recent victory. "That's why the Manchester is so important," she said; it was a token of the symbolic power ISLA could bring to a next, even bigger negotiation. ISLA leaders were communicating as *players*, not moral adversaries. A public interest attorney with ISLA pointed out "there's an inside game and an outside game"—invoking the same terms HJ advocates used to make their own plans. He said the inside game is "we want to be a partner . . . we've been a good partner [in the past], we've done this before— we are good at it—you are lucky to have it." ISLA's strategy sessions were sounding more like HJ's coordinating committee meetings, down to even the same metaphors.

The community of interest projected in this conversation soon became institutionalized. Just two weeks after the Manchester deal's announcement, ISLA participants codified membership and decision-making roles for the coalition. "Members" could vote on and be signatories to any potential agreements with the college's development office, and be appointed to negotiating teams. "Allies" could attend strategy meetings, but could not negotiate, vote on, or sign agreements. "Community residents" could have their own meetings and select representatives to attend strategy meetings, and be candidates for selection to negotiating teams. Negotiating teams included four organizational representatives and two community members. The ISLA coalition had in effect constructed concentric circles of affiliation and responsibility centered on a set of four shared interests. I did not hear any debate about whether or not the process was sufficiently community directed at all levels—as intern Enira had so avidly insisted on a year earlier. The community already was written into the decision-making process. The "movie" of the community and the alternate one about the four interests would each keep running on their different timelines, protected by confidentiality agreements all around. The community of identity's story was longer, and the community of interest's story more like a set of movies within a movie.

Is Style Just Another Stratagem for Entrepreneurs?

For a skeptical reader, it could look as if leaders in both coalitions manipulated scene style to entice participation from people whose support they needed. Why not treat scene style as a manipulatable cultural resource, like the frames or collective identities that social movement entrepreneurs craft to define grievances and mobilize supporters?[15] And putting it tartly, could it be that ISLA leaders cultivated a new taste for communities of interest when the prospect of winning something significant enticed them to leave aside the battles over identity? Researchers argue that advocates change strategies, including rhetorical ones, in response to changing political opportunities.[16] This skeptical line of argument would shift our attention back toward the entrepreneurial actor model with its focus on actors who *use* culture to take the best advantage of external opportunities. Let's see how that approach would play out.

First, there is little reason to reject the idea that sometimes, organizational leaders orchestrate scene styles intentionally. It makes sense to think Carol's tenant workshops invited the "we" of the community to complain about the property-owning agents of displacement because Carol figured that would appeal to working-class tenants whose support HJ would need. And it makes sense to think that when faced with the choice between an imperfect CBA and a new behemoth in the neighborhood with no benefit to speak of for ISLA's constituency, ISLA leaders would try to lead by compromising rather than building defensive solidarity and hardening boundaries. They wanted neighbors to recognize an interest in the agreement even if they were not going to identify with the developer.

Advocates have some amount of agency with scene styles, but they also wield that agency while standing and acting *within* a style, not from a "neutral" standpoint outside the world of styled action.[17] Social advocates are culturally cultivated, socially embedded actors; they don't stand outside the realm of culture, picking and choosing what they need with indefinite leeway. There are other good empirical and conceptual reasons not to overplay the role of deliberate, individual, conscious choice. Studies suggest that quite often, actors proceed with a scene style from nearby social cues and habit, not by a deliberate plan.[18] In conceptual terms it makes sense to think of scene style as a fuzzy and fuzzily perceived pattern—something actors know how to do and match more or less appropriately to a given scene, but not perfectly.[19] Style is not a firm rule nor a sharply delineated structure, so one cannot follow "it" absolutely consistently even if one wanted to, because there is not such a unitary "it."

Acknowledging that actors have agency and choices does not obviate the notion that action comes in styles that have a fuzzy logic of their own. The weight of previous decisions, and perceptions of what has worked before (like CBAs or broad-based coalition building for that matter) freight the decisions down the line.[20] Answering convincingly the question of why ISLA leaders switched to a community of interest when they did would require that we compare well-matched transition points from many coalitions. More interesting in this study is that faced with a potential deal with a property developer, ISLA leaders settled into a recognizable pattern, if not their most privileged one. There is a limited number of styles for acting.

In crisp terms, the scene style controls the actor as much as the actor controls the style. In the theory of action that informs this study, actors gravitate toward "packages" or chains of action; the scenarios we have seen already bear out the insight.[21] Grasping how chains of action unfold, and how those chains are patterned, we can understand puzzles and frustrations that bedevil even skilled entrepreneurial social advocates.

HJ coalition leaders' efforts to use the community of identity style *itself* strategically ended up backfiring. Those efforts also revealed just how deeply HJ leaders were cultivated in, and maybe confused by, assumptions that accompany a community of interest. Advocates like Carol assumed that proponents of a community of identity would say their peace and then stay in their compartment. As one steering committee member said to dissenter Terry, "We need your passion!" In the same spirit, others on the committee said it was fine for tenant advocates to push stridently for more than the coalition would likely get in terms of affordable housing mandates. The subtext in both cases was supposed to be that tenant advocates could perform stridently, all the while *accepting* the likelihood of compromises and satisficing in the zone of aspiration. But in a community of identity, members perform as authentic voices of the community, not stage-positioned bargainers playing "bad cop" and then "good cop." The misunderstanding exploded in coalition members' faces, as we see shortly. The (dubious) assumption that advocates could readily and agreeably compartmentalize a community of identity shows that scene style, the community of interest in this case, can deeply shape ways of being present in a social situation. It is not just a cultural garment one might put on or take off as occasions demand.

For ISLA advocates, being strategic with scene style risked a lot of inconvenience and at least a little self-questioning. When they presented their tentative CBA to neighborhood resident members, ISLA leaders led in line with a community of interest. They took on board that community's characteristic dilemma. They likely would have avoided the dilemma if given the choice—in some abstract world of act-by-act decision making. Who would want to cozy up with an opponent after months of fighting? One neighbor remarked as much: it would be hard for the group to endorse the Manchester project just after having fought it. But once acting as a community of interest, ISLA leaders found themselves caught up in the art of securing a deal, and the political tension of attending to the developer's terms in order to get the deal, while attending to their own constituency at the same time. They had to balance an insider versus outsider strategy. Once having orchestrated the scene, leaders themselves had to follow the script with its squirm-inducing moments. They did not manipulate relationships moment by moment or even meeting by meeting for best effect.

When we focus on chains of action rather than imagining advocates exert their will act by act, it is easier to grasp that scene style includes an emotional impact. The proud and protective anger of a community of identity would not so easily dissipate, any more than would advocates tune out the drumbeat, as Mary put it, of a community of interest's exciting, enervating, external deadline-driven campaign. At the last city hall hearing on the Manchester, after ISLA advocates had officially withdrawn their previous objections to the development, ISLA ally Francine told me softly that she felt sick to her stomach. So advocates sometimes may orchestrate a scene with a style for strategic ends. That does not make style itself less real, less causally important, or less emotionally powerful. Whether intentionally orchestrated or generated by habit, scene style is a patterned *chain* of actions, dilemmas, and consequences that individual advocates do not parse or rearrange at will.

The same insight illuminates the question of whether or not ISLA leaders grew a community of interest for ISLA because concrete, new opportunities had emerged. Studies referred to earlier point out that a change in external conditions—a perceived division between elites or shift in competing groups, for instance—produces a change in the political opportunity structure, prompting savvy advocates to push new strategic story lines about who we are, what the problem is, and what we should do about it. In this logic, the question of "how" recedes, and strategy is not so much a chain of action with its own patterns and rhythms but instead a more or less rational response advocates make to an external, structural constraint—like a puzzle piece that fits into a preexisting puzzle. On that logic, did ISLA advocates "get practical" and ditch some of the wrangling over who can speak for the community when there appeared a real opportunity to win something they wanted?

ISLA's timeline from 2010 onward strongly suggests not. The coalition's antidisplacement efforts had been germinating a community of interest months *before* the Manchester development literally bulldozed its way onto ISLA leaders' agenda. And then only after successfully concluding an agreement with its developer did ISLA leaders receive the big signal that the college was interested in negotiating an agreement too. If anything, ISLA members at strategy meetings had already started projecting what new opportunities *might* materialize *if* they positioned ISLA as a reputable player worth the college's time. They started living in a new future of their own collective projection.[22] Present caught up with future when the Manchester developer sought a CBA worth a great deal of money, in effect ratifying and also resourcing ISLA advocates' process of collective redefinition, which had already been happening for nearly a year. ISLA coalition members talked their way to a set of interests that expanded the coalition to new kinds of members, while maintaining "the community" as the ultimate source and arbiter of those interests. None of this would have been easy to predict two years earlier, when ISLA members were on the lookout for critically aware community members who did not want their asses kicked. Following styled action need not be a substitute for studying what gets achieved in the name of an organization or coalition. But it certainly enriches our ability to interpret and explain important, puzzling aspects of what happens along the way.

How Scene Style Can Break or Make a Coalition

Chapters 3 and 4 portrayed scene styles as patterned responses to tests. We can think of compartmentalization and alternating movies as responses to a kind of test too—the challenge of making two (or more) scene styles cohabit one problem-solving effort. As action unfolds, it is always possible that advocates fail that test, and we can say that is what happened in the HJ coalition, just as its MIHO campaign was accelerating. The coalition fractured, as some organizational representatives diminished their organization's involvement in the coalition, or departed it altogether and joined in forming the new HRN coalition. We are going to follow the clash between differently styled action at HJ coordinating committee meetings and the emerging HRN coalition. Then we try out an alternative explanation of what happened to HJ.

Scenario: A Unity Meeting

Coordinating committee members had just taken turns lauding the Housing Summit with the mayor—the discussion that opened chapter 3. Now it was time to engage the endorsers—people who represented organizations supporting the MIHO campaign on paper and received email updates from Francis.

Keith said, "What if we had an expanded steering committee meeting and invited them!"

Question from the table: "What do we tell them?"

Ralph, a policy researcher: "Don't screw us!"

Keith suggested that "we should just have it [the endorser's meeting] here, not make it a big deal." He proposed wording the invitation to the tune of "We need to move forward on this, and it would be great to have you join us."

It would be a "unity meeting."

Two weeks later at the unity meeting, about two dozen coordinating committee regulars along with representatives of endorsing groups listened to Keith recount a brief, upbeat history of the MIHO campaign. He described getting city council members to sign HJ's Housing Pledge. "One we cornered in the hall, and she said, 'Do you want me to sign? I'll sign it now!'" HJ advocates brought a Housing Pledge placard to meetings around town that were set up to build support for the campaign.

> Keith: "This has been a great symbol [and] momentum builder." He said that we "came back and showed the mayor, 'You said get eight (council members' pledges); we got nine.'"

Now Roger brought up the recent summit on housing.

> "We learned we need a broad coalition." He started enumerating the participants: "union members from different ethnic backgrounds—a painter, a city official . . ."

> Terry, cutting in: "Don't forget the homeless!"

> Roger, in slower, lower tones: "I was talking specifically about the workers." He acknowledged that a homeless person was among the speakers.

Carol pitched in that preservation of old, cheap apartments was a large issue in their discussions with the mayor's office, as was homelessness. Now a representative of LAPO said she had looked at the mayor's five-year plan and saw there were two buildings downtown that were being redeveloped. She was concerned that residents had to move out of these two former hotel buildings and would not be allowed back in.

> Carol: "We're not involved in it, but the housing authority has bought other land so that people can [move there]. . . . The mayor has said that they will try to accommodate" current residents and "want to minimize displacement."

> Question from the room: "Housing Justice is not taking a position?"

> East Los Angeles community organizer: "Why not?"

> Carol: "As endorsers, you signed onto the three-point plan. If we raised hands, you all would probably be against the [Iraq] war, and for another presidential candidate, but we're not going there. We have JUST enough energy for the three-point plan."

A college professor who I had not seen before emphasized how many homeless people that even a housing preservation policy would not help.

> Carol, slowing her speech: "Let me back up. We take no position on Mason Downs" (the redevelopment in question). She went on to explain the mayor's position.

The LAPO representative acknowledged that the mayor's new plan included "some of what we want," but was not entirely happy with either the mayor's plan or the conversational agenda.

> LAPO representative: "the preservation [component] is not good, and the trust fund [component] is not good. . . . We made the plan better, but it is pretty weak. I know it's not the point of this meeting, but we need to [speak out about] the mayor's plan."

> Darwish of Poor People for Change: "I second."

> Terry, forcefully: "Third!"

> College professor: "Fourth."

> Director of Terry's homelessness organization: "Fifth."

> Carol, without missing a beat: "OK. We should keep analyzing it."

Unity was fast dissipating.

Carol now toured us quickly through the sheet with HJ positions contrasted with the mayor's positions on affordable housing mandates. At several spots, she emphasized the MIHO campaign's attention to the "point" in the three-point plan that called for preserving old, low-rent apartment buildings. Yet the tenant and homeless advocacy group representatives in the room did not sound impressed.

> Question from the floor: "How did we reach the figure [the proposed quota of low-income targeted apartments per building]?

> Woman from Community Action League: "We had a retreat. . . . We arrived at it."

> Terry: "You usually push for more than you think you are going to get."

> Carol: "This is really Left!" She said that when she tried out the figure of 25 percent, people said that it was just too radical.

> Charlie from BCTU said, "We gotta focus on the people who have the toughest time finding affordable housing—the elderly, the homeless, and low-income workers." He went on to observe that some of the toughest pushback on HJ's proposals came from neighborhood councils, whose participants worried a lot about losing "the character of the neighborhood." He portrayed HJ as a sharp negotiator, keeping the most marginalized tenants in mind while pursuing a proposal that could really win. Playacting a conversation with a neighborhood council stalwart, he said, "OK, you want

your single-family neighborhoods?" Answering the rhetorical question, he pointed out that affordable housing quotas would apply only to large apartment complexes, not blocks of single-family housing. "This is what we've got to say to get this passed."

Terry: "A lot of us are concerned about [low-income people]." She asked what is going to happen if the city council doesn't even approve HJ's proposed quota.

Charlie paused, looking flustered at the question. "I'm just one member of the coordinating committee, but—we'd better talk about it."

To this point, it looked like clashing economic constituencies. The LAPO representative wanted the coalition to criticize the mayor's affordable housing plan and the initiative to redevelop two SRO hotels that might create displacement and more homelessness too. The attendees who affirmed her comments in quick succession all represented or supported groups that advocate for low-income and homeless people. In his preplanned capsule presentation of the coalition, Roger, on the other hand, said, "We learned we need a broad coalition, from low-income workers to middle-income folks." Maybe HJ's intended appeal to a large, cross-class constituency simply made some members feel too much of a tension between sustaining their own groups' agendas and collaborating with organizations pursuing differently phrased (if overlapping) goals and aspiring to wider constituencies. That is one reason coalitions get stressed and dissipate.[23]

But why did they articulate low-income and homeless people's interest the way they did? Students of class-based coalition building maintain there are different ways to represent the same social stratum. There is more than one way for advocates for low-income neighborhoods to value alliances beyond their locales.[24] More puzzling still is that LAPO's representation had already stopped attending coordinating committee meetings several months before the unity meeting. If coalition work really demands that staff members juggle their own organization's sustenance with the potential gain they get from putting time and energy into combined efforts, why did the LAPO staffer take precious time to come to a meeting with coalition endorsers and derail the proceedings, knowing that denouncing the mayor's proposals "is not the point of this meeting"? It would have been at least as "skilled" to sustain a polite, paper endorsement of the coalition, take whatever benefits might result, and save time to advocate elsewhere for the most precariously housed people.[25] I argue that style shaped the "calculus" driving the majority and dissenters in different directions on HJ strategy.

A Clash of Scene Styles

DUELING DILEMMAS

The style-hewn character of the conflict became increasingly obvious the longer the meeting went on. Roger thought the point of the coalition was to win a MIHO by building a broad-based coalition. Carol said we have "just enough" energy for the three-point plan. Even Charlie, more explicitly focused on low-income people, said there were just certain things "we've got to say to get this passed" and overcome neighborhood councils' opposition. Each implied that the coalition was an indefinitely expanding circle of advocates and their constituents who shared an interest in a MIHO, did not obligate each other to other issues, and said the things that need saying in order to increase support, fend off skeptics, and win. That is what a community of interest does.

In contrast, the two loudest dissenters spoke for a social category and implied that a good coalition identifies strongly with it, drawing hard boundaries around the category and rationales used to protect it, as a community of identity does. Community organizer Keith said, "If it's only low-income advocates, this probably is not happening, so we need more than low-income advocates." Terry retorted that the coalition's current ideas about affordable housing quotas would position it "to the right of the (local) Democratic Party"; there needed to be boundaries. Keith responded in the spirit of a diverse community of interest: "We need your passion!" Supporters did not all have to argue the same things at city hall, he added.

As the crescendo of tensions mounted, a LAPO member in turquoise stretch pants clutching a Betty Boop purse showed up at the door and heightened the drama: "Aren't we fighting for low-income people?!" And if we were not, "then you're leaving me out!" Darwish, director of Poor People for Change, added that "when people hear 'low income' and think it's a bad thing, you are talking racial." He said the coalition should be most concerned with the people who most need housing and criticized HJ's way of aiming for breadth by "not turning off middle-class people." As for the upcoming city council hearing on a MIHO, he asserted, "We'll be talking about low-income, and if anyone doesn't like it, f–'em." Conversation and unity drained away shortly after that declaration as attendees started getting up to leave.

The debriefing at the next committee meeting supports my interpretation. Keith said, "It seemed like talking past each other." That is my analysis too. The representative from an affordable housing developer said Terry had accused others around the table of "saying we don't need housing for working class and homeless—but that's who our [affordable housing nonprofit's] constituency *is!*" "We could make this a poor people's issue—but we decided to put a poor person's face, a working-class person's face, and a middle-class person's face on it." She went on to say it would not have been possible to get as far as they've gotten already without that broader appeal. Roger chided that "you don't show up at the end of the party and ask to change the menu. . . . You have to have a level of trust and faith." Another housing developer described that sort of trust in remarkably clear terms:

> "I always thought in this coalition if you don't like where we are going, you can get off here." He said that if the policy that HJ pushes for ends up being only 10 to 15 percent of the AMI, "WE will pull out. That's always been our prerogative. . . . We've committed to this, that's what we bought into. I'm not going to raise issues we discussed twelve months ago."

Mary explained that the point of the unity meeting was to strengthen coalition connections around what was actually a "risky" undertaking—in other words, to build *trust*. It was a community of interest's version of an "outsider strategy," unifying the outsiders trying to push policy-making insiders.

The trust that most HJ advocates presupposed was not the same as the trust Terry had in mind. There were "serious issues that could break your coalition apart—a serious breach of trust," Terry remarked, saying HJ leaders had arrived at proposals without consulting with members. Terry was speaking from the terms of a different dilemma altogether. To her, a worthwhile coalition would coordinate itself differently. She accused HJ leaders like Carol and Mary of speaking "for" the community without even being adequately in touch, much less *from* the community. No wonder it felt to Keith, and probably Terry too, like they were speaking past each other. The debriefing meeting ended no more conclusively than the unity meeting, but I noticed that over the next several committee meetings, several representatives had stopped attending.

A BREAKAWAY COALITION: HRN

The HRN coalition went public early in 2010. It included five, onetime organizational members of the HJ coordinating committee. A sole member of HRN continued to collaborate with HJ, while the other four distanced themselves from HJ's leadership and remained paper endorsers only. The dissenting organizations had worked on and off as an informal caucus within HJ. Shortly after the HJ's kickoff rally, a LAPO leader helped write the "housing preservation platform" for the caucus. Participants from the other organizations had considered themselves a "subset" of HJ that would focus efforts on the point in the HJ coalition's platform that demanded the preservation of housing for the lowest-income residents. HRN's first big public event was a five-hour town hall with a city councillor. Hundreds of participants took buses to a midtown auditorium to testify to the realities of rapacious landlords, roach-infested apartments, and inattentive oversight bureaucracies. They insisted the council person accede to a list of protections for renters.

The kickoff meeting of the HRN coalition, ritualized figuratively and literally the map and bonds of a community of identity. In an opening exercise, attendees placed post-its on a big map of the county, signifying where they lived. Referring to the post-laden map, a facilitator from LAPO said, "This is where the battle over land is happening. . . . We're the ones who've been fighting and keeping our neighborhoods as they are. . . . Even though we don't have housing in [the wide swaths of unposted spaces on the map], the housing we have here . . . are *our* communities and have been our communities for years." Roughly two-thirds of the attendees identified as Latinx people from low-income neighborhoods; most others identified as LAPO members, with the plurality African American. Concluding the five-hour event with a closing ritual, a meeting facilitator asked us all to join hands in a huge circle. He intoned, "We've been here before." He recited the mostly Spanish surnames of a multiracial band of people who were some of the earliest nonnative inhabitants in Los Angeles. We belonged here, the facilitator said, and always had. A new community of identity was born.

And that community had a right to housing. The coalition's name itself made a claim that HJ coalition leaders like Carol had treated skeptically without rejecting outright. The sober-sided Protestant pastor who introduced HJ's own kickoff rally two years earlier introduced himself by saying that he and his colleagues in Jewish, Muslim, and Christian traditions all felt the obligation "to view quality and safe affordable housing as a basic human right." A longtime veteran and downtown tenant member of LAPO put it somewhat more directly but no less eloquently that "housing is a human right, not a privilege." Carol, on the other, hand said that "when people hear that 'housing is a right,' they think 'well—maybe—not.'" Did the HJ coalition's tensions reflect members' disagreements over what counts as a right?

FRAMING DISPUTE OR STYLE DISPUTE?

In dispute with LAPO and other dissenting representatives' claims, Carol had argued at the unity meeting that HJ's current demands were "as far left as we can go" and still have a chance of winning the MIHO. Charlie agreed they were "left" in contrast with what the property-friendly Central City Association was saying about a MIHO. Terry disputed those assessments and emphasized that even the Democratic Party's demands were more radical. This all might reflect what social movement scholars call a "framing dispute."[26] Apart from attracting larger publics and fending off detractors, frames have consequences for cohesion among groups in a coalition.[27] I proposed in chapter 1 that while advocates craft claims strategically and intentionally at least sometimes, they do so in a meaningful, cultural context.[28] I heard a dispute over "frames" within a larger clash between two lines of styled action. The context behind the framing dispute became clearer at a coordinating committee discussion—held a month before the explosive unity meeting—on how to talk about affordable housing policy to the media.

Carol led a presentation contrasting two ways of "framing" housing issues; the term from social movement studies had entered activist parlance.[29] PowerPoint slides attributed a "social issue frame" to advocates who carry "values" such as "human rights" and "justice." Carol affirmed this frame, adding, "It's a social justice issue, right? That's what got *me* into it." Succeeding slides presented an alternative, "consumer issue frame" attributed to "everyone affected by the housing situation," and driven by values such as "choice, free market, family and child balance." Carol argued, and a majority around the table agreed, that the coalition should speak to people who held the "consumer" frame. She added, "If you have signs that say, 'housing is a human right,' that's not going to work!" Yet Carol had just affirmed the "frame" that represented "human rights." She did not say she disagreed with the notion now; she said it would not *work*. Carol referred to research showing that ordinary people care about homelessness, and added, "We should be talking about homelessness" and poor people, but in the context of "people" in general because "people care about the *people*. They don't care about the *category*."

The most crucial meanings that advocates like Terry and Carol would dispute were *the meanings of engaging in framing activity itself*. That dispute was the deeper source of the dispute over whether or not to call housing a human right in public. Carol implied that she personally agreed with the frame that housing is a human right and the most subordinated category (homeless people) needed to be explicitly part of any solution. But speaking as a participant in a community of interest, Carol bid other HJ participants to use the framing most capable of generalizing support for a housing ordinance. She assumed that the act of framing meant roughly what it also means to academic, social movement researchers. Keith assumed the same thing: that if advocates want to win, they want to frame issues to appeal to a big audience. At the unity meeting he pushed the value of "messaging," and the "message" that HJ had decided on is "housing for everyone—we want housing for the cook, the dish-washer. The trick is how do you do it without losing your core values." He went on to explain that a media consultant had said at a training workshop he attended that "low-income housing" turns people off. Yet "'housing for seniors'—yeah! . . . They are exactly the same thing!"

They were *not* the same thing to everyone around the table. For advocates who preferred to work as a community of identity, the very fact of engaging in strategic framing activity implied a distance from what matters. It would be inauthentic. The LAPO representative at the unity meeting said that HJ should "not [be] so focused . . . on politically palatable ways of framing the issue." It should not, in other words, do what the entrepreneurial actor model assumes advocates do. The rhetoric should not be made to appeal to indefinitely ex-panding circles of potential supporters as well as gatekeepers; it should reflect the most pressing, authentic needs of the social category that advocates are trying to protect. *She did not say that housing for the poorest should be framed strategically*; she could have. Rather, she said that HJ should be "fairly aggres-sive" and not use "buzzwords like 'affordable housing.'" Both sides could agree privately that "housing is a human right," but at the coordinating committee they were understanding that statement *in the context of different styles of col-lective action*. Each style gave the act of strategic framing activity *itself* different meaning and value.

At least some HRN participants would have converged with HJ coalition leaders on the same frames in the abstract. The problem is that we only hear and speak frames from inside a style of interaction. Style differences between HJ and HRN mattered more than this convergence of frame language. When a facilitator asked participants at HRN's kickoff meeting to say why they sup-port the new HRN coalition, a participant from LAPO answered, "We should be able to live where we want to live," and another, longtime LAPO member said, "Guarantee we always have a supply of low-income housing." Those are the same words HJ leaders used to justify their bid for a region-wide "three-point plan" instead of a few low-income housing enclaves: HJ leaders' three-point plan included a proposal to preserve existing low-income housing units everywhere. If we attend only to frames and semantic differences between frames, it is hard to understand why there was such bitter disagreement now. A LAPO leader told me privately, both *before* the organization rejected the HJ coordinating committee and *after* the HRN was emerging, that not only HJ's position on preservation but other HJ positions too actually were in her organ-ization's interest. We don't have to rule out the possibility that advocates for extremely low-income, ill-housed people wanted to focus more on their con-stituency's interests than HJ's larger community of interest. But that by itself does not explain how they *related to* their own constituency, or why they would viscerally reject HJ leaders' vision of a housing policy that spoke to homeless and low-income people's needs *among others*. Something else mattered, and that was the style by which HJ coalition leaders coordinated coalition building along with the alternative style that drove the dissenters.

Scene style influences coalition solidarity. How, if at all, does it matter for goals and successes?

6

What Is Winning?

ACTIVISTS AND RESEARCHERS all want to know about what makes advocates' campaigns successful. Which combinations of factors lead to things advocates and their constituencies want, such as new policies, new rights, and more representation? Yet, we also should ask why advocates have the goals they have to begin with, and what counts as winning. Neither of these is so obvious. Remember how Ethan of ISLA sounded oddly distant from HJ's affordable housing campaign. At a meeting, he had mentioned it in a conversational FYI comment about what was new in the housing advocacy world, on the way to an ironic takedown of "the new urbanism" in city planning. This was at a meeting of advocates who wanted to increase housing options for low-income people, so it seemed like an odd bypass. Why wouldn't some ISLA members be more enthusiastic about the citywide affordable housing mandates? Wouldn't that help ISLA win what it wanted?

Comparing two coalitions with somewhat different goals is counterintuitive. As its sponsoring organization's director told me at the start of the campaign, HJ planned to "focus like a laser" on a citywide MIHO. ISLA advocates, on the other hand, sought affordable housing amid other public goods, all for a small clutch of neighborhoods. They fought for a CBA from the developer of the Manchester as well as a college whose building projects were expanding into ISLA neighborhoods.[1] The goals of HJ and ISLA coalitions worked at different geographic scales. Using both cases to build up a general explanation of why campaigns succeed or fail would be wrongheaded, but that was not my own goal.

Instead, I use scenes from the two main coalitions to show just how different their campaigns were and why that matters, even though both fought for affordable housing. Accomplishments make sense only inside strategic arcs;

scene style shapes the strategic choices advocates make. Scene style inflects the *meaning* of particular strategies and goals as well as winning itself. This chapter presents two trajectories of collective problem solving that unfold on varying timelines, toward tentative and evolving goals. The two coalitions and their trajectories reveal different trade-offs that go with each, differently styled line of action.[2]

None of this is to imply that goals and outcomes themselves don't matter. In fact, accumulating evidence shows that different styles do shape outcomes that matter to advocates and the scholars who study them. There is much more to find out about how style contributes to outcomes as scholars usually treat them. The point is that we learn valuable and practical things when we understand particular outcomes *in the context of strategic arcs* that make those outcomes more, or less, meaningful to advocates and their constituencies.

Outcomes or Different Kinds of Success?

Which grassroots problem-solving efforts have the best outcomes? Practical-minded people and policy makers want to know, and it is not so easy to find out. The trouble is partly a matter of finding good evidence. It is partly also that the question itself is a lot more complicated than it looks. As for evidence, we can read about social advocates' efforts to improve a locale's environment, reform its police force, regenerate job opportunities, or steer urban development in equitable directions.[3] We can read cases that reveal "best practices" too.[4] There are fewer studies, though, that look *systematically* and comparatively at what makes local advocacy on issues such as affordable housing succeed.[5] When we turn to those systematic comparisons, the complexity of the "outcomes" question becomes glaring. Twenty years ago, sociologists had done few systematic studies on what makes social movements win new regulations and rights, achieve representation, or deliver other tangible outcomes that advocates and larger publics care about. Since then, more systematic comparisons have appeared. The point here is not to review them all, but only to summarize several characteristics of these outcomes studies enough to clarify how my approach differs.[6]

First, from William Gamson's (1975) foundational work on social movements in the 1970s and onward, studies of outcomes often have pictured a social movement as an individual actor writ large—an entrepreneur we figuratively can point to, rather than entwining and sometimes opposing lines of styled action. These studies frequently focus on a national or nationwide collective actor battling the state for new or different policies, rights, or regulations, even though a good deal of social movement organizing in the United

States over the past several decades has been local.[7] This means that at the outset, a lot of the curiosity about outcomes has addressed a different level of institutional change than what housing advocates in this study hoped to achieve.

Second, scholars usually approach the question of outcomes by asking which combinations of important factors produce which kinds of outcomes.[8] What are the ingredients of success? This analytic choice, like the decision to treat a social movement as a unitary subject, comes with benefits and drawbacks. In this "causal combinatorics" mode, the investigator uses cases to represent different combinations of factors or variables.[9] The investigator supposes these different collections of factors have led to different outcomes of the same class of event—a new political right or no new political right, a scheduled vote in the legislature or no vote, a win or a loss. Factors that such studies invoke include an organization's mobilizing capacity, use of protest tactics, or savvy framing strategy, or the degree of unity or division between the governing elites it confronts.[10]

To follow this route, we have to assume we know which actors and relationships count as part of the social movement we are trying to evaluate. And for this study's purposes, we have to treat the social movement as a unitary actor. If we can agree on those moves, the benefit of this strategy is clear: we get purchase on the big, practical question of why some advocates are better than others at solving their chosen problems. An exemplar of this causal combinatorics mode is Daniel Cress and David Snow's (2000) comparative study of fifteen local homeless social movements organizations. Like much other research on social movements, it invokes a collective, entrepreneurial actor, a social movement, or movement organization that has intentions the way a person does.[11] More complicated than some of the outcomes research, this study names four potential outcomes of homeless people's social movements, alliteratively tagged as representation, resources, rights, and relief. Different organizations in the study brought different combinations of organizational, strategic, and political factors to bear on their struggles. A combination of organizational stability and articulate framing mattered a lot for several of these r-word outcomes. Causal combinatorics assumes we can hold the *meaning* of an outcome constant while we assess which sets of factors produce it.

What if the same outcome has different significance in different organizations? That is what my research found. Studies that turn observed action over time into factors and outcomes are not set up to apprehend those different meanings. My alternative mode of comparison uses a theoretical category—like "civic action" or "style"—to compare different chains of action and consequences, instead of comparing different outcomes to the same class of event—policy change or no policy change, for instance. That way, we can understand an "outcome" inside the sequence of meaningful action in which it occurs—rather than pulling it out and treating it according to the scholar's own need for a clean model. I compared different chains of meaningful action, in HJ and ISLA coalitions, in terms of the common theoretical category of scene style. Different cases stand for variation inside a category—style—not different combinations of factors.

Different comparative modes come with different trade-offs. Comparing chains of action loses the power of a broad overview that may explain successful and failed outcomes across many cases. Comparing chains of action does, however, reveal important things about outcomes. Qualitatively rich studies of social movement organizations, volunteer groups, and nonprofit organizations tentatively suggest strengths and weaknesses of different scene styles for several outcomes of interest.[12] Two are especially relevant here. Neither would count as *final* ends or final successes for a lot of advocacy campaigns— the way that winning a new right might be a final end, for example—but advocates like the ones from ISLA and HJ work hard toward these ends. Further comparative, qualitative work can substantiate these tentative patterns.

First, acting as a community of interest, advocates are more likely to access governmental resources successfully than if they act as a community of identity. One snapshot of evidence for that style contrast comes from the HJ coalition: HJ leaders and the loyal majority of representatives valorized a quiet partnership with the mayor's office at the outset, while HJ dissenters considered such a partnership much more skeptically. Remember the scene from the contentious town hall with mayoral staff portrayed in chapter 3. Dissenters sounded little interested in securing goods from the mayor's office through collaboration on the mayor's terms.

Previous research also suggests style impacts efforts to get groups mobilized for a political coalition, whether or not the campaign wins. In this study, ISLA advocates selectively bracketed their longer-term, community struggle and carved out space for diverse, local groups to converge on a small slate of *issues*, including housing and jobs. They succeeded in mobilizing a more influential constituency that shared an interest in a CBA even if not all were so committed to a longer-lasting community of identity. They won an agreement from the Manchester developer and later the college on that basis.

What's most striking here is that these advocates clearly *knew* how to form a community of interest. Theoretically they could have been doing that all along, perhaps winning more short-term goals in the process. But they did not. All the more reason to supplement conventional questions about outcomes with research into what goals, outcomes, and success *mean* to advocates and their constituencies.

Two Styles of Projecting Success

A Pragmatist Approach: Timelines of Success

Following the action with HJ and ISLA coalitions made vivid how different styles of collective action induce different ways of defining a goal, and different criteria for what counts as meeting a goal. Styles cultivate goals on different timelines. Causal combinatorics explains coalition success or failure in terms of factors like savvy alliance building with governmental insiders, or effective framing, without considering the temporal context. In this mode, sociologists turn processes into abstract factors that play their role whenever they do, somewhere between chosen starting and end points for the subject in question. But individuals and groups continually project for themselves a future state of affairs, either more or less fully consciously. Sociologists have been thinking more about how people's imaginations of time itself influence their action. Our anticipation of a future state of affairs is embedded in and has some shaping influence on what we are doing *right now*.[13]

Dewey's pragmatist vocabulary makes the insight useful for thinking about social advocates' goals. Participants entangled in the midst of unfolding, collective action do not orient to a single, generic, omnipresent end or goal such as "affordable housing" in the abstract. They orient toward what Dewey (1939) called an "end-in-view": a goal that means something specific inside a particular timeline. An end-in-view, part of action in everyday settings, may transform depending on what happens over time, as actors recalibrate after advances or upsets. Differently styled problem-solving efforts transpire on longer or shorter "trajectories."[14] These are contexts that *shape a goal's particular meaning* for those pursuing it. As sociologist Josh Whitford (2002, 343) points out, actors don't choose single ends, one after another. Rather, "actors choose *processes*, so ends are meaningless without means-to-ends. Ends flow from means as effect from cause, the choice of a different means implies a different end state (and vice-versa)."[15]

The idea of an end-in-view helps us think about advocates' goals from the standpoint of unfolding action. People working together may project many ends in view, some more intermediate, and some longer term, yet all imagined on an arc stretching into the future. Accessing state resources or producing a mobilization for a campaign can be seen as intermediate ends in view—real and consequential goals for advocates even if they are not the longer-term ends of winning a campaign or protecting the community. The more common approach treats social advocates' goals from the standpoint of abstract principles in mission statements or advocates' own retellings of "a successful campaign" at some point after action is completed.[16]

Thinking of goals as ends-in-view helps explain why ISLA's Ethan was so little interested in HJ's MIHO campaign. HJ advocates' ideal of more affordable housing was one that ISLA participants could share in the abstract. But ISLA's own end-in-view for housing made sense inside a much *longer* and localized trajectory of community subordination and resistance. Participants assumed that trajectory would keep unfolding through time whether or not the city council voted for new housing mandates. ISLA advocates would say they were "in it for the long haul." Success, like the deal ISLA wrested from the Manchester's developer, would be a noteworthy marker in a long struggle, not a final end in itself. The HJ coalition's end-in-view, a MIHO, on the other hand, was a much more consequential, time-marking end in relation to the HJ coalition. In fact, winning a MIHO would *end* the coalition. HJ did its problem solving on a what participants projected as a shorter trajectory.

Explanations of success and failure risk obscuring real, consequential differences in goals and the significance of success. By comparing outcomes, we think we are comparing like with like when, from the advocates' point of view, we sometimes are not. Comparing trajectories, we better understand otherwise puzzling difficulties in collaboration between organizations.

In Hot Pursuit of Shifting and Just Good-Enough Goals: The Community of Interest in the HJ Coalition

Several months after HJ launched its "outsider strategy" with town hall meetings, the coalition made a remarkable advance. A crisis followed almost immediately, and the coalition started planning for a big shift in strategies. Coordinating committee members began considering new goals for HJ, but continued acting as a community of interest. The way that new goals emerged tells us a lot about how a community of interest relates to goals and strategies, and how it projects success.

In May 2009, the city council voted unanimously for a "framework" for a MIHO. That was not the same as a vote for an ordinance itself. Still, as HJ's coordinating committee convener told me over coffee, "We felt this momentum and a lot of excitement, and people felt like we're moving. . . . It's the first time we ever got something on paper." Council member Hernandez, magnet for so much worried second-guessing at the coordinating committee, had warmly mentioned HJ by name during the voting session. And for community organizers in the coalition, the vote was especially good news. On HJ leaders' urging, the framework included the language and numbers that would mandate more housing for the organizers' blue-collar constituencies in places like South Los Angeles, not just the higher-income groups alluded to in some of the comments by staff from the mayor's office at community meetings. The convener explained that for the first time in her tenure with HJ, staff "could sit back and think about what should come next."

Then a large property developer sued the city. The developer wanted to thwart a mixed-income housing policy already in force in one particular city district. The policy had been written into that district's official planning document, assessing fees for residential developments that failed to offer their quota of affordable apartments. The developer won the suit; the court decided those fees were illegal. The city attorney's office appealed the ruling and lost. The lawsuit portended a negative legal precedent for MIHOs, freezing HJ's existing strategies.

In fall 2009, at the next coordinating committee meeting I attended, Mary drew up a list of things HJ could do next. Committee members were most keen on supporting the city attorney's appeal of the recent ruling to the state supreme court. Next on their list was meetings with city council members' offices. Meantime, public interest attorneys were helping the committee figure out how they could accomplish what the MIHO was supposed to accomplish and in a way that could survive legal challenges. Maybe HJ would push the city to institute developer fees that could be channeled to affordable housing construction on the grounds that more housing options constituted a compelling public good. Maybe the coalition could simply pursue a more limited MIHO in hopes that a broader ordinance would get a legal pass from the state legislature or courts later on. Or maybe it would focus on a MIHO just for owner-occupied housing, like condominiums in the central city, not the rental housing where a majority of Angelenos lived. The recent legal case would not apply to owner-occupied homes.

In other words, coalition participants were willing to try different strategies to arrive at some sort of affordable housing ordinance, with different combinations of actors. HJ's incipient efforts toward "outsider" strategies the previous spring had now taken a U-turn toward what was perhaps the consummate insider strategy: reliance on courtroom action. "Success" might mean winning in court, not at city hall. A new attendee from a council of labor unions argued for moving cautiously, saying that the committee really needed to know more about what council members were thinking before pushing, and meeting facilitator Mary agreed. Both were saying, in effect, that it was time to figure out all over again who stood where in the concentric circles of close allies, more distant supporters, and adversaries, rather than to dig in heels and push the issue with city council members, as one attendee suggested. As Mary put it, "We have to figure out what we are pushing for." Short- and medium-term goals were shifting, but HJ advocates still acted as a community of interest.

Hypothetically, the developer's lawsuit could have spurred the coalition to remap itself as a threatened, resisting community. HJ advocates could have hardened the boundaries between "we" and "they."[17] HJ's constituent groups could have begun cultivating popular commitment to the idea that housing is a human right, the way members of the coalition's former, dissenting organizations did. At the following month's meeting, a list of potential strategies written with a felt pen onto a sheet on the wall included "organize low-income communities." What committee members talked more about, though, was legal recourse. We did not discuss community organizing during my time with the HJ coalition, which ended soon after this meeting.

What is most striking is that HJ advocates assumed it would be *alright* to shift their strategic goals toward different constituencies and players. Committee members did not even discuss how far the new aims should deviate from the old. Reaching success was a matter of *satisficing*, finding a good-enough goal involving affordable housing, not holding out steadfastly for one particular version of that goal. Relations between short-term goals and the shared interest were relatively fluid, mutually dependent, and negotiable. Different, plausibly acceptable strategies might rely on quite different sets of players, such as mobilized tenants, city council members, attorneys, state legislators, and state supreme court justices. That does not mean HJ was willing to adopt just any strategy at all. Recall how dissenter Terry on HJ's coordinating committee got little response when she promoted her version of an "outsider" strategy—organizing tenants to confront city agencies rather than unite behind the mayor's housing initiative. Still, strategies could shift between players, constituencies, and forums of contestation quite quickly without grossly threatening the *mode of strategizing*, the community of interest. The coalition even flirted with the idea of raising the socioeconomic "floor" of its chosen constituency by redrafting MIHO proposals for owner-occupied units that would attract a quite different social stratum from that of working-class tenants who had figured importantly in HJ's plans.

Advocates had assumed that strategies in pursuit of a MIHO, whether insider or outsider, would play out on a relatively short timeline. When HJ's efforts were close to winning the requisite number of city council member endorsements to pass a vote, coordinating committee members had said that property owners were just beginning to fight. Yet HJ leaders already had mapped out a roughly eighteen-month campaign to pass an ordinance they said would produce by far the largest affordable housing mandate in the United States. Given the aspiration here, it was an ambitious timeline.[18] Rhythms of a community of interest unfold to a campaign drumbeat, as Mary put it, and surge to little crescendos with public events. We could say advocates fit the entire HJ campaign onto a timeline with a relatively quick crescendo of success. At the last meeting I attended, Mary said, sounding tired, "It's clearly going to be a longer fight" than the coordinating committee had planned, even though with the campaign's ambition and commercial developers' likely resistance, this should not have been that surprising.

Some individual members of HJ's coordinating committee remembered at least one of the two prior campaigns named "Housing Justice" over the previous ten years. But committee members rarely referred to the earlier campaigns in my earshot. When they did, these came up briefly, fleetingly, as editorial comments. Once, a community organizer on the committee complained about gadfly Terry's blustery approach, saying that "we've worked toward this for ten years" and Terry was now threatening to derail the campaign. Another time I heard vocal coalition leader Carol say quickly, in one of those characteristically abbreviated references for in-the-know players, that a council member was hedging on committing to a MIHO because he felt "burned" by the campaign several years earlier. These comments suggest that some *individuals* came to committee meetings informed by a longer-term memory and even a ten-year struggle. Up until the chilling lawsuit, however, *the way members worked together* depended little, if any, on members' knowledge of prior campaigns.

Action instead depended on short-term knowledge: good, useful participants were the ones who kept keep track of which city council members had committed to supporting a MIHO this time, and which needed pressure from which ethnic or neighborhood constituencies. A city-approved MIHO could end the campaign, and along with it, the need for the HJ coalition in its current form. Two preceding campaigns on affordable housing-related issues, constructed as communities of interest, had disbanded at the conclusion of their respective campaigns. One had won, and the other lost, but either a win or loss would extinguish the reason for collaborating, and the current HJ campaign would be no different. Coordinating committee participants could go back to the other coalitions and organizational efforts waiting to fill in their always-packed schedules. HJ staff person Mary could simply continue working for Western Housing Association. Other HJ staff such as coalition convener Francis and office colleagues were hired on short-term contracts with no guarantee of renewal. It so happened that the staffer who replaced Francis was herself leaving just as the coalition was refiguring strategic goals after the lawsuit; her contract term was over, and WHA was not offering money to extend it. The community of interest projected a definitive outcome, successful or not, on a relatively short timeline.

The idea of a goal itself varies depending on style. Acting as a community of interest, HJ had worked toward the goal of a MIHO, but the form that goal might take and constituencies it would benefit could vary. Both the goal and coalition fighting for it could change in even startling ways, depending on how the ongoing pursuit of a shared interest unfolded in the context of blocks and threats. Winning even a version of a MIHO that would leave some organizations' representatives unable to "go with the group," as Carol put it, would end the community of interest happily for most participants.

Fighting the "Hundred Years' War": The Community of Identity

In contrast with HJ's community of interest, communities of identity project a longer timeline of action. On that timeline, successes are never definitive—not as long as there is a community to defend from threats. Goals, as discrete ends-in-view, have less of a defining influence on the collectivity pursuing them than do goals for a community of interest, in which goals are a major part of the interest, without which there is no community. A downtown resident member of LAPO's housing committee put it starkly while reacting to my presentation on what made LAPO and ISLA different from a coalition like HJ. In the tone of an insider teasing a naïf, he told me, "We're fighting a hundred years' war!" Maybe he had a taste for drama, but I gathered he was not just being ironic.

ISLA participants articulated their relatively long timeline in both more and less ceremonial settings. Early in this study, when ISLA advocate Ethan introduced the new ISLA coalition with a slideshow, the show began with pictures of a mostly African American commercial district that state redevelopment authorities had designated "blighted" and obliterated in the 1960s, nearly a half century earlier. ISLA's kickoff meeting similarly started with a long historical narrative-cum-slideshow of neighborhood transitions and gentrification near the college. To fight alongside ISLA was to place oneself on the community's timeline—a trajectory made palpable by ISLA advocates' stories.

The community's timeline informed talk in less ceremonially scripted settings too; it became part of the everyday action. During the Manchester campaign, participants occasionally would recall in the middle of a meeting that the city planning department had a long record of approving nearly any new building that did not self-destruct. Early in the antidisplacement campaign when it seemed as if college officials were ignoring ISLA advocates or speaking dismissively, the conversation would lurch toward stories of disrespect from years past and promises seemingly broken. Advocates would remind each other, for example, of how the college's outdoor swimming pool, announced originally as a good to share with neighbors, in fact admitted only instructors, staff, and students; the pool was constructed many years before the ISLA campaign. These bit narrations filled in a map that oriented ISLA advocates' relations to each other as well as outsiders. The two previous rounds of affordable housing activism that some HJ advocates knew about or had joined, in contrast, almost never entered ordinary, coordinating committee conversation. They were separate campaigns and communities of interest even if they included some of the same people representing the same groups. The campaign history HJ leaders did in fact tell at HJ's contentious "unity meeting" was only a year long.

When the timeline is a "long haul," it may seem to make any particular goal along the way more negotiable. But the opposite was true, because in a community of identity, the goals represent the will of a specific constituency (the community) even if its geographic boundaries are fuzzily defined. For ISLA's struggle with both the Manchester development and college, a CBA became the goal. A CBA might take a different shape, just as a MIHO might take a different shape, depending on what deals savvy negotiators on each side could strike. But the *beneficiaries* of the CBA would be nonnegotiable. And further, the range of other actors who might bring the goal to fruition were small. ISLA staff members availed themselves of legal advice from some of the same pro bono attorneys who assisted HJ. Even the most time-starved ISLA leader, though, would not allow a community strategy to transform entirely into fights centered mainly on courtrooms—as the HJ leaders seemed to be contemplating. The community needed to empower itself by organizing its local residents to speak out and ensure that closed-door negotiations had the community's approval.[19]

Francis from HJ once told me that LAPO "doesn't get many things passed, but they get what they want." While neither LAPO's housing committee nor other communities of identity in this study always got what they wanted, the comment turned out to be a helpful clue. Participants in communities of identity take their strategies as more of a reflection on *their collectivity* and aspirations than communities of interest do. The parties pursuing the strategies along with the beneficiaries of those strategies need to identify and be identified by others as community members. Satisficing is too open ended as well as potentially dissatisfying to describe relations between a community of identity and its strategies and goals. The range of potentially central players, constituencies, and forums cannot be as wide, and needs to include recognized members of the community. There is less leeway for the kind of shift in goals that HJ was contemplating.

A community of identity may significantly shift strategies and goals in the process of defending the community. The single-biggest change I saw during my time with ISLA, however, makes my point about the narrower leeway for problem solving. ISLA participants had hatched the Dreams for Draper project as a chance for a "win" along with a "positive" project that could signal to the city as well as the college, "Look what we can do, beyond complaining and resisting. We can create professional-quality neighborhood plans. We can be partners in planning." This positive strategy enlisted new participants—the urban planning students from a distant university, for example. They worked toward the short-term goal of a research-based report, and proposed redevelopment plans that might, in the much longer view, influence city planners and establish ISLA advocates' seriousness of purpose. This strategy was not intrinsically incompatible with a community of identity. A roughly similar strategy and goal culminated in the Somos la Comunidad event.

Yet a crucial difference distinguished the two efforts. Dreams for Draper depended on outsider expertise that threatened community boundaries. The outsider students' lack of familiarity with the community made things more awkward still. ISLA advocates' way of coordinating themselves did not open them up to diverse sources of initiative or expertise. The HJ coordinating committee, on the other hand, considered new roles for attorneys, statewide bodies, and even entirely new constituencies as it continued pursuing an interest in affordable housing. Proposing a constituency other than the community for ISLA's efforts would have been at best a nonstarter. A community of identity produces nonnegotiable positions more readily. Put differently, the community gives itself less leeway for a distanced, ambivalent, or satisficing relation to its own strategies. Success plays to a stricter standard, or otherwise the community of identity threatens its authenticity as the community's voice.

Different ways of embracing a strategy became especially clear at the HJ meeting following the "unity meeting" that had been so disunifying. Terry had insisted that the coalition needed to stand firm behind higher quotas of housing for extremely low-income tenants in any proposed ordinance. For Terry it had been a nonnegotiable commitment, bolstered by her claim that even the local Democratic Party stood for more low-income housing than HJ seemed willing to endorse. For Carol, authentic commitments might have to live in tension with the need for deals that could keep those concentric circles of allies, supporters, and potential supporters close enough for a win. Carol had told Terry, "We all care deeply about low-income people. It hurts that we can't do more." Carol's identity as a community member was not at stake; her loyalty to a shared *interest* was, however. That loyalty might even overpower the coalition's sincere commitment to extremely low-income and homeless constituencies. Terry asserted that "people are not necessarily on board" with the coalition's proposed quotas of housing for different income brackets.

> Carol: "We know that! . . . We think we have a position that's as left as we can go—and we feel fine about that!"

Carol would make do with what she supposed was best for a shared interest. Terry would remain steadfastly for what she supposed was the most authentic voice of a community.

While a community of identity narrows the potential range of allies and tightens advocates' identification with the strategies they choose, it may also multiply the number of issues with which advocates are willing to strategize. When news of the hospital demolition reached ISLA leaders, they were busy getting the local college to commit to negotiations over future development plans. Leaders had followed developments at the Manchester site for several years, but had not realized that construction suddenly could begin. Potential negotiations with the college would produce goods far more extensive than what one apartment development site could offer, yet no one ever said or implied that taking on the Manchester was a choice or a matter of triage with a stretched staff's energies. There was peril in the community, and as a staffer had said, "We *had* to fight it." At the HJ coordinating committee's unity meeting, in contrast, the blow-up started when dissenting members, who preferred a community of identity, found out that the committee was not going to take a position regarding residents forced to vacate two SRO hotels. It was not the committee's focal issue, Carol reminded them; the MIHO was.

Strategies and Meanings in Everyday Action

HJ and ISLA advocates used strategies that would sound the same if described in organizational reports or interviews done after the end of a campaign. The coalitions' seemingly similar strategies had different meanings for the actors, though, and elicited different immediate responses. In chapter 3, I used "strategy" in its conventional sense, as a plan devised for a goal. Now it is useful to compare strategy in this sense with an academic version of the term. For several decades, researchers influenced by culture scholars such as Pierre Bourdieu or Ann Swidler have conceived of a strategy as something more involved than simply a means toward an intentional goal. They theorize it as a culturally patterned way of organizing individual or collective action over time, whether or not it is entirely intentional.[20] Style turns strategy in the conventional sense into strategy in the more theoretical, cultural sense.

Strategy in the conventional sense is not a carefully calibrated object of study. Advocates decide on a "strategy" of demanding a meeting next week with a city councillor, or ponder the coalition's yearlong "strategy" to secure nine city council votes to approve a historic housing policy.[21] Depending on the metric we use, there could be many, many strategies in a two-year campaign, or just one "campaign strategy." To locate advocates' distinct strategies in the narrow sense of the term, we can follow social movement scholar Kathleen Blee (2012, 2013) and focus on "sequences" of interaction at meetings.

Sequences are simply conversations revolving around a particular topic, such as the need to hire a new campaign director, or the question of whether or not to mount a grassroots phone-in campaign to pressure city council members. Sequences may be long or short. Sequences treating the same topic may reemerge at multiple meetings. A topic, and therefore sequence, may emerge suddenly and then suddenly exit the stage in the middle of a sequence on a different topic. We will concentrate on sequences in which advocates are talking about or carrying out their strategies, whether or not they use that term explicitly for their plans.

Following are three sets of strategies, in the narrow sense of the term, that advocates discussed and carried out in both HJ and ISLA coalitions. Each became a different, meaningful line of action—a different strategy in the cultural, sociological sense—depending on the style in play.

Pondering Insider versus Outsider Strategies

Dissenter Terry argued with HJ coalition agenda setters such as Mary and Carol about the need for a "community strategy" or "grassroots mobilization." She criticized them for focusing too much on insider strategies. Terry and HJ leaders spoke past each other on the same topic because they understood strategies from inside different styles of action. Repeatedly Terry called her preferred plan of action an "outsider" strategy that brings ordinary tenants into angry, determined contact with city council members' offices. Mary and Carol both seemed to *think* they had addressed Terry's complaint. Both used nearly identical terms to respond. Mary replied to Terry's complaint with, "We've done a power analysis of who influences other people." Three meetings later, when another, short sequence of talk about insider versus outsider strategies came up, Carol said,

> "When we did our power analysis, we found out that labor is very important."

Different notions of outsiders produced the cross talk. It took repeated scans of field notes for me to figure out why Mary and Carol's use of a "power analysis" was not just a non sequitur response to Terry's call for an outsider strategy: they meant different things by "outsider"! For Mary and Carol, outsiders were people who do not make policy, including potentially powerful people such as labor leaders. They were "outside" the official legislative process in which interests are adjudicated, highlighted, or else unrecognized. Hence the reliance on a power analysis that rates how much influence different actors have with power brokers. It was on this basis that HJ leaders encouraged *legislative* outsiders to attend town halls to promote the mayor's vision of affordable housing.

For Terry, outsiders were something more like "the community." They were low-income tenants and homeless people. They were *social* outsiders— members of socially subordinate groups, not narrowly legislative outsiders who may actually represent relatively well-resourced organizations such as the federation of labor—whatever their own social background happens to be. Outsiders in Terry's sense would fight for the community's vision of its priorities, not the mayor's. Outsiderhood in each case is meaningful in relation to different social and institutional realities that we can see as social scientists, and that advocates experience and articulate in various ways.

Differences in preferred scene style gave the conversation between Terry and the other two its jarring disconnects. To Mary and Carol, gatekeepers with power over the housing issue, such as municipal legislators in this case, were central actors. They occupied the zone of aspiration; the point of a good strategy was to target them. To Terry, the community was a central actor. The point of a good strategy was to define and defend the community *against* threatening social forces represented by municipal legislators as well as police, exploitative property owners, and other social elites. During field visits to Terry's home organization, SHAPLA, I heard advocates defending and affirming the homeless community against threatening outsiders months before HJ's contentious coordinating committee meetings. They were propelling a community of identity, like the one pictured in the ISLA coalition. The same strategy on paper, an outsider strategy, would have advocates focusing on different kinds of allies, depending on the style.

Office Visits and Letter-Writing Campaigns

Both HJ and ISLA paired visits to municipal officials' offices with letter writing as a pressure strategy. Recall how HJ coordinating committee members frequently, seemingly obsessively, discussed the timing and purpose of visits to council members' offices. What did it mean that Hernandez does not want to talk to us this week? Members did not call these office visits a strategy, but the point did not need belaboring. The visits were one of the main strategies for reaching the goal of a majority vote on the city council for a MIHO. The point of a coinciding letter-writing project was equally unmistakable. Both were part of keeping up the drumbeat of pressure on the gatekeepers. Yet even straightforward-sounding strategies like these could mean different things in the context of different styles of action.

When HJ coalition leaders made office visits, they spoke on behalf of a coalition pursuing an interest. Who shared the interest? The coalition represented its constituency by way of letters signed by political and civic or religious leaders of publicly prominent groups in the city. The letters together communicated diverse rationales for the shared interest. A letter from African American leaders connected housing affordability to a longer struggle against housing discrimination. The letter from Latinx leaders emphasized the danger-ously overcrowded, unhealthy living conditions Latinos in the city dispropor-tionately faced. The letter from rabbis remarked on Jewish scriptural impera-tives to guarantee shelter and condemn evictions that leave people homeless. The point of these letters was not to announce cultural difference. Rather, HJ's office delegation visits and letter-writing strategies communicated that HJ represented a broadly diverse, collective "everyperson" of Los Angeles.

The topic of office visits came up at an ISLA strategy meeting too, a month before ISLA and the developer of the Manchester ratified their CBA. ISLA advocates had started visiting city planning commission offices in hopes of influencing their decision on the apartment complex. During one lengthy se-quence, what seemed like the same strategy on paper—office visits—began to sound different from the HJ coalition's visits in a subtle, important way. ISLA leader Francine had visited a city planner's office. She came back with the planner's friendly suggestion that the coalition select just "one good speaker and make four points and have six minutes" instead of fitting inside the usual public comment format of two-minute slots. SED leader Raimunda said it was crucial to "represent different parts of the coalition"—and up to this point, made the strategy sound like that of HJ—but then she added, "and one or two community members to make it *real*." She emphasized that "it's very important—none of *us* can represent close to them." This specified the mean-ing of contact with city officials. The communication act itself meant being a distinct community's voice, not the voice of an Angeleno everyperson. ISLA also paired the visits with a letter-writing project. Office staff prepared a tem-plate letter that *community residents* could send to the city planning depart-ment, embellished with whatever personal appeals they might like to add. The same strategy meant something different to each coalition's campaign coordi-nators and called forth different kinds of communication.

Small Committees Work Out the Details of a Deal

They may not have thought of it as a strategy, but the leading members of the HJ and ISLA coalitions all needed a plan for determining what could count as a worthwhile deal. Otherwise, neither coalition could claim to meet its goals. Comparing sequences from chapters 4 and 5, we find that different under-standings of group trust and legitimacy cast a very different light on both co-alitions' tendency to rely on small subcommittees to work out the details.

HJ leaders had maintained a policy committee, a subset of the coordinating committee. Formally, the coalition entrusted the policy committee members to figure out what quotas of affordable housing units at what income levels and what kind of buyout option for developers would produce the best deal for the coalition. At the blow-up meeting, Terry and other dissenters voiced their distrust of this arrangement. They said it left member organizations out of the loop, while producing a figurative ballpark of quotas for income levels that left them dissatisfied. Francis retorted that they could have read their email from the coalition if they wanted to be in the loop, and a seasoned coalition member shot back that maybe it was only Terry who was uncomfortable with the process. Carol summarized that everyone had to trust and "go with the group." The strategy of delegating policy details to a smaller circle ended up costing the coalition momentum, morale, and ultimately several important tenant organizations.

ISLA leaders followed a similar strategy in the Manchester campaign yet in a context that evidently gave them more legitimacy. A small group of ISLA staffers worked out a set of conditions with the Manchester developer and presented those to a gathering of neighborhood residents. Residents had asked skeptical, pointed questions, and one observed how awkward it was to make a deal with an entity they had opposed, but none challenged the legitimacy of the bargaining team. If a potential deal failed and the emerging community of interest with the developer collapsed, then, as SED's director teased, it would be time for plan B: break out the slogan-bearing T-shirts. The community of identity would endure, in other words. A history of routine appeals to the will of the community, by leaders and other participants alike, made it hard for even skeptical residents to delegitimate the provisional deal.

During the vetting, one ISLA leader asserted that the developer was never was going to set aside more than 5 percent of the upscale complex's units for affordable housing. No one challenged the claim. There is a truly striking contrast here: when HJ's coordinating committee debated what percentage of set-asides it should fight for, one experienced leader tried to mollify the dissenters, saying, "We could get an agreement [from city council] for 5 percent tomorrow if we wanted to." They were holding out for much more than that, of course; they were quite leftist after all, not just pushovers. Different circumstances will make "5 percent affordable housing" sound different, but still one can wonder how the same number could sound so *very* different. ISLA's 5 percent became part of a win that ISLA participants celebrated. HJ's "unquestionably more than 5 percent" did not enjoy the same trust and confidence. Dissenters interpreted the committee delegating strategy behind it as capable only of producing a raw deal since they deemed it inattentive to the will of the community.

A deal is a good deal depending on the style in play.

For either coalition, like any other that endures for a significant time, a variety of shorter-term strategies like office visits and letter writing live together in one campaign. Through the lens of style, we can see them as links in meaningful—styled—chains of action. The strategies can carry different significance and elicit different consequences even when they sound identical.

Following Action at a Distance: The Trade-offs of Style

Until now, we have been following the meanings of strategies, goals, and "success" from advocates' own points of view. This is a good place to step back and consider some practical trade-offs that come with styling collective action one way rather than another. *Trade-offs* are different from the *dilemmas* that chapters 3 and 4 followed. Advocates themselves talked about their dilemmas, if not in such direct terms. They puzzled and argued over whether to pursue an insider or outsider strategy, and whether or not their strategies were sufficiently rooted in the community. Dilemmas were built into styles of coordinating action because those styles unavoidably entangled advocates with social realities that complicated their way of acting.

Advocates rarely talked about trade-offs. Trade-offs are the largely unspoken risks of a style. Speaking about them would have been impolite and solidarity busting. Trade-offs are easier to see and talk about when we stand outside advocates' preferred style and think with comparisons. When advocates talked or implied something about trade-offs, it usually was to condemn the options they did not choose and affirm the ones they did. Considering trade-offs openly and deliberately would violate a taboo—something like the "sacred" of the group, as Goffman might have put it.[22]

Trade-offs in a Community of Interest: Risking Skewed Justice and a Lack of Accountability

Perhaps the most divisive trade-off for HJ leaders, when acting as a community of interest, emerged from their investment in broad-based coalition building. The upside seems obvious: a broad-based strategy potentially brings more supporters and more varied supporters than a narrower kind of organizing. The people who wrote HJ's coalition newsletters pointed out that everyone who depends on a robust economy benefits from companies that can more easily attract employees to the region if housing is affordable. On this thinking, there could be potentially many supporters beyond the "usual suspects" who get involved in campaigns for progressive social policy. But on the downside, a broad-based strategy for "everyone" could imply that financially strained office workers, laborers doubled up in apartments to save money, and homeless people teetering between shelters and the streets are equally aggrieved and in need of attention.

Dissenters in the coalition questioned this equivalence, pointing out a seemingly obvious fact: people with extremely low, unstable incomes are in worse straits than middle-income librarians or teachers. One suggested angrily that if HJ spokespeople did not talk forthrightly about the poorest, then "you're talking racial." HJ's community of interest constructed a general appeal; we want housing for everyone including the dishwasher, said community organizer Keith. Whether or not advocates were either intentionally or implicitly racist, the strategies they pursued as a community of interest could *sound* deceptively oblivious for not highlighting and prioritizing the poorest victims of Los Angeles' housing crisis. Given the racial contours of gentrification sketched out in chapter 2, the appeals for housing that a community of interest crafts for the Angeleno everyperson might sound tepid, not to mention too distant from the reality of Angelenos of color who lived near redevelopments, especially downtown. For the sake of redistributive justice (not a term committee members used), maybe HJ should have fought for a MIHO that would address the most urgent needs by offering more housing for residents of low-income, predominantly minority neighborhoods, even at the cost of distancing more economically stable groups from coalition demands.

The criticism reveals the trade-off. At contentious meetings, coalition loyalists addressed the trade-off in terms more moralizing than deliberative. Keith characterized dissenter Terry's criticisms as "ideology versus pragmatism." Context and tone communicated to me that the latter term was the moral high ground, and that Keith thought Terry had been impertinent and maybe offensive. Carol said that HJ's current MIHO proposal already leaned as far left as was possible if they wanted to win. Winning for her happened through give and take in the zone of aspiration; for Terry, it would occur by making the central boundary between us and them less porous as well as harder to move. "Ideology," "pragmatism," and "left" in this context are boundary-policing, jingoistic terms we will come back to in the concluding chapter. They protect rather than scrutinize the style in play. If a style of action breaks down, actors need to figure out some other way to coordinate action, otherwise the point of a group's existence is unclear. That is why I propose Goffman's Durkheimian metaphor: the group sacred is being violated.

Another trade-off for HJ's community of interest came with its strategy's time frame and demands on group trust. When dissenters Terry and several others at the coordinating committee complained that they had not been kept apprised of the shifting figures in HJ's MIHO proposal—the minimum quota of affordable housing that developers would have to provide, and for which income bracket of tenant—an HJ leader close to negotiations with city leaders said in effect "you have to trust us." He implied it was logistically impractical to tell all the community groups about every move in negotiations. Signing onto the coalition meant "going with the group," as Carol put it, and that meant assuming its leaders were fighting for what was possible. Given the seeming burst of enthusiasm from the mayor's office for an MIHO in later 2008 coupled with the impending mayoral election, the logistical argument made sense. The campaign was, after all, a project with a short-term goal for a coalition that did not need to endure indefinitely. On the other hand, Terry charged that leaders were in effect skirting accountability to supporters in community groups who did not know exactly how hard leaders were pushing for their priorities. The charge cast doubt on the legitimacy of HJ's entire broad-based, MIHO campaign strategy at that point. No wonder talk was so bitter and emotions were so explosive. Again, it was like a violation of what HJ leaders assumed was their whole way of coordinating action—a kind of group sacred.

When ISLA leaders presented a tentative agreement on the Manchester development to seventeen community residents, inviting them into a community of interest, they suddenly adopted the same trade-offs. They pushed what seemed possible to win, even if that meant eschewing a harder—some would say more just—line on the developer's offer of affordable units. In that scene they also tugged at residents to trust them rather than slowing the process to allow more critical pondering. The meeting had been called unusually quickly because *there was a rush* to decide on an agreement, and the seventeen people were those who were available on short notice.

Trade-offs in a Community of Identity: Risking Exclusivity and Freezing Time

Probably the most limiting trade-off for ISLA's community of identity was the immovable definition of the community that powered its strategy. On the one hand, this strategy gave ISLA advocates a privileged position as the truly legitimate voice of a socially bounded, fuzzily geographic constituency. Whether speaking from or for the community, ISLA advocates and close, vetted allies could speak much more authoritatively on the community's behalf in front of city leaders than would any more distant outsiders who claimed to know what was best for the community. They would be hard put to argue with authenticity, and even opponents at city hearings did not try to. At the final city hall deliberation, a Manchester developer's spokesperson said their team had listened to the community, and was making sincere efforts to be a good neighbor by scaling back and offering goods the community wanted. The community's definition of the neighborhood, theoretically, could have been up for debate, but it was not.

Other scenes showed the strains of a strategy based on projecting authenticity when it comes to attracting allies. When Frank from the job training nonprofit said he would not be able to summon laborers to attend hearings on the Manchester if ISLA was in effect shutting down potential construction work, the SED leader asked if he could support ISLA's alternative vision for development in the neighborhood. Frank said he could, but asked what was in it for the laborers. The community strategy threatened to exclude the kinds of allies who honor multiple commitments. These allies ask of any commitment, "What's in it for us?" The community strategy required allies make the community—as characterized by ISLA participants—the overriding priority. For potentially valuable, influential allies like Frank, that could be a tough deal. The risk of distancing or excluding potential allies outside the community was a big trade-off, but seemingly not worth a lot of breath. Recall how when Ethan quickly described the citywide MIHO strategy to fellow ISLA participants, he had made it sound distant from "this very specific area . . . where there is high displacement." Compelling as ISLA's cause could be, I noticed that relatively few citywide or regionwide housing or environmental organizations spoke up for it at city hearings.

Exploring and pondering ISLA advocates' definition of the community could sound impolite and a challenge to group solidarity. That is not just a guess. At ISLA's Lincoln neighborhood street fair, discussed in chapter 4, I saw how near I came to annoying Thalia and Francine when I asked about the coordinates of the community. Which streets were the boundaries? The gestures and tone of voice told me that my questions came off as supercilious—much as I had not meant them that way. I sensed they were too sharp and literal, or else just misdirected; they were clueless sounding about what really mattered.

Another trade-off resulted from the long timeline of ISLA's community of identity. On the one hand, planning for a "hundred years' war" makes good sense in the face of a powerful opposition—in this case, large property developers assisted by the politics of the municipal growth machine. On the other hand, a "war" understood in such prolonged terms may have to ignore or diminish changes in the "warriors" and turf, essentializing the community in the process. ISLA leaders defined their community of identity as a Spanish-speaking constituency that wanted to live in current neighborhoods indefinitely. "Proud members of this community" were not mobile, except under duress. There is no reason to think upward mobility is or should be a goal for all lower-income people, but it also would be wrong to assume that few, if any, Spanish-speaking people from immigrant families in South Los Angeles have middle-class aspirations and want to move to middle-class neighborhoods.[23] Communities change, in a crucible of individual residents' aspirations, regional and global markets as well as political economies. That fact sat awkwardly with ISLA advocates' efforts to valorize some current residents of a neighborhood, producing what I call a moral time freeze.

The essentialism of community freezes one historically specific, social and cultural profile of a locale as its proper and enduring condition over a long haul. The neighborhoods themselves, as ISLA leaders knew, were substantially African American a half century earlier. There still were "black homeowners" who ISLA advocates had learned would not necessarily support ISLA's antidisplacement work since gentrification might enhance their property values. When ISLA leaders spoke of the community, the tag would not normally include those African American homeowners. That makes sense if leaders are looking for the most likely supporters. It also privileges some residents over others in ISLA advocates' view of community. That is an inevitable trade-off for strategies that protect a community of identity. The community of identity envisions "a neighborhood that never changes," as sociologist Brown-Saracino (2009) put it in her study of gentrification.[24] In their view, ISLA advocates wanted to counteract the economic forces of the urban growth machine that values neighborhoods for how salable versus livable they are.[25] Property speculation kept property ownership in motion, making significant numbers of lower-income tenants in ISLA's neighborhoods move unwillingly. The community of identity places the driving forces of this process—developers and speculators—on the other side of its central boundary. The map counterposes this ceaseless, profit-making motion to a community whose residents want to stay put indefinitely—a stark scenario of opposition in a polar world.

7

Who Can Say What, Where, and How?

FOLLOW THE CLAIMS MAKING

ALONG THEIR different strategic arcs, LA housing advocates made lots of claims. There is always more than one kind of claim advocates could make about any condition, including the assertion that a condition others call a problem is really not a problem. Even a condition as seemingly obvious and important as a lack of housing for people who need it can be worded, felt, or judged differently, and of course solved differently too. What HJ advocates called a problem of too little affordable housing, some building industry advocates labeled an issue of too little housing in general or too little financial incentive to build for low-income people.

That is why we need to study how advocates "construct" social problems through claims making. Talk about social construction is nearly a cliché in social science after a half century of it.[1] It retains its hold on us because it helps convey a powerful, social science truth that departs from commonsense understandings: social problems come into existence when people make claims about conditions they consider problematic and in need of improvement.[2] Social advocates are in the business of turning conditions into problems through claims making.

Claims are demands, criticisms, or declarative statements that actors make in relation to public debate.[3] By definition then, claims makers publicize problems for collective problem solving. Claims making is different from a casual exchange of opinions among individuals.[4] It is a crucial part of civic action; it is part of collective efforts to improve some aspect of common life in society, however participants imagine society.

"People who work in Los Angeles should be able to live in Los Angeles" is a claim. I heard and read it during the 2008 campaign for a citywide MIHO. When Ethan from ISLA said the new urbanist model of city planning spotlights aesthetics and ignores affordability, he was making a claim. The statement that "the city has overdeveloped luxury housing by any measure" is a claim. The finding that "there are 28 percent fewer health care facilities here than the rest of the county" is a claim. Claims may communicate moral, political, or aesthetic preferences and matters of debate, like the first three examples, or be scientifically verifiable according to the best available, systematically collected evidence, like the fourth. If we want to understand how social advocates construct social problems, we have to take what the claims say, along with how and where they circulate, as being at least as important as whether or not they are verifiable. People may make those claims in formal, governmental settings like the city council chamber at city hall, where participants heard the first, third, and fourth examples, or much less formal and less public meetings of advocates, like the gathering that heard Ethan lampoon new urbanist city planning.[5]

To understand how social advocates construct social problems, we must do more than study claims. We must study claims *making*—the very social act of communicating claims in particular settings whether real or virtual. Often, casual observers and social scientists alike focus on the text of advocates' claims. We call them rhetorical appeals or ideologies, or use social movement scholars' notion of frame. This chapter looks closely at what advocates are *doing* when they make claims. The act of claims making unavoidably signals a claimant's social identity and reputation along with a message, because advocates develop and circulate claims inside ongoing relationships, real or imagined. So we will treat claims making, like relationship building, as styled interaction we can follow. That is why this chapter comes after the chapters that introduced styles and their strategic arcs.

Claims making happens in the context of not only a style of interaction but also a set of conventional categories for making claims. A *discursive field* provides those basic symbolic categories that advocates on multiple sides use to make claims about a problem. Scene style keeps some ways of talking about social problems outside the discursive field altogether, and relegates others to marginal enclaves or subordinate status inside the field. Following the action of claims making in the ISLA and HJ coalitions, we can learn how a discursive field works. The next chapter continues that conversation, using the topic of homelessness to highlight the perhaps surprising power a discursive field can have on our public speech.

Discursive Fields and How They Work

The Symbolic Categories We Usually Take for Granted

When advocates make claims about a problem, they enter an ongoing circle of real and imagined interactions with allies, opponents, and wider publics. They learn that certain categories of appeal—to fairness, compassion, or quality of life—are conventional for the issue at hand. We tend to talk about some problems as compassion and not fairness problems, for example. These symbolic categories orient us to the problem and suggest responses. If advocates use a symbolic category that is not conventional for the problem at hand, they risk sounding strange or impertinent, wasting time and losing their audience.[6] A simple cross-national comparison will help make the point.

It would not surprise many to hear someone say that homelessness in the United States is a compassion problem. Many, though certainly not all, also say that people become homeless through personal mistakes or character flaws; such a speaker imagines people who have became addicted to drugs and have lost their will to be productive. So we suppose that homeless people need more compassionate care or effective discipline in their lives, or maybe both. Talk of compassion and discipline both appeared in the website text of a large, nonprofit homeless service organization in Los Angeles that chapter 8 visits. The text explains that homelessness happens when individuals lack the structure and discipline to face their challenges. They need the caring "tough love" of professional and volunteer staff who enforce rules in homeless shelters, and help residents define and set goals for personal improvement.

But what if someone says that homelessness is a problem solved by inclusion in society? Relatively few people in the United States say that. To many ears, that would sound abstract and impractical. People have not been cultivated to that language for this problem, and would be more likely to say homelessness is solved by a change in the homeless person's personal habits, more compassion for the downtrodden, and/or a change in the availability of housing for disadvantaged people. An international nonprofit organization that originated in France does say homelessness is fundamentally a problem of inclusion in society and a "social emergency." Homelessness, as understood in this organization's mission statement, happens when society has "excluded" some people from the social ties that connect people as members of a political community. In this view, homelessness is more about (failed) social solidarity than about individuals with failings. The sight of people camped out on a Paris sidewalk, warming themselves over ventilation gratings on a winter's night, should elicit the reaction "Emergency! We need to call for help!" more than a compassionate "oh, how sad!" or tough-loving "oh, change your ways!"[7] Social advocates tend consistently toward a relatively few symbolic categories for making claims about housing problems. They avoid, react viscerally to, or just never think of others—like calling homelessness in Los Angeles a social solidarity emergency.

Field theorists say that a field's influence takes shape as relations of collaboration and competition or conflict develop around a shared stake or focus of attention.[8] In a discursive field, it is collaboration and conflict over what participants can say publicly about a social problem that matters.[9] The scale can vary. Researchers can study the discursive field that jells around one city's debates on the status of women, one industrial conflict, or one nation's collective memory.[10] Any of these applications can be defensible since it is up to the analyst to identify patterns of mutual attention toward a problem and designate them a field.[11] In this study, we see how discursive fields jell as collective actors focus on *problems*, not necessarily *issues* in the conventional sense such as "housing issues." That way, we can leave it an empirical question whether or not the field that develops around one problem involves the same symbolic categories, styles, or issues, as those of another contestation over a seemingly similar problem.[12] This study analyzes the discursive field that crystallized around the problem of the Manchester development, and the problem of instituting a citywide, affordable housing ordinance.

Why do advocates heed the categories circulating in the field, adapting or innovating instead of rejecting or transforming them? Why don't housing advocates come up with new ways of trying to convince the public as well as legislators that housing ought to be affordable and homeless people ought to have housing? How much leeway do social advocates have to innovate with the categories that organize most arguments in a discursive field?

The Social and Cultural Pull of a Discursive Field

A central theme is that the language that is prevalent in a discursive field strongly influences what advocates claim in that field, even if they may talk differently about the same topic outside the field. The field is not just optional terrain that advocates select; symbolically speaking, it exerts a gravitational pull. Chapter 1 introduced a more common approach to claims making: the social movement framing perspective that imagines social advocates as crafty entrepreneurs with leeway to piece together words and images to entice an audience. I mentioned the limits of this perspective when it comes to the question of how advocates make claims about problems. Here it is good just to add that strategic intent and skill *alone* would not easily explain why advocates often used just the same appeals in front of powerful decision makers at city hall as at informal activist meetings, or why they sometimes passed up alternatives seemingly more likely to appeal to the intended audience.

We can solve those puzzles by adopting a different picture of what claims makers are like. I argued that we learn more about how social advocates accomplish central tasks if we see them as socially embedded and culturally cultivated actors, not entrepreneurs with indefinite leeway to use their skills. This means that as advocates make claims, they become accustomed to and invested in big symbolic categories that preexist them, and make claims from mostly inside those categories.[13] Social advocates express themselves in shared, mostly preexisting categories so that their constituents, wider publics, and even competitors will understand, if not necessarily agree with, them and won't think they sound strange—the way calling homelessness a social solidarity problem would sound strange to most people in the United States. New claims makers learn the discourse of the field.[14] They are culturally cultivated.

Following advocates making claims about housing, I discovered something that previous studies of discursive fields have neglected: advocates inflect the main symbolic categories, making somewhat different claims depending on the setting. I discovered *patterns* of variation in social advocates' use of the same, symbolic categories for the same campaign but in different scenes. Goffman is the master proponent of the insight that different settings or scenes can elicit different modes of interaction from the same people. Studies of political, religious, and community service groups consistently bear out the insight.[15] The switches are not random but rather patterned by scene-specific expectations regarding who "we" all are, socially or institutionally.[16] That is what it means to say claims makers are socially embedded in distinct settings.

The question of "who we all are" matters especially when advocates make claims because they are representing more than private opinion. Though social advocates don't always bring groups of chanting supporters to a public debate, they *represent* a group, body of constituents, or entire population beyond an immediate scene of claims making. That is why when Francis and his HJ colleague went to the town hall on housing policy, pictured in the introduction, they were so confused at what they heard. City planning personnel were claiming exactly what *they*, HJ coalition advocates, claimed about the need for more affordable housing, in the same words. That violated the advocates' expectations about who we all are: city bureaucrats are not activists, even if they sometimes support the same policies. Those expectations come in patterns, and are none other than the maps that go with style. Style shapes social advocates' use of symbolic categories to make claims.

Now we can summarize more simply the cultural and social pull of a discursive field: when social advocates craft claims, they are not like freewheeling entrepreneurs trying out different rhetoric to see what produces a "sale." Claims makers make claims always in relation to others, real or imagined, as they perceive others in distinct scenes. Put simply, what advocates can claim about social problems depends on how they think they are connected to each other as well as to their audience.

That is why it makes sense to think of claims making and relationship building as closely paired, central tasks of civic action. And that is why advocates' puzzles and arguments over which claims to make quite often co-occurred with puzzles and arguments over how they should relate to or trust each other. Terry's explosive challenge to the HJ coordinating committee is a great example. Beginning as a criticism that the coalition's claims about how to increase housing opportunities were too timid, Terry's concern quickly segued into a seeming non sequitur: a criticism of committee relationships, which did not work as Terry thought they should.

How a Discursive Field Develops

In the discursive fields of this study, the shared stake was the matter of how to construct a housing-related problem. Parameters of acceptable claiming jell fairly quickly as newer participants are influenced by the established conversation and learn what can be said about a problem. They may notice reactions to what they later figure out are occasional mistakes.[17] Following the claims making, I discovered a surprising combination of continuities and systematic variation by social setting. The variation would escape notice or else look random to observers focused solely on overarching symbolic categories. Most previous studies of discursive fields built their arguments about a field of discourse from newspaper accounts, governmental documents, interviews, or secondary sources. This study draws systematically on internal documents from advocacy groups as well as audiotape or videotape of meetings at city hall, but depends heavily on everyday claims-making action too. I saw where advocates made claims and who they made them to. This combination of sources helps us discover how discursive fields actually work.

Under the influence of scene style, actors distinguish between *legitimate* symbolic categories and ones that they consider *illegitimate*, and refrain from using or even reject explicitly. Actors also distinguish between claims that are *appropriate* for a particular scene from those that are *inappropriate*—meaning they would violate the style of a scene. Finally, scene style can induce claimants to make some symbolic categories secondary or less salient than others that actors take to be more important, again because of expectations regarding who we all are in that scene. These features—legitimacy, appropriateness, and salience of claims—each are worth a bit more exploration.[18]

BOUNDING, OR WHAT CAN'T BE SAID ABOUT A PROBLEM: ILLEGITIMATE AND INAPPROPRIATE CLAIMS

Claims makers avoid entire symbolic categories, in effect putting up boundaries around what can or can't be said about a problem at all. Claims makers also avoid some particular kinds of claims in some scenes, dividing up the field internally. The first kind of rhetorical avoidance or rejection makes whole symbolic categories of claim *illegitimate*. I discovered how categories became illegitimate from tracking how claimants in the study talked across different scenes. Advocates' talk about compassion offers a good, quick example. ISLA advocates and local residents who identified with the coalition spoke caringly, as friends or neighbors in private informal scenes, about people displaced from their long-term homes by rising rents. By definition, this private conversation was not *claiming*. It was not talk launched in order to enter or imagine entering a public debate about displacement. Compassion-based *claims*, on the other hand, were exceedingly rare, and on the opposing side, extremely rare too, as if nearly all claimants had scripted and policed their sentiments. The shift in discourse between private informal and claims-making scenes is akin to what sociologist Nina Eliasoph has called "evaporation."[19] As ongoing interaction renders some entire categories illegitimate, the field acquires external boundaries.

In the second kind of rhetorical avoidance or rejection, claimants treat some claims as *inappropriate* for a particular scene. Even if fashioned with the right symbolic categories, those claims bear the influence of the wrong style for the scene at hand. During my rounds with housing advocates, claimants treated some style performances and claims as appropriate only in some carefully compartmentalized claims-making scenes. At the explosive "unity meeting," HJ advocates all were talking in terms of fair opportunities for housing, but some enacted the wrong style and turned "fair opportunity" into wrong-sounding claims for the scene. They were harshly censured by other coalition members for being impertinent, or seemingly clueless. In this way, a discursive field maintains internal boundaries.

SALIENCE: SOME CATEGORIES OF APPEAL ARE SUBORDINATE TO OTHERS

Analysts often suppose most fields maintain some kind of hierarchy. They make some discourses or practices dominant, or hegemonic.[20] Scholars of *discursive* fields point out that some discourses gain higher "stature" than others even apart from claimants' social structural positions.[21] Some themes in a discursive field are "recessive," less emphasized than others even if not illegitimate, and some discourses are more subculturally distinct than others.[22] In the United States, for example, political leaders frequently stress the rights and privileges of individuals regardless of the social context. It is mainly in subcultural, religious, or academic circles that we hear appeals to collective responsibility or communitarian sentiments. In the same vein of argument, illustrations below show how some symbolic categories can become less salient than others in a discursive field.

Scene style induces advocates to lower the salience of some categories of claim. Recall that scene style includes a shared social map with boundaries that separate "we" from "they" and "like us" from "not like us." Claimants may reduce the salience of rhetorical categories that they associate with a competing or conflicting "they" that is either physically present or imagined in their audience. Put metaphorically, style can produce an anti-magnetic effect. During debates over a new national constitution in post-Soviet Poland, for example, political leaders downplayed appeals to universalistic notions of citizenship because those appeals would risk associating them with (stigmatized) old Communists who invoked the same rhetoric.[23] In the United States, politically progressive religious activists have often avoided "sounding religious" because, they say, that is how religious fundamentalists sound.[24] To be clear, I do not mean to suggest we can strictly "determine" the ways claimants valorize and use symbolic categories simply by knowing the scene style they usually perform. Style works as a fuzzy, cultural parameter, not a strict program. Advocates enact it with some leeway for variation.

Now we can see the workings of discursive fields in contests over housing problems.

Claims about the Problem of a New Apartment Complex

Symbolic Categories

During the Manchester campaign, the vast majority of ISLA participants crafted housing claims from the categories of fair distribution of opportunity and quality of life, but primarily the former.[25] The central claim about housing, heard at ISLA meetings and city planning commission hearings, was that the Manchester would adversely affect neighborhood residents' housing opportunities. Meeting notes from early in the campaign stated that the development would "dramatically accelerate displacement in the area, bringing massive, market-rate development into an area severely lacking in affordable housing and experiencing rapidly rising rents." Talking points prepared for city planning commission hearings included the claim that the luxury apartments would not be affordable to many residents in South Los Angeles, since "here, 1 in 4 households is 'severely rent-burdened'" (meaning over 50 percent of their income goes to housing and utilities). Quality of life as an independently important claim was present but rare in the findings. One example comes in a laundry list–like letter, prepared by ISLA staff for tenants to mail to the city planning commission: "We are concerned about the loss of affordable housing in the area, gentrification, and the increased unhealthy air quality in the area that would result from the proposed project."

Two features of the Manchester episode support the idea that the contestation over the apartment complex was played out in a single, discursive field. First, ISLA made claims about the Manchester's health consequences, separate from housing. These health claims were also crafted with a predominant emphasis on fair distribution, with quality of life less salient. Meeting notes and flyers frequently mentioned that building the Manchester on a hospital site would result in lost hospital services in a locale "severely underserved medically." Others stressed that "there are 28 percent fewer health care facilities here than the rest of the county," before adding, "Because we have inadequate primary care, we suffer from higher rates of diabetes, hypertension, and HIV/AIDS." However local residents may have experienced inadequate health care privately, the *public wording* of these claims position health in relation to the distribution of health care opportunities—*because* they had inadequate primary care.

Second, these categories animated claims by skeptics as well as ISLA staff and uncritical supporters. As an agreement with the Manchester developer was being fleshed out, some ISLA participants and allies asked if the agreement would provide *enough* opportunity to low-income residents for housing and clinic access. At the last city planning commission hearing, a prominent housing advocate publicly questioned ISLA allies' acquiescence to a revised Manchester plan. She said the city had already allowed too many luxury developments to be built, and that organizations like hers would keep coming back to city hall "until low-income communities are treated equitably and fairly."

Pro-Manchester speakers *also* articulated fair distribution or quality-of-life claims.[26] This included the Manchester developer's employees and attorneys as well as business association allies, supportive local residents, and contractors and construction workers. A common quality-of-life argument was that the project would enhance shoppers' and commuters' experience of the neighborhood, and entice commuters out of cars and onto a nearby transit line. Many claimants underscored that the project would bring much-needed employment opportunities. The development team noted its plan to fill the jobs with local residents or at-risk individuals. Less frequently, speakers argued for fairly distributed goods in the form much-needed tax revenue that new, ground-floor businesses would generate, or else noted the developer's voluntary commitment to rent 5 percent of the units below the market rate. The fact that both skeptical ISLA participants and pro-Manchester speakers crafted claims using the two master categories strengthens my assertion that a discursive field contoured the debate.

How Style Shapes Claims Making: More Justice for a
Community of Identity

Claims about the Manchester at both city planning commission hearings and internal, coalition meetings bore the imprint of a community of identity. The master symbolic category of fair opportunity, "filtered" through style, became claims for more justice for a subjugated, distinct community. Claims consistently represented a self-identified collectivity resisting material injustices and indignities. A typical claim on talking points handouts stated, "The luxury apartments would not be affordable to us because [our area], which is mostly African American and Latino, has the lowest socioeconomic status in LA County." Meeting records show similar claims at ISLA's first, internal discussion about the Manchester: The development would "dramatically accelerate **displacement**" and have "serious effects on the health of low-income communities." These claims were not simply about fair distribution in general but instead about fairness for a distinct community; that was the nearly uniform style of the claims made.

Style helps explain why advocates often used fair distribution arguments for health concerns that participants likely *experienced* privately as quality of life issues too. Even if community members wanted a healthy quality of life, like people anywhere, *when individuals acted together as ISLA activists*, they shared a collective self-understanding as "the community" demanding justice in the face of external threats. Claims making already was embedded in this understanding of who we are to each other, and any such understanding limits what makes sense for actors to communicate.[27] Making community-specific claims against unjust external incursions was *already* central to ISLA advocates' social identity and how they wanted to be perceived by others, whether the claims were about housing or health.

The researcher separates out scene style and the claims people make while acting in that style, but of course in real life, the two come together. How can the researcher tell that the one influenced the other, and a broader symbolic category lay behind a specific claim? We can see the influence of ISLA's style of interaction operating by watching what ISLA advocates did when they encountered sympathetic statements crafted in a milieu with a different style. As natural experiments, these instances show how advocates work to make claims more appropriate to the style they prefer—even claims that are *already* about the fair distribution of opportunity. For instance, in the middle of the campaign, attorneys allied with ISLA drafted a letter to the city planning commission with appeals to fair opportunity. The draft warned that the Manchester's presence would contribute to the displacement of local residents and seemed commensurate with ISLA's concerns. Yet a campaign staffer revised it to emphasize more strongly a self-identified community's needs; the result sounded more like a letter from a community of identity. Unlike the attorney's first draft, the ISLA staffer's version prioritized community residents ahead of people simply working in the area, and added that the community already suffered comparatively high rates of chronic illness. The ISLA staffer's draft replaced a language of legal incentives with the claim that a severe shortage of low-income housing should compel the developer to change the building plan. Revisions comported more closely with a community of identity demanding justice.

A second illustration comes from the campaign's victory celebration, held at the new health clinic that ISLA had won in a CBA with the developer. Eager to be useful yet wary of posing inauthentically as a longtime community member, I produced a narrative timeline in the nonevaluative prose typical of social science monographs. Staff members borrowed from and revised my text to create educational display panels for the celebration. The revisions communicated in more evaluative, hortatory terms an effort of the community. My text had stated,

> "The Manchester appeared to be another in a line of development projects . . . that would increase rents and force increasing displacement of the surrounding neighborhood's residents, the plurality of whom are working-class people of color. . . . Attorneys with ISLA proposed alternative plans. . . . ISLA activists and residents attended public hearings and spotlighted the accelerated gentrification."

The final, revised text on the display panel presented an empathetic account told from the point of view a distinct community, united in resistance:

> "'The Manchester' appeared to compound the already disturbing level of displacement. . . . The community also feared that the new transit infrastructure . . . was being built not for them but to attract wealthier incoming residents and further advance displacement pressures on low-income residents. . . . Residents responded by organizing meetings, house visits and actions to counter the original plans."

In the final version, "disturbing" trends pit wealthier newcomers against a low-income *community*, not simply a neighborhood population. In my original draft, attorneys proposed an alternative plan, and ISLA activists and residents joined in. The final text highlights the proactive work of *residents* as a community, not attorneys in alliance with them.

Just as the style of a claim needs to be appropriate, the category in which a claim is made needs to be legitimate. Some ways of making claims about the Manchester could have sounded compelling in the abstract but became illegitimate. By following the action, we discover how discursive fields jell over time, as advocates exercise their sense of what is *wrong* to say about a problem.

How Some Categories Evaporate

WHY WASN'T THE APARTMENT COMPLEX A PROBLEM OF COMPASSION?

An entire symbolic category may challenge the style in which advocates prefer to make claims. The observer recognizes these illegitimate claims when interaction immediately around the claim indicates it was a kind of mistake and "should not have happened" in the scene.[28] In this case, the category of compassion became subject to an evaporation process, which narrows or even disappears options for advocates.[29] After its first appearance, the few later instances of compassion appeals suggest that these claims acquired illegitimate status. They are evidence of the kind of boundary drawing that keeps a discursive field marked off.

At the first meeting of ISLA's antidisplacement effort, an introductory speaker broke down crying as she recited to the workshop audience the story of having to move to a neighborhood with more affordable housing. The hurt she emphasized was personal. She had to abandon the neighborhood she knew from childhood—the neighborhood where her parents still lived, and the one that centered her life until now. Housing troubles can elicit compassion. Yet in the ongoing contention over the Manchester development, publicly announced claims for compassion became extremely rare after this kickoff meeting. In private chats before or after meetings, I occasionally heard ISLA staff and members say it was too bad that neighbors had to move away to more affordable neighborhoods. The emerging discursive field, however, was excluding compassion claims from legitimacy in claims-making scenes.

A supplemental review of all claims made by ISLA speakers and their opponents at municipal hearings supports my inference. Only four could be considered appeals to compassion. Three were made at city planning commission hearings, by construction workers advocating in favor of the project on the grounds that they needed work, or that "it will help me and my pals," as one said. The sole compassion claim on the ISLA side came from a parent distressed that her disabled child would lose her current site for pediatric care. Compassion claims nearly evaporated before entering the discursive field of the Manchester. They were interactional mistakes, committed by people (construction laborers and a parent) who had spent too little time to become embedded in the field and its conventional discourse.

Scene style helps explain why compassion claims evaporated. Bids for compassion like that of the teary woman become illegitimate when the style posits members as a resistant, proud community under threat from external forces of domination. It would strain the style's implicit sense of who we are on our map to make claims as if claimants were weakened supplicants seeking compassion rather than empowered resisters demanding justice. Routinely, residents and advocates worded their claims about displacement in terms of pride, not pathos; "proud member of this community" is what ISLA T-shirts and window signs announced, not a plea for help. It would take further research beyond the bounds of this book to be certain that scene styles among developer-allied groups similarly delegitimated compassion discourse, but evidence here is sufficient to demonstrate my argument about the mechanism: styled interaction can make a symbolic category evaporate.[30]

WHY WASN'T THE APARTMENT COMPLEX A PROBLEM OF CAPITALIST PROPERTY RELATIONS?

On one observed occasion, ISLA leaders treated another symbolic category as illegitimate: an appeal to social-structural change that goes beyond fair opportunity in the given property market. The rarity of the category and response to it suggests it may have evaporated between informal conversation or progressive advocates' private thoughts and the realm of claims making. At a general community meeting, participants discussed several new building projects in the neighborhood, including the Manchester. A meeting facilitator said that ISLA wanted to "preserve what we care so much about—our neighborhood, our businesses, our schools and families." One resident said that ISLA advocates ought to stop local property owners from selling to outside developers, and another proposed enlisting the neighborhood's city council person to regulate local property sales. The facilitator responded to the first resident, saying "sometimes property owners get great offers that they can't turn down." An ISLA advocate replied to the second resident by criticizing the council member's voting record and then changed the subject. The facilitator then made a pitch to "focus on the connections that we share as a community." Interaction at this meeting signaled, in short, that a capitalist property market was to be assumed and a critique of property rights was out of bounds.

A community of identity coordinates itself to defend the community against threats and build internal solidarity. Fairness for the community is different from social-structural change that would not *defend* the community so much as transform it fundamentally. Given a different kind of collective self-understanding—a different scene style—participants might assume what they are doing together is social critique in the interests of thoroughgoing social change. That is the "social critic" style—with its own characteristic map and bonds—familiar from some social movement efforts, but different from the more limited, if no less dedicated, defense of a community's cultural and geographic space.[31] While I occasionally heard scrappy, informal banter among ISLA leaders about greedy property-owning elites in Los Angeles, ISLA's public claims making about the Manchester did not include a critique of capitalist property relations.

The implicit convention against criticizing the system of property relations in ISLA meeting scenes is especially interesting given the reading material on offer in the ISLA staff office. I saw pamphlets from a network proclaiming a "right to the city," for example, that strongly implied urban property development should privilege its use value for current residents over its exchange value for investors. While fine on paper, such talk apparently did not seem appropriate in ordinary general meetings or strategy sessions with residents. In these forums, people could say big property owners were an intrusive "they" that threatened the community, yet that was different from saying property owners were incumbents of systematically exploitative property relations.

How a Legitimate Category Becomes Subordinate

Advocates can subordinate one category to another depending on how scene style induces them to map potential arguments. A category that claimants strongly associate with "people not like us" on their social map may be devalued as an appeal, and therefore less salient in claims. On the map of a community of identity, the community opposes outsiders who threaten it rather than identifying in solidarity with it. This helps us interpret the varying frequency of quality-of-life and fair opportunity claims.

Ethnographic evidence suggests that ISLA advocates consistently held quality-of-life arguments in lower repute, such that they needed to nest them inside primary claims about fair opportunity and rarely made them independently. Claimants take each other and themselves as objects with reputations; claimants may avoid categories that would easily associate themselves with the "wrong" side. ISLA advocates identified quality-of-life arguments with the negative side: the property developers and city planners on the other side of the community of identity's stiff boundary between "groups like us" and invasive outsiders. Here are just two brief examples.

At the strategy meeting that opened chapter 4, facilitator Ethan and other participants had positioned the topic of urban design as a distracting issue not worth much time. It turned out the planning department envisioned LA neighborhoods in light of new urbanist planning theory. Facilitator Ethan had characterized the "new urbanism" as planning that disregards the people who can't afford to live in pretty neighborhoods. He had devalued the quality-of-life goals of new urbanist planning, saying it was no "mystery" that ISLA participants shared them; they, too, wanted walkable neighborhoods with amenities nearby, but the real question was who could afford that. For groups like ours, Ethan said, new urbanist planning is something that outsiders, "they," propound that misses the point of "our" particular question about fair opportunity. Claims about what a city should be like, its quality-of-life features, should be obvious and not worth dwelling on.

A skeptic might say it is obvious that the aesthetic features or convenience of a locale do not matter much to people who desperately need affordable housing and fear being displaced. But both qualities were central when the same ISLA advocates put on the Somos la Comunidad event. ISLA members had complained about cracked, buckled sidewalks that could topple baby strollers and a surfeit of liquor stores. Speakers articulated these particular issues, plausibly quality-of-life concerns, as ones of fairness and opportunity. One woman told city planning staff and a city council member in attendance that "we" do not have the power or wealth of "you" city leaders sitting in front of us, and we do not want our kids growing up in an environment that denies them "opportunities for a decent life"; she turned potentially quality-of-life concerns into a distributional issue of opportunity.

Claims about safety or environmental sustainability elicited ISLA advocates' skepticism *when speakers justified them on quality-of-life grounds.* Just as ISLA staff's focus on the Manchester was intensifying, several longtime ISLA members and staff organizer Hortencia attended a forum put on to solicit people's comments on redevelopment plans for Balboa Boulevard, just a block from the Manchester. Urban redesign experts introduced the forum, saying the city could reduce car dependence on the massive boulevard, make it safer, and improve bicycling and transit options for Angelenos in general. The next speaker described how she enjoyed Sunday mornings by biking a route that ended with brunch at a hotel on the boulevard. These opening comments primed participants to take features of the boulevard's redevelopment as quality-of-life, not distributional, fairness issues. Participants then divided into discussion groups, seated at tables with maps of the boulevard and emoticon thumbtacks, to identify what they liked (smiley face) and did not like (sad face) on the map. Seated together at a table, Hortencia and ISLA members bestowed smiley thumbtacks only on a shopping arcade built by a nonprofit ally of ISLA as well as a school with a largely low-income minority student body. These were outposts of the community. When it was time for sharing from the tables, Hortencia said that her table's map sported mostly sad faces.

"Most of us are community residents. We ask who will benefit from this [planned] redevelopment. We need housing for people to enjoy living on the boulevard."

She said the community also wanted safer crosswalks, accessibility, "more clean streets, trees, all the things that you [want too]," but that it also was important for these plans to "integrate the needs of . . . so many long-term communities."

Design experts had expected the attendees to care about quality-of-life concerns—"enjoying" the boulevard. Yet Hortencia implied that even environmentally conscious redevelopment, if treated as a quality-of-life good, would only benefit others. At most, quality-of-life goods were obvious and unremarkable: "we want all the things you want," just as ISLA staffer Ethan had implied above. These two illustrations, from the Manchester campaign's intensive phase and twenty-two months before, strongly suggest that ISLA advocates consistently subordinated quality of life to fair opportunity when they spoke to a present or imagined audience of opposing actors on their map.

The tally of fair opportunity and quality-of-life claims at city planning commission hearings makes sense in this light. It strengthens the argument that scene style can affect the salience of different kinds of claims in a discursive field over time. Considerably more of ISLA or ISLA-allied claims made fair opportunity, not quality of life, into a dominant or independent theme. Furthermore, while ISLA advocates and allies made more claims over all at city planning commission hearings than did property developer spokespersons and allies, almost three-fourths (eighteen out of twenty-five) of the dominant or independent quality-of-life claims made by anyone *were made on behalf of the Manchester developer*. The tally here suggests that hearing quality-of-life claims emerge disproportionately from outsider opponents on their map could regenerate ISLA advocates' tendency to associate quality-of-life concerns with morally and politically suspect actors outside the community. ISLA advocates' future claims making, in response to what they still hear from the other side, may continue subordinating appeals to quality of life. Parallel field dynamics were shaping what HJ coalition allies and their opponents could say about a MIHO as a community of interest.

Claims about the Problem of Unaffordable Housing

Opportunity and Quality of Life in a Different Context

The master symbolic categories of argument in the Manchester campaign were dominant in HJ's MIHO campaign as well for what both HJ allies and opponents could claim publicly. For HJ, the essence of fair distribution appeals was that housing availability was deteriorating with the city's increasing rates of luxury housing development.[32] HJ advocates touted their solution in flyers, position statements, newsletters, and letters to city hall—a comprehensive strategy to "give people from all walks of life a place to live" and provide housing choices within the reach of "people currently priced out." One pagers summarizing campaign arguments stated that 90 percent of the new units built in the previous year were affordable only to those earning over $135,000. Business sector opponents overwhelmingly expressed fair distribution claims, contending that a mandate should not place the responsibility for affordable housing disproportionately on one sector. They maintained that limits on luxury housing production and failure to set aside funds to incentivize affordable housing production would unfairly burden the real estate and building industries. Such limits, they continued, would hamper the builders who play such a crucial role in providing housing opportunities.

Quality-of-life appeals by HJ advocates described socially and physically unhealthy living conditions.[33] Participants argued that if people are forced to the outlying suburbs in search of affordable homes, their lives become saddled with unbearably long commutes. Other lifestyle consequences follow, as people are unable to "participate in their communities" and spend less time with their families. "Many [workers] are living and raising children in overcrowded apartments that are cockroach infested and located in unsafe parts of town, far from where they work," one union leader wrote in a letter of support.

Most of these quality-of-life assertions were nested inside the primary appeal to the fair distribution of opportunity and thus less salient. In one-minute public comments, most HJ speakers made almost exclusively fair distribution claims. For instance, a labor leader emphasized that a lack of affordable opportunities forced construction workers to live outside Los Angeles, adding briefly the less salient quality-of-life claim, "and of course this is a contribution to traffic, pollution, and so many other issues." Only one speaker, a painter's union representative, gave a lengthy, independent quality-of-life appeal, describing overcrowding when "you have two or three women fighting over who's cooking . . . [and] kids in front of a television trying to do homework." He ended with an appeal to fair opportunity in the political process, stating that now that the city was finally addressing schooling and unemployment problems, it needed to make housing right too.

How Style Shapes Claims Making: Opportunity for an Indefinitely Expanding Community of Interest

The HJ coalition acted like a community of interest in most of the decision-making and public scenes connected with the MIHO campaign. In this case, the fair distribution of opportunities became fairness for an indefinitely expanding constituency of Angelenos "who work in Los Angeles and should be able to afford living there," as campaign flyers put it, rather than justice for a distinct, socially subjugated community. Letters of support each added another constituency to a diverse community of interest. The letters from African American civic and Latinx leaders both presented the signatories as dedicated to "making the city one of opportunity for all." Each connected a distinct group to a generalizable interest in affordable housing: the African American leaders talked about the history of redlining in African American neighborhoods, and the Latinx leaders described rates of overcrowding in Latinx households and the lack of housing affordability for Latinx renters. Both letters used signatories' racial or ethnic identification to articulate group-specific reasons for joining diverse others who shared the same interest in a specific *issue*.

In testimonies at city council, HJ speakers consistently presented their experiences as reasons for arriving at the shared interest. In a rare exception, one coalition representative promoted a "right of return" for people displaced by demolitions and conversions, implying something like a long-term community of identity. Otherwise, strings of two-minute statements before the council represented middle-class professionals who commuted long distances and low-income workers whose residences were at risk of demolition for condominiums. All positioned their particular experiences as *reasons for converging on the shared interest.* This was not the most obvious or natural way to promote affordable housing. Speakers who feared property demolition might have presented themselves as a group threatened by encroaching powers as opposed to a group advancing a citywide housing platform for everyone.

As in the Manchester campaign, ethnographic evidence suggests that advocates associated quality-of-life concerns with the "wrong" side. The category was less salient in their own claims. Chapter 3 showed that at coordinating committee meetings, advocates both loathed and feared neighborhood councils at least as much as big commercial real estate developers. They would recite in satirical singsong the claim by neighborhood council stalwarts that affordable housing developments diminish "the character of the neighborhood." They talked warily and ironically about these councils' pushback, as when Carol said that people would tell her she had been treated fairly well at a neighborhood council if no one had spat on her. It was as if HJ coordinating committee members were stung more strongly by rebuke from neighborhood councils than opposition from big property developers because their expectations for support from ostensibly grassroots, neighborhood assemblies were higher.

As with the Manchester case, a tally of fair opportunity and quality-of-life claims at city planning commission hearings makes sense in light of this aspect of scene style. HJ advocates and allies made more claims in all that their opposition did, but of all independent (not subordinated) quality-of-life claims made, twenty out of twenty-four were made either by neighborhood council representatives (eighteen) or individuals identifying with a locale (two). Affordable housing of course *can* be a quality-of-life matter. Outside this discursive field—after HJ's bid for a MIHO failed—an HJ leader made an elaborate pitch in quality-of-life terms for affordable housing development using dozens of PowerPoint slides.

Could It Be a Problem of Social Interdependence?: A Niche Appeal with Limited Salience

Just as with the Manchester campaign, a discursive field around HJ's MIHO campaign maintained some leeway for rhetorical variety. Following the fortunes of one particular rhetorical appeal teaches more about how a community of interest uses its discursive options. Rhetoric highlighting social ties and interdependence appeared early in the campaign. It is the closest LA housing advocates came to making housing issues into a social solidarity problem the way French homelessness advocates did. This appeal emerged in the comments of one of HJ's most prominent allies but never became one of the master categories. An internal document from over a year before HJ's campaign launch featured this category amid other ideas on a list of potential campaign messages. The list included the statement, "The housing crisis is tearing up the social, economic and civic fabric of Los Angeles." The first kickoff rally speaker, a Protestant pastor, said the same thing: as housing becomes increasingly less affordable, "the very structures of our society . . . are being threatened."

The same appeal emerged in only a handful of instances over the campaign's eighteen months, but each time articulated by speakers that coalition leaders respected. At a housing summit with the mayor, after appealing to both opportunity and quality-of-life concerns, a labor leader declared that the city owed decent affordable homes to the health care workers and janitors who we depend on to take care of as well as clean up after us. A support letter from rabbis used Jewish legal tradition to argue that landlords are obligated not to cause their tenants' homelessness and "a functional society" ensures everyone has decent housing. The category of social interdependence remained marginal, limited mainly to communications from the pastor mentioned above, the labor leader, and the rabbis' letter.

In a community of interest, the social interdependence category was acceptable in a limited way. It could help portray diversity in HJ's campaign without becoming a main theme. After all, an appeal to social interdependence would comport awkwardly with a style that bids participants to see themselves as members of *distinct* groups that converge. An appeal to social solidarity—the social fabric—in contrast, invites participants to identify with the social whole, diminishing their distinctiveness as African American, Latinx, or Jewish interest groups converging on a shared interest. Yet this category must have had some special appeal, because staff made a point of updating members about whether or not they had secured endorsements from "labor" and "Jewish groups," and ran the letters through multiple drafts. It makes sense if we think about what social interdependence rhetoric might signal about the speaker in the larger field, instead of focusing on the rhetoric itself. Publicizing distinctive, subcultural rhetoric from the tradition that honors the dignity of labor or the legal tradition of Judaism could signal to a wider public the *diversity* of the HJ coalition. A wider public hears that this community of interest is broad based. The logic would be, "Different kinds of groups see the value of our platform; your group can too!"

The contrast with ISLA's campaign bolsters my point. When ISLA advocates acted as a community of identity, they did *not* solicit claims that could suggest internal cultural diversity. Quite to the contrary, good speakers might be different kinds of people—health care providers, community organizers, or parents—but *all* spoke on behalf of the same social object—the community. The logic was different: "The community demands justice and respect; we must give the community what it deserves."

How Scene Style Can Induce Internal Boundaries in the Field and Segregate Issues

Even when HJ coalition members constructed their claims from a legitimate symbolic category, those claims still might challenge the scene style in play. They might be *inappropriate* in the scene at hand.

My chats with HJ staffer Francis revealed that while he was intensely committed to housing opportunity and HJ's success, privately he felt especially warm to tenant groups like onetime coalition members SED or LAPO. In the scenes I saw, participants in these two organizations acted as a community of identity, not interest. What Francis said about housing politics at city council sounded more like what participants in a community of identity would say too:

> Francis: "It's audacious, what they're trying to do with rent control—to basically take away [renters' protections]." He repeated, like someone observing a wonder of nature, that it's a huge move and also "very insulting." I was surprised he put it in such personal terms and wasn't sure what to say.
>
> Paul: "Yeah, insulting for renters or people who care about tenants."
>
> Francis said it was an insult to the good people who rent.

Francis articulated fairness for renters not so much as an *issue* in which Francis had an interest but instead as a matter of people with whom he *identified*. In coordinating committee scenes, however, I never heard Francis talking about housing opportunity in this way. He spoke the way most others did, about how best to make affordable housing mandates into a winnable issue at city hall, not how to defend tenants' dignity.

Conversation over dinner nine months later only reinforced the hunch. Characterizing the tenant groups as "my peers," Francis said he agreed with their approach and that HJ was taking a "politically safer" approach that collided with what he saw as "my role in this movement" over the longer haul. All the same, he observed that as a coordinating committee leader, he needed to finesse the difference between tenant groups' perspectives and those of other HJ leaders. HJ coalition leaders did occasionally orchestrate scenes for a community of identity, such as in the tenant workshops discussed in chapter 5. In the coordinating committee scene, however, the "we" was no longer "the community" but rather the larger imagined constituency for a MIHO.

Claims from a community of identity, welcomed at tenant workshops, got censured or even silenced. After HJ's ill-fated unity meeting, for instance, the representative from a nonprofit housing developer had argued with Terry, the homelessness advocate, over how to present the coalition's "face" to the wider public. Terry had maintained that HJ's campaign should speak stridently on behalf of housing for poor and homeless people. The developer affirmed the committee's decision to "to put a poor person's face, a working-class person's face, and a middle-class person's face on it." The committee's majority, in other words, wanted the campaign to represent the potentially broad appeal of HJ members' shared interest. Terry shot back in the terms of a community of identity: "You don't want to hear what *the community* is saying?" (emphasis added). Then a coalition leader curtly dismissed Terry's line of reasoning. Even when invoking the category of fair opportunity, claims from a community of identity could be inappropriate when launched outside the appropriate scenes for them.

Internal boundaries between scenes ended up segregating issues beyond the MIHO, which some committee representatives cared about, making some claims inappropriate. When LAPO advocate Deborah insisted at one meeting that the coalition speak out against the demolition of a downtown apartment building where low-income people (the community) lived, staff person Carol insisted that HJ would not take a public stance on the issue. It was inappropriately beyond the focus of obligation for HJ coalition members—the MIHO. The tenant leaders persisted. Carol responded, "OK, we should keep studying it," and then changed the subject. Similarly, coalition leaders decided HJ should not go on record endorsing a protest over policing tactics, even though policing deeply concerned LAPO, the coalition's leading tenant organization. Policing fell outside the agreed-on interest of the coalition. A staff person said that HJ leaders "encouraged members to go as individuals," not as HJ representatives. Acting as a community of interest, the coalition obligated members' reputations on one issue only.

———

Advocates launch claims about problems in a symbolic and social context that informs what they can say, to whom, and where. They word their claims in relation to real and imagined participants or audiences in distinct scenes. Conceiving of them as culturally cultivated, socially embedded claims makers rather than culture-wielding entrepreneurs can solve some puzzles. We can understand why left-progressive advocates like the ISLA leaders would be lukewarm at best about claims that emphasize environmental sustainability—which usually are considered "progressive" too. We can see why social advocates like HJ coalition leader Francis would not necessarily consider it a victory when municipal planners used the same arguments HJ used to promote affordable housing. Next, we see why LA housing advocates in this study did not often talk about homelessness as a "housing" problem.

8

How Homelessness Does Not
Become a Housing Problem

Separate Problems?

One way to find out how a social problem gets constructed is to focus on the rhetoric and imagery of a nationally publicized *issue*.[1] That approach has the virtue of scale: it aims to grasp a nationwide debate, not just the debate that concerns one neighborhood invaded by a stucco giant. This study's smaller-scale, comparative approach ultimately helps us understand what it took for housing advocates to consider a problem to be a *housing* issue to begin with. This chapter explores how, if at all, housing and homelessness advocates made claims about both homelessness and housing problems together. After all, isn't homelessness really a housing problem?

In 2010, as I was making my rounds in the field, the presidentially appointed United States Interagency Council on Homelessness (USICH) implied as much. It issued a remarkable plan for ending homelessness and preventing it in the future, marking the federal government's final break with the emergency service approach to homelessness conjured in the 1980s. The USICH's (2015, 14) plan embraced a simple insight: "Homelessness is a housing crisis and can be addressed through the provision of safe and affordable housing."[2] One of the strategic plan's four big objectives was to "provide affordable housing to people experiencing or most at risk of homelessness." The document predicated this goal on the observation that "for most people, the threat of homelessness stems from the gap between their current income and the cost of housing" (38). Just as striking, the plan's first big objective called for increasing collaboration between governmental agencies and "people with first-hand experience of homelessness, businesses, nonprofits, faith-based organizations, foundations, and volunteers" (33). This was a call for *civic* and not only governmental action that connects homelessness to affordable housing. This chapter looks at the cultural conditions that shrank opportunities for civic actors to expound on that connection out loud.

A lot of people in the United States may be readier to make the connection between homelessness and housing than we would think. On the one hand, the route of HomeWalk, an annual five-kilometer walkathon fundraiser for homeless services, was watched over by three-story pylons bearing this statement: "The central antidote to homelessness is not a police sweep or a shelter bed, it's housing." HomeWalk organizers from the United Way charity must have assumed that this was either new information, or a salutary reminder for walkers or the news media covering the walk. Yet there is evidence that at least urban dwellers see a collection of factors behind homelessness and they name social-structural opportunity a cause more frequently than homeless individuals' personal characteristics. Studies suggest that people's private attitudes in the United States toward homelessness are multifaceted and conflicted.[3]

All the more reason to move beyond a focus on private attitudes, and ask whether or not people's civic efforts can connect the reality of homelessness with an argument for affordable housing. Could Angeleno social advocates do what USICH's new report called for? Could advocates make claims about homelessness and housing *together*, routinely, in public places?

Many of the advocates did make fleeting claims about homelessness or homeless people. Yet they did not talk much about homelessness as a *housing* problem, even though it may seem like the most urgent one. Here is where investigating discursive fields and style can help. I will compare ISLA and HJ coalition members' claims about homelessness with those of professional-led volunteer efforts organized to address homelessness as a problem in itself. Connecting homelessness closely and forthrightly to housing would take cultural work that most housing advocates and homeless service personnel in this study did not do. It is likely that I did not find all the scenes in Los Angeles where advocates or service workers *may* have been linking the two, at least in passing. The range of scenes I studied nevertheless suggest that in Los Angeles, cultural conditions conspired to make homelessness a marginal topic across different quarters of the housing advocacy world. And homeless service workers talked little, if at all, about affordable housing as a public issue. Following the claims-making action leads to *part* of the reason that homelessness remained relatively separated from housing as a problem to housing advocates during this study.[4] To be clear, the point is *not* to ask why self-identified housing advocates did not mount campaigns specifically about homelessness or work in homelessness advocacy organizations. The question is why did housing advocates only rarely and briefly treat homelessness as a housing problem in their deliberations, strategy sessions, or big public events. The end of this short chapter suggests additional tools of cultural analysis that can illuminate the disconnect. These in turn enrich our understanding of how a discursive field works.

From the many scenes followed in this study, I found exactly one in which participants talked at length about the plight of homeless people *and* advocated that people in general treat homelessness as a *housing* problem. We go there first.

How Cultural Context Separates Homelessness and Housing

When Connecting Homelessness to Housing Takes Awkward, Boundary-Straddling Work

Caring Embrace of the Homeless and Poor (CE) worked to convince a wider public that affordable housing is the answer to homelessness.[5] It was a loose-knit group of religious congregational leaders and housing and homelessness advocates. Between five and twelve core members gathered monthly for meandering meetings facilitated generously by Theresa, social outreach coordinator at a liberal Protestant church near the college whose expansion plans concerned the ISLA coalition. The regular participants came from theologically liberal and conservative Protestant Christian congregations, joined occasionally by service and advocacy organization leaders, and three times by a synagogue social outreach group member. Theresa routinely introduced CE's monthly meetings with this story: congregational leaders had initiated CE when they noticed more apparently homeless people in their South LA neighborhood, and then began meeting monthly to consider responses to homelessness that were caring rather than stigmatizing for homeless people.

CE's main project during this study was a public education campaign urging local religious congregations to think about homelessness as a massive, urgent housing problem for Los Angeles. Called the Nails Project, the consciousness-raising campaign urged local religious congregations to collect a total of seventy-four thousand nails to symbolize each person homeless on an average night in the city at that time. CE planned to publicize the collection and then donate the nails to Habitat for Humanity, a large nonprofit organization that builds houses for low-income families. In addition, CE designed an educational presentation for congregations that was intended to dispel what Theresa and an HJ advocate advising her considered widespread myths about homeless people—that they are homeless *because* they are addicted to drugs or won't look for decent-paying jobs, for example. The point was to advocate affordable housing as the real solution to homelessness and get members of religious congregations to agree. Remarkably, "homeless people" and "affordable housing" cohabited these presentations.

Theresa was good at multiple dramatis personae. She was a core participant in ISLA during its ongoing antidisplacement campaign and counted herself a supporter of the HJ coalition too. She invited Francis of HJ to CE's monthly meetings, and sought his expertise on the facts of housing and homelessness. At ISLA meetings, Theresa sounded just like other members. She denounced the unfairness of displacement as well as the role of real estate developers and the college in gentrifying surrounding neighborhoods, and asserted the need for more housing opportunities as well as the value and valor of standing with the community.

Participating at a CE meeting was like being in two movies running concurrently—one about social activists and another about charitable volunteers. Theresa herself could sound as if she were playing two roles simultaneously, each character undercutting the other. During CE meetings and in flyers written for church audiences, Theresa affirmed repeatedly that "the solution to homelessness is affordable housing." During those same meetings, Theresa and others also said, repeatedly, that "if every church, mosque, and synagogue takes a homeless family," homelessness would disappear in Los Angeles. The attentive attendee at CE meetings would come away with an odd double message about what it would take to end homelessness: The real solution to homelessness is to institute more housing opportunity, and the real solution also is voluntary caring for homeless families. Theresa had been an activist a long time. It is unlikely she was just confused.

It makes more sense to say Theresa was speaking in (at least) two colliding discursive fields. Among affordable housing advocates, homeless people were part of the larger constituency for housing mandates, not a strongly distinct category. Among religious congregations, homeless people were a distinct object of compassion discourse. Neither Theresa nor the other CE participants tried reconciling the two discourses. Evidence suggests that few congregations would be ready to go even as far as CE had in making homelessness a housing problem. Though Theresa was unusually well connected in both church and advocacy circles, CE's educational presentation on homelessness received only a handful of invitations from congregations, and the nails collection lagged many months behind group goals.[6]

CE's experiences suggest the power of a discursive field. Claims makers could promote more broadly distributed housing opportunities, treating housing primarily as a fairness problem, as both HJ and ISLA did. Or they could promote charity and caring for homeless individuals, treating homelessness as a compassion problem. Outside CE, only a special subset of housing advocates would publicize and emphasize at length that *homeless people need more housing opportunities* or *homelessness is a fairness problem.* Let's go back and see what happens when a community of either interest or identity takes on the issue of homeless people inside the field of debate about affordable housing mandates in Los Angeles.

When an Interest in Housing Subsumes Homelessness

"Don't forget the homeless!" Terry had warned, interrupting another committee member at HJ's ill-fated unity meeting. Taken aback, the committee member said he was focusing on the presence of laborers and then added that a homeless worker had addressed the convocation too. Terry, a vocal advocate for homeless people, had questioned whether or not HJ coalition leaders' strategy adequately represented low-income people, the community. When several advocates including Terry wanted HJ to speak out in opposition to the mayor's plan to redevelop two SRO hotel buildings downtown, Carol answered that in the mayor's office, "there is concern for not wanting to make anyone homeless," and the office would try to offer alternative housing and "minimize displacement." A reasonable listener could infer that at least a few tenants might be left homeless or shunted from one shelter to another for a short time when their formerly low-cost apartments got redeveloped. A housing advocate might wonder just what Terry and other critics at the meeting wondered: Why would housing advocates, of all people, not want to speak out against a redevelopment project that could leave some people homeless?

HJ passed up a chance to address this potential increase in homelessness as a troubling issue for housing advocates. When a couple of HJ members pressed the point, Carol narrated the situation as a matter of conserving the focus, time, and energy for the shared interest that gave HJ its reason for being. She said, "We have *just* enough energy" for the affordable housing platform amid a lot of other interests that some, if not all, members might share as well. Affordable housing was the problem, and HJ's platform, including the proposed MIHO, was the interest. HJ leaders could rightly expect members to promote the shared interest, but could not rightly prevail on them to do more than that.

Communities of interest aim to generalize an interest in an issue to an indefinitely expanding audience of potential supporters rather than affirm many issues that all concern one self-identified community. Homeless people could benefit from an MIHO in the same way that other lower-income constituencies would benefit. For the community of interest, there was no contradiction between believing that the solution to homelessness is housing, and paying relatively little direct attention to homelessness or homeless people as aspects of a housing problem. As the logic goes, homeless people as a group need not elicit more specifically directed attention than the African Americans, Latinx people, or Jews, whose leaders had endorsed a MIHO. All endorsed the general interest; homeless people would make the convergence simply that much larger. If homelessness were going to enter the discursive field of the debate over affordable housing, HJ's community of interest offered a route that subsumed homelessness under "people who need affordable housing."[7] But there was at least one other way that the seventy-four thousand homeless Angelenos might enter the discursive field around the proposed housing mandate.

Making Homeless People into a Community

By chance, Terry's homeless advocacy organization, SHAPLA, became part of the study several months before research with the HJ coalition began. A SHAPLA staffer kindly welcomed me to the organization's "housing committee." I would see him again in HJ's staff office four months later and then much later at LAPO; it was Francis. I saw for myself that SHAPLA's housing committee worked as a community of identity. Terry's interaction with HJ's coordinating committee fit the same scene style, with its sharp boundaries between an authentic, resistant "we" and oppressive "they," and a sense of solidarity with the community across different issues.

SHAPLA's community was homeless people. I wondered why, on the one hand, Francis told the committee at my first meeting that we should "be more action oriented," yet he also let one participant, Sheila, self-described as formerly homeless, go off on long, angry rants at meetings. To judge from people's facial expressions, her diatribes tugged at everyone's patience. Sheila had lived with her children for months inside her old Chevy, which she let us know multiple times, was cleaner inside than any of those homeless shelters. She said shelters gave their guests bus tokens so they would take a ride to somewhere else. At one shelter, she explained, they offered guests a single paper towel to dry off after a shower when people really needed two. There was plenty to be outraged about. Then I realized after the second meeting—especially after Francis exclaimed, "Democracy! I love it!"—that Sheila represented what another SHAPLA participant enthused about at a city hall lawn encampment: the "voice of the (homeless) people." She lent authenticity.

In hindsight, it was easy to predict that the routine at SHAPLA's housing committee would not effectively overcome the community of identity's dilemma of being authentically *from* or *for* the community. Fully legitimate spokespersons ideally would be authentic—that is, homeless. That was good reason to heed recently homeless Sheila, but she was unlikely to be abided for long outside a small enclave of advocates in solidarity with homeless people.[8] One study cited above suggests at least indirectly that a designated, homeless spokesperson may induce less empathetic reception by a general audience than someone who comes off as a respectable professional. [9] That means public communication connecting homelessness with affordable housing would circulate further and faster by messengers speaking effectively *for* homelessness people even if less authentically *from* the community.

Like the leading participants in ISLA, Francis preferred spokespeople *from* the community. He ventured to me over coffee one day that "before we say what the community needs, we should ask the community." We should not just ask the "ten people around this table," as Francis put the same thought at a meeting. If the community of identity is homeless people, it would be especially challenging to find spokespeople either for or from, though. The communities of identity that ISLA and LAPO members constructed were at least fuzzily geographic, and at least implicitly, ethnically or racially distinct, and some members were extremely longtime residents. A homeless community of identity would be harder to speak for in a way that conveyed authenticity when the community itself was transient, and thus not so easily characterized by predominant ethnic or linguistic characteristics that others in solidarity might adopt. Some members of the homeless community might even cease to carry the defining identity and no longer honor it, as Sheila still did, if they become housed. For authenticity from such a diffuse constituency, one would have to wait for self-identified homeless people to show up and then appreciate the free expression of a voice from the community.

With greater geographic and implicitly racial specificity, LAPO cultivated leaders who could speak effectively for a community that included homeless people without marking them very distinctly. LAPO general meetings did authenticate homeless voices as fully a part of LAPO's "downtown community," yet LAPO also defined that community to include participants who lived in old, residential hotels as well as on the streets and in shelters, so the specificity of homeless people was not highlighted. Leaders and other participants spoke of LAPO's community as "low-income people who lived downtown," whether housed, sheltered, or unhoused. At meetings, leaders made a point of *not* drawing distinctions that would divide members of the community— homeless or housed, for example. All deserved respect as members of the community and needed to support each other, as a leading facilitator would say. Those were the people who could vote on proposals at LAPO meetings. The SHAPLA housing committee's "homeless community" was hard to give social locators. During my study, LAPO leaders made relatively few claims about homeless people as a distinct category.

The HJ coalition, SHAPLA, and LAPO all argued consistently for a fair distribution of housing opportunity. For HJ advocates, extremely low-income homeless or housed people, along with blue-collar workers, teachers, librarians, and anyone else whose household brought in less than $135,000 a year, would benefit from HJ proposals for mandates to increase affordable housing opportunities. As SHAPLA and LAPO advocates put it, in turn, the homeless and downtown communities needed housing, period. Everyone should have a right to housing—one way of assuring a fair distribution of housing opportunities. But given the way style worked in the discursive field around the MIHO proposal, leading advocates of these organizations made few claims that could encourage much broader publics to both recognize homelessness as a distinctive problem *and* connect it directly to the problem of affordable housing. The seventy-four thousand homeless people sank into a larger interest constituency, all of whom would benefit from a MIHO, or else became part of a culturally marginal or highly specific community whose supporters, like those of any community of identity, needed to identify closely with them in order to be taken as allies. Who, then, would help a broader public connect homelessness and housing together? The CE group made limited headway with its "split personality" strategy. What about people who focus exclusively on homelessness by serving homeless people?

Homelessness as a Separate Problem

Discourses of Compassion and Awareness

The category of compassion quickly evaporated from ISLA advocates' arguments after their antidisplacement campaign's kickoff meeting. It did not emerge at all in public claims about the MIHO campaign during this study. Yet compassion along with the theme of awareness were prominent, if not exclusive, appeals in claims about homelessness inside a large fundraising effort.

At the United Way's second annual HomeWalk fundraiser in 2008, walkers all received a nameplate to wear. The back side of the plate carried a story about a homeless person helped by one of the organizations cosponsoring the five-kilometer walk. Like the previous year's walk, this one followed a loop that began and ended in a field with booths set up by homeless service provider organizations—nonprofits and several governmental agencies. Each booth had on hand a plastic-encased sheet with a story like the one on walkers' nameplates about someone homeless the organization had helped. As the HomeWalk event presented it, homelessness was about individuals with stories, individuals who needed help, individuals we walkers might momentarily become aware of, feel for, and identify with. This year's featured speaker, *Los Angeles Times* columnist Steve Lopez, talked about the homeless musician Nathaniel Ayers. As moviegoers might recall, Lopez had met Ayers playing violin in an underpass downtown, and became friends with and supported

Ayers in finding a place to live.[10] Portrayed in the movie as grudgingly attentive and annoyed with his inconvenient new friendship with Ayers, Lopez ultimately manifests compassion in the modern US sense of the term.[11] At the previous year's HomeWalk, featured speaker Mayor Antonio Ramón Villaraigosa told participants that "today we walk, but this walk is about walking and demonstrating our compassion, our commitment that in this city of the angels, we care. . . . We're going to fix this problem of homelessness and poverty." At both HomeWalk events, prominent speakers claimed homelessness as a matter of compassion for individuals.

I walked and chatted with walkers in teams of youth group members, religious congregants, corporate employees, and surprising to me at first— nonprofit service providers. I saw no walkers representing either the HJ or ISLA coalitions—except Holly, the new interim director of SHAPLA. When Holly or Terry were promoting affordable housing, they advocated stridently and contentiously for housing opportunities for homeless people. But no one at the walk was talking that way. What was Holly even doing here? Why were homeless service professionals walking? Weren't they quite "aware" already?

The walkers and booth staff I chatted with along with the public education pylons lining the walk all helped me figure it out. *Housing* was not an "awareness" problem, but homelessness was that as well as a compassion problem. The walkers, including the homelessness professionals, had signed up to be human signposts. I never heard anyone saying during the affordable housing campaign that Angelenos or even city officials needed to become more "aware" of housing inequities, but I heard repeatedly at the walkathon that homelessness called for awareness. Theresa and participants in CE used the same rhetoric to promote the Nails Project: the public finally would "see" Los Angeles' massive homeless problem in the form of seventy-four thousand small, metal representatives. That is why Holly from SHAPLA was there—not because she necessarily thought a fundraising march could make much difference for the homeless community her organization wanted to represent. It was rather that she, like the representatives from homelessness nonprofit groups at the walk, was publicizing the issue of homelessness itself. People I met during the walk and at a variety of information booths said the same thing:

> A single walker from a small nonprofit called Housingworks carried a hand-painted sign that said "homeless people needed houses." I sidled up alongside him as we walked Draper Boulevard:
>
> Paul: "So if enough people march, do you think it'll change policy in LA?"
>
> Housingworks guy: "I hope—well, raise awareness. There are a lot of homeless people!"

I noticed a large team of walkers, all wearing aqua-colored T-shirts that said "Kyle and team, established 1986." It turned out to be a group of family and friends of a young man who had died of heart failure. I wondered why they chose the march for a collective walking memorial.

Paul: "Do you all follow homeless issues in Los Angeles?"

Walker: "No. His [Kyle's] mother was the most involved in this stuff."

I stopped to read the one-page testimony at the booth sponsored by a large homeless shelter downtown. A twenty-something woman staffing the booth smiled and offered casually, "Sign up with us. We're a really cool organization." I chatted with her partner.

Paul: "What do you think is the best thing about these events?"

Booth partner: "It brings attention."

Within this momentary, annually assembled public of several thousand volunteer walkers, several messages at the HomeWalk events did connect homelessness with the need for affordable housing. The connection was made *silently*, on both a walker's homemade sign and one of the educational pylons set up alongside the walking route. Included in a short laundry list of "things you can do" about homelessness was "promote the building of permanent, supportive and affordable housing in your neighborhood." Featured speakers did not *voice* that claim, however, and did not say that we as Angelenos or any other constituency should work *together* to solve the problem of homelessness.[12] HomeWalk was not set up to encourage participants to *say*, own, or work collectively with the idea that homelessness and affordable housing were connected, the way Theresa's CE group was—much as Theresa's statements about congregations adopting homeless people could undercut that claim. Like many other onetime or short-term volunteer events, HomeWalk was organized to carry out a task—fundraising—and call attention to an issue (homelessness) without cultivating further collective effort. It was up to individual volunteers which message to take away, if any, about things they could do to end homelessness.

Plug-in Volunteer Responses to Homelessness: Fundraisers and Underwear, with Little Claims Making

For walkers, HomeWalk's five-kilometer fundraising jaunt ran on a distinct scene style in which far more people participate than either the community of interest or identity.[13] This is *plug-in volunteering*. For many people in the United States, civic action *is* "volunteering," and volunteering means the short-term, task-oriented, can-do kind that researchers call plug-in.[14] Plug-in volunteers sign up for volunteer time slots, show up on time, and carry out tasks under instruction from volunteer coordinators who may be nonprofit staff or governmental employees. Tasks could be picking up litter on the beach, tutoring a child one hour a week in an after-school program, or serving dinner twice a month at a homeless shelter. In the case of HomeWalk, volunteers signed up for a five-kilometer walk, securing "sponsors" who paid for the volunteer's symbolic labor of walking by donating to the United Way nonprofit charitable organization that put on the HomeWalk event.

As close-up studies of volunteering point out, this is a style that downplays claims making in favor of *doing*.[15] A good volunteer believes in "*doing* instead of talking"; understanding those two as a sharp dichotomy is in fact one of the core characteristics of plug-in volunteering. Why talk about environmental policy when you could be recycling, cleaning up a beach, and doing your part right now to improve the environment? Why argue over solutions to homelessness when your church could be housing a homeless person right now or raising money to end the problem? When acting as plug-in volunteers, we don't see conflicts of interest or identity; those are not on our map. Acting as volunteers, it makes sense, then, to claim simply that a problem needs compassion by way of one-to-one tutoring, meal serving, or mentoring, or *awareness* that emerges when a wider public hears that something needs fixing. Brief introductory remarks by a Los Angeles County supervisor at the second HomeWalk were practically a doxology of the plug-in volunteer approach:

> "Each individual has a story, who needs help, and a hand up. If each and every one of us took responsibility for one homeless person, we could end homelessness. When you go, one person at a time, one foot in front of the other, we can make a difference."

A short-lived effort by Los Angeles' largest homeless service-providing organization aimed initially for a different approach. TWH's director initiated the Faith Brings Us Home project in hopes of convincing some religious congregational leaders to embark on building housing for homeless people on or over their underutilized parking lots. At the project's first luncheon, a few months before the HJ coalition's kickoff rally, forty congregational leaders and homeless service providers heard a speech about the role of churches in US social reform. At the second meeting, about twenty-five religious leaders and homeless service providers heard a long, peppy testimonial by the director of Caring Sunday, an annual, citywide help-a-thon. Caring Sunday staff spent months connecting plug-in volunteers with thousands of local opportunities to donate groceries, pull weeds, paint an elderly person's house, send a computer to a youth center that needs one, or carry out some other onetime charitable task on that one Caring Sunday every year. All that activity all over town would "build community through helping," as the website put it. If any more of these planned, quarterly luncheons took place, I never heard about them.

In their own terms, participants in Faith Brings Us Home ratified that plug-in volunteering was the most realistic approach for their congregations, and the first and perhaps last step to solving homelessness. A rabbi attending the meeting said he had come to realize that congregations each have their own way of doing things. From there, he deduced that it was best to start with projects that the majority of a congregation found "doable," like collecting protein bars and soap, because congregants often said they wanted to be able to give something useful to the homeless people on their daily rounds. The rabbi also talked a bit about his synagogue's participation in community organizing and then asked how many others' congregations were similarly involved. One woman raised a hand.

> Rabbi: "A protein bar or bar of soap is only the merest Band-Aid. To make change happen, . . . we need to get into the political process."

The pastor of a westside Presbyterian church thought little tasks would whet volunteers' appetites for more ambitious kinds of problem solving around homelessness. "My church was asked to contribute three hundred socks and underwear. . . . When you get it down to clean socks and underwear, people like to do that—people like it. They feel good about it. . . . They can get more involved [in other projects] later. It leads to bigger, more interesting things."

Taking the power of scene style seriously, we have to be more skeptical of the pastor's idea. He was articulating a theory popular among some activists, on which the empirical research record is ambiguous at best, that casual task-oriented volunteering induces volunteers to "scale up" to more collective and politically consequential civic action.[16] In contrast, I argue that volunteer scenes *by themselves* suppress opportunities to make connections to a "bigger" world of public claims making and collective action for institutional change.[17] They coordinate interaction for "doing, not talking," carrying out charitable tasks that need relatively minimal verbal elaboration. A simple claim will do. Homeless people need socks and underwear, *now*.

Maybe talking is overrated. Don't people who live on city sidewalks, and lack regular access to showers and washing machines, need clean underwear? Not everyone can or should get involved in claims making about homelessness and housing, or any other problem.

But scenes that suppress claims making allow misunderstandings to fester. That is especially the case when people playing scripts from two different scenes run into each other on the same city block. In the middle of Faith

Brings Us Home's second luncheon, one of two African American pastors interrupted the can-do tone of the largely white, lunch affair with perplexing news, to which I heard perplexingly little response:

> The pastor of Downtown Church on Seventh and Montgomery reported that "there's a movement downtown" of people who are concerned because people come to offer people food. The food ends up on the street, it's a mess, and it causes "health issues." "Food just shows up, and an easy way to kill off homeless people is to poison the food and distribute it." He did not say who this "movement" was, nor what anyone was doing about potential health issues.

> The attendee next to him, executive director of a prominent, Korean community services agency, said, seemingly in response, "I like the idea that [downtown] is a little cleaner now, safer," but that she got an unfriendly response from people downtown. That didn't feel good to her. She sounded hurt and bitter. She did not elaborate.

No one asked her to. No one asked the pastor of Downtown Church to say more about the idea that volunteers would poison giveaway food. There was no discussion. The luncheon facilitator told us now we would hear a presentation from the director of Caring Sunday.

It would be hard to find a starker illustration of a volunteer scene suppressing claims making in favor of tasking. The community services director and "movement downtown" came with different understandings of what volunteer-hosted meal giveaways accomplish, but apparently this was not the place to explore them. A scene styled for charitable volunteering does not normally include the role of critical observer; that is just not part of the script. In a scene styled by a community of identity, on the other hand, outsiders are usually suspect to some degree, no matter how they understand their own motives. That is true whether they are a big property owner or individual, each of whom, sincere in their charity, wants to "take responsibility for one homeless person," as the county supervisor put it.

I tried to initiate the conversation myself with the Downtown Church pastor after the lunch.[18] He told me that the "movement" considered the volunteer food giveaways on his block as an environmental as well as health issue. The charity service resulted in food and Styrofoam containers strewn about the street.

> Pastor: "We don't know where this food comes from. We don't know who prepares it."

> Paul: "I thought people needed a permit to distribute food."

The pastor said he didn't know, but guessed that "a lot of the people don't have a permit. . . . I'm just trying to represent what people were saying."

Paul: "They do sound like very serious—reasonable—concerns."

The pastor said some of the people voicing these issues, raising the specter of poisoning homeless residents, were involved with LAPO. LAPO participants and food-bearing volunteers apprehended homelessness from different worlds of style as well as different discursive fields.

Plug-in Volunteers with Service Providers: Specialized Service, with Little Claims Making

"What do you think about boundaries?" Cindy asked startlingly. Tom, a college student, said that they help ensure mutual respect. Cindy picked up a copy of last Friday's *Los Angeles Times*, showed us an article on homelessness, and pointed out the child in the picture—an obvious subject of concern and attachment. She talked more about boundaries. "There's manipulation. Manipulation is a survival strategy." "Boundaries" appeared on a sheet we would sign, listing roughly thirty things we were not supposed to do with homeless people, such as: don't talk about your own personal problems, don't invite them to your house, don't give them money, and don't touch them other than a handshake or to administer CPR.

Two Danish college students, a research assistant, and I were all taking a brief orientation before starting outreach volunteer stints. One of TWH's biggest draws for volunteers was the ride-along program with the homeless outreach service. TWH outreach workers would fan out in little white trucks to districts of the county that had contracted with TWH for its mobile staff to locate homeless people and invite them back to TWH shelters. For outreach volunteers, the route started with Cindy, the coordinator who scheduled volunteers, took their signed agreements to abide the "don'ts," and gave informal tours of the central TWH facility. Cindy was informing us about homeless people's survival strategies without sugarcoating them. She was modeling TWH's "tough love" approach.

A few statements gleaned from across a total of fourteen field sessions in TWH scenes could be considered *claims* about homelessness or affordable housing as public problems. A formal tour of TWH's central facility described TWH's services for homeless people in some detail, but the guide made no statements on behalf of TWH about homelessness as a public problem, or relations between homelessness and the availability of housing. Cindy said in our first conversation, though, that Los Angeles County had a total of fourteen thousand shelter beds yet ninety-one thousand homeless people, "so it's a big problem," and left it at that. Intriguingly, she also quoted the TWH director on how to address homelessness: "Shelters are not working. Transitional housing is not working. We need affordable housing. So he might be able to give you a bigger picture." A new branch of the TWH organization in fact was now planning affordable housing developments, and TWH endorsed the HJ's three-point plan for housing policy. Quite possibly in *other* scenes, beyond the congregational volunteer network and outreach volunteering opportunities, the "bigger picture" Cindy alluded to was informing claims about homelessness and housing. In the outreach volunteer scene, alongside TWH staff, those claims were extremely rare.

Four-hour sorties with lunch breaks and commutes between Hollywood and Inglewood left a lot of time for casual chat. We talked about music, Los Angeles, or outreach staff's clinical master's programs and future plans. On his first outreach sortie, my research partner got a description of municipal ordinances regarding public sleeping. An outreach worker explained:

> It's illegal to sleep on the sidewalks downtown except between the hours of 9:00 p.m. and 6:00 a.m., and that every so often LAPD will go down there and, at 6:01 a.m., start arresting homeless people for sleeping on the sidewalk and then checking for outstanding warrants on any of them.

To this, I replied, "Charming."

And she said, "Yeah, really," and gave a short exasperated "heh."[19]

The criticism implicit in the outreach worker's three-word commentary here was the most obvious claim about a public problem from among the few candidates we picked up in field notes from these volunteer stints.

Cindy and the outreach staff all referred to homeless people as "clients" whether or not they already were receiving any service from TWH. That along with Cindy's talk about boundaries at the volunteer orientation was a big clue. During outreach sorties, whether accompanied by several volunteers, myself only, or my research partner, staff spoke frequently in human service vocabularies or else from their professional experience. They talked about homeless people as individuals with personal problems, tough circumstances, and occasional breakthroughs (a clean shirt or an optimistic demeanor), and those attributions all seemed accurate. Staff worked hard at tuning in to their clients or prospective clients. Assiduously they would try, over weeks' or months' time, to develop a relationship with an evidently homeless individual, hoping to coax a new enrollee in TWH's program of shelter, employment readiness, and personal change. Staff kept little notebooks stashed in dashboard ashtrays and at the ready in back pockets. They took notes on each of their encounters with homeless people, tracking their progress in nudging potential clients toward the program. One found out that a man on a street corner in Inglewood was a soccer fan and vowed to buy him a sports magazine as an innocent opening to conversation.

Staff monitored the people who had become regulars during outreach, rather like a doctor doing hospital rounds or probation officer checking in.

Steph (suddenly, as we're driving): "There's Sharon, on the corner, she's with someone."

Herman: "Do you want to stop?"

Steph: "Yes, I want to check on her." Stephanie already knew that Sharon was pregnant. She asked Sharon if she had gone to her court hearing.

Sharon, half gruffly: "No, you gonna call the police?"

Stephanie said no, she just wanted to know. She told us that Sharon had been booked on "Proposition 36," which meant that she would get services if she had made her court date, but having missed her court date, Herman added, "she would go to jail." Stephanie said she didn't look as much as six months pregnant, and Herman said, "She's carrying a crack baby in her stomach."

Staff made first contacts in a matter-of-fact way, sparing euphemisms. Herman would hand people a flyer, and casually describe the shelter as a place to "pick yourself up" or "get your life in order." Staff attended to some regulars like Sharon elaborately, while others seemed to be on indefinite "check-in" status. In one Hollywood park, we checked in with a thin woman with sundamaged skin, a former model who, the team explained, was telling the truth when she said she used to own mansions in the hills. Allison talked about the woman's "triple morbidity" and said in the truck on the way back to the shelter that people with a drug addiction are the hardest clients to work with. If you don't have a diagnosed medical condition as well as the drug habit, the mental health clinic wouldn't help.

> They would have to call police authorities if they really thought someone was an imminent danger to themselves. It is a difficult call, she said, because you do want to create a relationship. Making the wrong judgment call about getting legal authorities involved might make things worse. Allison commented, "We have to come from a place of respect"—respecting the clients and their decisions, while wanting them to seek help and get services too.

This was a different line of work from constructing claims about social problems.

TWH's homeless-centered volunteer scenes engaged short-term tasking or else opened a short window on the gritty realities of homeless service. The annual volunteer HomeWalk performed the transubstantiation of leg power into money and awareness. None of these volunteer scenes made social space for volunteers to connect homelessness to housing as public problems out loud.

In most of this study's scenes, in fact, it was hard for advocates to develop explicit claims about *both* homelessness and housing, and connect the two at any length. On paper, advocates as well as governmental officials have considered homelessness a distinct problem while also saying that the long-term solution to homelessness is affordable housing with support services. I am suggesting that discursive fields and style, working together, have helped keep homelessness and housing separate, foregrounding one while marginalizing the other and cultivating advocates in quite different rhetorical appeals for each. Civic actors either could fight for more affordable housing, subsuming the distinct category of homeless people into a larger public of inadequately housed people, or turn homeless people into a marginal and perhaps precarious community. Or else they could focus in on the personal needs of homeless individuals by tasking or applying human service expertise, leaving the housing theme for others to take up.

The Benefits of Conceptual Pluralism

This chapter and the last one take claims makers as culturally cultivated and socially embedded. We can say at the same time that social advocates try to make their messaging strategic. They sometimes rummage around for usable slogans, within limits. It should be possible to study strategic framing work without discounting the cultural context that empowers and limits what advocates can consider strategic, and where, to begin with. It should be possible, too, to focus in on the images and reputations that social problems scholars find when they study the construction of different social issues, without ignoring or discounting a broader cultural context that keeps different images stuck to different issues.[20]

To take the case of the Manchester campaign, framing scholars might note that campaign leaders actively framed "talking points" to sway commissioners at city planning commission hearings. Before one hearing, for example, the director of a powerful organization in the coalition concluded, "We do want a variety of speakers to represent different parts of the coalition . . . and one or two community members to make it real, . . . [like] somebody who needs health care, somebody who needs a job." It is equally important to ask which cultural categories and styles of action shape what advocates can imagine as strategic or appropriate to begin with. The ISLA director's self-conscious strategy to "make it real" materialized in claims about unfairly distributed housing chances. It is not just natural that this would be more strategic than framing appeals to city council members in terms of compassion or quality of life. Further, the director's comments show she was assuming that claims for fairness and opportunity sound "real" when they are represented by members of "the community," not by Angelenos, or people who work in the city and therefore should be able to live in the city—as HJ advocates would have put it.

Strategic framing happened and is worth studying on its own terms. It also happened within a discursive field, through styled interaction. These induced leaders to select from what was potentially a larger universe of discourses or strategic frames. An HJ leader said after a kickoff rally that the three-point plan was the "glue" to hold together different constituencies in the campaign. This sounds like an unremarkably logical strategy. Yet Manchester campaign participants eventually included labor, community, and religious organizations, just as HJ did. These groups did not always work together or even agree with each other, but I never heard leaders speak of their framings as glue for a coalition. I would argue that having styled their campaign mostly as a community of identity, Manchester leaders needed to treat their public statements as representing the authentic will of a self-identified community of fate, not a temporary convergence of groups with disparate interests.

Cultural context can induce advocates to pass up opportunities for strategic framing. Limiting the examples here to the Manchester campaign, Why would the ISLA leader quoted just before think that claims about a distinct community's needs would sound more compelling to planning commission members drawn from across the city than claims framed in terms of what was good for Angelenos at large or the regional environment? It is not clear either why the ISLA staffer who revised the supportive attorneys' letter would suppose that government employees would be more moved by community-centered appeals than the original, legalistically framed statement. But rather than force a choice between one framework or another, future studies might draw insights from both, investigating further how scene styles constrain strategic framing. Maybe some styles induce more rigid constraints than others.

Future research can borrow valuable insights from the venerable, constructionist approach to social problems as well. Some constructionist approaches examine rhetorical tropes, imagery, or typifications that embody advocates' claims.[21] Problems become typecast politically too, "owned" by some political groups or identities, and shunned by others.[22] It is not hard to imagine the images that contribute to making fair opportunity or compassion feel different when we hear about them, and may help make housing and homelessness feel like different problems too. Research mentioned before finds that homelessness conjures up feelings of disgust and, for some people in the United States, images of personal failure. These are components of a more basic typification: homelessness implies a condition of *persons*. Housing, on the other hand, conjures up *facilities*, material infrastructure. In theory, either category may involve rights or opportunities. Observations here and studies cited earlier suggest that groups that approach the social world in terms of structured access to facilities—in the United States, politically progressive groups—will "own" a problem tagged with the word "housing" more than they will a problem tagged as "homelessness."

These ideas about typification also contribute a thicker understanding of meaning making in a discursive field. Informed by metaphors of battle or struggle, some scholars see discursive fields as sites for launching symbolic salvos, dominating or being dominated by others. That story line fits some of what happens in a discursive field, after the fact. The account here presented discursive fields as products of ongoing interaction. That implies that actors in the field are becoming socialized, learning to typify arguments, issues, or people in particular ways; that is part of what one field theorist called the "semiotic" import of fields.[23] Advocates for more housing learn to make fair opportunity arguments, but only very rarely arguments about the injustice of property rights. Over time, claims makers may pick up that assertions about housing issues need to be fair opportunity arguments. By the same logic, people already predisposed to particular kinds of argument may attach to some issues rather than others. Advocates who gravitate toward fairness arguments may tend to favor housing issues and be less likely to attend to concerns that sound like homelessness, since those conventionally are not about fairness.

There is more to learn about how issues, symbolic categories of argument, and political valences become stuck together or detached. Generations of social thinkers from Karl Marx onward have pondered the social organization of political ideas. Investigating discursive fields and styles, we can renew and refine inquiry into what sociologists have called ideologies, hegemony, cultural systems, or strategic frames. Rather than suppose that sociology already sports too many culture concepts and ought to settle on one, it is much more useful and generative to treat culture as multifaceted.[24] In tandem with a respectful pluralism, I suggest humbly that it is worthwhile to keep specifying what was once called the amorphous "mist" of culture.[25] Different tools of cultural analysis, combined judiciously, give richer and more practical analyses of conditions that have kept claims about homelessness and housing hard to work with together.

9

Hybrid Problem Solving

CREATING AFFORDABLE HOUSING

A Box Too Big

Keep following housing advocates in the United States and you inevitably arrive at nonprofit housing developers who produce what the housing advocates are fighting for. Like social movement organizations, nonprofit organizations aim to address social problems, are not agencies of the government, and as the name implies, do not follow all the ordinary routines of profit making in the marketplace. Some social movement organizations *are* nonprofit organizations. To go with the common usage, however, "nonprofit organization" will refer only to organizations whose staff makes a living by producing goods or services conceived of as benefiting society, and do not aim to make a profit for shareholders. Many scholars associate nonprofit organizations with "the nonprofit sector" or civic sector, one of the three sectors of public life along with government and the commercial or market sector.[1] Assigning organizations to a single sector can be misleading, though. That opens up a valuable opportunity to clarify "civic" beyond all the confusing language and imagery that go with the term—a major goal of this chapter.

Some research treats the civic sector as an institutional compartment of society that cultivates special virtues and skills. Typical candidates are public-spiritedness along with an ability to be a good listener or run a meeting efficiently.[2] Many researchers have expected the civic sector to host public-spirited, egalitarian collaboration between people.[3] In theory, the civic sector cultivates skills frequently devalued or suppressed in the other, less participatory or less public-minded institutional realms of modern society. In this view, the civic sector is society's guarantor of democracy, the realm in which the will of everyday people really matters. The ideal representative of the civic sector in these studies, the hardy, local volunteer group, would be easy enough to find in Los Angeles.[4] It could be the church-based social outreach group that was collecting socks and underwear for homeless people. Or it could be the volunteers who staffed a trailer-cum-kitchen, inside which they rolled and foil-wrapped burritos to distribute at homeless encampments throughout the city.[5]

Other researchers use "the civic sector" as a technical, not theoretical, tag. It is the collective term for organizations that legally are nonprofit enterprises, certified under Section 501(c)(3) of the United States Code because their managers have demonstrated on paper that their organizations exist to serve some public good. In this usage, the connection between "civic sector" and "good for democracy and society" is more attenuated although not wholly absent.[6] The ideal representative is a hospital or private university. Organizations with this designation are exempt from taxes on their earnings.

This quick terminological tour leads back to a point briefly implied in the first chapter: the civic sector "box" is too big and generic for this study. It can be a useful category for some kinds of research, depending on what we want to know. *If* we think that a large, diverse collection of groups really has some basic thing in common, it can make sense to classify those groups inside a "sector" of society. Doing that clears the way to comparing societies or historical periods with larger smaller, more or less diverse civic sectors. The trouble is that this is an extremely big *if*, and it requires trade-offs even bigger than the ones we make when we designate some collective effort as a social movement or social movement organization. Many nonprofit organizations, like private universities and hospitals, are not set up primarily to address social problems. We are concerned with the subset of nonprofit organizations whose staff do see themselves as addressing social problems directly by providing goods or services like affordable housing. These organizations have a mission—one that at least some of the public would find morally "magnetic" and indisputably appealing.[7]

This study's nonprofit housing developer organizations and their staff would match this description. At one of WHA's annual conferences, a keynote speaker and one of the few people wearing a tie, talked about how housing related to global warming, and how tightening state and federal housing budgets meant that developers needed to *share* their experiences and know-how more intensively. The appeal to collaboration would only make sense if affordable housing developers see themselves as advocates who share a commitment to a cause, not simply competitors for shrinking pots of money—though they were that too. It makes sense to think that a lot of affordable developers did in fact care about the cause of housing lower-income people, especially given that they signed up for a part of the housing industry that generally is less profitable than market-based real estate development.[8]

Instead of treating all nonprofits simply as interchangeable incumbents of a sector, recent ethnographic and historical accounts look more closely at their everyday workings.[9] These accounts suggest that the blanket label of "civic sector" obscures the different kinds of work that nonprofit organizations do. Some of that work is freely initiated and driven by missions that nonprofit professionals devise as people concerned about problems like unaffordable housing: civic action. Yet some of it is highly scripted by governmental mandates and the impersonal logic of the market. Working for a nonprofit affordable housing developer means juggling the different roles accompanying these scripts, and at the one I studied, the juggling act never stopped. Some of the staff said they enjoyed it, like the finance officer who told me gleefully, "We have fun here. . . . It's different every day!" In fact, it often was different from hour to hour, and sometimes hard to follow. The name for the juggling act is "*hybrid* civic action."[10] That means that some of the action was civic by this study's definition, while some looked and sounded much more like what governmental agencies do to address social problems, and some of it looked and sounded like what businesses— property owners or managers—do. Beyond clarifying a complicated process that creates a home for some low-income people, why should we bother looking at hybrid civic action closely?

First, we see important political and practical differences between *nonprofit* goods and service providers and the *social movement* groups they sometimes ally with. The category of "the civic sector" encompasses both and would obscure those differences. Those differences matter; it turns out that nonprofit housing developers manage enervating dilemmas that impinge little, if at all, on grassroots social movement organizations.

A deeper reason to follow hybrid civic action is to see what makes civic different from noncivic action. Clarifying the practical meaning of "civic" in the nonprofit world is far more than a dry academic exercise. Popular social critics and promoters of civic engagement drench the topic of civic in simple, romantic notions of what is "local" and "voluntary." In commonsense thinking, we suppose that civic action is both.[11] Both descriptors do point vaguely toward something important in civic action, but neither is precise or reliable. Scenarios from fieldwork on nonprofit housing development will challenge commonsense, overidealized notions of civic that inflect scholarly discussion as well as popular and political conversation. The close juxtaposition of civic and noncivic in hybrid civic action will give us better ways to discern whether or not, and how, nonprofits express the will of people in their immediate locale, and whether or not they pose an effective alternative to governmental action, as some commentators argue. All that should help clarify how civic action really works.

We focus mostly on a locally prominent and successful, nonprofit afford-able housing developer, HSLA. At the end we compare HSLA briefly with efforts by an ISLA committee to administer the housing provisions of the CBA that ISLA's campaign won from the Manchester apartments developer. This was a different kind of hybrid. ISLA's affordable housing work for the com-munity ultimately was both financed and constrained by a big, for-profit real estate developer—the Manchester property owner.

Hybrid Civic Action

Contracting and Its Dilemmas

Many grassroots efforts mix civic and noncivic action at least a little. Social movement organizations like LAPO or SHAPLA as well as coalitions like HJ or ISLA had staff people who issued paychecks, paid rent on office space, filled out requisitions for catered sandwiches and chips now and then, and did other administrative things that sustain their organizations but do not relate directly to collective, social problem solving. But the participants in this study, like the great bulk of leading staff persons and participants in the organizations, un-derstood themselves primarily as civic actors, and civic action took most of their time. It would be misleading to call these organizations *hybrid* just because one or a small handful of staff in the organizations had mainly admin-istrative jobs that kept their organizations' heating and lights on, employees paid, and guests fed snacks. The collective efforts in this chapter are different, being much more thoroughly a mix of civic and noncivic efforts.

Chapters 3 and 4 showed that different styles of civic action each face a distinctive dilemma. Nonprofit affordable housing developers face other char-acteristic dilemmas. One is set for them by a web of state regulations that govern different aspects of affordable housing. The web can become a constricting tangle for nonprofits. Another dilemma—a set of them, really—derives from a funding structure that can induce even socially conscious, committed develop-ers to remain fairly distant from the people or locales they serve—more like the commonly held image of a state agency than a locally based civic group. Nonprofit housing developers, just by virtue of the professional work they have chosen, cannot sidestep or switch these dilemmas. We need more studies before we can identify widespread patterns of hybridity. My time with housing developers is enough to indicate, though, that there is a distinct kind of scene along with a way of combining scenes that goes with hybrid civic action. First we should clarify why nonprofit affordable housing developers have special dilemmas to begin with.

Housing is expensive. Nonprofit housing professionals must raise the money it takes to buy the land, then hire the contractor, architectural firm, construction workers, and building managers, and sometimes pay the salaries for the supportive human service workers that staff some affordable housing developments. They may also cover moving expenses for current tenants who have to leave a building that a developer like HSLA is going to gut and rebuild. If the developer does win the grants to build the housing, it then enters a world of Twister-like tasks. Or as HSLA's receptionist said unprompted on my first day as a volunteer staff person, "Oh, it really is a pain! I mean, it's good to have housing for the low-income people, but . . ."

The world they enter is the "contracting regime."[12] Put simply, the US federal government stopped designing and building housing for low-income people in the mid-1980s. Instead, nonprofit organizations like HSLA contract for grants, loans, tax credits, and other kinds of funding from multiple sources in order to do what federal and state or municipal government working in concert used to do.[13] The massive change in the way US society provides housing for some low-income people unable to afford market rates reflects a massive institutional shift that has restructured the way the United States provides for human needs more generally. Federal legislators' zest for *devolution* since the time of President Ronald Reagan has shifted more and more formerly federal responsibilities to states and local governments. When affordable housing developers apply for grant money from governmental grant programs, they are usually applying for state- or municipal-sponsored grants. And the move from direct governmental responsibility for low-income housing to a shifting patchwork of contracts with and grants to nongovernmental (frequently nonprofit) housing organizations represents just one of many instances of a *privatization* of formerly governmental responsibilities that has altered the social contract in the United States. Countries around the globe have experienced similar transformations since the 1970s, sometimes heralded with appeals to greater civic responsibility and empowerment like the ones people have heard in the United States.[14] In the contracting regime, nonprofit professionals rather than governmental agency employees increasingly are the ones who design and deliver public goods and services.[15] For nonprofit professionals like the housing developers I studied, the contracting regime induces dilemmas between roles traditionally assigned to government and those we expect of self-directed, grassroots advocates. Two dilemmas were especially prominent in my field sites.

Dilemma: Equity versus Responsiveness

When nonprofit housing professionals use tax money to provide a good (housing) that government used to provide, they must treat potential clients equitably. They can't brazenly discriminate, play favorites, or pay for goods that recipients don't need with the public's money. But as nongovernmental organizations, they also have the leeway to pursue missions that are responsive to the particular cultural or individual character of the people they serve.[16] Nonprofit staff may voluntarily charter an organization with the mission of serving a particular population (elderly people, Asian Americans, or disabled people, for instance) as opposed to only the most general population.[17]

The dilemma of equity versus responsiveness played out in the way HSLA staff chose applicants for their apartments. Nonprofit staff at HSLA followed the criterion of equity by devising application and publicity guidelines that would not unfairly benefit one ethnic group or one kind of Angeleno over another if all in question need housing. They worked with an active eye toward fair housing legislation, which since 1968, has forbidden racial, ethnic, and other kinds of discrimination in the housing market.[18] HSLA practiced responsiveness in part by maintaining a community liaison who kept abreast of local civic organizations, including occasional social movement activity, that might affect life in the particular neighborhoods with HSLA developments. Nonprofit professionals want to be responsive, but usually they cannot make cultural or individual particularity a basis for privileging some recipients of service and disadvantaging others; that would be inequitable. Balancing equity and responsiveness is tricky.

Dilemma: Disembeddedness versus Responsiveness

Relying on short-term contracts introduces a second dilemma that affects nonprofit developers whether their contracts are paid by governmental bodies or philanthropic foundations. Policy makers in Sacramento or Los Angeles, and executives in foundation boardrooms, continually filled or drained their pools of grant money in line with changing priorities. From a nonprofit staff's point of view, making a living and keeping an enterprise going by winning grants under these conditions means working under constant uncertainty. Sustaining oneself and the organization requires being willing to remain disembedded from any particular constituency. One cannot be too attached to any particular group, social category, or need, for who can know what next year's call for proposals will be? A call for proposals might prompt proposals to house homeless vets, families, or low-income seniors. A nonprofit that writes grant proposals to house only a limited range of constituencies reduces its chances of staying afloat financially. On the other hand, applying for a great variety of grants, addressing many different constituencies, would require being able to show convincingly on paper that the organization can be responsive to each of many different cultural or demographic categories of need: housing for low-income elderly, families with small children, and homeless vets.

A distinct batch of conundrums ensues. I will call the batch, collectively, the dilemma of disembeddedness versus responsiveness.[19] Participation in a system of limited, unpredictable short-term funding makes nonprofit professionals like those at HSLA into sellers in the marketplace, competitors whose survival depends on avoiding an exclusive affinity for any particular service clientele. We see how each dilemma plays out by following HSLA staff as they select tenants and develop plans for a new housing development.

Following Hybrid Civic Action at HSLA

The Lottery and the Dilemma of Equity and Responsiveness

On my first day at the office, Nora had scheduled a phone consult with a friend in the real estate business. She wanted advice on how to choose among applicants for one of the apartments in HSLA's new Hollywood Apartments development, a three-story stucco building with small, sunny porches and a facade with square-shaped splashes of earth-toned colors, ready for occupancy in just a couple months. She invited me to listen in and ask questions. A lot of applicants were going to be disappointed, or worse. There were 1,267 applications for 32 apartments. Nora told me that choosing applicants on a first-come, first-served basis would not work. "There are community groups that will get everyone they know and all stand in line together—if they really know the system they can work it, so that they all get housing, and none left for anyone else. There goes your 'fair housing.'"

The realtor suggested holding a lottery with a small cast of carefully selected attendees in a carefully selected location. He explained that each application would get a number, and we would put each number into a bingo machine. We asked who should attend the lottery drawing.

> Realtor: "There will be an owner's [from HSLA] representative. Is there city money in this?"

> Nora: "Yep."

> Realtor: "You want to have a council person's representative, and someone from the city."

He added that HSLA also should hold "community meetings" to "educate" prospective applicants about how to apply, how affordable housing works, and what kind of income qualifies applicants for the affordable rents.

> Paul: "Where does this [lottery] actually happen? What is the audience— what is the social scene like?"

Realtor: "Very good question. I don't recommend an audience. It is good to do in the [Los Angeles city] council man's office."

Paul: "Does anyone make a stink and go complain?"

The realtor answered that if we have held community meetings, then people will understand the process and there would not be much complaint.

Realtor: "Have management [HSLA's chosen management company] take the lead because they are not as close to the community as HSLA."

Figuring out the action in HJ and ISLA scenes could be challenging on occasion, yet hybrid civic action frequently was a far higher magnitude of challenge. As I debriefed with Nora and HSLA's community liaison Nathan, I slowly came to understand it: the selection process was sort of like a TV game show, but with a high-minded purpose and for a private audience. It was a creative attempt to balance equity and responsiveness. Nora told us all to dress up for our morning of spinning the basket; this was a lottery with serious, even life-changing consequences.

On the responsiveness side, Nora told me that HSLA indeed had held community meetings, including with Spanish translators, about its new development to help potential applicants understand the process. Relatively speaking, HSLA was "close to the community," as Nora's real estate friend put it. The meetings were run by Angelenos United, a community organizing coalition that got low-income Latinx churchgoers in South Los Angeles fired up about supporting HJ's three-point plan for an affordable housing mandate before the big fracture in the HJ coalition. HSLA rented an office near the new apartment development to receive applications so that it would be easy for local residents to apply. In these and other ways, HSLA staff built responsiveness into the selection process.

Choosing a lottery system to begin with was also a way to safeguard *equity*, with a commitment to fair housing law, as Nora implied. A first-come, first-served process would have allowed ethnic-based community groups to fill that line with their own well-networked members. A HSLA staffer told me that according to the local housing authority, favoring applicants located in a building's neighborhood would not by itself constitute discrimination because geographic residence is not a protected category. The Hollywood Apartments, however, were located in a heavily Armenian immigrant part of town. If application procedures seemed to elicit a preponderance of Armenian applicants, they could *look* unfair and invite the charge of discrimination along with time-consuming legal battles, whether or not the charge was justified. Nora had reason to be concerned. Community meetings in other neighborhoods were not only a device to ensure responsiveness but also a means of broadening the potential pool of applicants in the interest of fairness. The management office taking the applications was not just in the neighborhood but down the hall from that district's city council man's field office too. That was by design. As the financial officer put it, association with the city council office lent "legitimacy" to the selection process, diminishing the chance that an applicant would complain that it favored some kinds of applicants over others.

In all, HSLA staff tried to make the selection process equitable, and also enhance the *perception* that it was equitable and above reproach by applicants, a vast majority of whom would not get an apartment. The financial officer told me that the lottery would be videotaped, and that two applicants already put in requests for a copy; one wanted it posted on YouTube. Filling the Hollywood Apartments with tenants required a complicated dance of commitments, perceptions, and organizational self-protection.

The business end of the Hollywood Apartments introduced yet more complexity. Incomes and assets reported on applications needed to fall below a ceiling since the premise of affordable housing is to offer opportunities that compensate to some degree for low-income tenants' inferior position in the housing market—a matter of equity. As Nora explained it after the phone call to her friend, HSLA "needs to have affordable units, but we also need the cash flow to make the deal possible." That is where the financial officer's job came in; he was the one who would figure out how many apartments to offer at what rent levels. A range of rents would qualify as "affordable" to tenants earning between 20 and 60 percent of the average monthly income in the region.

Balancing equity and responsiveness thoughtfully made financial officer Ricky's job into a matter of playing "good cop" and "bad cop" at the same time.

> Ricky: "Even if an apartment is, say, a hundred dollars a month, they need to make enough income to cover that rent. There's still rent. . . . If you want people to pay no more than 50 percent of their income in rent, if it's a hundred dollars a month, they need to make so much a year because after rent they have to buy groceries, for instance."

> Paul: "Yeah, the federal limit is 30 percent of your income."

> Ricky: "I'm OK with 50 percent. Because some people are paying 80 percent (now), so 50 percent is a relief."

Sometimes there are surprises. Ricky said that he went to inspect an apartment once and saw a Mercedes parked in the driveway.

> Ricky: "I want it to be fair, by ethnicity and gender—if they're good tenants, great. . . . That's why I want to do home visits. See if they're pack rats. . . . It's only thirty-two units. I don't want to give housing to people who don't need it."

Nora, Nathan, and Ricky all displayed at one point or another their desire to go beyond the call of duty to help out their tenants. Nora told me that she saw a haggard mom with (she presumed) an autistic kid having a meltdown, standing in line with their application for an apartment; she wanted so badly to just give her one of the thirty-two units in Hollywood Apartments. Ricky wanted to be responsive to prospective tenants hurting from paying an unsustainably high proportion of their earnings to current landlords. He told me that when a construction contractor asked him why he wanted granite countertops installed in the kitchens of a newly refurbished building (on that part of that day, Ricky was acting as liaison to the contractor), he had replied flatly, "Why shouldn't homeless people have nice countertops like everyone else?" He also wanted to be fair and safeguard the principle that affordable housing should go to tenants limited in what they can afford. Inspecting apartments—a role classically played by invasive landlords or cold, bureaucratic social workers— was part of Ricky's solution to the dilemma of equity and responsiveness.

All in an Hour's Work: Hybrid Civic Action Unfolds in Quilts of Scenes

Work at HSLA was a complicated dance, balancing governmentally guaranteed rights and the community-minded concern that often goes with notions of civic. How did they do it? As the quilt metaphor suggests, action over even brief periods at HSLA unfolded in a patchwork of different scenes, some civic, some noncivic, and some both. The scene could change quickly, lurching from one patch to another. Sometimes it was like we were in a volunteer group meeting, then suddenly a government agency, and then twenty minutes later, a small business. Each of those scenes ran on different expectations about who we are in relation to the wider world, and how we depend on each other—different styles of interaction.

Participants in quilts of action know implicitly that they will need to shift frequently between a small batch of styles. Eliasoph's (2011) youth empowerment projects are a great example. African American high school–age participants in a youth club knew implicitly that in the course of one afternoon meeting, they would need to act like civic volunteer do-gooders visiting bedridden hospital patients, then switch suddenly to acting like well-behaved clients (not civic actors) of social workers, and then for short moments their scholarly or civic achievements were victories for their whole "community"—and they were then members of a community of identity. At HSLA, action bunched up into several different scenes each with a different style or hybrid of styles. That is how work unfolded all day. Here is just one hour's worth.

When I checked in for a short afternoon stint at the HSLA office, on a June day in 2008, HSLA director Nora asked what I had seen the previous day at HSLA's property management office. I was watching/helping staff vet applications for the Hollywood Apartments. I had seen a lot of applicants checking what rank their application had received from the lottery. I added that it seemed like many of the applicants did not understand the lottery. Indignant, Nora told me that HSLA had received a fair housing complaint. "There are always complaints, no matter what system we use," she said. This time, a complainant had called a local fair housing agency to say that a staff person in the property management office told her she would not get an apartment "because she's an African American." Nora pointed out that the third-ranked application on the long list of entries was "something like 'Keisha.'"

> Paul: "It was a rainbow of people coming in. A lot of Armenians, but a lot of others too."

> Nora: "Well that's the neighborhood . . . and that group [Armenians] is well organized."

But as for discrimination against an African American, Nora disagreed.

> Nora: "I mean, *c'mon*! The guy doing the interviews is African American . . . and the third name on the list *sounds* . . ." (She threw both her arms up in the air; I inferred that Nora was quite sure the third-ranked applicant was an African American.)

Though miffed, Nora took the complaint seriously. She abided by HSLA's obligation as a housing provider to follow regulations that prohibit racial discrimination. Nora gave me the job of finding the fair housing office's number and phoning up to "do a little PR" with the complainant's case manager. I would say I was calling "to make sure that you have what you needed" to make a determination about the complaint and find out if the complainant's case was still open. Nora said nothing to imply that she thought that antidiscrimination law itself was unfair. Here was a scene in which action was scripted largely by governmental regulations, not self-organizing, grassroots problem solving. This was in effect a "test" of HSLA's operating procedures, parallel to the tests of style we saw emerge in the ISLA and HJ scenes. Nora responded with one of the styles of action familiar to HSLA staff: they knew how to act like careful subjects of governmental regulation.

Now Nora realized she had run out of things for me to do. Nora asked staffers if they could find some project for me. At that point the scene shifted abruptly. I was not a subject of governmental regulation anymore. I had jumped into a new patch or scene of action, and soon I needed help simply to understand "what's going on here," as Goffman ([1974] 1986) put it.

Queenie volunteered that I could take over her new project. She was lining up a HSLA tenant to give a testimonial. HSLA staff wanted a cameo story about a tenant's life experiences to present at the groundbreaking ceremony for a newly planned affordable housing complex a mile and a half away. So I could interview the tenant, find out where he came from originally and what he did for a living, and write it all up as an engaging story for the ceremony.

As with so much of the work at HSLA, I just did not *get* it. The task was to write up the personal story of a tenant of *one* apartment complex so as to grace a groundbreaking ceremony for a *different* apartment complex? Who would hear this story? Why would this mystery audience *care* about a random tenant's personal tale? Queenie explained that the testimonial could "put a face on" affordable housing and supportive services, adding that buildings like the one under construction served to "fix situations."

Paul: "Personal situations?"

Queenie, seeming at a loss for words: "Well—doing good."

Trying valiantly to clue me in, she said the point of the testimonial was to feature "someone who was helped" by living in a HSLA building. The testimonial should convey the message "to support affordable housing and support programs like ours." The building was financed in conjunction with Southland Foundation Land Trust, and Queenie said it was important "to talk up" the foundation, since its money helped make the new apartment complex possible.

Finally, I put it together: Queenie was saying that when HSLA placed people in an affordable development, it was *helping* them, "doing good" in general, the way volunteers in the United States typically talk about helping the needy. HSLA was like a collective volunteer; it never occurred to me that staff at a housing developer with millions of dollars in contracts would act volunteer style. But that was not all; this volunteer map of who we are worked alongside a different one orienting the same scene. On that other map, HSLA was like an employee relating to a boss who has the power to control the employee's livelihood; this was not the world of civic action anymore. Associating Southland Foundation with doing good, personified by the happy HSLA tenant who lives better by paying low rent, would in some small way massage the foundation's reputation by association with a heartwarming scenario, all the while positioning HSLA as an effective contractee worth the money. Happy tenant, programs like ours that do good, funder with the power to choose projects, and ceremonial setting—this chain of meanings went together unre-markably for Queenie, but took real effort for me to assemble.

Volunteer-style civic action and a noncivic concern for a marketable reputa-tion in the world of foundations guided the scene I was entering. Queenie offered just the same analysis yet in far simpler terms: "Working on spread-sheets and forms [to stay financially viable] is the *job*—but you should want to know how your work has benefited the community." In roughly an hour, I had gone from pliant subject of state mandates to collective civic volunteer-cum-grant-seeker in a tight market for funding, all in the same sixth-floor of-fice space.

Revisioning the MacArthur Park Apartments: The Dilemma of Disembeddedness and Responsiveness

The Los Angeles Housing Department had smiled on HSLA's proposal to empty out, gut, and renovate a hundred-year-old apartment building as afford-able housing for extremely low-income seniors. Then state-level evaluators turned it down. The pseudonym for this development honors the city park that sits nearby, in a largely Central American immigrant neighborhood a few miles west of downtown. HSLA staff learned of another call for proposals and were now rushing to complete one with a new vision for the old building. The new proposal was not for housing extremely low-income seniors. Staying *dis-embedded*, pivoting quickly to new populations when necessary, was part of hybrid civic action. The new call for proposals solicited ideas to build housing for "homeless seniors"—a different, if overlapping, social category. These pro-posals would need to plan not only housing but also the counseling and human support services that this targeted population likely would need. Nora decided the new call for proposals was worth a try and secured approval from HSLA's board of directors, "all in a matter of a few days," she told me.

Having newly adopted a constituency, staff's job was now to show that they could be responsive to *that* constituency's particular needs. HSLA had never submitted a proposal to build for homeless seniors or a population needing supportive services. What did its staff know about homeless seniors? Nora and Nathan, who worked on the early proposal drafts, were learning a lot, fast. Reading over the early drafts of the new proposal, I puzzled over how these housing professionals happened to know that there was a low-cost, psycho-logical services provider and senior day center within a half mile of the apart-ments. I thought housing developers were in a different line of work.

Paul: "There just happen to be these service providers in this area . . . and you knew about them already?"

Nora: "It was a referral. St. Francis [a Catholic-sponsored, low-cost health clinic] told us about them."

Paul: "You must have done a lot of quick reading of websites."

Nora: "It was a lot of phone calls and reading websites quickly."

Paul: "You have to be poised for quick changes."

Nora: "Bureaucracy wouldn't work here."

A quick switch of projects and fast-approaching deadline made it only more challenging to learn enough about a population that homeless advocates and social service workers would have spent years trying to understand.[20] That is the dilemma, disembeddedness and responsiveness, but to Nora it was an interesting new learning experience: "It's very exciting. When you listen to what Sara Teitelbaum says, you find out that homeless seniors is a big population." Someone at a state agency had told Nora that this population was a big priority for funding right now.

Positioned amid the work of meeting governmental guidelines and sustaining a cash flow, the civic part of the hybrid action here sounded, again, like ordinary volunteering. Classically, community service volunteers understand themselves on a map full of needy populations: each groupings' needs may be unique, but all are worth being met. Volunteers in clubs like Rotary International organize fundraisers for a succession of unrelated needy groups or invite monthly, luncheon speakers to talk on a variety of unrelated, charitable causes. The point is to be of service to a locale, to be charitable, good people *in general*, no matter what the issue.[21] Nora related to homeless seniors as one, important needy social category among other important needy categories out there. One could learn about and become interested in them, the way community service volunteers do, not as a community of identity to whom one attaches deeply and protects. Unprompted, Nora told me at work one day that she used to be an investment banker. "It went from 'how can I take all your money and invest it?' to 'how can I help you?'"

Nonprofit housing development faces special dilemmas, but nonprofit professionals in some ways sound like volunteers. Are they just doing volunteer-style helping amped up with a lot more technical skills, money, and multitasking? What exactly makes them different? Overidealized notions of civic action and oversimplified thinking about social sectors have made this surprisingly difficult to address. The lack of clarity about what civic and hybrid civic are sounds like an issue for academic specialists, but it has perilous, practical consequences. The fuzziness invites unrealistically high expectations for nonprofit approaches to social problems.

High Hopes for the Nonprofit Approach to Problem Solving

Virtuous Locals versus Their Governments?

Some theorists and commentators assume the nonprofit approach to problem solving benefits society because nonprofits, at least if they are local organizations, run on locally cultivated virtues and skills. The scholarly version of this civic localism often pulls imagery selectively from Tocqueville's *Democracy in America* to make the point.[22] Communitarian social thinkers such as Peter Berger and Richard Neuhaus (1977) have recirculated that imagery, writing that local communities cultivate moral sensibilities and virtues that don't find fertile grounds in other spheres of modern society. Eminent sociologist Amitai Etzioni (1996) celebrated local communities for safeguarding "the moral voice" that motivates people to take responsibility and solve some social problems themselves. Many people have heard or perhaps adopted some version of the idea that longtime inhabitants of a local community grow into being good citizens who know what their community needs, rightfully suspicious of outsiders who presume to know better. To find civic virtue, go to a New England town hall meeting or church-run homeless shelter, goes the thinking.

These sensibilities closely complement the argument that these theorists and a much larger collection of policy makers make that nongovernmental approaches to social problems are better than the ones legislators devise. On this view, nonprofit organizations *must* be more efficient than government agencies, more connected to the people's will, or both.[23] Etzioni contended, for example, that a "community devolution" could be a good thing when it comes to problems that local people would address more sensibly than governmental officials.[24] The idea is that moral and civic virtue develop locally, not through nationally directed, governmental effort. The thinking depends on a simple, sectoral notion of society that we should treat skeptically. Civic localism and skepticism of larger governments both assume that whatever is *not* the federal government *must* be more locally rooted and locally sustainable, and therefore better. The contrast between inefficient, clueless centralized government and local, virtuous nongovernmental effort animates a potent cultural story, and sometimes wins elections, but in the case of nonprofits, it obscures at least as much as it illuminates.

Nonprofit Housing Developers to the Rescue?

Two decades before the federal government stopped planning housing projects, the distinction between bumbling, top-down planning and virtuous, local initiative already resonated in debates over housing. A historian of public housing has written that "top-down, state-centered planning" was discredited by the late 1960s, largely because of public housing projects.[25] Policy makers, planners, and some social scientists called for an end to massive housing projects and leveling of entire neighborhoods, which they saw as the sour fruit of centralized planning. Their idea was to integrate low-income people into neighborhood life rather than sequestering them in bleak, high-rise towers that only reminded residents they were "wards of the state."[26] Neighborhood preservation and rehabilitation became the guiding priorities of federal housing policy. These complemented the community empowerment motif enshrined in mid-1960s' poverty legislation, which called for low-income people to organize themselves in local community action projects and determine their own destinies—a goal that theorists Berger and Neuhaus lauded too.[27]

The critique of centrally planned housing projects spread beyond planning specialists and federal policy makers. As early as 1966, a *New York Times* correspondent described public housing projects in Brooklyn as "monsters devouring their residents, polluting the areas about them, spewing out a social excrescence which infects the whole of our society."[28] In the succeeding decades, politicians would score points perhaps less poetically for identifying government-built housing with crime and indolence. City dwellers would disparage the housing projects as crime ridden, disorderly, and ugly to boot.[29]

Enter the local, nonprofit housing developer. During my time with the HJ coalition and nonprofit HSLA, proponents of affordable housing did point out that their developments fit in with their surrounding neighborhoods. No more high-rise monuments to monitorial modernism brought to you by the government. Two- and three-story stucco apartments with gabled, tiled roofs graced the roster of award-winning buildings at WHA's annual conference. The proposal for the HSLA housing development that I assisted with as a volunteer grant writer included plans for liaison with an inclusive social service provider and employment opportunities all just several blocks away. It seemed like the point was very much to integrate residents into the neighborhood and even empower them. An on-site resident's council would give residents a voice in running the building.

How does the optimistic take on nonprofit problem solving play out with HSLA? Did HSLA's work in fact grow out of locally bred values and traditions? With the criticisms of governmental planning in mind, we can ask even larger questions. How did HSLA's housing development practices depart from long-criticized, top-down planning methods? How did HSLA staff actually empower or speak on behalf of the socially marginalized tenants of its buildings?

To the first question, observations above suggest a skeptical response. There was nothing distinctively local about HSLA staff's volunteer-helper orientation. The scenarios above suggest that Nora, Nathan, Ricky, and Queenie all felt a sincere interest in doing good. It would be hard, though, to find *locally cultivated moral understandings* and traditions behind their work. In no way should it dishonor Queenie's or Nora's self-stated, helping orientation to observe that it is a generic, modular, transposable ethic, not one deeply rooted in a locale or people. An Armenian immigrant in one of HSLA's buildings had a colorful life story that could lend human interest, by association, to a new HSLA project elsewhere and also be transposed to "programs like ours," as Queenie phrased it. Nora learned from research conducted at another nonprofit organization that homeless seniors could be a worthwhile and gratifying focus for a housing developer's help. In both cases, social beneficence is an *abstract* quality, not a local tradition. It exists in general, and then attaches, temporarily, to particular categories of people or projects. With no criticism of the ethical impulse intended, I point out that this is distinct from the communitarian theorists' vision of morality that is organic to a locally particular people.

To the second question, about an alternative to top-down planning and administering, the best way to find out is to look closely at how HSLA staff made claims and created relationships—with funders, local citizen groups, residents, and tenants. It turns out that entrusting a lot of the administrative work of affordable housing to nonprofit organizations displaces some of the top-down planning associated with government but does not make it disappear. Nonprofit housing development does not really bring home building "closer to the local community," as one might suppose a civic effort would. In the case of HSLA, it makes more sense to say that nonprofit housing development ended up making the local nonprofit developer more governmental and sometimes more commercial. Depending on one's vision of a good society, that is not necessarily a bad thing, but it is quite different from the idea that nonprofits are fundamentally different from state agencies or businesses. It blasts the popular distinction between distant, unworthy government and local, grassroots, nonprofit efforts.

Hybrid Claims Making and Relationship Building

Making Claims to Governmental or Market Specifications

HSLA staff participated little in public rallies or activists' meetings, and did not engage in city hall deliberations during my time with them. To find claims making at HSLA, the best place to look is the long grant applications that staff wrote to fund housing projects. On the one hand, staff made claims, just as HJ or ISLA participants did. ISLA advocates made claims about local housing conditions, and so did HSLA's grant applications. ISLA's general and strategy meetings, information sheets, and testimonies included talk about "displacement," and so did HSLA's grant applications. HJ advocates wrote and spoke of its beneficiaries in terms of social categories—retirees or low-wage workers, for example. HSLA's applications did too—extremely low-income people or seniors, for instance. Reference to expert knowledge graced the communication of all three.

Still, important differences between HJ's or ISLA's claims and those from HSLA reflect differences between civic and hybrid action. Civic action is collectively self-coordinating action; people work together to organize themselves. But the claims that HSLA staff made in their grant applications were part of a much less self-coordinating process. Claims in applications followed a format determined by the city housing department, not HSLA. Applications responded to calls for proposals to fund housing for particular categories of people determined by the city agency, not the nonprofit. The application form asked questions about, for example, "the population the project intends to serve and how the decision was made to serve this population," "the physical and socio-economic characteristics of the surrounding community," and the project's "public benefit" and "impact on the neighborhood." City agency staff would score applications in a competitive process to produce a winner; different parts of the application were worth different amounts of points. HSLA did *hybrid* civic claims making.

Of course, nonprofit staff were free to apply or not for funding. In that way, they had the leeway of civic action. They may have decided that they really did feel committed to the category of people they applied for money to build for— the way volunteers come to care about the people they serve over a period of time. Nora was edified to learn that housing for homeless seniors was a fast-growing need. We should not think of *hybrid* civic claims making as simply uncharitable underneath it all or not in the public interest. It is more helpful to understand it as melding civic-sounding motives to a funding process that imposes governmental standards and practices on nonprofit organizations.

CUT AND PASTE: REPORTS, NOT ARGUMENTS

These differences between civic and hybrid ways of making claims only really hit me as I did an unexpected kind of wordsmithing for HSLA grant applications. The process itself could be exhausting, as represented in these field notes from the first day of work on a grant application to the Los Angeles Housing Department.

> I actually did work on them for three hours straight. Got bugeyed. . . . I overheard one side of maybe five phone conversations but did not keep track of any. I was engrossed in the application, trying to synthesize and parse from the earlier application they wrote to the Community Redevelopment Agency in 2007. It was a tremendous amount of repositioning, selective deleting, re-categorizing, and some writing from scratch, though not so much of that.

Drafting narratives for grant applications to build the MacArthur Park apartments engaged me in the same engrossing process. It was not exactly "writing" but instead more like micromanaging sentences and paragraphs. My field notes tried to summarize my experience of it:

> You get into managing text, and trying to figure out how to cut and paste and suture and compose in relation to other blocks of text, with a title/ subtitle format that will create order out of mess, and it is hard to break away from the whole combined puzzle. . . . You cut and paste the part about MacArthur Park neighborhood poverty from some other application, and the part about people being displaced. . . . It is social movement talk turned into text management.

Grant applications called for claims that *report* or give *overviews*, more than they try to *convince* the way civic actors traditionally would. Applications called for standardized information, more than in forums where two or more sides use facts to argue a viewpoint. The information that grant applications called for is more amenable to cutting and pasting because standardized facts about a neighborhood (social composition, amenities, and the number of transit stops) are supposed to be the same for any reader, probably over many months' time. Civic actors, in contrast, might want different facts depending on the audience, proximity of a campaign to political events on the calendar, or other contingencies.

The difference between this hybrid claims making and more thoroughly civic, citizen-driven claims making is like the difference between taking an open-book essay exam and participating in a public debate. The exam gets graded, by predetermined criteria at one point. HSLA staff wrote with an eye for criteria—the eight questions—in hopes of doing well on the "exam" and winning the money. When HJ or ISLA coalition advocates launched claims about displacement, gentrification, or the benefits of affordable housing, in contrast, those claims entered an ongoing debate. In the process, housing advocates might *change* what they say—within the parameters of a discursive field and style—and revise claims *depending on what opponents or bystander publics say*. It is not a one-shot exam. Civic claims making is a more open-ended process than hybrid claims making.[30]

REPRESENTING THE LOCALS?

A more subtle but important difference between civic and noncivic action also matters here. By definition, civic actors make claims about conditions that they consider problems and want to convince others to take as problems too. The claim represents a constituency of people who care already, and projects that to an audience that *should* care.

ISLA and HJ advocates purported to speak on behalf of distinct constituencies—the community that demands justice for Latinx neighborhoods in South Los Angeles or community of Angelenos who share an interest in affordable housing mandates. HJ staff crafted and recrafted talking points for use at city hall, in letters from African American leaders or Latinx businesspeople, or for interviews with the press; my records include multiple drafts to prove the point. That sounds sort of like the text-management work that I dubbed "cut and paste." But they drafted and redrafted claims in relation to specific grassroots constituencies that they wanted the claims to represent. Sometimes, especially at the start of the campaign, they experimented with new claims, trying to hit the right note. A year before HJ's kickoff rally, for example, HJ staffers tried out campaign slogans at a "messaging brainstorm":

> You think we're good enough to clean your floor but not good enough to live next door.

> We're good enough to clean your floor AND good enough to live next door!

> It's not just about buildings; it's about people/neighbors.

> Development is pushing people away from their jobs.

> This isn't about statistics; it's about our lives.

> The only permanent housing is jail.

> Twelve million dollars for dog parks, zero for us. [31]

Whether cheeky or earnest, the claims that HJ advocates projected were *coming from a "we" that the claims represent.*

But who exactly was represented by HSLA's claims? Assertions in nonprofit HSLA's grant applications did not come from or represent local people *to* some larger public. There was no smaller "we" trying to convince the public or its leaders regarding the solution to a problem. Rather, claims in grant applications offered an *overview* of conditions ostensibly true for all observers, for any combination of "us." This is, classically, how *governmental* administrators communicate. They speak as outside managers rather than participants in a fray in which citizens are arguing, compromising, and figuring things out.

This may sound like a condemnation of HSLA's communication or perhaps the entire grant application process. But I intend it only as a description that alerts us to some differences between civic and state-driven forms of communication. The point is not to nominate "good" and "bad" actors here. Neither is the point that HSLA claims relied only on facts, while HJ and ISLA claims eschewed facts. Recall that ISLA, for instance, mobilized facts about health care disparities in Los Angeles County, and HJ referred frequently to the facts regarding housing built and housing needed in different income categories. These facts became part of claims about conditions "we" see as problems that "you" should see as problems too. All three parties' assertions referred to factual information. The point is that they related *differently to* the facts.

Talk of "displacement" is a good illustration. Until I started watching and working alongside HSLA housing developers, I had assumed that the word "displacement" was intrinsically a criticism, not a description. I thought it was a term for criticizing gentrification from an activist sensibility. I figured that was why it was a victory for ISLA when college officials changed stances and agreed that displacement was happening. That is why I was surprised that an application to a city agency for affordable housing funds could use the term prominently. Wouldn't a city agency prefer a neutral, nonpolitical-sounding application? Yet on HSLA's first application to fund the MacArthur apartments, Nora amended my draft's answer to the question of why HSLA chose its target population (seniors) with the phrase "the need to minimize permanent displacement." The existing template I was redrafting already noted that seniors have a difficult time finding affordable apartments. Nora also appended a sentence further down the page that seniors were affected by an increase in "profitable conversion to condos and lofts." This sounded exactly like what HJ said in activist settings about no more conversions or what LAPO said about "no more displacement." I wasn't really expecting this and asked about it.

> Paul: "I wasn't sure if it might sound too controversial or political to bring up about conversions."
>
> Nora: "No"—nodding.
>
> Paul: "This sounds exactly like what Housing Justice says."
>
> Nora: "Yes, they [the city housing agency] want to stop conversions that displace people."

Nora did not say "we are against displacement," the way ISLA advocates routinely did. She said the state agency had a priority. The "need to minimize permanent displacement" was not a claim *on behalf of* displaced people. It was a fact ratified by the municipal agency. HSLA was not trying to convince a larger public that displacement is a problem in need of solving, though staff individually made it clear that they thought that. It was trying to score well on

the agency's "test" by offering a good rationale for the population it was proposing to house.

Though they did not clearly represent a particular constituency, claims in
HSLA grant applications did come implicitly from a point of view—one that
surveys general features and summarizes them from above. It shows in HSLA's
application for a grant to fund construction of the "first version" of the MacArthur Park apartments—the version that would have won money to house low-
income seniors.[32] Parts evidently had been cut and pasted from at least two
other HSLA grant applications. The cut-and-paste ethic made quick pivoting
from one request for proposals to another more feasible, as the contracting
regime demands. First came a description of "physical and socio-economic
characteristics of the surrounding community":

> MacArthur Park was established in 1885. . . . Neon signs, believed to be the
> first in the United States, adorn the rooftops. . . . MacArthur Park is an
> urban oasis with a lake and paddle boats, a large, sand playing field. . . .
> MacArthur Park/Westlake is known as the most densely populated area
> "west of Manhattan" and is one of the most impoverished neighborhoods
> in Los Angeles.

Next is an excerpt from the section portraying public benefits of the
project:

> The [MacArthur Park apartments] food bank is a public benefit that any
> member of the community may patronize. . . . The project will redevelop
> a building which has long been an eyesore on the block. . . . [A] high
> percentage of the resident population has been transient and very difficult
> to manage, evidenced by the high number of eviction proceedings initi-
> ated by the management agent over the years as well as the high number
> of calls to LAPD.
>
> Development of [the MacArthur Park apartments] complements efforts
> to eradicate area crime, some of which was generated by residents of the
> existing residential hotel, and contribute the stability of a strong, senior
> residential community.
>
> The project offers the opportunity to achieve a mutual goal shared by
> HSLA and LAHD: to find an appropriate solution to a property with a
> troubled past and uncertain future.

And finally, here is a short segment portraying the neighborhood impact of
the new development:

> The [MacArthur Park apartments] will add to the renaissance currently
> underway in the MacArthur Park neighborhood. First, an investment by

LAHD in this project will leverage City investments already made and committed to physical improvements, recreational programs, and crime fighting.

The text of the grant proposal is a dispassionate overview of demographics, social and economic conditions, and public facilities. Possibly excepting the mention of a food bank, the material about public benefits assumes a reader who views the neighborhood and housing project as *objects* seen from above. Though there is no explicit "we," there is an implicit viewpoint—that of people who would be interested in reducing crime, improving architectural aesthetics, and/or finding a better and more financially sustainable use for a building. While lower-income people care about crime and neighborhood aesthetics too, one still can ask who would be expressing concerns about the currently existing building's residents who were "hard to manage" and involved in crime. The proposal sounds like it speaks to people who would see the neighborhood and apartment project as things *to be dealt with*, to be ameliorated—from outside. It speaks administratively. That is normal for state actors; it is not what we usually expect of civic actors.

The proposal speaks a bit in a commercial voice as well, depicting a historic neighborhood with vintage neon signs and paddleboating. These passages reworked text from an older proposal, for a Community Redevelopment Agency (CRA) grant, written to address a question about the market appeal of the proposed development. Particularly pertinent, the proposal noted that the MacArthur Park apartments would complement ongoing investments by the CRA in aesthetic, streetscape improvements. In other words, the MacArthur Park apartments would complement other efforts to upgrade the neighborhood and make it more commercially viable.

Hybrid Relationship Building

HSLA needed to maintain a complicated set of relationships with tenants, funding partners, social service providers, and local civic associations. HSLA staff might sustain a single relationship using several different styles—perhaps even simultaneously. Relations with tenants are a good example.

MANAGING, ADMINISTERING, AND HELPING TENANTS—ALL AT THE SAME TIME

Part of Ricky's job was to make sure that a prospective tenant had enough monthly income to pay the rent. Prospective tenants for HSLA's buildings needed vetting the way tenants for any ordinary apartment would. Administering the process in line with state and federal regulations was more complicated than that, though. Nora outsourced one entire HSLA scene to another location, where employees of an apartment management company interviewed tenants and checked their documents with those guidelines in mind. For a week I watched as Russian- and Spanish-speaking applicants for the Hollywood Apartments managed with varying degrees of English-language proficiency to navigate the fifteen-minute interview.

One couple brought their own translator, who kept asking the management employee Janice to repeat herself.

> Janice: "The next form is the child support questionnaire, even if he doesn't receive child support, he signs it."
>
> Translator: "Child support?"
>
> Janice: "He doesn't receive child support? He needs to check no and sign."
>
> Janice: "The next form is the nonemployment affidavit."
>
> Translator: "Slow, I don't understand."
>
> Janice: "Next form is stating he has no more than $5,000 in the bank account."
>
> The translator doesn't understand. Janice repeats more slowly, several times.

It is easy to see why at least a few applicants would be mistrustful of the process and inclined to threaten with lawsuits. The trouble is that being more responsive and having better-trained translators on hand for multiple languages would cost money that would have to come out of the grants that pay for the housing project, leaving less money for something else equally necessary.

Janice was the management company's compliance specialist. HSLA depended on her to make sure that tenant selection complied with the rules. Janice explained on my first day in the company office that if the company selects a tenant who earns an income higher than what an apartment is slated for, then the whole building may be called "out of compliance" with the law. Affordable housing built with tax money is supposed to go to people in income brackets that are too low to cover ordinary market-rate rents safely. The out-of-compliance designation would endanger the nonprofit's access to state funds set aside for financing the building that housed a tenant over the income limit.[33]

> Paul: "So in a way you're doing some of the government's work."
>
> Janice: "It's a program for low-income families, trying to build themselves up and get out of low-income housing."

In this scene HSLA was like a collective, outsourced social worker, earning money from government funds to administer tenants. When HSLA staff or employees of the management company talked of tenants "gaming the system," it made sense given the scene. Here were professionals who saw themselves as responsible for *administering* things fairly—not part of the usual imagination of what civic actors do. Recall that Ricky wanted to do home inspections to make sure there was not an expensive car parked in an HSLA apartment's driveway. Janice talked occasionally in the same conversational register: "A lot of times, someone claims zero income, but they're getting social security on the side," she observed. She told me how one time, applicants attested to a low monthly income, submitting pay stubs that were all suspiciously written for exactly the same amount of wage; closer inspection revealed the stubs were written to different people. The applicants turned out to be affluent, and had hoped to make a lot of money living in a cheap apartment and renting out their own more expensive residences. And like social workers, HSLA staff had administrative leeway to determine for how long tenants deserved affordable housing. Would a tenant with an increase in income have to move out? Janice explained that it would be up to the owner's (HSLA's) "judgment that they feel they [the tenants] don't need low-income housing anymore. If they [HSLA] don't think they are losing tax credits, then they usually won't evict."

> Paul: "So it's up to the owner to decide if they want to do "good" [by offering a low-rent apartment] for someone even poorer?"

> Janice: "Yes."

HSLA's own financial stability would help determine if it should evict a more well-resourced current tenant in favor of one who falls into a low-income bracket.

In short, administrative and managerial duties sometimes ran the scene, crowding out the volunteer helping impulse that HSLA staff like Queenie or Nora expressed with such sincerity. At HSLA, "helping" had its own full-time staff person.

THE COMMUNITY LIAISON

As the community liaison, Nathan orchestrated a great deal of HSLA's helping. The tag suggests distance between HSLA and whomever might be the community. Civic efforts like ISLA or HJ coalitions would not have a community liaison. Each already claimed to be the voice of a community of some kind—a "we"—no need for an intermediary. All the same, Nathan kept up an ambitious docket of projects that often he himself conceived of as helping what he called the community. In that way, he was the primary civic actor of HSLA.

Nathan's weekly to-do lists were filled with meetings of local associations. Just as a US small business proprietor might join a local volunteer club in order to do good but also develop a good reputation that could facilitate more business later, Nathan kept a peripatetic meeting schedule that gave HSLA a civic presence and reputational goodwill.[34] For a different part of this study, I saw him, for instance, at the monthly meetings of a MacArthur Park neighborhood improvement coalition that met at a tamale restaurant that operated as a nonprofit organization to train Latin American immigrants in food service.[35] The attentively self-curated local notable who ran the restaurant, a youth arts program director, two local beat police officers, a parks district employee, a local elementary school principal, and assorted others met monthly. Nathan updated the group on HSLA's plans for affordable apartment developments in the neighborhood. He cultivated relationships with neighborhood institutions like some of the ones represented in this coalition, along with others much less commercial, including several with an explicitly political mission. He told me, for instance, about a new grant awarded to a HSLA-led team, which included a low-income public health clinic, a Central American immigrant and workers' rights organization, and two others, that is "for the community," and would pay for a thousand units of broadband access, youth training program, local inventory of services, low-cost computer purchasing program, and free internet access.

Paul: "This is for people in one of your buildings?"

Nathan: "This is for the community. . . . It's not our core business, but it's something I wanted to do."

Paul: "Nice to have the leeway to do that kind of work."

Nathan sometimes could sound like an ISLA advocate. He looked skeptically on people who only spoke *for* the community rather than *from* it, but as we see soon, his activities as community liaison were more in line with the *volunteer* spirit of Nora or Queenie, or social service, than the oppositional community of identity that ISLA's Ethan or Victor were leading. At one of HSLA's buildings, he designed a food giveaway program—for the community, not only the residents—that would save building staff the bother of storing food. I helped him give out bags with turkey and canned groceries before Thanksgiving one year to a line of people that stretched around the block. The building hosted an after-school educational program too, run by its own staff, intended to introduce underprivileged teens to a broader world of career possibilities than they might imagine otherwise. To introduce urban planning professions, the program tapped Nathan and a university professor to lead a neighborhood surveying walk. At first it seemed just like the neighborhood walks that ISLA leaders put on to teach local residents and students how to identify the traces of power and privilege behind the features of the built environment. But Nathan's walk was a striking contrast.

This was not so much about celebrating "our turf," and pointing out indignities and injustices, as when ISLA led tours for students. For Nathan, it was more an opportunity to model professional success to the underprivileged. He introduced himself to the high school students thus: "I work for Housing Solutions for Los Angeles. We build low-income housing." The survey walk proceeded without empowering euphemisms, and on the walk, Nathan pointed out now and then that "this is one of our buildings." When one of the walkers said he did not know why they were doing this surveying walk, Nathan explained, "There are a lot of little local restaurants and their business is hurting. . . . This is to figure out if it's because of parking or access to transportation." Whether or not Nathan thought privately that endangered business related to something more social-structural or disempowering, he did not bring it up that afternoon. We stood on the sidewalk across the street from Pueblecito. Nathan and the restaurant proprietor, a wearily smiling older man, faced us.

> Nathan said, "We own this building. . . . It has the restaurant on the bottom, and it has low-income apartments for senior citizens and families. You would never know it [from looking at the building]. . . . There are a lot of possibilities in life. I grew up in a neighborhood like this one. . . . I went to school to become a planner. . . . Now I have the luxury of passing out little cards with my name on them."

> Nathan introduced the proprietor and told us Pueblecito is a great place to eat. He said, "They're providing food, they're providing culture—we don't want to lose them," and concluded that "the message is: eat at Pueblecito."

Had an ISLA advocate been leading the tour, the message would have been: proud members of this community resist displacement.

EMPOWERING TENANTS?

Fieldwork at HSLA began just a month after the big kickoff rally for HJ coalition's affordable housing campaign. HSLA was a prominent member of WHA, which sponsored HJ and paid staff salaries. Yet over the several months' time during which I was a volunteer worker, I never heard anyone say that HSLA staff—or residents of HSLA buildings—should get involved in the campaign. The coalition's proposed MIHO would have benefited HSLA by guaranteeing more opportunities to apply for grants. It also would have benefited residents who potentially might identify as inadequately housed people who needed or deserved better chances. Nora mentioned to me once, offhandedly, that some-one from HJ had called to see if she could attend a coalition event. She sup-ported the cause but did not really have time. I recalled, then, that while vol-unteering in the HJ office, telephoning housing developers to turn them out for HJ's kickoff rally, I had gotten a similar message from the HSLA staffer I called. Unlike staff in some other hybrid civic, nonprofit organizations, HSLA workers did not pursue efforts explicitly aimed at "empowering" their clients to speak up for funding that could have benefited them at least indirectly.[36]

Behind the scenes, Nathan got involved in the kind of local empowerment efforts that a community of identity pursues. In a few scenes outside the office, HSLA became a quiet ally. Nathan encountered other characters from my study, making for fascinating comparisons. He told me, for example, that "a bunch of nonprofits" including HSLA, a local low-cost clinic, two low-income tenant organizations, and SHAPLA planned a "workshop day kind of like the one that Ethan from SED did, the first day I met you, except bigger—for a lot more people."[37] The workshop, "for people in the community in general," would discuss "the role of the CRA" and highlight "what the community wants—no, *needs*." Ideally, these needs would inform the CRA's plans to reno-vate a decommissioned theater near the MacArthur Park apartments. Nathan said he did not know if the community would have real decision-making power," but hoped the CRA would invite the coalition of groups speaking on the com-munity's behalf to judge proposals for renovating the theater building.

Terry, SHAPLA's gadfly from HJ coalition meetings, had joined the newly emerging coalition, by invitation. Nathan chuckled, "She tried to take over the meeting, saying, 'This is what I want.'" He said, "She wants to get us [HSLA] out" of the group, adding that "they [SHAPLA] come in as an invited mem-ber," not like "us" who are "the people who created it." Terry and SHAPLA "aren't involved as having constituents or a base." I was still trying to figure out why she wanted HSLA out of the effort and tried out an interpretation.

Paul: "She's not crazy about developers."

Nathan: "She's not crazy about any kind of developer, nonprofit or for profit. She actually said to me at one point, 'You can take *that* to your people.'"

In contrast, he said, "We're [HSLA] in the neighborhood, we're on the ground—we're giving out food . . . dealing with people's real problems. . . . SHAPLA doesn't have a take on what people here need."

What Nathan was narrating to me was hybrid civic action. His criticism of Terry sounded like ISLA members' criticism of people who only speak for the community without being from it. Nathan talked community empowerment, yet at the same time created and promoted programming that served "needs"— or addressed "people's real problems," as he put it—the way social service professionals and volunteer helpers serve homeless people's needs. The timeline for satisfying human needs is individual, and cyclic, repeating on a daily basis. The timeline for a community of identity that wants to empower itself is a long, projected history of collective struggle—the hundred years' war mentioned earlier. The individual human needs that HSLA was in touch with by way of Nathan's valiant efforts were not the needs—usually cast as *demands*—that SHAPLA or ISLA would even consider fighting for. Civic, community empowerment, and social service provision co-organized HSLA's work in the neighborhood, in Nathan's view.

Pushback more potent than Terry's limited Nathan's involvement in the community coalition. At a neighborhood improvement meeting, a half year after HSLA and other organizations hatched their coalition, I asked Nathan for an update. Squinting mischievously, he said, "We're not really involved." The CRA included coalition participants' ideas in its plan to redevelop the theater, but there was no official CBA. Additionally, a CRA staff person had phoned him, sounding annoyed that HSLA was involved in this community coalition at all. Nathan explained, "CRA is one of our major funders," and it thought of this community coalition as basically a pain. So, I summarized, CRA was annoyed with the coalition, not HSLA. Yes, that was it. Nathan said, "I do it on my own." The dance of perceptions and expectations in the contracting regime shifted Nathan into individual, unofficial support for the local coalition.

Beyond "the Civic Sector"

When we follow action instead of following a sector, we see that governmental ways of making claims and relating to people do not disappear when the government contracts with nonprofits. Governmental practices simply get outsourced and become patches in the nonprofit's unfolding quilt of action. HSLA professionals imbued their work with a transposable volunteer-helping ethic that serves the community in general. Staff organized themselves as professionals using hard-won resources to help people with housing problems. But at the same time, a lot of the claims and relationships that went into this helping were shaped by governmental directives and sometimes reflected a commercial real estate sensibility too.

In some ways, HSLA was local. Its enterprise was locally based, not a regional or national enterprise. Nathan energetically kept up HSLA's relations with local leaders and local notables—Pueblecito restaurant's proprietor, the upbeat youth arts program director, and the overworked guy from the free clinic who organized local residents to challenge the CRA during his precious off-hours. In other ways, HSLA staff were outsiders wielding abstractions of limited, if any, use to the people they housed; their grant applications' claims about housing and neighborhood conditions read like governmental reports, an apartment manager's files, or real estate ad copy. Staff expressed genuinely charitable motives and went out of their way to help hurting individuals, yet they also vetted and monitored their tenants closely, dispassionately, and annually. That is hybrid civic action.

In their LA office, HSLA staff practiced a soft-spoken version of what political anthropologist James C. Scott (1998) has called "seeing like a state." The narratives I worked on for the MacArthur Park apartments took a broad, managerial overview of the local population, not one rooted in ongoing local conversation or contestation. Applications for funding took their cue and housing priorities from city hall, or the California state agencies in Sacramento, not from the neighborhood that would receive the new housing. Well intended as it may be, affordable housing under the contracting regime depends on abstract expertise more than the local knowledge that scholars like Scott, or communitarian thinkers like Berger and Neuhaus, all celebrate. Nathan and Nora had enough local know-how to know that the St. Francis Rehabilitation Center was a half mile from their new housing development. And they knew that it could sound good to write St. Francis into the part of their grant proposal that described services HSLA would offer to special needs tenants. At the same time, it is not obvious that MacArthur Park needed housing for homeless seniors more than for other identifiable groups—but this group was big and underserved in the state at large. They needed to live *somewhere* in decent, safe housing. Plunking dozens of poor, high-needs people down in one building, in a neighborhood already remarkably poor, might only further strain an already-stressed, local social ecology. Disregarding local relationships means ignoring what makes any neighborhood sustainable over time, as urban theorist and activist Jane Jacobs (1961) famously pointed out. Affordable housing development by way of the contracting regime turns out to be rather like monocultural foresting.[38]

As long as there is a contracting regime apportioning limited funds for affordable housing, what might be the alternative? Grants made with public tax money come with governmentally determined priorities that may enforce a one-size-fits-all approach to housing. Yet if a state funding agency does *not* prioritize especially underserved or fast-growing homeless populations, why would affordable housing developers who need to keep balance sheets in the black ever build for those populations, especially if others take less staff time to write proposals for and are cheaper to house too? If statewide or even citywide calls for proposals don't rotate housing priorities—housing for homeless seniors, low-income seniors, families, and veterans—then some groups may get left out altogether. Should those groups do with fewer opportunities because they are inconvenient?

In the sunniest view, when hybrid civic action builds affordable housing through the contracting regime, it combines neighborly virtues of localism with the largesse of tax money and a respect for equal opportunity. Illustrations from HSLA suggest a different picture: hybrid civic action leads actors through difficult dilemmas, played out in a patchwork of suddenly shifting scenes. The actors do not always act like people cultivated by, rooted in, and responsible to a distinct locale; they can't, since they also carry out governmental and occasionally commercial roles, and depend on governmental or private money. While illustrations here hardly exhaust the world of nonprofit housing in Los Angeles, they do also indicate that nonprofit developers are likely to encounter a lot more demand than their efforts can possibly meet, as long as they are negotiating dilemmas and making ends meet in a shrinking welfare state.

For some observers, the big problem here is dependence on external money. Some left-progressive critics argue that the only good nonprofit is one that sidesteps the money train of the contracting regime and acts like a social movement organization, not a hybrid social service agency. In the case of nonprofit housing development, that would mean organizing tenants to demand collectively that housing is a right.[39] But the research record is ambiguous on the funding question. Sometimes governmental funding does not discernibly affect the political aspects of a nonprofit's mission.[40] But sometimes, participating in the contracting regime transforms an organization's strident social critique into a depoliticized, social service mission; for example, feminist consciousness-raising at a battered women's shelter gives way to individual-centered counseling.[41]

Maybe the problem is more complicated. If so, a popular, US cultural story does not help. The story has it that participation in public life is either voluntary, virtuous, and internally motivated—thus civic—or else coerced, corrupted, and externally funded, and hence noncivic. Scenes from nonprofit housing development suggest this binary hides much more varied and complex relations between civic action and funding sources. Nonprofits *do* plan housing developments with funding in mind *and* their staff do attach classically civic-sounding motives to their work. I did see evidence that developers avoid action that would upset funders, such as Nathan's careful dance with the CRA. But it also is possible to pursue a consistent, civic mission with external funds—albeit within parameters that civic actors do not set. ISLA advocates initiated this kind of hybrid as they carried out the terms of their

CBA agreement with the Manchester property developer. That effort invited other dilemmas.

Different Hybrid, Different Dilemmas

ISLA coalition's CBA made ISLA representatives into de facto partners with the Manchester developer in a community of interest. ISLA members would help choose tenants for that 5 percent of the Manchester's apartments that would rent at below the market rate as per the agreement. Members also would help administer seed money to initiate other affordable housing projects in the neighborhood. Once perceived as a menace, the Manchester developer was now a *collaborator*. Work with the CBA generated distinctive dilemmas for an ISLA committee.

The ISLA coalition itself was not a home-building enterprise, and its staff salaries did not depend on grants from a statewide or nationwide contracting regime for housing. Staff did not need to stay perpetually flexible and ready to retrain themselves for new service populations, unlike Nora of HSLA who found it stimulating to learn about homeless seniors, never having built for them previously. When ISLA representatives planned for their new roles as affordable housing administrators, they depended especially on technical know-how from a new affordable developer in the coalition, CGTC, which had shared, then acquired several staff formerly with a founding member organization of the coalition. CGTC worked as a community of identity in its monthly meeting and strategic planning scenes, sharing not only the same personnel but also same notion of community with other ISLA representatives, the community that would last beyond and set limits on the community of interest with the developer.[42] At the time of the Manchester CBA, CGTC's funds came from a foundation grant awarded to promote housing stability in the community as well as money from a different CBA, paid by a different developer in lieu of building affordable housing.

No dilemma of disembeddedness versus responsiveness shadowed ISLA's work with the Manchester. In hindsight, though, it was clear that ISLA would encounter new predicaments as soon as the city planning commission had ratified the CBA. They surfaced as a newly appointed ISLA committee began envisioning ISLA's practical roles in the CBA. For brevity's sake, I pick out some relevant themes from just one of the committee's earlier meetings, in 2011.

Committee members including Raimunda of SED, Thalia of CGTC, and Francine agreed with a consultant they brought on board that housing developers working with the CBA needed several skill sets. They needed not only to understand the complicated world of affordable housing development but the tenant's perspective on housing too, and just as important, have "experience doing grassroots work," as Thalia and the consultant noted. This was, after all, neighborhood-based development, the consultant said. Here was another chance for an ethnographer to let on to genuine puzzlement about who the neighborhood was, with an annoyingly naive question.

> Paul: "So 'neighborhood-based' means a developer who is actually in the neighborhood, like CGTC—not one that just happens to want to build in the neighborhood?"

> Thalia said that yes, CGTC, or a community development corporation, and the consultant said that it means a developer with "a connection to the neighborhood. . . . You're going to have to decide what that connection is, the quality of it."

It was not going to become much clearer than the time, several years earlier at an ISLA street fair, when Thalia and Francine talked to me about the boundaries of the Lincoln neighborhood. Community members just knew. In any event, ISLA's participation in administering the CBA, like the agreement itself, was on behalf of the community.

That means ISLA staff could consider equity and responsiveness somewhat differently from how HSLA did. The dilemma did not go away, but "responsiveness" meant attending to constituents the way a community of identity does. We could call this a dilemma of "equity versus the community." It emerged in the discussion on how to select tenants for the Manchester's reduced-rent apartments. Thalia proposed that ISLA draw on a list of tenants in need of more affordable local housing—tenants who belonged to CGTC or the cooperative land trust. The consultant thought this would work because there was supposed to be a preference for displaced, formerly local tenants when the subsidized, Manchester apartments were getting leased up. Yet the consultant also brought up the equity implications of a tenant "list": "How does that meet fair housing standards?" She preferred to talk in terms of a "marketing plan"; the phrase itself sounds more like a broadcast pitch instead of a narrowcasting invitation. Thalia spoke more from the "responsiveness" angle, concerned for the community, while not ignoring equity. The CBA set aside money for a (legal) "compliance reviewer." Thalia wondered if some of that large sum could not be redirected, within the CBA's terms, to help ISLA or CGTC members—the community—position themselves for strong applications.

> "So there's a whole group of our members and mother members that could be ready. So we have this relation with the developer; I want to move this from a compliance relation to getting our members stable. . . . You get this

a lot in affordable housing, where you don't get many of the local community."

ISLA's version of responsiveness was different from HSLA's. The heavily Armenian neighborhoods surrounding the Hollywood Apartments were not HSLA's community but rather one among others to try being responsive to. Thalia, on the other hand, assumed the point was to try to prioritize the most threatened or already-displaced members of ISLA's community—without violating basic fairness. Thalia wanted to help "people from our community going into those units—not violate fair housing, but maximize the opportunity for our people to get in. . . . CGTC wants to do a training to get our people out in front."

The "civic" part of hybrid civic action in HSLA scenes was not the same as civic action in scenes where ISLA was working with the Manchester CBA either. HSLA's public-facing work was about doing good in general. The assumption, similar to what casual volunteering supposes, was that there are lots of needs out there; the benefactor picks one to work on, the way Nora picked the housing needs of homeless seniors. Meeting those needs, and doing it fairly, was the greatest good. But the civic aspect of ISLA's work with the CBA was rooted in a particular community, not the general population of Los Angeles. The consultant proposed the CBA was "an opportunity to develop a new model that doesn't depend on big tax credits"—in other words, that does not depend on the contracting regime and its ethos of compliance with regulations. The committee wanted to institute an ethos of community empowerment instead. Francine said this was "an opportunity to build community capacity."

Community empowerment would have to happen within the bounds of a CBA as opposed to the contracting regime. That too would involve a dilemma—we could call it "community versus collaboration"—built into this private-funded method of creating affordable housing. The problem came up most starkly as the committee discussed the seed money program for developers. Members originally imagined putting this part of the CBA into effect by establishing a loan program for affordable housing developers. Running such a program would require making judgments about deservingness among organizations all identified with the community. And loan payments would return to a fund with the developer's name on it, ultimately a symbol of the developer's largesse. Members proposed instead to distribute the seed money as grants, not loans, to facilitate community-oriented nonprofit housing developers. Rather than loan worthiness, the seed money program's selection criteria could emphasize a developer's creative plans for building its own community-serving capacities as it built housing for local, low-income tenants of color. The idea was to empower rightly oriented nonprofit developers, strengthening the community versus sustaining a pot of money in the developer's name.

Research with ISLA ended before the Manchester opened its affordable apartment units. These observations are enough to suggest that ISLA's civic-commercial hybrid worked somewhat differently from the state-civic hybrid of HSLA. ISLA preserved its community-driven approach to the problem of displacement—within quite narrow parameters though. While ISLA advocates would not put it quite this way, their work indirectly facilitated the continued operations of a large property developer who previously had shown little concern for the community priorities that ISLA promoted.

But beyond the dilemma that ISLA members themselves experienced, of working with a former challenger, there was a big trade-off for ISLA and housing advocates at large. CBA-style agreements access private money, turning it into homes for lower-income people, without instituting a potentially unpopular tax. By definition, CBAs link affordable housing opportunities to sites that developers have already determined to build, for developer (and market) reasons. Stocking a neighborhood or city with more affordable housing through CBAs keeps those developers steering urban development. The community becomes a kind of transaction cost on the way to further development that feeds the urban growth machine. Neither communities nor the broad public decides where affordable housing will go next. It depends on which developer happens to be building big, and is willing to offer or submit to an agreement. Thalia had recognized the problem already, telling me over coffee one day that the CBA device, helpful as it can be, is not a long-term strategy for securing housing for a city's low-income citizens.

What Civic Really Is

To understand the civic, scholars and popular commentators often have relied on misleading images and misplaced moral fervor. Nonprofit organizations have gotten caught up in the crosswinds of idealization and critique, elevated or disparaged in sometimes empirically unsupportable ways. The scenarios and discussions in this chapter have called out these empirical problems.

For some writers, *local* voluntary public action is by definition civic, and laudable, and nonprofit housing developers are local. But HSLA did not clearly speak either from or for any local constituency. Neither did its hard work to build more housing depend on special local customs and traditions of the sort that communitarian thinkers uphold. Its beneficent reputation did likely depend at least partly on the indefatigable community liaison. It is true that local staff probably would find out more easily than faraway agencies how far the nearest adult day center was from a planned apartment complex. Yet an internet search and a couple short videoconferences might also have done the trick.

For others, *nongovernmental* public action is by definition civic, and laudable, and nonprofit housing developers are not the government. Here is where sectoral thinking plays its biggest role. Money for something expensive like housing has to come from somewhere, and government money from taxes is a big source. Reducing government's role in how exactly that money is spent—a primary goal of the contracting regime—does not diminish all the less direct ways that governmentally set priorities, criteria, and safeguards enable as well as constrain nonprofit organizations that apply for grants. We might say the money empowers "local" initiative or at least initiative in a different sector. Yet we might also say the contracting regime makes nonprofits more like outsourced governmental agencies that monitor their clients the way traditional social workers do. It is worth adding that if the taxpaying public supports equal opportunity in housing and agrees that residential racial segregation is unacceptable, then the governmental regulation of civic responsiveness is hardly a bad thing. The problem is making government into the stock, bad guy character in the story and relying on a reverse valorization of the other parties, meanwhile forgetting how housing nonprofits depend on relationships with governmental agencies.

Finally, for some critics, real civic action leaves *money*, at least large sums of it, out of the picture. Money corrupts civic and political missions, goes the thinking. While the research record on that claim is mixed, as noted above, the contrast between ISLA and HSLA shows that it is entirely possible to pursue a civic approach to affordable housing while drawing on outside money, and from a for-profit company no less. The money does of course come with strings attached, which rope the nonprofit into offering or managing housing on some of the granting developer's terms. If there is no for-profit housing or other commercial development, there is no CBA. In the case of foundation-funded affordable housing, homes become available in line with private donors' ideas about needs, rather than private entrepreneurs' ideas about where and for whom to build. Whether initiated by foundations and donors or entrepreneurs, neither process is steered by public input. At the same time, it would be wrong to say that neither HSLA nor ISLA hosted any civic action.

The best way to understand civic is not by looking for what is voluntary and local, nongovernmental, or free of outside money. It is better to follow and interpret collective, problem-solving action.

Conclusion

BENEFITS OF A BIGGER BOX

AROUND THE WORLD, researchers are using something like the conceptual box of civic action to study social advocacy and participatory planning.[1] What do we gain from adopting this alternative to the view of social advocates as strategic entrepreneurs? And what might social advocates or broader publics gain from the move toward concepts of style, scene, or discursive field? It is good to consider these questions the way pragmatist thinkers and especially Dewey would, which is to say they are related. It will help to start with the idea that scientific inquiry is more like a dialogue than a grand collection of correct answers to test questions.

Our sociological questions only rarely are answered purely with facts, much as facts must be central in any answer. Credible claims *about* facts emerge through dialogue, not through the force of facticity. Once-accepted claims may lose their legitimacy in light of continued dialogue about more or different evidence; scientific truth is a controvertible consensus. That is why philosophers talk about communities of inquiry.[2] These exist to assess and dispute claims about facts in light of evidence scholars bring to the table. A community of inquiry looks for a good "fit" between claims and evidence.[3]

Nothing in this dialogic view of knowledge production should sound controversial. Acting on it can expand our conceptual imaginations—but in sometimes challenging ways. A big reason is that "fit" turns out to be an ambiguous criterion. Questions of fit will not always resolve with more evidence. The specialist's name for the problem here is "underdetermination." Feminist epistemologist Helen Longino (2002, 126) puts it this way: "Data alone are consistent with different and conflicting hypotheses." And so background assumptions fill in the underdetermination gap between empirical evidence and knowledge claims.[4] Sometimes those background assumptions keep us from noticing evidence or patterns in evidence that could suggest new hypotheses. Even the most carefully considered research hypotheses take for granted some operating assumptions about what people or societies are like, or what action is like. These assumptions keep us from checking out other hypotheses, not because those others are less scientifically valid, but because background assumptions work like a kind of collegial subconscious that tracks our imagination in certain directions and obscures others.[5]

The entrepreneurial actor model sometimes has worked in this way. And as case chapters pointed out, it *would* be possible to fit some of the study's evidence into the kind of claims that model can sponsor. To do that, though, we would need to shave off a lot of important findings. Some of the big puzzles that prompted this study would remain; background assumptions might keep us from even recognizing them. Any community rests partly on background knowledge, but a community of inquiry, especially in Dewey's (1927, 168; 1938, 490) view, ought to be able to examine that knowledge critically, potentially freeing up new hypotheses and alternative lines of inquiry to consider. Communities of inquiry do not just assess facts but instead, occasionally, entire preexisting conversations about facts.[6] That is what critical "literature reviews" are good for, and that is what the review of the entrepreneurial actor model and its silences was doing in chapter 1. It suggested an alternative view: that actors are socially embedded and culturally cultivated.

Claims about civic action do not have to invalidate established insights anchored in the entrepreneurial actor model. Broader than any single line of research or theory, the model has proven useful for important questions and likely will continue to do so. It just depends on what questions we ask. Rethinking a preexisting scholarly conversation does not mean replacing or defaming it, but promoting intellectual pluralism, opening way for new concepts and questions that are "generative" for further inquiry, as Dewey would put it. We should see underdetermination as an opportunity to highlight powerful patterns with different conceptual frameworks, not a liability that we suffer while trudging on down our customary conceptual paths.

Underdetermination became an opportunity to see the puzzle of the HJ coordinating committee's blow-up argument in a new light. A more well-established approach would focus on ideologies or frames, and treat the explosive argument as a "framing dispute." Committee members were disputing how "left" to frame their prognosis for the affordable housing problem. The civic action approach illuminated something else: that claims making depends on claimants' assumptions about relationships. Sensitized by the alternative insight, I saw another pattern come into view that would not have stood out otherwise.

The dispute over how to frame affordable housing was interspersed with a dispute over how committee members should relate to each other. Both kept

coming up together in committee conversation. At one of those difficult meetings, for example, members debated how to message about low-income
people's housing needs. In the middle of that discussion, seemingly non sequitur, Terry said there was a "disconnect" between the steering committee and
groups it claims to represent. It sounded at first like a new topic. She reported
that someone who had been on the committee a long time still "had no idea
what the process was" for deciding how many affordable units should be mandated for each income bracket. Dispute over how we relate to each other and
our constituents wove into a dispute over framing the pitch for affordable
housing. To Terry and other dissenters, the trouble with HJ's frame was connected to trouble with a scene style that centers the participants on relations
with gatekeepers, bids them see themselves as an organized interest group, and
privileges broad-based appeal to an expanding audience. Coalition leaders had
chosen a framing that ignored the category of homeless people. Terry called
it "insulting": it dishonored her community. To her, the framing implied there
was something wrong with the way advocates were relating to each other on
the committee, not just something wrong with their perceptions of issues.
According to the committee majority, on the other hand, the problem was that
Terry just did not understand how relations should work. As one member
remarked, Terry needed to trust the committee or else she shouldn't be on it.
Throughout this sequence, disputes about claims were also disputes about
styles of relationship. The study's initial, rough field hypothesis about claims
and relationships turned out to be generative for the study.

Using the civic action box and central concepts I put in it, this study helps
us address questions that professional advocates and active citizens as well as
scholars ask. They go beyond the world of housing advocacy.

Practical Findings on Coalitions and Social Advocacy

What makes advocacy coalitions break apart? Advocates themselves would
likely point to conflicts over ideas, constituencies, or personalities. It is not
always easy to agree on how to word the claims or whose voices to represent.
Sometimes, individual advocates are lightning rods, susceptible to the charge
that they are abrasive, out of touch with constituents, or unable to compromise. I heard disagreements and complaints like all these, front stage or backstage, in HJ circles. Research footnoted in chapter 5 puts these divisions in academic terms as differences in underlying social and economic interests,
conflicts over collective identity, or disagreements over frames. Studies have
paid less attention to taken-for-granted, less "declarative" cultural understandings that coalition members rely on to coordinate action together.[7]

The HJ coalition's experience suggests that disagreements over how to co-ordinate action mattered a great deal. Sharp differences in preferred scene style, in other words, can corrode or snap the ties that bind a coalition. Dis-agreements over the *meaning* of the act of framing were part of the conflict. A style comes with a dense web of meanings, not only about relationships at one point in time, but about what participants consider the right strategic arc.

The bigger box also helps explain why seemingly related issues can be hard to articulate together in a campaign. In this case, the dynamics of discursive fields made it difficult for LA housing advocates to elaborate links between homelessness and housing. They divided housing and homelessness into largely different spheres of rhetoric and social reputation. A discourse combin-ing housing and homelessness was nearly screened out. For the influential housing advocates involved in HJ, too much attention specifically to homeless-ness risked violating a community of interest's way of strategizing. In other settings where homeless advocates promoted affordable housing too, a search for authentic voices mattered more than an effort to broaden the circle of voices speaking up for the housing needs of homeless people. For many of those professionals and volunteers focused directly on homelessness, the dis-cursive field was different. Homeless people had immediate needs that actors understood through appeals to compassion—nearly absent from housing ad-vocacy—or its bad-cop cousin, tough love, or else in terms of professional, human services discourse. In these scenarios, affordable housing for homeless people was a more distant topic—something to work on elsewhere, later, maybe, in another discursive field where fairness talk was dominant.

Parallel dynamics may limit advocates' ability to combine other seemingly related issues. It does not take the demolition of a clinic by a developer to see how housing and health could be connected, especially in urban neighbor-hoods across the country where people endure the hazards of substandard housing. In the past several decades, national health research and advocacy organizations have wanted more grassroots civic actors to see that connection, and have offered funding to local advocates who take up health alongside the other issues. Local advocates have responded, but the grant money does not produce claims all by itself. Style and issue reputation are important cultural parameters on how advocates take up the cause of health. The scenes from ISLA suggest that piecing together a regional coalition that unites housing and health-oriented advocates in a common cause might be challenging if the reputation of "health" is strongly tied up with quality of life rather than op-portunity and justice.[8]

Understanding these cultural parameters makes it easier to understand why grassroots housing advocates would not claim more forthrightly that people need housing that is affordable *and* environmentally sustainable. To some observers and maybe some advocates, it is still common sense that affordability is more important. Environmentalism has long been tagged as a middle-class and white person's concern in the United States, not a necessity for low-income people.[9] Yet some advocates fight for environmental *justice*, and define "the environment" as "where we work, live, and play," rather than the realm of rare species and extreme sports. Studies repeatedly have shown that low-income people of color are more likely to suffer environmental hazards than whites.[10] Other scholars point out that when advocates take on multiple issues, their organizations benefit from access to new expertise, new resources, and new pools of supporters.[11] Why wouldn't grassroots affordable housing advocates do more to make common cause with environmentalists at least rhetorically? At a general meeting of the land trust organization CGTC, staffer Victor made a point of saying that we were not tree huggers, thrusting his arms out in embrace of an imaginary trunk. Why would this image of environmentalism endure?

In the case of the Manchester conflict at least, implicit cultural conventions were at work. They protected advocates from sounding just like their opponents when much is at stake. Protecting meaningful communication and group solidarity with one's own allies and constituents mattered at least as much as the potential new resources and support networks that could come from promoting an additional issue; the entrepreneurial actor model would weigh the goods differently. The signal concepts of this study offer good clues. A community of identity acts in sharp opposition to groups that members see as exploiting or displacing them. ISLA advocates heard property developers and their allies talk relatively frequently in quality-of-life terms. As chapter 8 noted, issues develop reputations in discursive fields. In the field of debate over housing problems in Los Angeles, environmental issues acquired a quality-of-life reputation. Advocates for the community would be all the more likely to distinguish themselves by subordinating quality-of-life appeals and "environmental" issues too, *if* those came with a quality-of-life reputation.[12] Community-based housing advocates risk underestimating the potential of allying with environmental groups that do make quality-of-life appeals. They might also undercut their own ability to publicize the idea that multiply marginalized people deserve an environmentally sustainable quality of life as much as other people.[13]

Finally, some critically minded scholars and citizens might argue that local social advocates ought to tie housing unaffordability more explicitly to large social forces that make some people's homes into other people's commodities. Ultimately, that is not a story of insensitive outsiders and victimized residents but instead the relationships of property in a racialized, capitalist society. This broad overview has plenty of support from sociological studies of urban life. Versions of it also appear in flyers and newsletters like the ones I saw one day in the reception area of an ISLA member organization's office. An internal memo from early in HJ's MIHO campaign pointed in a similar direction, characterizing opposition to a MIHO as "classist," "racist," and dedicated to unrestrained markets. It is worth remembering just how *rare* this critically analytic language was in general meetings, committee meetings, strategy sessions, and large public forums of the campaigns. Advocates, some of whom agreed with the critical analysis on their own time, contributed to marginalizing its terms in campaign settings. The takeaway in the simplest terms is that what people can say to each other depends on how they think they are connected to each other. Housing advocates invoked discourse that could be spoken and heard given the connection—the style of relationship—operating in a scene. It is a matter of what advocates can say, where, and to whom, and not what they think in their heads. A different discourse might challenge the grounds of solidarity necessary for communication to happen at all.

But that does not mean academic-sounding concepts are simply impractical. It all depends on where and to whom we are speaking. Academic-sounding concepts *can* be practical in some settings. That is part of what is refreshing about Dewey's approach to the question of a practical social science. It is more subtle and layered than either the populist call for "relevant" research or the quite different view that social science must be a walled-off professional realm.[14] On the one hand, Dewey advocated that social researchers take our problems from the other communities and society in which we participate.[15] On the other hand, he thought it a mistake to assume that research problems come predefined.[16] Rather, social researchers need to articulate our problems to each other in an unapologetically conceptual language, using categories that others in the community of inquiry can grasp and talk about. That way, we can make useful comparisons and generate more inquiry. In contemporary terms, researchers say we need to "case" our subject matter or put it in a category, and there is usually more than one scientifically interesting way to do that. This study conceptualized its cases in terms of civic action. If it had cased the empirical material primarily as "housing movements" instead, I would have featured different comparisons and contrasts, and asked different questions.

Social inquiry can start with everyday people's problems, and proceed in a reflexively refreshed, scientific language that helps organize discoveries that are useful for both scholars and nonscholars.[17] But then, suppose we want to communicate potentially useful research findings on coalition building. How do we talk?

Communicating Findings with Social Advocates
Tips for Success?

One way that researchers relate to the social advocates we write about is by putting findings in a report that conveys advice. Campaigns organized by both major coalitions in this study have been written up in reports on successful advocacy.[18] These publications serve important informational and maybe solidarity-building purposes that academic publishing would not often satisfy, though academics may read them too. It could be tempting to read these as lessons for future advocates; one of the two illustrations I use here is pitched that way explicitly. Both outline strategic arcs that end with outcomes the authors present as victories for the campaigns. While informative and interesting, these retellings would not likely clue advocates in to the dilemmas and tensions one discovers by following the action. Attempting to follow a strategy presented as a straight line of decisions leading to success, an advocate may get frustrated. The strategy *itself* produces dilemmas and trade-offs, curves and forks in the road, even apart from the pressure of confrontation with an opposition. Let me illustrate this notion.

One report sketches the first HJ campaign, preceding the one I studied by the same name. It won the first affordable housing trust fund. Describing what this book calls a community of interest, the report narrates a strategy "to bring together different constituencies, with different interests, around the common goal." It goes on to explain that "we had an 'outside/inside' strategy. The coalition would be built 'outside' City Hall before and during the election. When the new administration was sworn in, the campaign would go 'inside' and focus on getting the actual votes." Put in skeletal terms, the HJ campaign I studied—the last in a series of three—combined outside and inside strategies too, though in tandem more than in succession. But the paired strategies meant systematically different things to two factions of the campaign. Carol, Terry, and Mary kept talking past each other about them.

Maybe even more to the point here is that outside and inside strategies were not simply complementary options on a menu of strategic plans. Together they constituted the defining, ongoing *dilemma* for this style of advocacy. HJ advocates fretted repeatedly about whether or not their intense focus on city council members was leaving too little time for mobilizing tenants and Angelenos at large (seen as outsiders); recall that the coordinating committee facilitator said even her housemate had never heard of HJ. It is possible that clashing scene styles did not mark HJ's first campaign. It is even plausible that actions and expectations lined up closely enough that actors could all agree to make a clean switch from the outside to the inside strategy. The point, though, is that an advocacy group searching for practical tips would miss *patterns* of improvising and agonizing that end up being integral to this style of advocacy. To be forewarned of these patterns is to be forearmed—which is not to say the battle therefore is won. If researchers do want readers to take their accounts as conveying advice—and this author did not expressly say as much—readers may get more from an account written in the vein of dilemmas or trade-offs than best practices.

Similar limitations characterize another report, which features the ISLA campaigns. Based on interviews with the main actors who retold the campaign several years after the fact, the report raised a crucial question for the advocates that I too found central: Who speaks for the community? The report pitched this as a question that skeptical outsiders used to question ISLA's ability to represent the community. It implied there was in fact an "authentic community" since it observes that ISLA organizations had "deep roots" in it. I found that advocates spent much more of their time trying to negotiate the dilemma of "from the community versus for the community" than they spent considering external skeptics' challenges. In a section that offers pointers for future activist campaigns, the report advises advocates to build coalitions that integrate diverse strengths, empower community voices with communication skills, and work on finding a good frame. A civic action viewpoint might well affirm all these, but then ask, "How?" And that brings us back to following the action and searching for patterns.

When outcomes rather than chains of action are the focus of the case, we may end the story too soon. We lose out on the lessons that may emerge from sequences snipped off the chain of action covered in a report—ones that transpired after the success that defines the report's purpose. When Thalia of CGTC told me that winning CBAs is not really a long-term strategy for increasing affordable housing, she added that developers had begun using the CBA as a device to buy off community advocates. "When do you want your CBA?" they would ask. Sometimes it is more useful to discuss the trade-offs of different styles of action than to identify lessons in success. A case study that is defined by an outcome will conclude with that outcome as a definitive end. A case study defined by chains of action may treat the same outcome as an "end in view"—one that means something specific within that longer chain. A widespread understanding of success happens to comport with how HJ imagined its trajectory: a campaign that sweeps to its victory, a policy change in this case, and then no longer needs to exist. But for ISLA's antidisplacement campaign, the victory of a CBA was more like a way station on what advocates projected as a much longer arc.

The meaning of an outcome itself should not be taken for granted. Dewey affirmed the point, criticizing research designed only to follow a track toward a preconceived end—a researcher's idea of what counts as an important or successful outcome.[19] Presenting an advocacy campaign in this way truncates meanings that matter to practitioners, and have the power to produce frustrations and unintended consequences.[20] Seeing the fuller pattern in the way a researcher potentially does, even if that means adopting some research language, may indeed be practical.

Invitations to Dialogue

TALK ABOUT PATTERNS OF ACTION, NOT JUST IDEAS AND PEOPLE

Dialogue about research that has "followed the action" may help social advocates account more effectively for their actions and frustrations in trying to get along. This by itself won't guarantee any outcomes or solve all the many puzzles of coalition building. For that matter, "getting along" may sound like a minor human relations issue. But the research literature noted in chapter 5 shows repeatedly that influential coalitions with a real chance to create significant social change have blown apart or dissipated over the failure to do what coalitions, by definition, try to do: get along across social, cultural, or political differences. LA housing advocates not only experienced but also commented on at least some of the problems I saw. They tended to ascribe the frustrations of claims making and relationship building to wrongheaded ideas or else difficult individuals. Dialogues based on this study's findings would be much more about types of action or relationships, not types of ideas or people, not successful versus unsuccessful strategies. Here are two instances where, in retrospect, I see openings for dialogue about patterns of action.

During his time with the HJ coalition, Francis clearly thought a lot about the coalition's tensions. He saw some of the same lines of battle I did, though he understood them in different language. Over dinner one night, around the time he was leaving HJ, Francis told me that when the explosive unity meeting happened, "Carol was totally blindsided." She had no idea that endorsers would come and be angry about the organizational process of HJ, in other words. She had thought sending email updates was enough to keep groups engaged—what Francis himself had said in the coalition's defense at the meeting. But now he added that "email is not [a means to] engaging people, to ask their opinions."

I commented it sounded like Beth worked from "a different model." Francis agreed. I said that it was "not the model of consensus democracy and lots of participation." This was early in the study, and later, in ISLA and LAPO scenes, it became clear that what I would come to call a community of identity was not necessarily strong on consensus decision making. Meeting formats actually involved a lot of tutelage, not just egalitarian self-expression, even though that mattered too—sometimes. Still, I said something about ways of working together, and *that made sense to Francis* and in terms of my own developing analysis.

Here was an opening for an invitation I would be able to offer "next time," informed by knowledge of patterns I became clearer on in the years after that spaghetti dinner. Ideally if the talking partner takes up the invitation, a longer exploration of style could result—much as we might want to use plainer terms such as model, group format, or ways of working together. The dialogue might explore conflicting assumptions about who matters most in a campaign, or what the style framework calls advocates' maps. The miscues and cross talk reported in chapter 3 already suggest that the HJ majority and dissenters had different ideas of "success" born of different styles of action along different strategic arcs.

Francis and other HJ participants talked about what I tentatively called a clash of "models" as a clash of personality types or ideologies. Francis joked that he identified with the tenant groups because he was really "just a six-year-old antiauthoritarian." At the unity meeting and debriefing that followed, actors attributed their explosive tensions to differences in *ideology*. Community organizer Keith called Terry's criticisms a matter of favoring "ideology" over "pragmatism." Terry scored the coalition's stance as being "to the right of the Democratic Party." Carol and Charlie had affirmed it was really quite "left." Months later, a LAPO member of the new HRN coalition characterized HJ's split as a matter of differences in "philosophy," and so did a leader of LAPO.

Yet during the arguments that Terry, Keith, Carol, and Charlie considered to be disagreements over ideologies, no one was really talking about things we think of as ideological. No one was hashing out belief systems, philosophies, or party lines—other than the slam about being to the right of the Democratic Party. Explaining disagreements in terms of ideas may be common sense for people like social advocates who often define *themselves* in terms of ideas, and the same could be true of academics.[21] Inducing a dialogue that contextualizes ideas within forms of *action* and relationship is a fresh as well as more empirically sound departure.

A language that points to style, not ideology in isolation, opens advocates' access to less-remarked-on patterns. A clash between those patterns contributed mightily to HJ coalition's loss of publicly visible supporters. Granted, it may be an awkward-sounding conversation at first simply because it is less familiar than criticizing difficult coalition partners or ideas, not to mention well-financed opponents. Making research findings into material for sustained dialogue rather than (translated) advice does risk inconvenience and awkwardness. Yet if a lot of social advocates already are thinking and talking about how they, their allies, and competitors do things together frustratingly, the conversation is not necessarily so strange.

ACKNOWLEDGE THE TRADE-OFFS OF DIFFERENT STYLES, DON'T MORALIZE THEM

Nathan, of the nonprofit HSLA, told me twice about arguments with gadfly Terry of SHAPLA. They sparred over the new coalition that Nathan had helped put together to inject community voices into plans for redeveloping a movie theater. The coalition hoped to get the CRA and a city council member on board. Reviewing my notes, I recognized another invitation to dialogue for future researchers who encounter a pattern similar to the one I saw unfolding between Nathan and Terry. This conversation would be about tensions between hybrid civic action with its mix of governmental and civic volunteer-helper perspectives, and civic action that promotes a community of identity. Sincere proponents of either could easily misunderstand and mistrust each other. In this study, advocates sometimes touted their own strategy and disparaged others, but that did not make proponents of other strategies disappear. Why not try figuring out how one strategy might complement another in a bigger division of civic labor?

In Nathan's terms, the conflict was between what everyday people "need" and what outsiders think they should want. Nathan planned for the theater redevelopment coalition to hold a workshop at which CRA officials could hear "what the community wants—no, *needs*." Nathan hoped that the workshop would produce "community input" that the CRA could use while judging proposals for redeveloping the defunct theater. He sounded less concerned that community residents control the process than that they "prove to the [city] council" that the community has needs. Terry of SHAPLA attended a meeting that planned this workshop, and in Nathan's words, had tried to take it over, push her own demands, and get HSLA off the coalition altogether. Retelling the encounter to me, Nathan had said that HSLA was on the ground, dealing with people's problems, while Terry's organization did not know what people in the neighborhood really needed.

The same tension came up in another conversation about this new coalition. Nathan did not want to "ruffle feathers with the [city] council or the CRA," but on the other hand, some people "want the world!" He told me that if he wasn't on such bad terms with Terry, he would ask her, "How are we going to build without them [the CRA]?" Nathan again characterized his side as the one in touch with people's needs:

> I actually work in the community. I do the food bank.[22] I'm frequently there after dark—I'm with the kids." Terry in contrast had this "overarching view versus what people want."

He said it was a matter of "elite consciousness versus what people really want." "People have real wants, real feelings, real lives, and we [HSLA] want to have a community forum. . . . It's not what *we* think, it's what they need." The shock theater of taking over a meeting is bound to offend whomever set the meeting up. Put in these terms, the rightness of Nathan's approach was compelling and hard to dispute, but that was part of the problem; the other side had a point, too.

The big workshop did happen, two months later, and it showed me why Terry's own perspective was worth considering. A CRA official presented slides captioned with obscure developer talk. As a Spanish-speaking attendee pointed out, it would not have made sense to most blue-collar immigrant neighbors in the room even if they spoke English. A city official speaking on behalf of the CRA mentioned that "unfortunately for nonprofit developers, they get caught up in the rules of the funders—sometimes they get funding for singles, sometimes for families, . . . so you as a community should tell us what kind of affordable housing you want to see here." In other words, with the best of intentions, nonprofit developers relying on the contracting regime might not get funding to provide what "the community" wants. The "you" in the room divided into breakout discussion groups, and they did not all share identical ideas about what they wanted either. One wanted housing with "100 percent" of units set aside for low-income people, several wanted low-cost health services installed in the former theater, and one group (the only one designated as "English speaking" as well as an apparently white majority) wanted renovations to "reflect the culture" of the neighborhood. To the extent that HSLA's nonprofit charter gave it a constituency, it was "the public" in general that would benefit from the goods HSLA was chartered to provide, and none of the breakout groups were more essentially "the public" than the others. Governmental entities such as the CRA officially would need to take all these disparate "stakeholders" into account too.

In this context, Terry's skepticism about what nonprofit developers can really accomplish for local low-income residents made sense even if she communicated it ungraciously to Nathan. It made sense to look beyond food banks and piecemeal housing projects to redevelopment agendas and who controls them. Nathan's language of "elite consciousness" versus real "needs," common as it is, moralizes the trade-offs instead of representing them usefully. Talk of human "needs" too easily naturalizes relationships and conditions that have resulted from political processes—which means they could be changed.[23] Yet it is true too, as Nathan said, that lots of neighborhood residents needed more food. He was there in the neighborhood distributing it to families, while Terry was not.

What would a more useful conversation sound like? It might clarify, first, that Nathan and Terry *both* worked for and not from the community. Neither had a lock on neighborhood authenticity. Each worked on different strategic timelines. Nonprofits address "real-world" needs with housing developments, but often they are doing that as managerial *outsiders* accountable to no particular community. To advocates like Terry, deeply cultivated in the notion that good problem solvers empower the community, that will look obvious and suspect. Nathan was a *liaison*—a go-between from an outside entity, serving populations with (outsider-defined) needs, not communities with demands. Terry's approach was parallel in at least one way: she too assumed she knew what was *really* best for the neighborhood. A brave dialogue would float the idea that both Nathan and Terry traded on a notion of community, whether a community of needs or identity, that risked essentializing and oversimplifying a population. Instead of presuming that a neighborhood's needs are uniform or only one strategy can address them, it makes more sense to dare talking about trade-offs.

Self-critical collaboration between nonprofit staffers and local advocates for a community of identity is not crazy to imagine. The CGTC land trust fused nonprofit know-how with the voice of ISLA's community. And nonprofit employee Nathan himself told me he could appreciate what community organizers like Terry were doing, because "it's what I saw growing up. . . . I would love to be able to do it, but I'm with a nonprofit developer. . . . We got CRA funding, and our building wouldn't be possible without it." It is about trade-offs, not essentially good or bad choices. Appreciating different timelines with different goals may work better for a diverse urban redevelopment coalition than expecting everyone to fit onto the same strategic arc with the same identity.

When frustrations emerge, it is good to ask if these come from clashing styles of action instead of assuming they result from ill-willed actors or bad ideologies. Terry had said and Francis had implied that several of the representatives in the HJ coalition thought that Carol was abrasive, making the coalition more difficult to work in. Coalition members might have advanced the cause of affordable housing more by scrutinizing the trade-offs of a community of interest strategy as opposed to personalizing the terms of disagreement. Personal attacks tend to end conversations; disagreements over style do not necessarily.[24]

Things felt at least as tense when the director of the Korean community services agency took offense at the Faith Brings Us Home meeting and reiterated her irritation to me privately. She said that her efforts with homeless people were unwelcome downtown. Hearing, even secondhand, the charge that donated food might poison homeless people, a community services director understandably could feel hurt and excluded. It might be more productive all around, though, if would-be servers from outside a neighborhood learned to recognize a community of identity's response to the server-served relationship. The community's strategy for dealing with charitable outsiders probably felt as justified to local advocates as the director's charity felt sincere to her.

———

Each of the campaigns that we have followed aimed to make ordinary living somewhat better for Angelenos. The advocates all experienced victories and disappointments as they traveled their different strategic arcs, with emotional highs and lows along the way. Thanks to the office visits and letter campaigns, the testimonies from ordinary Joes and authentic members of the community, the insider and outsider strategies, and efforts from and for the community, the city of Los Angeles had come quite close to adopting a MIHO during this study, and some South Los Angeles residents got affordable housing unavailable when the study began. This is not the stuff of high drama. To paraphrase philosopher Michael Walzer (1992), doing civic action is like speaking in prose. Though not epic poetry most of the time, it is a big part of what makes democracy a "way of life," as Dewey (1927) asserted, not only a form of governance.

In the time since my fieldwork, prospects for alleviating Los Angeles' housing crisis remained uncertain. A stream of news stories was pointing out the lack of affordable housing in the city. The problem animated documentaries and became a talking point for candidates in local election campaigns. Homelessness was at least as visible on broad, less-traveled sidewalks, under bridges, and beside the Los Angeles River, and abundantly deplored. Couldn't anyone do anything? Housing advocates were pushing on in their different ways. Voters approved a proposition that would *raise taxes* to build permanent, supportive housing for currently homeless Angelenos. It takes a differently focused study to determine how much the heightened public debate and new tax could have been due to housing advocates' efforts versus those of other advocates or other factors. It makes sense to think, however, that without advocacy, unaffordable housing and homelessness would have been only less audible in public debate, and the city would have been only further away from doing things to address these problems.[25]

At this writing, the COVID-19 pandemic and its baleful economic consequences already had dramatized how indispensable governmental action can be. Yet that made civic action no less important in the short term or long run, and no less urgent to assess thoughtfully. On one day alone, the global pandemic had prompted Angelenos, like so many others in the country, to a wide spectrum of civic initiatives.[26] Volunteer projects continued to collect face masks for nurses and doctors. The country was now several weeks into protests at statehouses—and beaches, near Los Angeles—where bands of angry, sometimes armed participants demanded an end to the stay-at-home orders that prioritized public health over jobs, incomes, and investments. And that day, grocery store workers went on strike to publicize the underrecognized new health risks of serving the public. Were volunteer, protective wear collection drives generating interest in existing campaigns for new, national health care guarantees? Would grocery store and medical workers' claims build into pressure on legislators to increase labor protections nationwide? How, if at all, did it matter that statehouse protesters' seemingly grassroots civic action was in some cases coordinated by a parent project funded by extremely wealthy, conservative donors?[27] The pandemic, like the global crisis of habitability that it has prefigured vividly, only underscores how vital our questions about civic action will continue to be.

Civic action is not intrinsically good or bad, polite or risky, enlightened or reactive, humane or hateful. Neither is it necessarily a substitute for governmental action; in the United States, growth in civic action has accompanied growth in governmental initiatives.[28] Civic action comes with no guarantees. LA housing advocates fought for more power over decisions about housing made, or allowed, by local government and private developers. When governments institute new policies to address social problems, such as through affordable housing mandates, it is often because of the pressure of civic action. Yet civic action is not necessarily always "progressive." Sometimes people engage collective problem solving with the goal of reducing citizen steering power. During the time I researched and wrote this book, increasing numbers of people around the world were telling survey researchers they would prefer an authoritarian leader to democratic governance.[29] That was increasingly what a variety of countries were getting, sometimes by way of democratically organized elections. Does that mean many people have given up on the idea that by working on problems collectively, ordinary people might help steer society? Do they think civic action is dispensable? That impulse is incompatible with many visions of democracy that include collective, civic problem solving with a significant political role. Nothing in this book should be taken to imply that civic action by itself can or should solve all, or even most, social problems. But what a tragedy if many people were to decide that civic action of any sort really is not worth the trouble.

We need studies that illuminate how different kinds of civic action work, wherever they unfold. We need to understand which kinds are likely to expand or shrink the circle of inclusion. We need people who figure out what civic action can and cannot do to bend history's arc toward greater justice, solidarity, and sustainability. There is a lot to do.

Putting Together the Study

Beginning with a Topic and a Rough Picture

In a previous book, I had studied how different kinds of social ties develop inside and between religiously sponsored civic groups.[1] At the outset of this study, I wanted to understand civic advocacy better, taking advantage of the possibilities hosted by a huge metropolitan area with many, many advocacy organizations. Some colleagues and I wrote a proposal to fund network survey and ethnographic research on civic relationships, and received partial funding along with funding for a partial continuation. There was a companion goal: to understand how discourses about a social problem would develop and circulate among social advocates. Recent work in cultural theory had implied that social advocates' discourses and their ways of relating to each other developed *together* in some way not yet well specified.[2] From this initial, partially funded research there emerged several lines of argument that would be anchored in different combinations of data.

This book lays out the arguments that developed from ethnographic research and the archival research that grew out of the ethnographic work. Ethnographic and archival evidence substantiate the four, central arguments summarized in chapter 1, all of which are grounded in my pragmatist, civic action approach to social problem solving. Another line of argument combined data on the network structure and meanings of civic relationships, drawing on a network survey of LA housing organizations along with selected ethnographic cases. Details of the survey as well as preliminary findings on how network ties and meanings related to each other in this organizational field are reported elsewhere.[3]

Ethnographers widely agree that we don't come to the field with a blank slate. Often we enter with a blurry, hypothetical picture of what we will find—a big guess. We may spend years sharpening our questions and coloring the picture in as we carry out fieldwork, and compare that picture against others circulating in our scholarly community of inquiry, to decide which best solves our empirical puzzles.[4] In the "picture" I began with, different kinds of relationship in advocacy organizations would orient advocacy groups to different discourses for articulating social issues such as housing.[5] Or in simpler terms, what advocates could say publicly about issues would depend on how they perceived their relations to other advocates.[6] There were different ways to conceive of this connection between advocates' discourse about social problems and the relationships in their organizations, and I hoped this project would clarify how this broadly sketched relationship worked, if in fact it did.

The puzzles I kept experiencing in the field over the next several years validated for me the possibility of refining and substantiating a theory based on my big hypothetical picture. The rough picture had emerged from conceptual innovations first hatched during the decade leading up to my first field sorties. The puzzles along with recent conceptual innovations strengthened my resolve to take an alternate approach to social problem solving, departing from academic understandings of social movements and collective action that had been dominant in US sociology for several decades.

These research goals reflect the view that social research is, at least potentially, an ongoing, disciplined, critical dialogue.[7] Quite often scholars relate to social research as an edifice-building or paradigm-protecting activity. Either of those research trajectories may lead to valuable findings.[8] Once we see social science as an ongoing dialogue as well, we may propose that some empirical puzzles invite our community of inquiry—our discipline, subdiscipline, or interdisciplinary circle—to rethink some of its basic presuppositions.[9] With evidence in hand, we bid our colleagues to go and look again, with a new conceptual framework, at existing as well as new empirical work. If altered conceptual starting points yield fresh, defensible interpretations, new causal explanations that stand up to skeptical scrutiny, or new and interesting questions, then the new conceptual framework is warranted. It certainly need *not* replace other frameworks in our scholarly storehouse, but it can augment them and bring more research questions into the dialogue than were circulating before.

Focusing on Housing Coalition Campaigns

There were many kinds of advocacy on which the larger project could have focused. Los Angeles offered up literally hundreds of housing-related advocacy groups. Collective action on housing issues became the focus of study.[10] Methodologists say that whether researchers entirely realize it or not, we set "relevance criteria"—essentially an implicit deal we make with readers about what degree of breadth is fair to expect of our research.[11] A focus on "housing" advocacy was one relevance criterion for including groups in my ethnographic research. I followed as these advocates addressed several other issues too because doing that made for good comparisons with efforts on housing, but I did not study peace advocacy, for example, since that was not part of any of these advocates' work.

The choice to follow the action of *coalitions* was another relevance criterion. Much advocacy in the United States is pursued by alliances of groups, not separate organizations, and yet coalitions remained underexamined in sociological work on advocacy when the study began.[12] Coalitions also would maximize the opportunity to follow different styles of relationship and different claims about housing. That would make it easier to learn about how styles of relationship relate to the claims advocates made about housing, especially when either relationships or claims were being stretched or breached.[13] And finally, the book's specific focus on coalition *campaigns* rather than organizations per se emerged along with the pragmatist focus on unfolding action. Comparing different kinds of action in different settings would yield the main conceptual contributions.

Comparative Logic

Casing

The question of how to categorize our research objects calls for decisions about *casing*. We need to decide what to say we have "a case of" before we can know what the conceptual contribution will be.[14] I *could* have conceptualized housing advocates' claims making and relationship building in terms of social movement research concepts, such as framing or collective identity, to name two prominent ones. But those moves, by themselves, would have *squeezed out* puzzles instead of teasing out those puzzles as opportunities to learn more about collective action. That was a big reason to case the collective efforts I studied as cases of civic action.

As the fieldwork proceeded, many emerging puzzles sorted pretty well into the two subject areas I hoped to understand better and relate to one another. Some puzzles were especially striking. One of those was the combination of unexpected continuities and surprising shifts in what advocates in the two main coalitions could claim, and where and to whom, about housing problems. None of the current concepts on offer could really explain, for instance, why advocates talked so similarly in their own meetings and at city hall, where one would expect much more self-consciously strategic discourse to please the powers that be and fend off opponents. The other started as the puzzle of a social explosion. For several months, advocates in the large and increasingly powerful HJ coalition had worked together on their affordable housing campaign. Whether a planned disruption or spontaneous outburst, tensions erupted at a meeting actually intended to display coalition unity for endorsers who did not normally attend these meetings. The follow-up meeting to process what had happened was even more bitter. Several organizations' representatives stopped attending meetings in the following months. I looked back at other scenarios from my field notes and noticed other strange disconnects. What made relationships so difficult?

Comparisons and Contrasts Lead to Explanations with Ethnographic Data

Puzzles helped drive an ongoing search for more sites. More sites would help me decide whether or not the tentative, rough picture I started with was worth keeping and filling in further, or whether it would be better to discard it for a different orienting picture. The ongoing search for comparisons would also help me refine claims about patterns.[15]

New research sites offered the possibility not only for solidifying and refining field hypotheses but bolstering them against alternative accounts too. Sometimes we look for contrast or negative cases in order to check out the possibility that a competing account from our scholarly community is at least as good as our own. We might call this the method of bravery, but we also hope that the negative or counterfactual case casts doubt on the alternative hypothesis, enhancing the credibility of our own.[16] So, for example, if we hypothesize that affordable housing advocates speaking at city hall feel constrained to appeal to either fairness or quality-of-life concerns, we might look for evidence of different but logically plausible rhetorical appeals to see how common they are. We look, then, for signs that the alternative appeals we find might have been a kind of rhetorical mistake—exceptions that "prove the rule" we are proposing. That is why I looked for appeals to compassion. It was reasonable to think advocates might elicit compassion on behalf of people lacking decent housing. I counted it as support for my hypothesis when the few compassion appeals I did find were either enunciated early in a campaign (before discursive norms jelled, as I argued in chapter 7) or offered by speakers far outside the circles of experienced advocates in the public controversy (a distraught local parent, not a professional advocate).

Social research textbooks used to say that ethnography is for description or finding out how people think. To *explain* the social world, however, they would say we need a study with many cases, measured quantitatively and compared statistically. Lively debates in the past two decades give us more options than that for thinking about how ethnographic evidence contributes to explanatory social science.[17] The comparisons and contrasts in this study unfolded with that end in view.

My ongoing search for ethnographic comparison cases and negative cases expanded until I felt confident that ample evidence bolstered this book's causal and interpretative arguments, while casting doubt on the ability of alternatives, especially the entrepreneurial actor model, to offer better accounts. Comparison and contrast along with evidence from other research substantiated the value of seeing *style* as a characteristic of a scene, not necessarily a whole "group" or coalition (chapter 5).[18] On the other hand, the same style might characterize scenes of organizations with quite different cultural or ethnic reference points (chapter 4). By the same moves, I discovered that the kinds of claims advocates made about housing problems depended at least as much on the style of the scene they were participating in, and discursive field they had participated in, as the speaker's coalition affiliation (chapters 5 and 7) or nature of the issue (chapter 7). A series of comparisons showed that the same goals and strategic moves "on paper" can mean something different depending on scene style (chapter 6).

Part of the overall comparison strategy involved a look at life inside selected organizations. Comparing campaign settings peopled by members of many organizations with settings inside separate, member organizations taught me more about how style works as well as how clashes of style affect participants. These comparisons between organizational and coalition campaign settings also helped me track how issues circulate, or don't, contributing to the arguments about discursive fields.

Observing sites beyond housing advocacy narrowly defined boosts my arguments and their practical relevance. I studied a collection of organizations and projects that focused on homelessness. Comparing them shows that this study's attention to discursive field and scene style yields a part of the explanation for why advocates often treated homelessness separately from housing issues in Los Angeles, even if the two issues seem intrinsically related (chapter 8). Another site beyond housing advocacy was that of the nonprofit affordable housing developer, HSLA. Comparisons affirm that whether or not action is civic depends on the *scene* of action, not the organization, the social sector the organization resides in, or its rootedness in a local community (chapter 9). The focus on scenes of action illuminates binds and tensions in nonprofit work that policy makers' pronouncements and social commentary frequently distort or ignore altogether.

Who Was the Ethnographer?

REFLECTIONS ON THE FIELD RESEARCH

LOS ANGELES still felt new to me when I began the research in late 2007. A year and a half earlier I had decided that a provisional move to Los Angeles from Madison, Wisconsin, would be a relocation after all.[1] The scale of the city was still disorienting to someone who had been living in a much smaller place. It took repeated misunderstandings for me to figure out that Angelenos considered a three-mile distance to be "nearby." I puzzled over why someone would choose to live in one place instead of another in the great urban basin. White and middle-class professionals had the privilege of wondering that about much wider swaths of streetscape than nonwhites and people on nonprofessional salaries. Even so, I wondered where that salary went.

Introducing myself at potential research sites, I said that I wanted to learn how organizations define and act on housing and related public issues. I wanted to understand this work from the viewpoint of people doing it. I said I thought they were doing important work—and that represented me accurately. I thought Angelenos should have affordable, decent places to live, though I did not have any firm ideas on the best way for advocates to work toward that goal. I asked to observe meetings and events, and participate to some limited extent. I also said I was interested in doing something useful for the organizations that hosted me. As I participant, I volunteered for tasks, did some office work, and did what others did at rallies and marches—listening, marching, chanting, schmoozing, and jumping up and down and screaming at one demonstration before a long town hall meeting. At meetings, I tossed in an occasional question or comment where doing so did not seem to stretch my implicit role in the scene. When attendees were voting on an endorsement or making a decision that they understood as the will of a distinct community, however, I refrained from participating. I understood myself as a curious, unassuming observer who often knew less than others about the issue at hand.

I wanted to understand patterns that, I thought, would generate a lot of the frustrations and joys that mattered to people in the field. That was part of what made the patterns worth studying to begin with. I also thought that we see these patterns in sharper resolution when we use scholarly lenses. The concluding chapter discusses this mode of research, at once problem driven and academic, and its practical possibilities. As for "doing something useful for the organizations that hosted me," I meant to be useful *as* someone with academic-related skills that advocates might find worthwhile on their own terms. Asking participants what they would like from me would be inviting them to spend more precious time on my account. So I watched and listened in the field, tried to come up with projects that I guessed staff would want, and then asked them without firm expectations that I had guessed correctly.

Projects took shape in various ways. A few times, opportunities presented themselves by way of established roles in the organization—that was the ideal way to contribute. In the ISLA coalition's Dreams for Draper initiative, for example, staff formed a research committee, and I then joined, more fully a participant than in most other sites. I shared thoughts on the trade-offs of survey and focus group research, and delivered notes on a focus group discussion. At LAPO, staff decided local tenants could use a manual of tenant rights and resources. I happily took up the invitation to join the small manual writing committee, learned about the relevant regulations with considerable help from LAPO activists and previous documents, and helped write several sections. At WHA, I took several short work shifts, phoning ally groups about HJ's big kickoff rally and doing other tasks. This work experience also helped me understand subtler aspects of relationship building in the housing advocacy world. At HSLA, I did not need to push the project idea at all. The available roles at HSLA's businesslike office made it natural, if still surprising, for the director to invite me to learn about HSLA by working there. I worked as a temporary, adjunct grant proposal writer and general tasker.

In other cases, projects took more creative role crafting. At LAPO, staff wanted the capacity to keep track of the hours and contributions of the many volunteers and interns who passed through. I offered to interview a variety of participants about their experience of intern work and then use what I learned to devise a "deliverable," as a staff member put it—something like what an outside consultant would produce. I produced an administrative form and simple way to integrate it into office routines. At the ISLA office, I offered to sort and organize the many paper files I had encountered while searching for records on the Manchester campaign. It was something staff said they wanted and did not have time to do. These were hardly Herculean tasks! I hope they conveyed my deep appreciation for being welcomed to these sites and saved staff some time.

From most scholars' point of view, the central thing I did was produce knowledge claims from field notes. In qualitative research circles, it is common to ask how a researcher's own qualities and capacities affect the process. I agree with the contemporary epistemological shibboleth of ethnography: all our knowledge is partial and to some degree uncertain. Researchers cannot be everywhere—logistically, socially, or philosophically. We see and learn from a standpoint—a collection of social positions we are accustomed to occupying. Qualitative social researchers' unlovely term for this is "positionality." But what are those positions exactly, and which matter most where? As ethnographer Lynne Haney (1996) has observed, we don't necessarily know. To presume otherwise is to contradict ourselves: if all social science knowledge is partial and uncertain, then why would we be certain about which positional attribute(s) shaped our viewpoint, and where? People in this book did not change their social positions moment by moment, but neither did they act the same, with the same identities, in every scene. They were not simple, unitary actors. I was not either. I might experience different misunderstandings in different settings.

Continually I tried to discover my misunderstandings, bias, and weak interpretations *through the ongoing test of relationships in the field.* I tried to correct those misunderstandings, in the field and on paper. I decided that the people in the field and the study itself would benefit more from my effort to grasp differences in meaning than an effort to discern exactly which differences in social position(s) would make me miss or misconstrue things in a particular setting. At the same time, I thought before and during field visits about how I might or did come off, to whom, and how that might affect the observations, and that was important to do too.[2]

One position I was quite sure I brought into the field was that of scholar. I did not aim to inject academic-sounding talk into the scenes I observed, unless I was invited to—which happened only at ISLA's research committee. But I did not aim to hide the fact of being a scholar either. That is part of the reason I thought it better, or more genuine, to contribute something useful *as* a person who has spent lots of time reading and writing for a living, rather than conceive of useful things that would somehow "make up for" my being a researcher or academic. Scholarship is part of the society in which we all participate, and even with the institutional status of academic, we construct some variety of relations with others.

I figured that some scenes would receive me not only as a researcher or academic but also white male one, potentially invasive and probably naive at best about some things. In other scenes—mostly professional and usually multiracial—I aimed never to impose, to learn the cues and be a quiet, respectful presence. When I related to nonstaff campaign participants who evidently had low incomes, carried minority racial or ethnic status, were inadequately housed, or placed themselves in several or all those categories—none of which would apply to me—I thought of myself as a quiet learner. In these situations, I bypassed temptations to identify quickly with others or send signals that, as a political progressive, I knew about what social disadvantage is like. The well-intended gesture risks dishonoring life experiences that often would be different from mine, sometimes more life endangering, and frequently met with fewer material or social resources. Do ethnographers need to be "closer" than that to the people we write about? Let me address the personal part of "closeness" before continuing on to questions of social and cultural distance.

My goal was not to get inside other people's heads or personal lives. I feel like I became casually friendly beyond conventional courtesy with at least several dozen people from among the groups I studied. I liked the people I met, and hope they found me to be decent company. But ethnographers do not necessarily become close pals, confidants, or partners in adversity with the people we research.[3] *It depends a lot on the research question.* My questions were about patterned relationships between words and action, action and action, and words and words in settings where people were planning and doing mostly public things for public purposes. I wanted to understand those relationships and their collective emotions partly through experiencing them myself; that is part of the reason we do participant observation. I did not aim to know a lot about people's private, idiosyncratic experiences of the patterns that mattered in this study. Some of those seeped out anyway. A participant in one organization confided that the group played favorites and she felt underappreciated. A staff person in another implied to me that frustrations had made him consider switching jobs. For a study driven by different questions, the individual impacts could have been hot clues to dynamics I would need to explore at length—easier when one is personally close to participants. Given my questions, they were clues only to the extent they signaled something about patterns of civic action, which I would investigate mainly by observing interaction. Those patterns are not feelings free. Chapters 3 and 4 discussed emotional tones that cogenerate different styles of action, and these emotions are products of interaction too, not just private sensibilities.

People in the field positioned me, taking cues from some of what I was giving off whether or not I always realized or intended it. Language politics and the politics of phenotype danced several different ways when participants spoke to or of me in ISLA scenes. I gathered from field interactions that most participants saw me as a primarily English-speaking white academic man who apparently understood Spanish to some degree and supported the cause in general. Several longtime local resident members of ISLA affirmed my Spanish speaking. I took it as a friendly welcome to one who appeared to be a native

English speaker. On the other hand, on two occasions an (evidently white) ISLA staffer translated my Spanish into Spanish for local residents. It was not a matter of bad acoustics in the room. I guessed, maybe incorrectly, that it could be hard for some to hear Spanish coming from me as ordinary communication rather than odd etiquette. A journalist from a Spanish-language newspaper interviewed me during the study (on a completely different topic) and informed me I could stop apologizing in advance for my Spanish. While his comment came after an email interview, it suggested that a fluent speaker found my Spanish adequately comprehensible in writing; it does not necessarily say much about speaking. I made sure not to lean on faith in my abilities at any rate. When I was not certain I understood what a Spanish speaker had said, I moved closer to the English-language translator, or in a few cases, availed myself of headphones provided for people who wanted translation at a large meeting. Sometimes translation was oversimplified or fragmentary; at one meeting, primarily Spanish-speaking participants complained bitterly about the same thing. On the occasions that I knew I was picking up more from a Spanish-language speaker than from the translation, my field notes followed the speaker.[4]

Another position that advocates explicitly constructed for me was that of "outsider with potential access to public forums." It was a reasonable way to see a professor who had said he hoped eventually to publish on what he learned, and in these instances, other aspects of my social background seemed less salient. HJ staff were concerned that I not reveal their emerging strategies for securing a positive vote on a MIHO at city council. An ISLA leader cautioned me not to share (with media people) anything I had heard at a meeting about the tentative terms of an agreement with a property developer. In my introductory announcement at meetings of each coalition, and then the few times this same issue came up hence, I emphasized that this was not a journalistic writing project and I would happily pledge not to talk about my work to media sources, for any reasonable amount of time they might suggest. I had asked permission to carry out participant observation that might last many months, and said it would be fine anytime to ask me to leave a meeting or end my research with them altogether, if they so desired. A facilitator of the LAPO housing committee asked me to leave a meeting. It turned out they wanted to talk about me, and decided to ask me to give a short talk on what I was finding. I asked them to take my talk as thoughts in progress, and learned important, helpful things from the responses to the talk I gave; this was fairly early in my relations with them. I continued attending committee meetings off and on for many months afterward.

I can only guess how my other social locations mattered, much as they almost certainly did depending on the scene. The privileges and perceptions typically available to white male academics like me likely made some of the lived meanings of tenanthood shared by lower-income Latinx and African American LA tenants inaccessible to me. Given the questions orienting *this* particular study, I was especially concerned that my social and literally geographic location might diminish the accessibility of meetings, especially ISLA and LAPO meetings. That too might be summarized as "white, male academic meets organizations oriented to lower-income tenants of color." The observation that I was an academic visiting field sites roughly five to eight miles from where I lived offers additional, useful concreteness and subtlety, once the listener knows that Los Angeles is highly class as well as racially segregated. In my neighborhood, one that evidently was majority white, homeowners like me needed professional-level salaries to make it work. The logistics of field access matter. In the case of ISLA-related scenes, I was probably less likely than other participants to be invited if staff called urgent strategy meetings at short notice or put on educational sessions geared specifically to local residents. My best guess is that *in these situations*, the logistics mattered more than the persona bred by my social background.[5] That still leaves the possibility that my social locations would induce me to misrepresent the action I was studying.

I developed the research design with all these potential limits in mind, but unfortunately cannot guarantee I have surmounted them entirely. The argument about how discursive fields work took two precautions. First, it depends heavily on public (city hall) testimony that was recorded exhaustively on audio or video. This was to lessen the chance that my observations would be skewed because I could not attend all coalition campaign meetings where claims making happened or claimants may have avoided certain kinds of rhetoric when my presence was obvious. Second, to lessen the effects of the field logistics on my ability to attend some meetings I knew about, I hired research assistants who could observe meetings I had hoped to attend but could not fit into my schedule of other fieldwork and teaching. To diminish the possibility of racial- and ethnic-based misinterpretations or overgeneralizations that could accompany the category "community of identity," I used observations from LAPO scenes, with their African American cultural resonances, as a comparison with the Latinx-identified scenes of ISLA. That still would not prevent me from misidentifying African American or Latinx cultural resonances. I hope that my previous reading as well as research encounters with African American political culture, and my previous reading about and experience with Latinx-affirming activists, both helped to some extent.[6] I hope my willingness to risk being awkward and learn from mistakes helped too. Again, to be a good interpreter, I tried to keep close track of my interactional mistakes when I realized them, and listened especially carefully when participants criticized others' interaction. Most of all, I have tried hard not to make claims about participants' personal experiences that my research roles and social perceptions would not likely access clearly.

It is worth emphasizing here that claims about LAPO are limited to general and housing committee meetings. This was not a study of the whole LAPO organization. Participant observers with different questions might want to know more about the organizational structure or other accomplishments of this striking, often effective group—more than what I have considered sufficient context for my arguments. I spent a lot more time than I may have needed to understand style and idioculture in the selected LAPO scenes. I tried to exercise an abundance of caution regarding what I might be misconstruing.

Reflecting on positionality is only one kind of reflexivity. I suggested above that it is just as important to reflect carefully on misunderstandings in interaction—usually realized only after the fact. We should do this so we can clarify *meanings* that powerfully orient action of the people we write about. Instead of presenting all those here, I have called attention to various puzzles over meanings—in ethnographic scenarios spread across the book—that especially perplexed and educated me on the way to developing arguments. The professionals at the affordable housing developer, HSLA, presented me with the most consistently confounding scenarios. In no other organizational setting did I frequently feel compelled to seek more help in understanding what participants were saying and doing.

NOTES

Introduction

1. I will use "social advocates" as the generic term for many of the actors in this study. By social advocate, I mean people who participate in collective action to improve some social condition, whether that means advocating for more housing, a better business climate for building housing, or any of countless other goods. The term is not intended to carry a lot of conceptual or interpretative weight. I do not use it in the vein of some US social activists who distinguish between "activists" in grassroots social change efforts and paid professional "advocates" who "advocate" on behalf of groups to which they don't directly belong. "Collective problem solvers" also would convey my intent well, but is too awkward.

2. On urban "scenes" along with their aesthetic and emotional attractions, see Silver and Clark 2016.

3. For a fuller elaboration on this definition and the gloss that follows, see Lichterman and Eliasoph 2014.

4. A society is "self-organizing" to the degree it hosts civic action. The "self-organizing," "self-steering" capacity of a society is Jürgen Habermas's (1987, 1984) characterization of civic activity.

5. For enduring, influential works on this topic from different scholarly generations, see Almond and Verba 1963; Verba, Schlozman, and Brady 1995; Putnam 2000.

6. See, for example, Berger and Neuhaus 1977; Habermas 1987; Wolfe 1989; Wuthnow 1991b.

7. For an extended discussion on this point, with international and US examples, see Lichterman and Eliasoph 2014.

8. Martens 2002; Hall 1999; Clemens 2006, 207–10.

9. Schlozman, Verba, and Brady 2013; Baggett 2000.

10. I have developed this argument at length elsewhere (Lichterman 2005, 2006, 2009). In short, many researchers have used the concept of social capital to mean the social networks, norms of reciprocity, and sense of trust they expect to find among individuals or groups in the sector of society they call "civic." The concept ends up accomplishing a kind of disappearing act: social capital is an abstraction that turns attention away from distinct practices of mutual obligation as well as different definitions of trust and loyalty that we will see within different forms of civic action in the case chapters of this book.

11. See, for example, McAdam, Tarrow, and Tilly 2001; Armstrong and Bernstein 2008.

12. See, for example, Brown 1997; Minkoff 2002; Baiocchi 2005; Fisher 2006; Marwell 2007; Armstrong and Bernstein 2008; Walker 2014; Ewick and Steinberg 2019.

13. Sometimes they do, though, as in the case of participatory governance that includes governmental agents or contenders for electoral or government agency offices. See, for example, Fung and Wright 2003; Baiocchi 2005.

14. See Klandermans 1992; Melucci 1988; Rucht 2004.

15. For helpful leads in this direction, see Cefaï 2002; Hilgartner and Bosk 1988.

16. In parallel fashion, social activists may publicize political claims in reaction to how "volunteers" approach a problem. In an earlier study, I found church-based critics of President Bill Clinton–era social welfare policy reform aiming some of their assertions against the notion, which they heard in their churches, that compassionate volunteers were better or more desirable than governmental agents in the role of caring for hungry or homeless people (Lichterman 2005). Researchers sometimes echo a "politics versus charity" or "contention versus compassion" terminology of the people they study (Poppendieck 1999; Blau 1992). They treat charitable volunteer groups as mistakenly ignoring the social structural causes of problems and therefore not worth including in the investigation—yet these groups represent a mode of collective problem solving too.

17. Ethnographic research always poses the question of what we "have a case of," and there is always more than one potential answer. Sometimes our audience will not recognize our discoveries as findings worth attending to unless we engage in "metacommunication," prompting critique or replacement of an academic subfield's widely shared categories and assumptions in order to grasp a discovery's significance. Metacommunication may result in choosing a less frequently used case—"civic action" rather than "social movement," for example—in order to parlay a discovery into a new set of questions for a field of research that could not apprehend them previously. See Lichterman and Reed 2015.

18. See Alvarez et al. 2017; Smilde and Hellinger 2011; Baiocchi 2005.

19. Duyvendak and Fillieule 2015; Cefaï 2002; Baldassarri and Diani 2007; Diani and Bison 2004; Diani and Pilati 2011.

20. See also Benford and Hunt 1992.

21. Sampson et al. 2005.

22. The proportion of events combining "nonpolitical" and "protest" action increased three-fold between 1970 and 2000. By my definition, a good proportion of these activities may be civic and interesting to compare, whether or not they include protest.

23. Traditionally the definition emphasizes contention with the state over resources or rights. Elizabeth Armstrong and Mary Bernstein (2008) argue for expanding the definition of social movement to include struggles for cultural recognition and efforts at cultural change. The next chapter discusses what both definitions have in common.

Chapter 1: A New Sociology of Civic Action

1. This statement expands the traditional understanding of "social movement" (Gamson 1975) to include contestations over cultural recognition and identity (see, for example, Armstrong and Bernstein 2008; Fraser 1997).

2. See McCarthy and Zald 1973, 1977.

3. The much-criticized classic study is Smelser 1962.

4. See, for example, McAdam 1982; Tarrow 1994; Kitschelt 1986.

5. Some of these studies, like mine, situate institutional challengers in thick cultural or situational contexts that shape them as much as the other way around. See, for example, Ann Mische's (2008) study of Brazilian youth activism in 1980s' and 1990s' Brazil, Steinberg's (1998, 1999, 2002) work on nineteenth-century English labor activists, Kathleen Blee's (2012, 2013) research on how grassroots activist groups emerge and occasionally transform their pathways of action, and Ewick and Steinberg's (2019) study of activists narrating collective identity as faithful dissenters inside the Catholic church.

6. See, for example, Melucci 1989; Jasper 1997; Taylor and Raeburn 1995; Guigni 2008.

7. See Armstrong and Bernstein 2008.

8. Armstrong and Bernstein 2008, 85, 93.

9. Research on social movement culture and emotions is too big an arena for a single review, but for reviews of notable studies and essays that continue to inform current work, see Morris and Mueller 1992; Johnston and Klandermans 1995; Goodwin, Jasper, and Polletta 2001; Polletta and Jasper 2001; Williams 2004; Polletta 2006; Snow et al. 2014. Below I discuss one particularly relevant part of this work that matters for my research: studies of strategic framing.

10. For a sample of statements, see McAdam 1988a; Jasper 1997; Goodwin, Jasper, and Polletta 2001; Guigni 2008.

11. See, for example, Armstrong and Bernstein 2008; Fligstein and McAdam 2012.

12. Skilled actors have a "highly developed cognitive capacity for reading people and environments, framing lines of action, and mobilizing people in the service of broader conceptions of the world and of themselves" (Fligstein and McAdam 2012,17).

13. Since others already have reviewed this work extensively (Benford 1997; Snow 2004; Snow et al. 2014), a brief, conversational overview suffices. In some studies, a "frame" is a cultural microstructure that organizes communication. More commonly, the term connotes a "picture frame" that marks off some aspects of reality while bracketing others (Williams and Benford 2000, 129). For an often-cited, compact treatment of the "framing" idea, see Snow and Benford 1988.

14. See Snow 2008; Snow et al. 2014; Snow et al. 1986, 467.

15. The framing perspective's progenitors understand it that way. See Snow et al. 2014, 29.

16. In signal statements, scholars combine interactionist presuppositions with the tendency to see social advocates as self-consciously "agentic." See Snow 2004, 385; Fligstein and McAdam 2012.

17. As the literature would put it, the framing was prognostic as well as diagnostic (Snow and Benford 1988).

18. See especially the argument in Eliasoph 1998.

19. See Fligstein 2001.

20. A sharper-edged critique would suggest that the skill explanation by itself can become uncomfortably teleological (see Steinberg 1998). To concretely picture that, let's assume that speakers at city hall or their leaders had the skill to frame the apartment construction / hospital demolition without compassion language. ISLA ultimately won its bid, and the commissioners demanded of the property developer an extensively revised construction plan. Yet, ISLA leaders could not know for sure what would happen, and were understandably nervous even if hopeful. So to put the question, How do we know ISLA leaders had skill at the outset? If we use their win as evidence that ISLA leaders had "skill," we are granting advocates the power to know the

future with transcendent certainty. If we don't make that move, then we simply return to my initial question: *How* do advocates know which kinds of claims will be appropriate or powerful— the ones we call "skilled" after the fact? Entrepreneurial models go quiet on that process.

21. See, for example, an interesting piece on the pitches that activists used to get people to join a nuclear disarmament campaign (Benford 1993b) or research on the stories that civil rights activists told about how they jumped into risky protest (Polletta 2006).

22. See, for example, McAdam 1988b; McAdam and Paulsen 1993.

23. See, for example, Weare, Lichterman, and Esparza 2014.

24. Diani 2003.

25. Personal conversation with HJ leader, January 2009.

26. See McAdam and Paulsen 1993, 663.

27. "Interpreters must command sufficient resources and numbers to provide a social/organizational base for mobilization. When this is the case, the ideational challenge inherent in fashioning an account . . . gets joined to a more narrowly organizational one. As a prerequisite for action, would-be insurgents must either create an organizational vehicle and its supporting collective identity or, more likely, *appropriate* an existing organization and the routine collective identity on which it rests" (McAdam 2003, 291–92).

28. For a similar point, see Luhtakallio and Tavory 2018.

29. Some scholars of claims making have criticized the social movement framing perspective for a static approach to language—one that assumes that a word or phrase consistently gives off the same meaning. They find in framing studies a default assumption that strategic entrepreneurs have indefinite leeway to frame messages to attract supporters. See Steinberg 1998, 1999, 2002; Hart 1996; Jasper 1997; Williams and Benford 2000; Eliasoph and Lichterman 2003; Williams 2004. Given that the framing perspective emerged in the 1980s from a "social-psychological turn" in social movement research (Oliver and Johnson 2000, 37), it may not be so surprising that it has attended less to what culture-oriented scholars tend to emphasize. While a few framing studies do suggest that broader ideologies constrain framing (Benford and Snow 2000), framing researchers say studies should spend more timing investigating broader cultural contexts that influence activists' sense of what is an appropriate frame. See, for example, Hart 1996; Polletta and Kai Ho 2006; Snow 2008, 5; Williams 2004; Lichterman and Dasgupta 2020.

30. For one statement of this concern, see Snow 2008.

31. On entrepreneurial model studies, see, for example, Noy 2009; Diani and McAdam 2003. Other network scholarship points out that network ties rely on varying meanings of relationship (Krackhardt and Kilduff 2002; Mische 2003, 2008; Weare, Lichterman, and Esparza 2014). Studies outside network scholarship make the same point: that relationships can *mean* different things even for members of the same organization or coalition. See Lichterman 1995; Clemens 1996; Polletta 2002; Roth 2010.

32. See Baldassarri and Diani 2007. Diani (2013) elaborates, for instance, on different "modes of coordination" in networks, shifting some analytic emphasis further toward kinds of relationships. In this scheme, "coalitions" coordinate action around a shared cause, beyond unscheduled, casual exchanges, and share a (limited) goal, while "social movements" coordinate action with a collective identity. Whether or not we go with these special definitions of coalition and social movement, Diani's framework directs us helpfully to kinds of interaction rather than merely the volume or frequency of them.

33. Lichterman 2006.

34. In traditional definitions (for example, McCarthy and Zald 1977), organizations are central to social movements. Some social movement scholars have pointed out that social activists of New Left, environmental, radical feminist, and more recently, alternative globalization and Occupy movements often have eschewed stable, resource-acquiring organizations for more ephemeral and flexible groupings, alternative subcultures, individually mounted visibility actions, flash mobs, or temporary campouts (Gitlin 1987; Melucci 1989; Epstein 1991; Taylor and Raeburn 1995; Lichterman 1996; Juris 2008; Lang and Lang/Levitsky 2012).

35. Left-indented blocks of text always represent excerpts from ethnographic field notes, unless otherwise specified. They quote or paraphrase conversation, or describe action.

36. Public Ally is a national program that sends young college graduates to intern at progressive organizations.

37. See Skocpol 2002, 1999; Walker 2014; Wuthnow 1998a.

38. See Lichterman and Eliasoph 2014, 809–10.

39. That does not mean they must be unpaid "volunteers" in the US sense, nor that they cannot also be governmental agents or employees. It means they have leeway to coordinate their efforts rather than being subject to inflexible legal mandates, or the (governmentally guaranteed) relations of private property and market exchange.

40. See, for example, David Pettinicchio's (2012, 2019) research on disability advocates—"institutional activists" in the US Senate and House of Representatives.

41. See Tocqueville (1835) 1969; Durkheim 1957. For US pragmatists' notion of a democratically self-controlling society, see Addams (1902) 2002; Dewey 1927; Follett (1918) 1965. See also Cefaï 2002. For critical theorists' vision of democratic publics, see Cohen and Arato 1992; Habermas 1984, 1987, (1964) 1989. On the "social control" theme in US sociology, see Sampson, Morenoff, and Earls 1999; Janowitz 1975.

42. For many, the conversation began with the publication of Robert Putnam's (1995, 2000) figures on association memberships. From there, one of US social science's biggest and most lively debates since the 1960s ensued. What did the figures mean, and what should be done? See, for example, Edwards and Foley 1997; Schudson 1998; Wuthnow 1998a; Cohen 1999; Skocpol and Fiorina 1999; Wilson 2001; Fishman 2004; Lichterman 2005, 2006; Somers 2005.

43. Sirianni and Friedland 2001; Putnam and Feldstein 2003.

44. Edwards and Foley 1997; Skocpol and Fiorina 1999; Somers 2005.

45. See Briggs 2008, especially 13–15, 23–24, 297–310. For another useful comparison of regional, civic collaborations, see Benner and Pastor 2015.

46. See especially Dewey 1922, 1927, 1938, 1939; Addams (1902) 2002; Peirce (1868) 1992; Joas 1996. It is important to recognize that these philosophers did not all share identical approaches to epistemological, substantive, or moral questions, and did not have identical understandings of social science; they did not all consistently embrace the term "pragmatist" either. "Pragmatism" is a rather loose constellation of orienting postulates, intellectual problems, and discussions concerning action, meaning, and knowledge claims, not "a method" or "a theory." I lean most here on Dewey's contributions to those discussions, and am emphasizing the broad commonalities that writers and readers who use "pragmatist" tend to associate with the term. See, for example, Lichterman 2015.

47. Volunteers at a meals program for people with AIDS avow religious teachings in some settings but not others (Bender 2003). Neighbors who shun talk of racism or corporate-caused environmental damage in public meetings or in front of media cameras condemn racial

discrimination and speculate about corporate malfeasance in casual conversations off the public stage (Eliasoph 1998). Religiously based community organizers and queer activists too promote self-critical, multivalent identities in small group meetings, while claiming homogeneous interests and unitary group identities in public campaign settings (Lichterman 1999; Wood 2002).

48. See Goffman (1974) 1986, 8–10.

49. Joseph Gusfield's (1980) study of drinking and driving offers a wonderful example: plaintiffs or defendants in court proceedings act systematically differently in the book-lined office chamber of a robed judge than when outside the courthouse.

50. Those patterns clue us in to causal mechanisms we can use to explain why action unfolded one way and not another. For extensive discussion on these points, see Lichterman and Reed 2015; Reed and Lichterman 2017, forthcoming; Reed 2011.

51. For a foundational statement, see Eliasoph and Lichterman 2003.

52. Eliasoph and Lichterman 2003, 739.

53. For practical guides to identifying different styles that researchers have found repeatedly, see Eliasoph and Lichterman (2003, appendix). See also the detailed table of style characteristics in Lichterman and Eliasoph 2014.

54. For a review and meta-analysis of studies, see Lichterman and Eliasoph 2014, 839–47. Earlier work observed that a style—"personalized politics," for instance—may require the cultural capital, the distinct self-presentation and articulation skills, that is more available to highly schooled or professional middle-class people than others (Lichterman 1996). Given the participants observed in this and other studies, it would be hard to say that about these two styles.

55. Dewey (1939, 248) put it this way: "There is no desire and no interest which, in its distinction from raw impulse and strictly organic appetite, is not what it is because of transformation effected in the latter by their interaction with the cultural environment." If we think otherwise, he argued, we surrender to a kind of "metaphysical individualism" that prefers commonsense understandings of purposive action over sociological analysis of it.

56. In the Deweyan understanding, actors' experiences and choices don't start out separate from larger contexts only to become "influenced" by them—as if contexts exist in a realm separate from the world of action. Styles of action are always "entangled" in those larger contexts and bear their mark.

57. That would not be *entanglement* but instead simply a result or reflection—one thing causing another thing. Dewey had something messier in mind.

58. If social and institutional realities were to shift fundamentally, we would expect the relatively few widespread styles of civic action (Lichterman and Eliasoph 2014) to alter or disappear, and others to emerge, as civic actors crystallize different accommodations to the impinging realities. The conjecture is worth more study, but comparative research offers some support for it already. In France, where political representation is not so routinely defined in terms of interest groups, and institutionalized racism works differently than in the United States, communities of interest or identity often look antidemocratic (Camus-Vigué 2000). Attempts to import these models of collective action from the United States are treated by social advocates with suspicion (Talpin 2017). In a similar vein, when a colleague and I (Lichterman and Doidy 2018) compared activism by socially marginal, inadequately housed people in Los Angeles and Paris, we found that LA activists expressed their radicalism as a community of identity while Parisian

activists, cultivated in French political culture, pressed fairly similar housing issues in a more universalistic style called "social critic" (Lichterman and Eliasoph 2014).

59. See Schlozman, Verba, and Brady 2013.

60. For an authoritative account of how this political form became institutionalized, see Clemens 1997.

61. For an in-depth study of this "astroturf" organizing and similar efforts, see Walker 2014.

62. Systematic survey research finds that people of a lower socioeconomic status have less time, fewer organizational skills, and less "social capital" for mounting collective action (Schloz-man, Verba, and Brady 2012; Wuthnow 2002). They may have a much less developed sense of entitlement to speak out too. For close-up studies, see Hart 2001; Warren 2001; Saegert et al. 2001.

63. In one case, for instance, a group of white, midwestern church volunteers took a clue from tensions they felt emanating from the community center director of a low-income Hmong and Black neighborhood. Their way of working together frankly was not working. They reorga-nized their whole volunteer project. Rather than coming to "serve those in need" as casual volunteers, they started collaborating with the center and each other as partners, producing public goods for the neighborhood rather than one-to-one helping service. See Lichterman 2005, chapter 6.

64. A focus on scenes and styled action differs from Blee's valuable approach in several ways. See Lichterman and Dasgupta 2020. In short, this study's approach highlights styles operating in different scenes. Blee's "emergentist" approach stresses a path-dependent process for a group as a whole, where "discursive rules" emerge over time.

65. Sociologists use the discursive field concept to mean some variety of things. In Christo-pher Bail's (2008) study of media coverage of Islam or David Snow's (2008) theoretical writing about social movement discourses, for example, "discursive field" refers to the sum total of discourses circulating about a specific topic. I follow Wuthnow's expansive, foundational work on the topic and Spillman's widely cited statement, both of which treat a discursive field as an enabling, constraining cultural *context* rather than a sum total of diffusing discourses.

66. Blee (2012, 2013) delineates this process in detail in her study of newly crystallizing grassroots activist groups in Pittsburgh. For a more theoretical version of the same point, see field theorist Martin 2003.

67. The notion of "discursive field," like "culture" more generally in current sociology, names a dimension of analysis. It refers to a set of symbolic patterns and meaningful practices that have their own influence on speech and action that is not completely or immediately determined by actors' social-structural interests or organizational positions outside the field (Smith 1997; Kane 1997; Sewell 1992; Alexander and Seidman 1990). This is important to note since other concepts of "field," valuable in their own ways, treat culture differently (see, for example, Bourdieu 1993; Fligstein and McAdam 2011). Analyzing the two primary campaigns in terms of *discursive* fields rather than some other kind of field, I focus on how actors collaborate and conflict over claims about problems.

68. See Emirbayer 1997.

69. This is a basic postulate of symbolic interactionism in sociology. For more conceptual discussion and sources on this point, and extended illustrations of how these perceptions took

hold in scenes from this study, see Lichterman and Dasgupta 2020. Interestingly, prominent studies on the entrepreneurial actor model (Snow et al. 1986; Fligstein and McAdam 2012) also base themselves in symbolic interactionist thought (see Snow et al. 2014; Fligstein and McAdam 2012, 17–18, 47). My cultural focus leads me to a different strand of that tradition.

70. For more discussion on the role of leaders and the limits in their ability to sidestep the style of a scene, see Lichterman and Dasgupta 2020.

Chapter 2: Placing and Studying the Action

1. Professionals in affordable housing say that rent is "affordable" if a tenant household spends no more than 30 percent of its income on it. Tenants who rent, along with homeless people, were the main constituency for housing advocates in this study.

2. See Logan and Molotch 1987, especially 50–66.

3. See Harvey 1989. For a concrete example, among others, see Pacewicz 2015.

4. See, for example, Perez 2004. Though scholars frequently use the term "gentrification" to connote the displacement of lower-income residents (see, for example, Brown-Saracino 2010; Mele 2000), the implicit critique is not universally shared. For a sunnier view of locally rooted businesses, arts entrepreneurs, leaders, and residents collaborating to "rebrand" their stigmatized neighborhood with a proud, ethnic identity, see Wherry 2011.

5. See Smith 2002.

6. See Charles 2003; Hwang and Sampson 2014; Krysan and Bader 2007; Quillian and Pager 2001; Sampson 2012.

7. Wyly and Hammel 2004.

8. For an extensive list of strategies and locales, see Annunziata and Rivas-Alonso 2018.

9. These claims are informed by timely analyses in Gottlieb et al. 2005.

10. See the review in Kahne 2018, 310.

11. See Gottlieb et al. 2005, 85–86.

12. See Kahne 2018.

13. See Saito 2012. See also Mike Davis's (1990) writerly account of some of these developments along with brazen land and water grabs, sweetheart deals, and other feats of sordid entrepreneurialism that preceded them.

14. See Kahne 2018, 311–12.

15. See Wu 2012.

16. See Steckler and Garcia 2008. This is using a conventional standard that no more than roughly 30 percent of income go to rent or 33 percent to homeowner costs.

17. This was one upshot of a lengthy report, appearing in early 2009, by investigators commissioned by one of the leading organizations in the ISLA coalition (author's file). In keeping with the decision not to use real collective or individual names, I decline to cite the report.

18. Beyond my observations as a resident, Juliet Kahne (2018) verifies the point.

19. See Fulton 1997; Purcell 2000.

20. See Saito 2012, 2019.

21. Residents, pundits, and some scholars have pointed to Los Angeles' "sprawl" as one big sign of an ever-present prodevelopment sensibility among city administrations and city planners. See Gottlieb et al. 2005. While recent developments quickly surveyed here suggest a more

nuanced picture, it is good to note that studies within urban planning do indicate that efforts to contain development in Los Angeles up to the time that this study began had often been more nominal than substantive. For instance, efforts to institute transit-oriented development in Los Angeles operate more as guidelines than enforceable requirements (Boarnet and Crane 1997). Moreover, well before HJ's campaign presented here, other California and prominent West Coast cities had instituted mandatory inclusionary housing requirements for developers, but efforts to pass similar measures in Los Angeles had floated around and failed since the early 1990s (Mukhija et al. 2010).

22. See Katz 2015, 2001, 2002.

23. One of those twelve, Rediscover MacArthur Park (RMP) coalition, appears only as a brief mention in chapter 9 and does not appear in the following descriptions. I attended a year's worth of RMP meetings along with wine- and tamale-tasting events at the nonprofit restaurant that hosted RMP, because the coalition's commercial-friendly approach to neighborhood development was so interestingly different from ISLA's equitable development, antidisplacement stance. RMP discussions produced a lot of neighborhood-booster talk about crime, new transit lines, and affordable housing—topics ISLA took up too in a different key. The contrasts helped me clarify what was distinctive about ISLA's work for and from "the community." For an initial analysis of RMP, see Citroni and Lichterman 2017.

24. Author's file; citation omitted to preserve confidentiality of coalition actors.

25. Steckler and Garcia 2008. Data produced quarterly by the California Association of Realtors, cited in the following news articles: Kevin Felt, "Housing Affordability Level Falls in Los Angeles County, Calif.," *San Gabriel Valley Tribune*, August 19, 2004; "Housing Affordability Index Falls Five Points in February, Affordability Gap between California and U.S. Now at 26 Percent," PR Newswire, April 4, 2002.

26. Steckler and Garcia 2008.

27. Author's file; citation omitted to preserve confidentiality of coalition actors.

28. This comes from a report by WHA (2004, author's file), the association of affordable housing developers that funded the staff of the HJ coalition.

29. Details of this second HJ campaign come from "Mahoney Proposal," City News Service, October 2, 2003; "Developers Seek Bonuses with Proposed Inclusionary Housing Law," City News Service, October 22, 2003; "Housing Policy," City News Service, April 15, 2004; "Officials Ponder Zoning to Reduce Home Prices," *Daily News of Los Angeles*, May 25, 2004; David Zahniser, "Zoning Proposal Opposed by Neighborhood Groups," Copley News Service, August 20, 2004; Rick Orlov, "Councils May Fight Zoning Plan," *Daily News of Los Angeles*, September 27, 2004; Rick Orlov, "Zoning Change Urged for More Low-Cost Homes," *Daily News of Los Angeles*, June 2, 2005.

30. Wardrip 2009.

31. Descriptions in this paragraph and the next one are not backed by citations out of deference to individual actors that actual sources would make too easy to trace.

32. In 1999, on a sample street in the Draper neighborhood, 10 percent of the residences housed or were being refitted to house students; in 2009, roughly 75 percent of the residences were student occupied according to ISLA advocates' research.

33. The typical field sortie (a meeting, rally, task activity, or stint in an office) lasted on average roughly two hours, and typically I would spend two or three hours expanding jottings into

field notes for every hour in the field. Accompanying the outreach work of The Way Home (TWH) staff with homeless people was different; outreach shifts lasted roughly four hours each.

34. For two years of ethnographic research, graduate assistants extended observations beyond what one ethnographer could do alone while keeping up teaching and service duties.

35. For a discussion of how I thought about and practiced reflexivity as a researcher during the study, see Lichterman 2017, as well as Appendix II.

36. See Emerson, Fretz, and Shaw 2011.

37. Coding for style benefited from heuristics established in the literature (Eliasoph and Lichterman 2003, 784–87; Lichterman and Eliasoph 2014, 842), aided by the insight that interactional patterns like style are easier to identify when violated or disputed (Goffman 1961, (1974) 1986, 308–77).

38. See Lichterman (2005, 274–79; 2012, 22). Saved from circularity, the causal logic is secure; others already have shown that scene style can work as a causal mechanism (Gross 2009; Reed 2011), shaping both strategic messaging and informal, exploratory communication (Lichterman 2005; Mische 2008).

39. This may not be true much longer. Clever matching and parsing work, assisted by computational linguistic methods, may make it possible to discern scene style from the texts of complex websites. See Lichterman and Eliasoph 2014.

40. The ethnographer needs to ply the constant comparative process sensitively, and generate good guesses about when and why the style may change amid one meeting; the same process makes it possible to reconstruct a change in style that may have occurred during meetings or events the researcher missed.

Chapter 3: Solving Problems by Fighting for an Interest

1. Plans for the MIHO campaign began months before news of a suddenly deepening recession. Strikingly, HJ advocates talked of the recession primarily as all the more reason to do what they were planning to do rather than a reason for new departures.

2. The history of interest-based politics is a huge topic beyond the scope of discussion here, but for an authoritative account of its institutional origins, see Clemens 1997.

3. Crises like these, whether externally or internally generated, do sometimes change participants' sense of what they are doing together as an organization, what their longer-term goals should be, and how they should relate to one another. See, for example, Blee's (2012, 2013) study of turning points in grassroots activist groups, or Lichterman's (2005) study for a look at how a network of church volunteers refashioned their relations to a low-income neighborhood to become a conduit for modest public goods rather than individual donations and one-to-one helping relations.

4. Each of the scholarly concepts here tags a research literature far too large to be reviewed usefully in one place. This study's relation to social movement frames and framing research is discussed in chapter 7. See also Lichterman and Dasgupta 2020. For an important statement on narrative in social movements, see Polletta 2006. For landmark statements and useful reviews from earlier and more recent work in the voluminous research on collective identity in social movements, see Melucci 1988, 1989; Taylor and Whittier 1992; Laraña, Johnston, and Gusfield 1994; Polletta and Jasper 2001; Snow, Soule, and Kriesi 2004; Fominaya 2010.

5. See Eliasoph and Lichterman 2003; Lichterman and Eliasoph 2014.

6. See Lichterman and Eliasoph 2014, 842.

7. Recent historical studies also cast doubt on the value of the simple sectoral distinction here. See, for example, Clemens and Guthrie 2010. See also the review of research on international as well as US cases in Lichterman and Eliasoph 2014.

8. SRO stands for "single room occupancy." An SRO hotel is a building that once served as a hotel but was converted into one-room apartments for long-term residents.

9. Research assistant Brady Potts attended and took the notes.

10. A less-studied dimension of scene style is "speech norms," which include the expressions of feeling and genres of verbal expression. See Lichterman and Eliasoph 2014, 814.

11. For other studies that manifest the increasing interest in the emotions of collective advocacy, see, for example, Goodwin, Jasper, and Polletta 2000; Polletta and Jasper 2001; Whittier 2009.

12. See extended descriptions of this tactic, a "public drama," in Wood 2002.

13. See Heaney and Rojas 2014.

14. A short list of examples in the United States includes a variety of issues: local community organizing, labor activism, municipal urban politics, and LGBTQ activism. See Lichterman and Eliasoph 2014, 842.

15. Fligstein and McAdam 2012.

Chapter 4: Solving Problems by Protecting an Identity

1. The distinction between this expressive politics and a more conventional, instrumental politics organized Frank Parkin's (1968) now-classic account of Great Britain's antinuclear movement of the early 1960s. It strongly informed studies of the US civil rights and student New Left movements of the 1960s and early 1970s (Breines 1982; McAdam 1982, 1988a; Gitlin 1987; Whalen and Flacks 1989), and the countercultural efflorescence of the same time (Gitlin 1987; Melucci 1989; Berger 1981).

2. See Gitlin 1987.

3. See Young 1990; Fraser; Taylor 1994; Kymlicka 1995.

4. See especially Taylor 1994; Fraser 1997.

5. For a start, see Honneth 1996.

6. See Gitlin 1994, 1995; Etzioni 1996.

7. See, for example, Hamburger 2018.

8. See Lilla 2017.

9. Bernstein 1997.

10. Levine 2017.

11. In this vein, see also McQuarrie 2013.

12. See some cases in Lee, McQuarrie, and Walker 2015; Eliasoph 2011.

13. From here on, when I represent actors invoking "the community" or refer to that subject myself, I will not use quotation marks since doing so may signal an editorial condescension that I do not intend. I will trust readers to keep in mind that what I am referring to is a social construction honored by those who identify with it. It has real, materially and emotionally palpable consequences, just as many social constructions do.

14. Lamont 1992.

15. This alludes to theorist Pierre Bourdieu's (1984) use of the phrase.

16. Levine 2017; Lichterman 1996.

17. For a classic statement here, see McCarthy and Zald 1977.

18. For an extended example, see Lichterman 1996.

19. See Wood 2002; Warren 2001; Hart 2001.

20. For a short list of examples, see Lichterman and Eliasoph 2014, 842.

21. For local antigentrification activism styled this way in Chicago neighborhoods and the tourist destination of Provincetown, Massachusetts, see Brown-Saracino 2009. In Japonica Brown-Saracino's excellent study, residents opposed to gentrification that she categorizes as "social preservationists" speak protectively on behalf of a particular ethnic and geographically local community's authenticity. They construct a community of identity that they themselves cannot really join. That is in effect the same position that ISLA leaders offered students: allies in support of others' community of identity. For similarly styled collective action on New York City's Lower East Side, see Mele 2000, especially 277–78.

22. Sociologists have different concepts for getting at different dimensions of organizational culture. Scene style is one of course, but other conceptual tools mine other dimensions. If we want to study the symbols, stories, or group routines that people share over time in one small group—a baseball team, for example—across different scenes of that group's action, then we are studying idioculture. For extensive, authoritative discussions, see Fine 1987, 2010.

23. Abutting that corner is a park known for large encampments of people in tents. I interpret the laughter as recognition of a prime address for homelessness in Los Angeles and perhaps the irony that some people can't say they have a "residence."

24. On US anti-intervention activism, especially focused on Central America, see Munkres 2003; Smith 1996.

25. On African American charismatic leadership, see Reed 1986.

26. For an academically worded version of the idea, see Smith 2007; Kivel 2007.

27. Length of residence in the LAPO community was much less celebrated or even re-marked. Some LAPO participants were temporarily housed or homeless, not long-term tenants. Unsurprisingly, then, "proud member of this community for x years" was not a feature of LA-PO's idioculture even though it was central in ISLA's. Idioculture researcher Gary Alan Fine (1983) explains that demographic and social structural contingencies indirectly or directly influence the symbols and practices that an idioculture preserves.

28. LAPO's "implicit" rather than explicit African American identity is not unique in grass-roots activism. A multiracial, environmental justice organization I studied over two decades ago similarly expressed its common commitment in African American cultural idioms while never claiming that "we are a Black organization." See Lichterman 1996. See a similar phenomenon in Mary Pattillo-McCoy's (1998) research on local civic groups in Chicago.

29. For the case of a suburban environmental group, see Lichterman 1996; Eliasoph and Lichterman 2003.

Chapter 5: Why Follow the Style, Not Just the Organization?

1. See Van Dyke and McCammon 2010.

2. See, for example, Rochon and Meyer 1997; Schlozman, Verba, and Brady 2013; Staggenborg 1986; Van Dyke and McCammon 2010; Warren 2001; Brenner and Pastor 2015.

3. See Obach 2004; McAdam 1988a; Ghaziani and Baldassarri 2011; Rose 2000; Lichterman 1995; Van Dyke 2003; Ferree and Hess 1994.

4. For an early example of this line of argument, see Lichterman 1995.

5. For the Boston coalition, see Beamish and Luebbers 2009. For examples of coalitions that dissipated or never jelled, see Bell and Delaney 2001; Lichterman 1995.

6. For a good view of the tensions here, see Moseley 2012.

7. Priming the listener with an organizational name is a "scene-switching practice," an interactional move that nudges the listener toward or away from the style appropriate for a particular scene. See Lichterman and Eliasoph 2014.

8. On the varied settings of complex organizations, see, for example, Thompson 1967. For applications of the insight to the world of civic action, see Mische 2008; Binder 2007; Lichterman 1999; Eliasoph 2011.

9. See, for example, Lichterman 2005; Eliasoph and Lichterman 2003.

10. Lichterman and Eliasoph 2014, 816.

11. For useful discussions of these telling, everyday glitches, see Goffman 1961; (1974) 1986, 308–44.

12. The attendees' comments quoted here were originally in Spanish; author's translation.

13. For other examples of nimble, style juggling, see Lichterman and Eliasoph 2014; Lichterman 2005, chapter 6. For more analysis of interaction dynamics in this as well as other scenarios where the juggling act was rough or failed, see Lichterman and Dasgupta 2020.

14. The neighborhood residents' comments quoted here were originally in Spanish; author's translation.

15. See Fligstein and McAdam 2012, 7.

16. For the classic piece in this line of work, see Kitschelt 1986. See also McAdam, McCarthy, and Zald 1996; Cress and Snow 2000; McCammon et al. 2007; Trumpy 2016; Ayoub and Chetaille 2017.

17. For more elaboration on culturally structured agency, see Sewell 1992.

18. See, for example, Lichterman 1996; 2005, chapter 3.

19. On style as a fuzzy cultural form, see Lichterman 2012. See also Cicourel 1993; Taylor 1993.

20. See Blee 2012, especially 36.

21. See Dewey 1939; Whitford 2002; Swidler 1986.

22. Mische 2009; Tavory and Eliasoph 2013; Mische, forthcoming.

23. See, for example, Obach 2004, 129.

24. On class-based coalition building, see Rose 2000. On low-income neighborhoods and wider ties, see Sampson 1999; Saegert, Thompson, and Warren 2001.

25. The most credible account I can piece together from the available documents is that the coalition had arrived three months earlier at ballpark figures on how much affordable housing to demand for different income levels. These probably would not change substantially if Carol was right that coalition leaders had already found out where the no-go zone was in their negotiations over a tentative proposal with the city hall officials who would help introduce it at city council.

26. See Benford 1993a; Benford and Snow 2000.

27. See, for example, Noy 2009.

28. When I mentioned framing strategies to a SED director, a social scientist herself, she laughed lightly and said unprompted that a lot of the organization's messaging happened by the "seat of the pants."

29. Carol implied she had learned the term at a media training workshop put on by union organizers.

Chapter 6: What Is Winning?

1. For more about CBAs, see the brief discussion in chapter 2. See also Saito 2012; Wolf-Powers 2010.

2. While each coalition hosted more than one style of action, a dominant style oriented the scenes in which core participants in each coalition made the big decisions about the coalition's direction.

3. See, for example, Wood, Davis, and Rouse 2004; Stuart 2011; Checker 2005.

4. See, for example, Briggs 2008; Sirianni and Friedland 2001; Putnam and Feldstein 2003. For a less hortatory, comparative study of civic partnerships for regional economic development, see Benner and Pastor 2015.

5. In their review of framing, Robert Benford and David Snow (2000, 624) argue that comparative studies of advocacy are, in general, rare due to the lengthy, labor-intensive research process that is required to do them. There certainly are comparative studies of advocacy groups and their cultures, though. Examples include Raka Ray's (1999) study of feminist activists in two Indian cities, Richard Wood's (2002) comparison of faith- and race-based activism in Oakland, California, or Susan Stall and Randy Stoecker's (1998) study of women's organizing in two Chicago neighborhoods. Such studies, however, often can be limited in how they can compare problem-solving processes among civic groups if the groups are not part of the same locality, or are not working on the same public policy goal or advocating at the same point in time.

6. For good reviews, see Guigni 1998, 2008; Earl 2004; Bosi and Uba 2009. A useful review would need to start with the question of what counts as an outcome to begin with, noting along the way that outcomes may be more complicated than a simple win or loss (Amenta et al. 2010; Earl 2004). Social movements' consequences for policy making have received more attention (Earl 2004; Amenta et al. 2010; Pettinicchio 2019), while impacts on popular culture, broadly circulating ideas, or institutionalized ways of doing things have received a lot less (Bosi and Uba 2009).

7. On this point, see Cress and Snow 2000. For examples of studies that cast a national, collective actor, see, for example, Amenta et al. 2010. For the less common, comparative look at how local social movements succeed or fail, see Cress and Snow 2000; Beamish 2015.

8. An important exception is Blee's (2012, 2013) work, which implicitly takes a view of outcomes closer to the one informing this book. Following group action closely, Blee charts the pathways by which local activist groups develop or drop issues and strategies; those decisions and turning points are the main outcomes of interest.

9. See Reed and Lichterman 2017.

10. This short list includes the three factors—organizational resources, political opportunity, and framing—presented in authoritative accounts (see, for example, McAdam, McCarthy, and Zald 1996), along with the continuing interest in the power of aggressive protest, already

apparent at the dawn of modern social movements research (Gamson 1975; see also Piven and Cloward 1979). The most sophisticated studies in this vein look at social movements' impacts on policy by breaking down that big question into multiple parts. Edwin Amenta and his colleagues (2010, 291) argue, for instance, that it is good to be precise about the goals or outcomes we want to explain. Rather than ask whether or not a social movement changed policy, it would be better to examine whether or not a social movement succeeded in getting its issue on a legislative agenda, influencing the content of a bill, influencing a vote on the bill, influencing implementation of a resulting policy, or any of those.

11. The study's explanation of differences between "direct" and "indirect" outcomes implies an organization is a unitary actor that does things: "Whereas direct outcomes are typically articulated as movement goals and are a reflection of a movement's primary ideological rationale, indirect outcomes are thought to reflect a movement's influence but are less likely to be ideologically based" (Cress and Snow 2000, 1065).

12. For a review of scene style and outcomes, see Lichterman and Eliasoph 2014, 847–49. That discussion treats both of the outcomes considered here.

13. Sociologists have been giving more attention to the role of future projections in how we act, individually and collectively. See, for example, Mische 2009, forthcoming; Tavory and Eliasoph 2013; Abbott 2001. A strong philosophical precursor to some of this discussion is John Dewey's *A Theory of Valuation* (1939).

14. Tavory and Eliasioph 2013.

15. Emphasis added. The insight has been core to contemporary sociological thinking about culture and action. See the much-cited statement in Swidler 1986.

16. These are often the approaches found in "case studies" that interview participants, read newspaper articles, or analyze organizational literature after a specific campaign or collective action episode has ended. Analyzing ends-in-view is not impossible when limited to such materials, but the tendency of the case study approach to focus on best practices, or identify common practices, often directs scholars to read a campaign from the standpoint of a win or loss. Tactical options and choices are analyzed in relation to the final outcome or whether it contributed to success/failure rather than in relation to other options available at the times of decision. See Bronfenbrenner et al. 1998; Brown and Zavestoski 2004.

17. That is one response among activists to failed aspirations. For instance, in medical advocacy, different interest or citizen advocacy groups have sometimes regrouped as an aggrieved identity—"treatment activists" or "disease constituencies"—after their concerns fell on deaf ears. See Epstein 1995.

18. One of the two *other* campaigns named "Housing Justice," mentioned in chapter 2, aimed to achieve less far-reaching institutional change in about the same amount of time.

19. As chapter 5 pointed out, participation by community members was written into the terms governing ISLA negotiations on a CBA with college officials.

20. Bourdieu 1977; Swidler 1986, 2001.

21. Researchers (see, for example, Jasper 2006) or advocates may want to call the first of these a "tactic," and only the second a "strategy." With the simple, plain-language definition I rely on here, both count as strategies.

22. Goffman wrote (1967, 91) that in his contemporary, secular world, people treated the self as a kind of deity, "a sacred object which must be treated with proper ritual care and in turn must

be presented in a proper light to others." I extend the insight to group self-understandings. Thanks to Christian Sperneac-Wolfer for pointing out Goffman's remark.

23. On upward mobility and aspiration among Latinx Californians, see, for example, Agius Vallejo 2012.

24. In her study of four gentrifying locales, Brown-Saracino identified a subculture of "social preservationists" who tried to protect the presence of some neighbors who were *different* from them in ethnic and class terms, and thus more "authentic." ISLA advocates and willing neighborhood residents, in contrast, identified with the same community.

25. See Logan and Molotch 1987. See also Čapek and Gilderbloom 1992.

Chapter 7: Who Can Say What, Where, and How?

1. Tracing the history of this social science rhetoric is a research project in itself, but for one early landmark, see Berger and Luckmann 1966.

2. For this book's purposes, we can sidestep the newer debate about whether we want to be "strict" or else "modified" constructionists who argue that we have to suppose some things really are problems because we can't investigate without assuming there's a reality there. That is where constructionism went from its early strict constructionist beginnings. Constructivist studies of social problems (Best 1995) have moved toward the intellectual mood of cultural sociology—emphasizing categories, not objective conditions, rhetoric not simple rationality (Miller and Holstein 1993; Holstein and Miller 2003; Kitsuse and Spector 1973; Best 1995).

3. Koopmans and Statham 1999.

4. That is one reason it is good to distinguish civic action from a cousin term, "the public sphere." Some researchers and theorists consider any conversation about public issues as "a site of the public sphere," one tiny contribution to the sum total of conversations about public-relevant topics, formal or informal. Public sphere and civic action overlap as empirical topics for writers who care about democracy, but not all conversations about politics or the public interest need to be considered part of sustained efforts to improve some aspect of society. See the discussion in Lichterman and Eliasoph 2014.

5. It is worth paying attention to claims making in more and less formal settings because all of them matter for sustained efforts to improve some aspect of society, and in any of them, people may be orienting their talk to a public debate. See Mische 2008; Polletta and Ho 2006; Williams 2004, 128.

6. See Spillman 1995.

7. See Cefaï and Gardella 2011, especially 45–55. The language of social emergency and social inclusion of the excluded was institutionalized in the mission statements of Samusocial de Paris, the founding organization of what became an international NGO dedicated to homelessness.

8. Diverse field theorists converge on this basic definition. See, for example, Bourdieu 1984; Fligstein and McAdam 2012; Martin 2003; Spillman 1995.

9. One of the prominent early statements calls it a "field within which discourse can be framed"—one that consists of "fundamental categories" that set the "limits of discussion" (Wuthnow 1989, 13, 555). Some work, like Bail's (2008) study of media coverage of Islam or Snow's (2008) theoretical writing about social movement discourses, defines "discursive field" differently, not as a forcefield that enables and constrains speech. In these accounts, it is more

a diffusion space where discourses circulate on some topic. That approach produces valuable findings but trains researchers' sensitivities for different kinds of questions.

10. See Ray 1999; Steinberg 1999; Spillman 1997. For other notable field analyses of political debates, see Wuthnow 1989; Zubrzycki 2001; Bail 2012; Spillman 2012.

11. Pierre Bourdieu and Loïc Waquant (1992) make this point authoritatively.

12. See Duyvendak and Fillieule 2015, 306; Blumer 1969.

13. See Spillman 1995. Spillman's (1997, 2012) research on the discursive field of national identity and business association discourse shows that symbolic categories sometimes endure a long time so that actors in successive historical events are cultivated by them; other research shows how "rules" of political discourse crystallize in organizational fields for years at a time (Armstrong 2002).

14. See, for instance, Martin 2003, 31. On discursive rules, see Blee 2012.

15. The physical and symbolic appurtenances of public settings often send signals about what kinds of claims are appropriate (see, for example, Gusfield 1980; McRoberts 2003; Lichterman and Eliasoph 2014).

16. Volunteers making free meals for sick people learn that it is OK to sound "religious" in some settings and not others (Bender 2003). Suburban environmental activists talk critically and politically in some backstage settings, but apolitically in front of journalists (Eliasoph 1998).

17. On discovering mistakes, see Goffman 1961, (1974) 1986. See also Blee's (2013) observations on how discursive rules emerge in activist groups, shaping what participants can say about options for group action. See also Lichterman and Dasgupta's (2020) different account of how group leaders orchestrate a style for specific scenes of interaction.

18. Two of these core characteristics, legitimacy and salience, come up in writing related to fields, and are plausibly common to many, existing discursive fields. See Bourdieu 1985; Emirbayer and Johnson 2008; Martin 2003; Spillman 1997, 2012; Steinberg 1999; Williams 1995. Appropriateness is harder to derive from previous studies of discursive fields because it depends more on a close look at everyday interaction.

19. Eliasoph observed that grassroots environmental group members could talk critically in private about corporate responsibility for toxic industrial waste, but in front of a media microphone, their critique evaporated, and the activists said they were just "moms" who cared. What Eliasoph called "political" evaporation we can conceive of as a subset of a more general process in play when people judge some categories of claim beyond the bounds of any public claims-making scene. The discursive shift may be in either a depoliticizing or politicizing direction. Studies have observed kindred shifts in speakers' propensities for making explicitly religious claims (Wuthnow 1991a; Lichterman 2005). The empirical section describes how scene style induces the shift.

20. See Bourdieu 1985; Steinberg 1999.

21. See Williams 2004. Many researchers treat social life as a series of competitions in fields where actors with different amounts of "capital" are competing for the most prestigious, commanding positions, whether in the field of real estate development or graduate sociology training programs. Social movements scholar Rhys Williams (1995, 128) notes that discourses, however, "cannot be bargained or traded as can capital" because their uses are context dependent. Discourses may be honored even apart from how much social, economic, or cultural capital their bearers have.

22. See Spillman 1997, 134, 93; Alexander 2003, 125.

23. Zubrzycki 2001.

24. Lichterman and Williams 2017; Lichterman 2005.

25. Only four public comments at city hall hearings did not involve either category. These were one-sentence statements at the end of the campaign made by ISLA participants publicly withdrawing objections to the project. Only eleven campaign documents did not involve either category.

26. Twenty-eight pro-Manchester speakers gave public comment. Only two made comments without reference to either category.

27. Symbolic interactionist theory and writings on social identity substantiate the point. For more discussion, see Lichterman and Dasgupta, 2020.

28. See Katz 2015.

29. This section borrows the "evaporation" metaphor from Eliasoph 1998. See Blee's (2013) somewhat parallel argument on "how options disappear."

30. See Lichterman and Reed 2015; Gross 2009.

31. See Lichterman 2005, chapter 4.

32. Every HJ document contained an appeal to fair distribution.

33. Sixty-eight HJ documents—or 55 percent of the total—involved appeals to quality of life.

Chapter 8: How Homelessness Does Not Become a Housing Problem

1. See, for example, Gamson and Modigliani 1989; Miller and Holstein 1993; Holstein and Miller 2003.

2. Homelessness previously had been considered a "short-term crisis . . . akin to a natural disaster," calling for emergency shelter and individual treatment (USICH 2015, 14). The amended, 2015 plan observed progress in reducing homelessness over the previous years.

3. Elliot Liebow's (1993) well-crafted close-up study of volunteering in homeless shelters revealed volunteers who viewed homeless residents as objectionable individuals in need of more discipline and better manners. Scott Clifford and Spencer Piston (2017) make a good argument that plain-old disgust prompts people in the United States to support punitive municipal policies that segregate homeless people from the rest of the public. Interestingly, disgust-afflicted survey respondents were not less likely than others to support increasing housing options or economic opportunity for homeless people. On recognition of social-structural as well as personal factors in homelessness, see Lee, Jones, and Lewis 1990. See also Pascale 2005.

4. While beyond the scope of this study to explore, it is likely that affordable housing and homeless service organizations occupied different organizational fields with different stakes and resource streams, in Los Angeles and nationally. As neoinstitutionalists remind us, organizational missions and formats have lives of their own; organizational conditions of course contribute to a separation between "housing" and "homelessness," and separate networks of communication would cultivate that separation too. Like the rest of the study, the argument in this chapter builds on the insight widely accepted in contemporary sociology that symbols and meaningful practices have some relative autonomy in social life and their own dynamics. They don't simply reflect the "harder" realities of organizational or network structure. Cultural

structures help shape what advocates consider *possible to say* about housing and homeless problems in different scenes; those possibilities are not fully determined simply by an advocate's
position in a field of organizations.

5. For more details on the group along with its participants and its work, see Lichterman
2012).

6. See Lichterman 2012.

7. The video that ran at the start of several HJ workshops I attended began with a slide calling
Los Angeles the "homeless capital of the world." It did not go on to discuss the condition or
problem of homelessness but instead shifted quickly to arguing the need for an affordable housing mandate. Rather than explore the connection between homelessness and housing, it subsumed homelessness under the problem of unaffordable housing.

8. Sheila also went to CE meetings and there launched animatedly bitter accounts like the
ones we heard at SHAPLA; Theresa negotiated several times with a polite call to move on.

9. On the "disgust" for homeless people, see Clifford and Piston 2017.

10. Lopez's relation to Ayers was portrayed in the popular film *The Soloist* (2009).

11. As Wuthnow explained (1991a), the mainstream US understanding of compassion features interpersonal, voluntary caring and the feelings that go with caring between individuals,
without an institutional context that would define how and for whom we should care.

12. The mayor emphasized compassion in his English-language remarks on homelessness.
Interestingly, his briefer comments in Spanish referred in passing to affordable housing (*vivien-
das asequibles*). Given the walking teams' organizational sponsors, it is safe to guess that only a
minority of the walkers would have understood the Spanish version.

13. Putnam's (2000) extensive study found that short-term volunteering (called here "plug-in
volunteering") was the most common form of civic engagement in the United States. It was the
only one for which rates of participation had not declined in the previous several decades.

14. See the extended discussions in Eliasoph 2011; Wuthnow 1998a. See also Lichterman
2006. As Wuthnow points out, the activity that many people in the US cultural mainstream
think of as simply volunteering dates to the 1970s. Before that, volunteering for middle-class
people in the United States more often implied membership in a sociable club of amateurs who
collaborated on charitable activities, "doing good" in general for a locale.

15. See Lichterman 2005, 2006; Eliasoph 2011.

16. See Stebbins 1996; Henderson and Presley 2003. Read carefully, the research record is
ambiguous on the empirical validity of the folk theory. Part of the problem is that prominent
studies often measure voluntary action by quantities of acts or skills, or intensity of attitudes,
without distinguishing clearly where acts occur and what they mean to actors. For example,
political scientists Sidney Verba, Kay Lehman Schlozman, and Henry Brady (1995) found that
the volunteer work of setting up a church food pantry or chairing a charity drive increases civic
skill, which in turn heightens one's sense of political efficacy and competence. Voluntary action
scholar David Knoke (1990) argues that if we consider taking a committee assignment or official
position in a voluntary organization as "volunteering," then volunteering has a positive impact
on political behavior (discussed in Wilson and Musick 1999, 142–43). As Knoke's own hedge
implies, it all depends on what we mean by volunteering. Taking on the vice presidency of a
community service organization is not the same as tutoring a child once a week for an hour, but
both could be called "volunteering" and may count that way in surveys. John Wilson and Marc

Musick's (1999, 144) review of research draws an appropriately ambiguous conclusion: "Studies suggest caution when generalizing about the 'benefits' of volunteering as far as democratic action is concerned. If an abundant supply of social capital is believed to be a necessary condition for democratic politics, then volunteering can certainly help supply it, but not all kinds of volunteering do it equally well." Indeed, some kinds of volunteering induce members to avoid or silence political activity rather than open to it (see Eliasoph 1998).

17. See Lichterman 2005, chapters 3 and 6.

18. I did the same with the director of the Korean social services agency. She did not comment on the claim about dangers for homeless people receiving free food. Sounding tense and wary of making accusations, and clearly working to avoid naming names, she implied vaguely that the city council district encompassing an area with many homeless people was hostile to working with outsiders.

19. These are excerpts from my researcher partner's field notes.

20. See, for example, Best 1995; Gamson and Modigliani 1989; Holstein and Miller 2003.

21. See Ibarra and Kitsuse 2003; Best 1995.

22. See Bélanger and Meguid 2008; Walgrave, Lefevere, and Tresch 2012.

23. See Martin 2003.

24. Smith 2016.

25. See Fine 1979.

Chapter 9: Hybrid Problem Solving

1. It is a widely invoked trichotomy. For varying versions of it, see Gramsci 1971; Habermas 1987, 1984; Wuthnow 1991b; Smith and Lipsky 1993; Cohen and Arato 1992.

2. See, for example, Berger and Neuhaus 1977; Wolfe 1989; Bellah et al. 1996; Putnam 2000; McFarland and Thomas 2006; Schlozman, Verba, and Brady 2013. See the review in Lichterman and Eliasoph 2014.

3. The classic source here is Tocqueville, and of course one can find important passages that support these writers' inferences in *Democracy in America* (see, for example, Tocqueville [1835] 1969, 515). The trouble is that these oft-cited passages celebrating the democratic virtues of civic groups come to stand in for Tocqueville's more complex and ambivalent argument tout court (see, for example, Putnam 1995).

4. In academic terms, I mean an "idealized cognitive model" (Lakoff 1987), the image we typically call to mind when we encounter an abstraction like "the civic sector."

5. The burritos-on-wheels effort graciously has served as a field site for several students in my undergraduate seminar titled Solving Social Problems.

6. Researchers also point out that the proliferation of related terms—civic sector, civil society, nonprofit sector, third sector, and voluntary sector—each have somewhat different lineages and only partially overlapping referents, as the contrast between a local volunteer group and nonprofit hospital helps illustrate. See Martens 2002; Clemens 2006, 207–10; Steinberg and Powell 2006.

7. On nonprofit organizations' missions, see Minkoff 2002. On morally magnetic missions, see Eliasoph 2011.

8. See Kautz 2002.

9. See Rudrappa 2004; Eliasoph 2011; Clemens and Guthrie 2011; Moseley 2012; Dasgupta 2013; Lichterman and Eliasoph 2014.

10. It could make just as much sense to say they pursue "hybrid *state* action" or "hybrid governance," but the "hybrid civic" tag is more helpful since part of the goal is to clarify what makes civic action civic.

11. This was especially the case in some of the popular response to Putnam's (1996) startling news of civic decline, though the tendency to view civic this way is much older in the United States.

12. The term is from Steven Smith and Michael Lipsky (1993), whose excellent discussion informs this synopsis.

13. There is no single, set path for building affordable housing. Developers of such projects typically have to bring together funding from a number of sources. As the Urban Institute reports, it is not uncommon for developers to have to rely on more than twenty different sources of funding to build projects. While some may assume that affordable housing development is a philanthropic enterprise, several other sources of funds are crucial. One source comes in the form of loans from banks or other lenders, though loans usually do not cover the full cost of construction, since lenders approve amounts based on future rental income, which is lower with affordable housing compared to other similar real estate projects. Another important source is tax credits from state and federal authorities, awarded to projects in which apartments will not rent for more than 60 percent—or sometimes some other percent value—of the area's median income. The federal Low-Income Housing Tax Credit is perhaps the most well known of these; tax credit programs issue credits through competitions since funds are limited. These tax credit programs are designed to encourage for-profit developers to build affordable housing, but they can also be awarded to investors who choose to finance a nonprofit's affordable housing project. Most often, such credits cannot fund the cost of a single project entirely or support all eligible development projects in a government authority's jurisdiction. Grants from federal block grant programs or local housing trust funds as well as charitable foundations sometimes play a role. Finally, developers frequently rely on the promise of rental assistance programs, like vouchers for tenants, to adjust rents as well as confidently assure investors and lenders that tenants will be able to lease such apartments. Ultimately, developers have to assemble a range of financial partners, often mixing government, private nonprofit, and private for-profit sources to fund projects. See Johnson, Steffel and Talen 2008; Blumenthal, Handelman, and Tilley 2016.

14. On welfare policy reform in England and the Netherlands, for example, see Verhoevens and Tonkens 2013. Governments in both countries argued, in somewhat different ways, that people ought to take up more of the responsibility of caring for each other instead of relying on a central government. People in the United States heard something similar when President Bill Clinton ended "welfare as we know it" in 1996; the new legislation gave religious social service organizations, congregations, and other citizen groups more opportunities to receive tax money to fund social service programs as alternatives to government-delivered services. Some social commentators, including the first director of the White House Office of Faith-Based and Community Initiatives, applauded the policy reform, saying it would put people more in touch with their fellow citizens, and cultivate a stronger sense of responsibility for and ownership of the society. See DiIulio 2001, quoted in Lichterman 2005, 283ff.

15. Nonprofit housing developers also receive grants and contract with foundations and other nonprofit organizations in the ongoing effort to cobble enough funds for the next housing project. While this too is "contracting," the use of tax money (contrasted with private foundation money) conditions the nonprofit organizations with a special, ongoing dilemma, described below, that perhaps feels like an imposed "regime," a challenging game plan that nonprofit actors did not entirely choose themselves. This is a good example of how nonprofit housing developers' action, no matter how mission driven, is hybridized and not entirely civic by my definition. The dilemma cuts deeply into actors' relative freedom to coordinate their collective work—a quality that we expect in civic action.

16. This brief discussion along with the phrase "equity versus responsiveness" is culled from Smith and Lipsky 1993, 121–26.

17. See Smith and Lipsky 1993. In Sharmila Rudrappa's (2004) study, for example, a nonprofit women's shelter for survivors of domestic abuse intended to serve South Asian women in Chicago.

18. In addition to ending discriminatory housing practices, the Fair Housing Act of 1968 requires that authorities investigate housing discrimination complaints brought forward by civil rights groups or individuals. In one of the field scenarios below, Nora asked me to call up one such investigative office. The act also requires that federal authorities work to "affirmatively further" fair housing—or in other words, institute efforts to actively desegregate housing markets. Actual implementation of such efforts has waxed and waned since the law's passage, but this requirement has been the basis for which "disproportionate impacts" cases—which challenge policies that otherwise appear neutral but unduly affect minority groups—have made their way through the courts. For more detail, see Massey 2015; National Housing Law Project, https://www.nhlp.org/wp-content/uploads/2017/09/AFFH-Part-I-An-Overview-for -Advocates-April-2016.pdf.

19. Unpredictable short-term funding induces other binds for nonprofits too, as when youth social work professionals at community centers (Eliasoph 2011) or domestic violence shelter staff (Rudrappa 2004) must document how many people they helped. We might say this disembeds staff from the caring relations their work bids them cultivate, while the contracting regime disembeds nonprofit developers from the "community" for whom they build housing.

20. Several months earlier, the *Los Angeles Times* reported findings from a study of elderly homeless people that a nonprofit homeless advocacy organization, headed by Sara Teitelbaum (pseudonym), had spent two years conducting. The study found homeless elders to be one of the fastest-growing and most vulnerable homeless populations at the time. A majority (62 percent) reported having a physical or mental disability. See DiMassa 2008.

21. See Wuthnow 1998a; Camus-Vigué 2000; Lichterman and Eliasoph 2014.

22. In Tocqueville's ([1835] 1969, 507) well-known account, local associations, whether devoted to building roads, erecting hospitals, or bolstering members' sobriety, all cultivated civic commitment by nudging people in the United States with "a thousand reminders" that they live in society.

23. This part of the critique would also resonate with a viewpoint we can call social democratic. It values participatory democracy, but is more ambivalent about the role of communal virtues and traditions in a pluralistic, open society. The social democratic argument, elaborated extensively by Habermas and based partly on Dewey's vision of public life, arrives at some

understandings and aspirations not so different from those of communitarians: governmental administration subordinates people, as objects to administer, and in modern societies it too often "colonizes"—diminishes, supplants, and disempowers—people's everyday worlds of meaning and value. By contrast, the civic realm is powered by a less predetermined process of collective learning and collective self-understanding, informed and refreshed by collectively ratified, evolving agreements about how best to run society (see Habermas 1987, 1984; 1975; Cohen and Arato 1992). Both the communitarian and social democratic visions share the same sectoral understanding of modern society—divided into state, market, and civil society. Both see the state encroaching on people's initiative in the civic sector, much as they disagree on the reasons and remedies. For a semipopular social critique that blends elements of both visions and has achieved some currency in local community development circles since the 1980s, see McKnight 1995.

24. Berger and Neuhaus 1977; Etzioni 1996.

25. Hunt 2009, 10.

26. See Ledbetter 1967, 501.

27. On shifting federal priorities for housing and community action projects, see von Hoffman 2000.

28. Friedman 1966, 644.

29. Goetz 2000, 2003.

30. Despite important differences, the civic action and framing perspectives share the notion that the participants may change their claims depending on what they hear back; they "counterframe" in relation to opponents.

31. These slogans come from an early, internal HJ coalition memo.

32. These are excerpts of answers to standard questions, described above, posed on the city housing department's grant application form for affordable housing developers. The excerpts come from the draft already in HSLA's files before I began revisions. I aimed to revise them very much in the spirit of the templates given me to work with instead of intentionally introducing changes and perhaps imperiling seasoned professionals' chances of winning the money they sought.

33. In California, developers apply to the California Tax Credit Allocation Committee to access the funds available in state and federal Low-Income Housing Tax Credit programs. The committee gives points to applications based on different criteria, such as location in high- or low-resource areas, or assistance to special needs residents, and awards grants based on the point totals. On distributing credits, the committee monitors such developments for compliance and standards for fifty-five years. Developers are assessed fines for different violations of compliance requirements and, per the Internal Revenue Code, the credits that have been awarded are potentially subject to "recapture" by the awarding agencies. See Ballard 2003. See also California Tax Credit Allocation Committee, https://www.treasurer.ca.gov/ctcac/.

34. This is an older style of volunteering, represented by clubs like the Rotary or Kiwanis, and centered on sociability more than the task-oriented, plug-in volunteering that people do in homeless shelters, for example. See Wuthnow 1998a; Camus-Vigué 2000; Lichterman and Eliasoph 2014. Few civic practices better exemplify Tocqueville's ([1835] 1969) classic observations on "self-interest properly understood." A business (or perhaps nonprofit organization) with a good reputation secures a public more positively predisposed to its business initiatives (or

locally sited affordable housing projects) later on. The former director of the Western Housing Association of nonprofit housing developers told me emphatically that what his member organizations needed most was "money, land, and public acceptance."

35. See Citroni and Lichterman 2017.

36. For examples of staff and clients of nonprofit social service organizations appealing to governmental officials for continued funding, see Marwell 2007; Eliasoph 2011.

37. That was the day of the long meeting and workshop that kicked off ISLA's antidisplacement campaign.

38. Scott (1998) uses massive forestation and monocultural farming as historical examples of state-sponsored planning that imposes standardization while destroying preexisting natural or social ecologies. I do not intend this as a precise comparison with affordable housing emplaced by the contracting regime. The part of the metaphor that works is the notion of residential developments whose location is less a function of deliberate thinking about a neighborhood's social life and more a function of impersonal forces—in this case, a housing market that leaves some neighborhoods with more dilapidated buildings that can be redeveloped as affordable housing.

39. See Kivel 2007. For parallel critiques of the "nonprofit industrial complex," see INCITE! 2007.

40. Chaves, Stephens, and Galaskiewicz 2004.

41. Rudrappa 2004.

42. Space limitations preclude a full exploration of CGTC's community of identity, but observations made obvious that the preferred style of action closely paralleled what I have already described.

Conclusion

1. Here are just a few representative works from varied national contexts. It would take far more space to survey the lines of research on social advocacy that focus closely on action without relying on assumptions about entrepreneurial actors. US cases include work by Blee (2012, 2013), mentioned throughout this study, on how grassroots activism emerges, Gianpaolo Baiocchi and team's (2015) work on the civic imagination in citizen associations, Amy Binder and Kate Wood's (2013) research on university activists, Ruth Braunstein's (2017) study of Tea Party and progressive religious activism, Braunstein, Brad Fulton, and Richard Wood (2014) on bridging practices in socially and racially diverse civic organizations, and Eliasoph's (2011) ethnography of civic empowerment projects. From Brazil, Mische's (2008) cases of youth activist networks and Baiocchi's (2005) research on participatory budgeting offer methodological and conceptual exemplars. David Smilde and Daniel Hellinger (2011) introduce a critical, "civil society" lens on civic and political participation in Venezuela under Hugo Chávez. In France, researchers at the EHESS and especially its Centre d'Étude des Mouvements Sociaux have inquired into civic action on homelessness, urban development, and other topics, informed by French pragmatic sociology (Boltanski and Thévenot 2006; Thévenot 2006) as well as the writings of Dewey and Goffman. See, for example, Cefaï 2002, 2015; Cefaï and Gardella 2011; Stavo-Debauge and Trom 2004. Some similar inspirations influence Eeva Luhtakallio's (2012) comparative work on advocacy around urban development and public space in Finland and France,

and Mathieu Berger's (2008) and Julien Charles's (2016) investigations of citizen planning fo-rums and other participatory or pseudoparticipatory spaces in Belgium. Sebastiano Citroni (2015) brings us comparative cases of civic action and sociability from NGOs and the culturally alternative spaces of Milan, Italy. In China too, researchers are using the lenses of cultural analy-sis and conceiving cases of civic action or something analogous as they study civic responses to an earthquake (Xu 2017), compare advocates' strategies to improve educational opportunity (Zhou 2018), or how farmers interact with governing agents (Hua, Hou and Deng 2016).

2. For classic pragmatist statements on the community of inquiry and its role in adjudicating research claims, see Peirce (1877) 1992, (1868) 1992.

3. Pragmatist C. S. Peirce's ([1877] 1992, [1868] 1992) oft-quoted foundational statements stress the encounter between "beliefs" and evidence. Dewey (1938) gives us richer and more realistic insights for understanding how social scientists juggle evidence and conceptual frame-works, and I will rely more on his thinking. See the discussion in Lichterman 2015.

4. As Longino writes (2002, 126), the "choice of hypothesis is not fully determined by the data. Nor do hypotheses specify the data that will confirm them."

5. Lichterman 2015.

6. This has been called "metacommunicative dialogue" (Lichterman and Reed 2015): con-ceptual critique that scrutinizes the foundational assumptions behind a line of research.

7. For a compendium of factors found to influence coalition endurance, see Van Dyke and McCammon 2010. For "declarative" versus more implicit forms of culture, see Lizardo 2017. On the power of more implicit forms of culture for alliance building, see Roth 2010; Lichterman 1995.

8. For more discussion on how health becomes part of social advocates' issue agendas, see Dasgupta and Lichterman 2016.

9. See Lichterman 1996; Rose 2000.

10. See, for example, Novotny 2000; Boer et al. 1997.

11. See Heaney and Rojas 2014; Jung, King, and Soule 2014.

12. Similarly, in Christopher Mele's (2000) study of urban change on Manhattan's Lower East Side, residents challenging gentrification mistrusted arguments appealing to quality of life.

13. Observations from ISLA's Manchester campaign warrant this hypothesis. Strikingly, in written and oral testimony for the deliberations at city hall, it was only the pro bono legal coun-sel and a couple of environmental advocates who connected housing affordability in the neigh-borhood to regional well-being. They made fair opportunity and quality-of-life concerns *both* salient and mutually reinforcing. In their view, the Manchester was not simply a neighborhood issue if its construction, and the likely tenant displacement in its wake, was going to increase long-distance auto commutes, thereby increasing air pollution, traffic woes, and other quality-of-life hazards far beyond the neighborhood. From a framing perspective, this argument could attract prominent allies far beyond the immediate locale as well as ones working on several is-sues besides housing. I wondered why ISLA leaders had not made more efforts in this direction.

14. One populist call for relevance is Peter Nien-chu Kiang's (2008) argument for a "com-munity invasion" that enlists social researchers to work on behalf of oppressed communities. Quite different is Bourdieu's contention on behalf of a social science that minds its field bound-aries and performs a heavy translation of actors' problems into Bourdieu's language for

analyzing "agents" deploying capital in fields. From that view, other ways of naming and analyzing action would cloud up sociology's project of demystifying social domination. See especially Bourdieu and Wacquant 1992.

15. Dewey 1927; 1938, 492–93, 499.

16. Dewey was arguing that when social science disciplines separated "practical" from "theoretical" social inquiry, both would suffer. The division relied on the faulty assumption that "problems are already definite in their main features . . . [T]he consequence of this assumption is that the work of analytic discrimination, which is necessary to convert a problematic situation into a set of conditions forming a definite problem, is largely foregone" (Dewey 1938, 493). Again the task of casing is crucial (see Ragin and Becker 1992), and that involves categorizing with terms from a community of inquiry.

17. Dewey 1938, 268, 464, 498–99.

18. Author's file. One case was a short report published by a nonprofit policy institute that seeks to inform urban advocacy and development practices. The other was produced by an applied research center. I refrain from citing either case study out of deference to coalition players who may prefer anonymity.

19. In Dewey's terms (1938, 496), social research that takes some ends as given or naturally worthy "excludes ends (consequences) from the field of inquiry and reduces inquiry at its very best to the truncated and distorted business of finding out means for realizing objectives already settled upon."

20. Glaeser's (2005, 2011, 2014) conceptual and empirical discussions of action-reaction effect flows are especially helpful here.

21. The sociological sin here is "intellectualism." See especially Bourdieu and Wacquant 1992.

22. HSLA hosted and financially supported a food bank in one of its affordable developments. That is where I helped Nathan distribute grocery bags with turkeys and canned vegetables to residents and neighbors before Thanksgiving in 2009.

23. See, for, example Haney 2010.

24. This is not to say that talking about style differences would guarantee a resolution. The research record does suggest that talking openly about those differences and negotiating them as *collective* problems rather than failings of individuals *can* sometimes keep a coalition together (see Beamish and Luebbers 2009; Lichterman 2005), while obtuseness about them can lead demonstrably to aborted opportunities (Lichterman 1995). Talking accurately about sources of division is worth a try. In my (limited) experience, social advocates pick up on something like style without a lot of elaboration. For example, Theresa of CE told me she was impressed but uncomfortable with a highly scripted meeting run by community organizers at a Catholic church, where a pastor, trying to act his part conscientiously, forthrightly put the question of endorsing HJ's three-point plan to a city council member who already had affirmed the plan. The council member affirmed it again to a cheery, collective outburst from the pews. Theresa associated this whole "top-down," scripted affair with the Catholic church, in contrast to the less collectivistic ethos of her liberal Protestant congregation. Bypassing the topic of religious ideology, I suggested the meeting's style was different from what she was used to, and she agreed.

25. In 2016, Angelenos passed Proposition HHH to raise tax money to house homeless people. At this writing several years later, homelessness continued to be decried as a local crisis.

26. I picked May 1, 2020, for this anecdotal evidence.

27. Isaac Stanley-Becker and Tony Romm, "The Anti-Quarantine Protests Seem Spontaneous. But Behind the Scenes, a Powerful Network Is Helping," *Washington Post*, April 22, 2020.

28. See, for example, Wuthnow 1991b.

29. For survey research on this topic, see Foa and Mounk 2016.

Appendix I: Putting Together the Study

1. Lichterman 2005.

2. The theoretical work was Eliasoph and Lichterman 2003. See also Lichterman 1996; Eliasop 1998.

3. Chris Weare constructed the network survey with input from the research team. Weare directed the survey; Weare and Nicole Esparza analyzed the network survey data. For a description of the network survey and procedures for implementing it, see Weare, Lichterman, and Esparza 2014. For findings on the relations between network structure, culture, and styles of action, see Weare, Esparza, and Lichterman 2011; Weare, Lichterman, and Esparza 2014; Lichterman, Weare, and Esparza 2014. Periods of ethnographic research and analysis of field data and archival data continued outside periods of National Science Foundation funding for the project. Substantial parts of this book's conceptual contributions, including the pragmatist story line and approach to discursive fields, emerged after the end of the second National Science Foundation funding period.

4. This process is "abduction," so named by Peirce, and detailed in erudite as well as practical terms by Richard Swedberg (2014). For the relation of abduction to "grounded theory" research, see the clear discussion in Timmermans and Tavory 2012. Abduction describes what many ethnographers actually are doing when they go into the field, better than "induction," the term ethnographic methodology texts often use to name the process of discovery. In induction, the researcher starts by trying to bracket received conceptual notions and simply see what's there in the field in order to produce new concepts "from the ground up." The classic statement of this perspective is Barney Glaser and Anselm Strauss's (1967) guide to the production of grounded theory. For other important practical and theoretical statements, see Strauss and Corbin 1991; Glaser 1978; Strauss 1987.

5. The first National Science Foundation grant proposal for this research (Crigler et al. 2007) worded one of several master hypotheses thus; this particular hypothesis derived principally from Eliasoph and Lichterman 2003.

6. For similar wording, see Lichterman 1999, 105.

7. Pragmatist philosophers Dewey (especially 1938) and Peirce ([1877] 1992, [1868], 1992) shared the vision of science as a dialogue with a community of inquiry over evidence, concepts, and the fit between the two. Feminist epistemologists such as Longino (2002, 1990) developed a similar picture. For much more development of these points, see Lichterman 2015; Lichterman and Reed 2015; Reed and Lichterman 2017, forthcoming. As for the larger purpose of the dialogue—improvement in the conditions of collective and individual life—one intellectual source is Habermas 1972.

8. These two metaphors can describe different moments of a social science centered on paradigms. Edifice building pictures the valuable work of accumulating knowledge within a given paradigm of questions and orienting assumptions; it is the "normal science" (Kuhn 1962)

that many of us engage a lot of the time. In ethnographic research circles, it may be represented most commonly by "grounded theory" research that brings new empirical categories and dimensions to established subfields of a discipline. For the classic statement, see Glaser and Strauss 1967. Paradigm protecting could roughly describe research intended to fend off alternative paradigms by *improving* the paradigm we work in without transforming its core assumptions. Projected in epistemologists' debates a half century ago (see Lakatos and Musgrave 1968), this vision of knowledge production drives Michael Burawoy's (1998) version of the extended case method in ethnography. For the longer lineage of this method of inquiry, see Evens and Handelman 2006.

9. This is metacommunicative dialogue—a dialogue that questions the conceptual terms we use to sift and compare evidence. See Lichterman 2015; Lichterman and Reed 2015.

10. Many thanks to Chris Weare for suggesting this thematic focus at the outset.

11. See Lichterman and Reed 2015.

12. See, for example, Van Dyke and McCammon 2010.

13. See Becker 1999; Lichterman 2005.

14. See Ragin and Becker 1992.

15. This ongoing search is the time-honored "constant comparative method," core to the process of discovery in ethnographic research (Glaser and Strauss 1967; Strauss 1987).

16. The proper name of the logic is "analytic induction." See Katz 2001, 2002, 2015; Lichterman and Reed 2015.

17. See the discussion in Lichterman and Reed 2015. For varied examples, see Burawoy 1998; Swedberg 2014; Katz 2001, 2002, 2015.

18. See Lichterman and Eliasoph 2014.

Appendix II: Who Was the Ethnographer?

1. The decision was difficult; schooling opportunities in Los Angeles were a big factor. The metropolis also offered a bounty of field sites for an ethnographer interested in social advocacy.

2. For a much more extensive development of this paragraph's argument about positionality and the need to reflect on our interpretations as well as social positions, see Lichterman 2017.

3. In a similar spirit, ethnographer Mario Small (2004) has pointed out that participant observers do not necessarily aim for whole-life portraits of subjects known intimately, in the manner of some second Chicago school works. There are other standards for a good ethnographic study.

4. I did not encounter the kind of translation described in Doerr's (2018) study of social activist translators who go beyond denotational meanings, turning their craft into a kind of political empowerment project for underrepresented voices

5. This guess has to be based on the evidence available. Both of the main coalitions' staff were multiracial; LAPO staff and core members together were multiracial, though majority African American. That does not mean people did not "notice" or have opinions related to my evident background. Having spent many months with the two main coalitions, my best guess is that I gained trust as it became and remained clear that I was trying to be useful, and was not informing any potentially unfriendly outsiders about the goings-on in coalition settings.

6. Lichterman 1996.

REFERENCES

Abbott, Andrew. 2001. *Time Matters: On Theory and Method.* Chicago: University of Chicago Press.

Addams, Jane. (1902) 2002. *Democracy and Social Ethics.* Urbana: University of Illinois Press.

Agius Vallejo, Jody. 2012. *Barrios to Burbs: The Making of the Mexican American Middle Class.* Stanford, CA: Stanford University Press.

Alexander, Jeffrey. 2003. *The Meanings of Social Life.* New York: Oxford University Press.

Alexander, Jeffrey, and Steven Seidman, eds. 1990. *Culture and Society: Contemporary Debates.* New York: Cambridge University Press.

Almond, Gabriel A., and Sidney Verba. 1963. *The Civic Culture: Political Attitudes and Democracy in Five Nations.* Princeton, NJ: Princeton University Press.

Alvarez, Sonia E., Jeffrey W. Rubin, Millie Thayer, Gianpaolo Baiocchi, Agustín Laó-Montes, and Arturo Escobar, eds. 2017. *Beyond Civil Society: Activism, Participation, and Protest in Latin America.* Durham, NC: Duke University Press.

Amenta, Edwin, Neal Caren, Elizabeth Chiarello, and Yang Su. 2010. "The Political Consequences of Social Movements." *Annual Review of Sociology* 36 (1): 287–307.

Annunziata, Sandra, and Clara Rivas-Alonso. 2018. "Resisting Gentrification." In *Handbook of Gentrification Studies,* edited by Loretta Lees and Martin Phillips, 393–412. Cheltenham, UK: Edward Elgar Publisher.

Armstrong, Elizabeth A. 2002. *Forging Gay Identities: Organizing Sexuality in San Francisco, 1950–1994.* Chicago: University of Chicago Press.

Armstrong, Elizabeth A., and Mary Bernstein. 2008. "Culture, Power, and Institutions: A Multi-Institutional Politics Approach to Social Movements." *Sociological Theory* 26 (1): 74–99.

Ayoub, Phillip M., and Agnès Chetaille. 2017. "Movement/Countermovement Interaction and Instrumental Framing in a Multi-Level World: Rooting Polish Lesbian and Gay Activism." *Social Movement Studies,* 1–17.

Baggett, Jerome P. 2000. *Habitat for Humanity: Building Private Homes, Building Public Religion.* Philadelphia: Temple University Press.

Bail, Christopher. 2008. "The Configuration of Symbolic Boundaries against Immigrants in Europe." *American Sociological Review* 73 (1): 37–59.

———. 2012. "The Fringe Effect: Civil Society Organizations and the Evolution of Media Discourse about Islam since the September 11th Attacks." *American Sociological Review* 77 (6): 855–79.

Baiocchi, Gianpaolo. 2005. *Militants and Citizens: The Politics of Participatory Democracy in Porto Alegre.* Stanford, CA: Stanford University Press.

Baiocchi, Gianpaolo, Elizabeth A. Bennett, Alissa Cordner, Peter Klein, and Stephanie Savell. 2015. *Civic Imagination: Making a Difference in American Political Life*. New York: Routledge.

Baldassarri, Delia, and Mario Diani. 2007. "The Integrative Power of Civic Networks." *American Journal of Sociology* 113 (3): 735–80.

Ballard, Megan J. 2003. "Profiting from Poverty: The Competition between For-Profit and Nonprofit Developers for Low-Income Housing Tax Credits." *Hastings Law Journal* 55 (1): 211–44.

Beamish, Thomas D. 2015. *Community at Risk: Biodefense and the Collective Search for Security*. Stanford, CA: Stanford University Press.

Beamish, Thomas D., and Amy J. Luebbers. 2009. "Alliance Building across Social Movements: Bridging Difference in a Peace and Justice Coalition." *Social Problems* 56 (4): 647–76.

Becker, Penny Edgell. 1999. *Congregations in Conflict*. New York: Cambridge University Press.

Bélanger, Éric, and Bonnie M. Meguid. 2008. "Issue Salience, Issue Ownership, and Issue-Based Vote Choice." *Electoral Studies* 27 (3): 477–91.

Bell, Sandra J., and Mary E. Delaney. 2001. "Collaborating across Difference: From Theory and Rhetoric to the Hard Reality of Building Coalitions." In *Forging Radical Alliances across Difference: Coalition Politics for the New Millennium*, edited by Jill M. Bystydzienski and Steven P. Schacht, 63–76. New York: Rowman and Littlefield Publishers.

Bellah, Robert N., Richard Madsen, William M. Sullivan, Ann Swidler, and Steven M. Tipton, eds. 1996. *Habits of the Heart: Individualism and Commitment in American Life*. Berkeley: University of California Press.

Bender, Courtney. 2003. *Heaven's Kitchen: Living Religion at God's Love We Deliver*. Chicago: University of Chicago Press.

Benford, Robert. 1993a. "Frame Disputes within the Nuclear Disarmament Movement." *Social Forces* 71 (3): 677–701.

———. 1993b. "'You Could Be the Hundredth Monkey': Collective Action Frames and Vocabularies of Motive within the Nuclear Disarmament Movement." *Sociological Quarterly* 34 (2): 195–216.

———. 1997. "An Insider's Critique of the Social Movement Framing Perspective." *Sociological Inquiry* 67 (4): 409–30.

Benford, Robert, and Scott Hunt. 1992. "Dramaturgy and Social Movements: The Social Construction and Communication of Power." *Sociological Inquiry* 62 (1): 36–55.

Benford, Robert, and David Snow. 2000. "Framing Processes and Social Movements: An Overview and Assessment." *Annual Review of Sociology* 26 (1): 611–39.

Benner, Chris, and Manuel Pastor. 2015. *Equity, Growth, and Community: What the Nation Can Learn from America's Metro Areas*. Berkeley: University of California Press.

Berger, Bennett M. 1981. *The Survival of a Counterculture: Ideological Work and Everyday Life among Rural Communards*. Berkeley: University of California Press.

Berger, Mathieu. 2008. *Bruxelles à L'Épreuve de la Participation: Les Contrats de Quartier en Exercices*. Brussels: Région de Bruxelles-Capitale.

Berger, Peter L., and Thomas Luckmann. 1966. *The Social Construction of Reality*. New York: Random House.

Berger, Peter L., and Richard J. Neuhaus. 1977. *To Empower People: From State to Civil Society*. Washington, DC: American Enterprise Institute.

Bernstein, Mary. 1997. "Celebration and Suppression: The Strategic Uses of Identity by the Lesbian and Gay Movement." *American Journal of Sociology* 103 (3): 531–65.

Best, Joel, ed. 1995. *Images of Issues: Typifying Contemporary Social Problems*. New Brunswick, NJ: Aldine de Gruyter.

Binder, Amy. 2007. "For Love and Money: Organizations' Creative Responses to Multiple Environmental Logics." *Theory and Society* 36 (6): 547–71.

Binder, Amy, and Kate Wood. 2013. *Becoming Right*. Princeton, NJ: Princeton University Press.

Blau, Joel. 1992. *The Visible Poor: Homelessness in the United States*. New York: Oxford University Press.

Blee, Kathleen M. 2012. *Democracy in the Making: How Activist Groups Form*. New York: Oxford University Press.

———. 2013. "How Options Disappear: Causality and Emergence in Grassroots Activist Groups." *American Journal of Sociology* 119 (3): 655–81.

Blumenthal, Pamela, Ethan Handelman, and Alexandra Tilley. 2016. "How Affordable Housing Gets Built." *Urban Wire* (blog), Urban Institute, July 27.

Blumer, Herbert. 1969. *Symbolic Interactionism: Perspective and Method*. Englewood Cliffs, NJ: Prentice Hall.

Boarnet, Marlon, and Randall Crane. 1997. "L.A. Story: A Reality Check for Transit-Based Housing." *Journal of the American Planning Association* 63 (2): 189–204.

Boer, J. Tom, Manuel Pastor, James L. Sadd, and Lori D. Snyder. 1997. "Is There Environmental Racism?: The Demographics of Hazardous Waste in Los Angeles County." *Social Science Quarterly* 78 (4): 793–810.

Boltanski, Luc, and Laurent Thévenot. 2006. *On Justification: Economies of Worth*. Princeton, NJ: Princeton University Press.

Bosi, Lorenzo, and Katrin Uba. 2009. "Introduction: The Outcomes of Social Movements." *Mobilization* 14 (4): 409–15.

Bourdieu, Pierre. 1977. *Outline of a Theory of Practice*. New York: Cambridge University Press.

———. 1984. *Distinction: A Social Critique of the Judgement of Taste*. Cambridge, MA: Harvard University Press.

———. 1985. "The Social Space and the Genesis of Groups." *Theory and Society* 14 (6): 723–44.

———. 1993. *Language and Symbolic Power*. Cambridge, MA: Harvard University Press.

Bourdieu, Pierre, and Loïc Wacquant. 1992. *An Invitation to Reflexive Sociology*. Chicago: University of Chicago Press.

Braunstein, Ruth. 2017. *Prophets and Patriots: Faith in Democracy across the Political Divide*. Berkeley: University of California Press.

Braunstein, Ruth, Brad Fulton, and Richard Wood. 2014. "The Role of Bridging Cultural Practices in Racially and Socioeconomically Diverse Civic Organizations." *American Sociological Review* 79 (4): 705–25.

Breines, Wini. 1982. *Community and Organization in the New Left, 1962–1968: The Great Refusal*. New York: J. F. Bergin.

Briggs, Xavier de Souza. 2008. *Democracy as Problem Solving: Civic Capacity in Communities across the Globe*. Cambridge, MA: MIT Press.

Bronfenbrenner, Kate, Sheldon Friedman, Richard W. Hurd, Rudolph A. Oswald, and Ronald L. Seeber, eds. 1998. *Organizing to Win: New Research on Union Strategies*. Ithaca, NY: ILR Press.

Brown, Michael P. 1997. *RePlacing Citizenship: AIDS Activism and Radical Democracy.* New York: Guilford Press.

Brown, Phil, and Stephen Zavestoski. 2004. "Social Movements in Health: An Introduction." *Sociology of Health and Illness* 26 (6): 679–94.

Brown-Saracino, Japonica. 2009. *A Neighborhood That Never Changes: Gentrification, Social Preservation, and the Search for Authenticity.* Chicago: University of Chicago Press.

———, ed. 2010. *The Gentrification Debates.* New York: Routledge.

Burawoy, Michael. 1998. "The Extended Case Method." *Sociological Theory* 16 (1): 4–33.

Camus-Vigué, Agnčs. 2000. "Community and Civic Culture: The Rotary Club in France and the United States." In *Rethinking Comparative Cultural Sociology: Repertoires of Evaluation in France and the United States,* edited by Michèle Lamont and Laurent Thévenot, 213–28. New York: Cambridge University Press.

Čapek, Stella M., and John Ingram Gilderbloom. 1992. *Community versus Commodity: Tenants and the American City.* Albany: State University of New York Press.

Cefaï, Daniel. 2002. "Qu'est-Ce Qu'une Arène Publique?: Quelques Pistes dans une Perspective Pragmatiste." In *L'héritage du pragmatisme: conflits d'urbanité et épreuves de civisme,* edited by Daniel Cefaï and Isaac Joseph, 51–82. Paris: Editions de l'aube / Centre culturel international de Cerisy-la-Salle.

———. 2015. "Outreach Work in Paris: A Moral Ethnography of Social Work and Nursing with Homeless People." *Human Studies* 38 (1): 137–56.

Cefaï, Daniel, and Edouard Gardella. 2011. *L'urgence sociale en action: Ethnographie du Samusocial de Paris.* Paris: Découverte.

Charles, Camille Zubrinsky. 2003. "The Dynamics of Racial Residential Segregation." *Annual Review of Sociology* 29 (1): 167–207.

Charles, Julien. 2016. *La participation en actes: Enterprise, ville, association.* Paris: Éditions Desclée de Brouwer.

Chaves, Mark, Laura Stephens, and Joseph Galaskiewicz. 2004. "Does Government Funding Suppress Nonprofits' Political Activity?" *American Sociological Review* 69 (2): 292–316.

Checker, Melissa. 2005. *Polluted Promises: Environmental Racism and the Search for Justice in a Southern Town.* New York: NYU Press.

Cicourel, Aaron. 1993. "Aspects of Structural and Processual Theories of Knowledge." In *Bourdieu: Critical Perspectives,* edited by Craig Calhoun, Edward LiPuma, and Moishe Postone, 89–115. New York: Polity.

Citroni, Sebastiano. 2015. *Inclusive Togetherness: A Comparative Ethnography of Cultural Associations Making Milan Sociable.* Brescia: Editrice La Scuola.

Citroni, Sebastiano, and Paul Lichterman. 2017. "Cultural Entrepreneurialism for Civic Causes in Milan and Los Angeles." *Etnografia e Ricerca Qualitativa* 3:471–85.

Clemens, Elisabeth S. 1996. "Organizational Form as Frame: Collective Identity and Political Strategy in the American Labor Movement, 1880–1920." In *Comparative Perspectives on Social Movements,* edited by Doug McAdam, John D. McCarthy, and Mayer N. Zald, 205–26. New York: Cambridge University Press.

———. 1997. *The People's Lobby: Organizational Innovation and the Rise of Interest Group Politics in the United States, 1890–1925.* Chicago: University of Chicago Press.

———. 2006. "The Constitution of Citizens: Political Theories of Nonprofit Organizations." In *The Nonprofit Sector: A Research Handbook,* edited by Walter W. Powell and Richard Steinberg, 207–20. New Haven, CT: Yale University Press.

Clemens, Elisabeth S., and Doug Guthrie. 2010. *Politics and Partnerships: The Role of Voluntary Associations in America's Political Past and Present.* Chicago: University of Chicago Press.

Clifford, Scott, and Spencer Piston. 2017. "Explaining Public Support for Counterproductive Homelessness Policy: The Role of Disgust." *Political Behavior* 39 (2): 503–25.

Cohen, Jean L., and Andrew Arato. 1992. *Civil Society and Political Theory.* Cambridge, MA: MIT Press.

Cress, Daniel M., and David A. Snow. 2000. "The Outcomes of Homeless Mobilization: The Influence of Organization, Disruption, Political Mediation, and Framing." *American Journal of Sociology* 105 (4): 1063–104.

Crigler, Ann, Nina Eliasoph, Paul Lichterman, and Chris Weare. 2007. "The Dynamics of Civic Relationships: A Proposal for Strengthening Qualitative Research through Methodological Innovation and Integration." Proposal submitted to the National Science Foundation, Grant #SES-0719760, Washington, DC (awarded July 2007).

Dasgupta, Kushan. 2013. "Mapping Group Identity in Community-Based Labor Advocacy." Paper presented at the annual meeting of the American Sociological Association, New York.

Dasgupta, Kushan, and Paul Lichterman. 2016. "How a Housing Advocacy Coalition Adds Health: A Culture of Claims-Making." *Social Science and Medicine* 165:255–62.

Davis, Mike. 1990. *City of Quartz: Excavating the Future in Los Angeles.* New York: Verso Books.

Dewey, John. 1922. *Human Nature and Conduct: An Introduction to Social Psychology.* New York: Henry Holt and Company.

———. (1925) 1958. *Experience and Nature.* 2nd edition. New York: Dover Publications.

———. 1927. *The Public and Its Problems.* Athens, OH: Swallow Press.

———. 1938. *Logic: The Theory of Inquiry.* New York: Henry Holt and Co.

———. 1939. *Theory of Valuation.* Chicago: University of Chicago Press.

Diani, Mario. 2003. "Leaders or Brokers?: Positions and Influence in Social Movement Networks." In *Social Movements and Networks: Relational Approaches to Collective Action,* edited by Mario Diani and Doug McAdam, 105–22. New York: Oxford University Press.

Diani, Mario. 2013. "Organizational Fields and Social Movement Dynamics." In *The Future of Social Movement Research: Dynamics, Mechanisms, and Processes,* edited by Jacquelien van Stekelenburg, Conny Roggeband, and Bert Klandermans, 145–68. Minneapolis: University of Minnesota Press.

Diani, Mario, and Ivano Bison. 2004. "Organizations, Coalitions, and Movements." *Theory and Society* 33:281–309.

Diani, Mario, and Doug McAdam, eds. 2003. *Social Movements and Networks: Relational Approaches to Collective Action.* New York: Oxford University Press.

Diani, Mario, and Katia Pilati. 2011. "Interests, Identities and Relations: Drawing Boundaries in Civic Organizational Fields." *Mobilization* 16 (3): 265–82.

DiIulio, John. 2001. "John M. Olin Foundation Lecture on the Moral Foundations of American Democracy." Princeton University, Princeton, NJ, April 27.

DiMassa, Cara Mia. 2008. "L.A.'s Elderly Homeless Population Is Growing." *Los Angeles Times*, March 20.

Doerr, Nicole. 2018. *Political Translation: How Social Movement Democracies Survive.* New York: Cambridge University Press.

Durkheim, Émile. 1957. *Professional Ethics and Civic Morals.* Translated by Cornelia Brookfield. London: Routledge.

Duyvendak, Jan Willem, and Olivier Fillieule. 2015. "Patterned Fluidity: An Interactionist Perspective as a Tool for Exploring Contentious Politics." In *Players and Arenas: The Interactive Dynamics of Protest*, edited by James M. Jasper and Jan Willem Duyvendak, 295–318. Amsterdam: Amsterdam University Press.

Earl, Jennifer. 2004. "The Cultural Consequences of Social Movements." In *The Blackwell Companion to Social Movements*, edited by David Snow, Sarah Soule, and Hanspeter. Kriesi, 508–30. New York: Blackwell.

Edwards, Bob, and Michael W. Foley. 1997. "Social Capital and the Political Economy of Our Discontent." *American Behavioral Scientist* 40 (5): 669–78.

Effler, Erika Summers. 2010. *Laughing Saints and Righteous Heroes: Emotional Rhythms in Social Movement Groups.* Chicago: University of Chicago Press.

Eliasoph, Nina. 1998. *Avoiding Politics: How Americans Produce Apathy in Everyday Life.* New York: Cambridge University Press.

———. 2011. *Making Volunteers: Civic Life after Welfare's End.* Princeton, NJ: Princeton University Press.

Eliasoph, Nina, and Paul Lichterman. 2003. "Culture in Interaction." *American Journal of Sociology* 108 (4): 735–94.

Emerson, Robert, Rachel Fretz, and Linda Shaw. 2011. *Writing Ethnographic Fieldnotes.* Chicago: University of Chicago Press.

Emirbayer, Mustafa. 1997. Manifesto for a Relational Sociology. *American Journal of Sociology* 103 (2): 281–317.

Emirbayer, Mustafa, and Victoria Johnson. 2008. "Bourdieu and Organizational Analysis." *Theory and Society* 37 (1): 1–44.

Epstein, Barbara. 1991. *Political Protest and Cultural Revolution.* Berkeley: University of California Press.

Epstein, Steven. 1995. "The Construction of Lay Expertise: AIDS Activism and the Forging of Credibility in the Reform of Clinical Trials." *Science, Technology, and Human Values* 20 (4): 408–37.

Etzioni, Amitai. 1996. *The New Golden Rule.* New York: Basic Books.

Evens, T. M. S., and Don Handelman, eds. 2006. *The Manchester School: Practice and Ethnographic Praxis in Anthropology.* New York: Berghahn Books.

Ewick, Patricia, and Marc W. Steinberg. 2019. *Beyond Betrayal: The Priest Sex Abuse Crisis, the Voice of the Faithful, and the Process of Collective Identity.* Chicago: University of Chicago Press.

Ferree, Myra Marx, and Beth B. Hess. 1994. *Controversy and Coalition: The New Feminist Movement across Three Decades of Change.* Woodsbridge, CT: Twayne.

Fine, Gary Alan. 1979. "Small Groups and Culture Creation: The Idioculture of Little League Baseball Teams." *American Sociological Review* 44 (5): 733.

———. 1987. *With the Boys: Little League Baseball and Preadolescent Culture.* Chicago: University of Chicago Press.

———. 2010. "The Sociology of the Local: Action and Its Publics." *Sociological Theory* 28 (4): 355–76.

Fisher, Dana. 2006. *Activism, Inc.* Stanford, CA: Stanford University Press.

Fligstein, Neil. 2001. "Social Skill and the Theory of Fields." *Sociological Theory* 19 (2): 105–25.

Fligstein, Neil, and Doug McAdam. 2012. *A Theory of Fields.* Oxford: Oxford University Press.

Foa, Roberto S., and Yascha Mounk. 2016. "The Democratic Disconnect." *Journal of Democracy* 27 (3): 5–17.

Follett, Mary Parker. (1918) 1965. *The New State: Group Organization the Solution of Popular Government.* University Park: Pennsylvania State University Press.

Fraser, Nancy. 1997. *Justice Interruptus: Critical Reflections on the "Postsocialist" Condition.* New York: Routledge.

Freire, Paulo. 1970. *Pedagogy of the Oppressed.* New York: Herder and Herder.

Friedman, Lawrence M. 1966. "Public Housing and the Poor: An Overview." *California Law Review* 54 (2): 642–69.

Fulton, William. 1997. *The Reluctant Metropolis: The Politics of Urban Growth in Los Angeles.* Baltimore: Johns Hopkins University Press.

Fung, Archon, and Erik Olin Wright. 2003. *Deepening Democracy: Institutional Innovations in Empowered Participatory Governance.* New York: Verso.

Gamson, William A. 1975. *The Strategy of Social Protest.* Homewood, IL: Dorsey Press.

Gamson, William A., and Andre Modigliani. 1989. "Media Discourse and Public Opinion on Nuclear Power: A Constructionist Approach." *American Journal of Sociology* 95 (1): 1–37

Ghaziani, Amin, and Delia Baldassarri. 2011. "Cultural Anchors and the Organization of Differences: A Multi-Method Analysis of LGBT Marches on Washington." *American Sociological Review* 76 (2): 179–206.

Gitlin, Todd. 1987. *The Sixties: Years of Hope, Days of Rage.* New York: Bantam Books.

———. 1994. "From Universality to Difference: Notes on the Fragmentation of the Idea of the Left." In *Social Theory and the Politics of Identity,* edited by Craig Calhoun, 150–74. Oxford: Wiley-Blackwell.

———. 1995. *The Twilight of Common Dreams: Why America Is Wracked by Culture Wars.* New York: Metropolitan Books.

Glaeser, Andreas. 2005. "An Ontology for the Ethnographic Analysis of Social Processes: Extending the Extended Case Method." *Social Analysis* 49 (3): 18–47.

———. 2011. *Political Epistemics: The Secret Police, the Opposition, and the End of East German Socialism.* Chicago: University of Chicago Press.

———. 2014. "Hermeneutic Institutionalism: Towards a New Synthesis." *Qualitative Sociology* 37 (2): 207–41.

Glaser, Barney. 1978. *Advances in the Methodology of Grounded Theory: Theoretical Sensitivity.* Mill Valley, CA: Sociology Press

Glaser, Barney, and Anselm Strauss. 1967. *The Discovery of Grounded Theory: Strategies for Qualitative Research.* Chicago: Aldine.

Goetz, Edward G. 2000. "The Politics of Poverty Deconcentration and Housing Demolition." *Journal of Urban Affairs* 22 (2): 157–73.

———. 2003. *Clearing the Way: Deconcentrating the Poor in Urban America.* Washington, DC: Urban Institute Press.

Goffman, Erving. 1961. *Encounters: Two Studies in the Sociology of Interaction*. Indianapolis: Bobbs-Merrill.

———. 1967. *Interaction Ritual: Essays on Face-to-Face Interaction*. Chicago: Aldine.

———. (1974) 1986. *Frame Analysis: An Essay on the Organization of Experience*. Boston: Northeastern University Press.

Goodwin, Jeff, James M. Jasper, and Francesca Polletta. 2000. "The Return of the Repressed: The Fall and Rise of Emotions in Social Movement Theory." *Mobilization* 5 (1): 65–83.

———, eds. 2001. *Passionate Politics: Emotions and Social Movements*. Chicago: University of Chicago Press

Gottlieb, Robert, Regina Freer, Mark Vallianatos, and Peter Dreier. 2005. *The Next Los Angeles: The Struggle for a Livable City*. Berkeley: University of California Press

Gramsci, Antonio. 1971. *Selections from the Prison Notebooks*. Edited by Quintin Hoare and Geoffrey Nowell-Smith. New York: International Publishers.

Gross, Neil. 2009. "A Pragmatist Theory of Social Mechanisms." *American Sociological Review* 74 (3): 358–79.

Guigni, Marco. 1998. "Was it Worth the Effort?: The Outcomes and Consequences of Social Movements." *Annual Review of Sociology* 24:371–93.

———. 2008. "Political, Biographical, and Cultural Consequences of Social Movements." *Sociology Compass* 2/5:1582–600.

Gumperz, John J. 1982a. *Discourse Strategies*. New York: Cambridge University Press.

———, ed. 1982b. *Language and Social Identity*. New York: Cambridge University Press.

Gusfield, Joseph. 1980. *The Culture of Public Problems: Drinking-Driving and the Symbolic Order*. Chicago: University of Chicago Press.

Habermas, Jürgen. 1972. *Knowledge and Human Interests*. New York: Beacon Press.

———. 1975. *Legitimation Crisis*. Boston: Beacon Press.

———. 1984. *The Theory of Communicative Action, Volume 1: Reason and the Rationalization of Society*. Boston: Beacon Press.

———. 1987. *The Theory of Communicative Action, Volume 2: Lifeworld and System: A Critique of Functionalist Reason*. Boston: Beacon Press.

Hall, Peter Dobkin. 1999. "Vital Signs: Organizational Population Trends and Civic Engagement in New Haven, Connecticut, 1850–1998." In *Civic Engagement in American Democracy*, edited by Theda Skocpol and Morris P. Fiorina, 211–48. Washington, DC: Brookings Institution Press.

Hamburger, Jacob. 2018. "Focus: Liberalism and Identity Politics." Tocqueville21. Accessed January 4, 2019, https://tocqueville21.com/focus/focus-liberalism-and-identity-politics/.

Haney, Lynne. 1996. "Homeboys, Babies, Men in Suits: The State and the Reproduction of Male Dominance." *American Sociological Review* 61:759–78.

———. 2010. *Offending Women: Power, Punishment, and the Regulation of Desire*. Berkeley: University of California Press.

Hart, Stephen. 1996. "The Cultural Dimension of Social Movements: A Theoretical Reassessment and Literature Review." *Sociology of Religion* 57 (1):87.

———. 2001. *Cultural Dilemmas of Progressive Politics: Styles of Engagement among Grassroots Activists*. Chicago: University of Chicago Press.

Harvey, David. 1989. "From Managerialism to Entrepreneurialism: The Transformation in Urban Governance in Late Capitalism." *Geografiska Annaler: Series B, Human Geography* 71(1): 3–17.

Heaney, Michael T., and Fabio Rojas. 2014. "Hybrid Activism: Social Movement Mobilization in a Multimovement Environment. *American Journal of Sociology* 119 (4): 1047–103.

Henderson, Karla A., and Jacquelyn Presley. 2003. "Globalization and the Values of Volunteering as Leisure." *World Leisure Journal* 45 (2): 33–37.

Hilgartner, Stephen, and Charles Bosk. 1988. "The Rise and Fall of Social Problems: A Public Arenas Model. *American Journal of Sociology* 94 (1): 53–78.

Holstein, James A., and Gale Miller, eds. 2003. *Challenges and Choices: Constructionist Perspectives on Social Problems*. New York: Aldine de Gruyter.

Honneth, Axel. 1996. *The Struggle for Recognition: The Moral Grammar of Social Conflicts*. Cambridge, MA: MIT Press.

Hua, Ruoyun, Yuxin Hou, and Guosheng Deng. 2016. "Instrumental Civil Rights and Institutionalized Participation in China: A Case Study of Protest in Wukan Village." *VOLUNTAS: International Journal of Voluntary and Nonprofit Organizations* 27 (5): 2131–49.

Hunt, D. Bradford. 2009. *Blueprint for Disaster: The Unraveling of Chicago Public Housing*. Chicago: University of Chicago Press.

Hwang, Jackelyn, and Robert J. Sampson. 2014. "Divergent Pathways of Gentrification: Racial Inequality and the Social Order of Renewal in Chicago Neighborhoods." *American Sociological Review* 79 (4): 726–51.

Ibarra, Peter, and John Kitsuse. 2003. "Claims-Making Discourse and Vernacular Resources." In *Challenges and Choices: Constructionist Perspectives on Social Problems*, edited by Gale Miller and James A. Holstein, 17–50. New York: Aldine de Gruyter.

INCITE!, eds. 2007. *The Revolution Will Not Be Funded*. Cambridge, MA: South End Press.

Jacobs, Jane. 1961. *The Death and Life of Great American Cities*. New York: Random House.

Janowitz, Morris. 1975. "Sociological Theory and Social Control." *American Journal of Sociology* 81 (1): 82–108.

Jasper, James. 1997. *The Art of Moral Protest: Culture, Biography, and Creativity in Social Movements*. Chicago: University of Chicago Press.

———. 2006. *Getting Your Way: Strategic Dilemmas in the Real World*. Chicago: University of Chicago Press.

Joas, Hans. 1996. *The Creativity of Action*. Translated by Jeremy Gaines and Paul Keast. Chicago: University of Chicago Press.

Johnson, Jennifer Steffel, and Emily Talen. 2008. "Affordable Housing in New Urbanist Communities: A Survey of Developers." *Housing Policy Debate* 19 (4): 583–613.

Johnston, Hank, and Bert Klandermans, eds. 1995. *Social Movements and Culture*. Minneapolis: University of Minnesota Press.

Jung, Wooseok, Brayden G. King, and Sarah A. Soule. 2014. "Issue Bricolage: Explaining the Configuration of the Social Movement Sector, 1960–1995." *American Journal of Sociology* 120 (1): 187–225.

Juris, Jeffrey. 2008. *Networking Futures: The Movements against Corporate Globalization*. Durham, NC: Duke University Press.

Kahne, Juliet. 2018. "Gentle Gentrification in the Exceptional City of LA?" In *Handbook of Gentrification Studies*, edited by Loretta Lees and Martin Phillips, 310–28. Cheltenham, UK: Edward Elgar Publishing.

Kane, Anne. 1997. "Theorizing Meaning Construction in Social Movements: Symbolic Structures and Interpretation during the Irish Land War, 1879–1882." *Sociological Theory* 15 (3): 249–76.

Katz, Jack. 2001. "From How to Why: On Luminous Description and Causal Inference in Ethnography (Part I)." *Ethnography* 2 (4): 443–73.

———. 2002. "From How to Why: On Luminous Description and Causal Inference in Ethnography (Part II)." *Ethnography* 3 (1): 63–90.

———. 2015. "Situational Evidence: Strategies for Causal Reasoning from Observational Field Notes." *Sociological Methods and Research* 44 (1): 108–44.

Kautz, Barbara Ehrlich. 2002. "In Defense of Inclusionary Zoning: Successfully Creating Affordable Housing." *University of San Francisco Law Review* 36:971–1032.

Kiang, Peter Nien-chu. 2008. "Crouching Activists, Hidden Scholars." In *Engaging Contradictions: Theory, Politics, and Methods of Activist Scholarship*, edited by Charles R. Hale, 299–318. Berkeley: University of California Press.

Kitschelt, Herbert P. 1986. "Political Opportunity Structures and Political Protest: Anti-Nuclear Movements in Four Democracies." *British Journal of Political Science* 16 (1): 57–85.

Kitsuse, John, and Malcolm Spector. 1973. "Toward a Sociology of Social Problems: Social Conditions, Value-Judgments, and Social Problems." *Social Problems* 20 (4): 407–19.

Kivel, Paul. 2007. "Social Service or Social Change?" In *The Revolution Will Not Be Funded*, edited by INCITE!, 129–50. Cambridge, MA: South End Press.

Klandermans, Bert. 1992. "The Social Construction of Protest and Multiorganizational Fields." In *Frontiers in Social Movement Theory*, edited by Aldon Morris and Carol McClurg Mueller, 77–103. New Haven, CT: Yale University Press.

Koopmans, Ruud, and Paul Statham. 1999. "Political Claims Analysis: Integrating Protest Event and Political Discourse Approaches." *Mobilization* 4 (1): 203–21.

Krackhardt, David, and Martin Kilduff. 2002. "Structure, Culture, and Simmelian Ties in Entrepreneurial Firms." *Social Networks* 24 (3): 279–90.

Krysan, Maria, and Michael Bader. 2007. "Perceiving the Metropolis: Seeing the City through a Prism of Race." *Social Forces* 86 (2): 699–733.

Kuhn, Thomas. 1962. *The Structure of Scientific Revolutions*. Chicago: University of Chicago Press.

Kymlicka, Will. 1995. *Multicultural Citizenship*. New York: Oxford University Press.

Lakatos, Imre, and Alan Musgrave, eds. 1968. *Problems in the Philosophy of Science*. Amsterdam: North-Holland Publishers.

Lakoff, George. 1987. *Women, Fire, and Dangerous Things: What Categories Reveal about the Mind*. Chicago: University of Chicago Press.

Lamont, Michèle. 1992. *Money, Morals, and Manners: The Culture of the French and American Upper-Middle Class*. Chicago: University of Chicago Press.

Lang, Amy, and Daniel Lang/Levitsky, eds. 2012. *Dreaming in Public: Building the Occupy Movement*. Oxford, UK: New Internationalist Publications.

Laraña, Enrique, Hank Johnston, and Joseph R. Gusfield, eds. 1994. *New Social Movements: From Ideology to Identity*. Philadelphia: Temple University Press.

Ledbetter, William H. 1967. "Public Housing: A Social Experiment Seeks Acceptance." *Law and Contemporary Problems* 32 (3): 490–527.

Lee, Barrett A., Sue Hinze Jones, and David W. Lewis. 1990. "Public Beliefs about the Causes of Homelessness." *Social Forces* 69 (1): 253–65.

Lee, Caroline W., Michael McQuarrie, and Edward T. Walker, eds. 2015. *Democratizing Inequalities: Dilemmas of the New Public Participation*. New York: NYU Press.

Levine, Jeremy R. 2017. "The Paradox of Community Power: Cultural Processes and Elite Authority in Participatory Governance." *Social Forces* 95 (3): 1155–79.

Lichterman, Paul. 1995. "Piecing Together Multicultural Community: Cultural Differences in Community Building among Grass-Roots Environmentalists." *Social Problems* 42 (4): 513–34.

———. 1996. *The Search for Political Community: American Activists Reinventing Commitment.* New York: Cambridge University Press.

———. 1999. "Talking Identity in the Public Sphere: Broad Visions and Small Spaces in Sexual Identity Politics." *Theory and Society* 28 (1): 101–41.

———. 2005. *Elusive Togetherness: Church Groups Trying to Bridge America's Divisions.* Princeton, NJ: Princeton University Press.

———. 2006. "Social Capital or Group Style?: Rescuing Tocqueville's Insights on Civic Engagement." *Theory and Society* 35:529–63.

———. 2009. "Social Capacity and the Styles of Group Life: Some Inconvenient Wellsprings of Democracy." *American Behavioral Scientist* 52:846–66.

———. 2012. "Religion in Public Action: From Actors to Settings." *Sociological Theory* 30 (1): 15–36.

———. 2015. "A More Dialogical Community of Inquiry, or, Dredging the Collective Collegial Subconscious." Paper presented at the Pragmatism and Sociology conference, University of Chicago, August 21.

———. 2017. "Interpretive Reflexivity in Ethnography." *Ethnography* 18 (1): 35–45.

Lichterman, Paul, and Kushan Dasgupta. 2020. "From Culture to Claimsmaking." *Sociological Theory*, advanced online publication doi: 10.1177/0735275120947133.

Lichterman, Paul, and Eric Doidy. 2018. "Luttes pour le logement à Paris et Los Angeles. Une comparaison des méthodes de politization." In *De l'autre coté du miroir: Comparaisons franco-américaines*, edited by Daniel Sabbagh and Maud Simonet, 159–72. Rennes: Presses Universitaires de Rennes.

Lichterman, Paul, and Nina Eliasoph. 2014. "Civic Action." *American Journal of Sociology* 120 (3): 798–863.

Lichterman, Paul, and Isaac Ariail Reed. 2015. "Theory and Contrastive Explanation in Ethnography." *Sociological Methods and Research* 44 (4): 585–635.

Lichterman, Paul, Christopher Weare, and Nicole Esparza. 2014. "Culture and Networks in Everyday Interaction: Ambivalent Ties in a Housing Coalition." Paper presented at the American Sociological Association annual conference, San Francisco, CA.

Lichterman, Paul, and Rhys Williams. 2017. "Cultural Challenges for Mainline Protestant Political Progressives." In *Progressive Religion and Social Activism: New Stories about Faith and Politics*, edited by Ruth Braunstein, Todd Nicholas Fuist, and Rhys H. Williams, 117–37. New York: NYU Press.

Liebow, Elliot. 1993. *Tell Them Who I Am: The Lives of Homeless Women.* London: Penguin Books.

Lilla, Mark. 2017. *The Once and Future Liberal: After Identity Politics.* New York: HarperCollins.

Lizardo, Omar. 2017. "Improving Cultural Analysis: Considering Personal Culture in Its Declarative and Nondeclarative Modes." *American Sociological Review* 82 (1): 88–115.

Logan, John, and Harvey L. Molotch. 1987. *Urban Fortunes: The Political Economy of Place.* Berkeley: University of California Press.

Longino, Helen. 1990. *Science as Social Knowledge: Values and Objectivity in Scientific Inquiry.* Princeton, NJ: Princeton University Press.

———. 2002. *The Fate of Knowledge*. Princeton, NJ: Princeton University Press.

Luhtakallio, Eeva. 2012. *Practicing Democracy: Local Activism and Politics in France and Finland*. New York: Palgrave Macmillan.

Luhtakallio, Eeva, and Iddo Tavory. 2018. "Patterns of Engagement: Identities and Social Movement Organizations in Finland and Malawi." *Theory and Society* 47 (2): 151–74.

Martens, Kerstin. 2002. "Mission Impossible?: Defining Nongovernmental Organizations." *Voluntas* 13 (3): 271–85.

Martin, John Levi. 2003. "What Is Field Theory?" *American Journal of Sociology* 109 (1): 1–49.

Marwell, Nicole P. 2007. *Bargaining for Brooklyn: Community Organizations in the Entrepreneurial City*. Chicago: University of Chicago Press.

Massey, Douglas. 2015. "The Legacy of the 1968 Fair Housing Act." *Sociological Forum* 30:571–88.

McAdam, Doug. 1982. *Political Process and the Development of Black Insurgency, 1930–1970*. Chicago: University of Chicago Press.

———. 1988a. *Freedom Summer*. New York: Oxford University Press.

———. 1988b. "Micromobilization Contexts and Recruitment to Activism." *International Social Movement Research* 1:125–54.

———. 2003. "Beyond Structural Analysis: Toward a More Dynamic Understanding of Social Movements." In *Social Movements and Networks: Relational Approaches to Collective Action*, edited by Mario Diani and Doug McAdam, 281–98. New York: Oxford University Press.

McAdam, Doug, John D. McCarthy, and Mayer Zald, eds. 1996. *Comparative Perspectives on Social Movements: Political Opportunities, Mobilizing Structures, and Cultural Framings*. New York: Cambridge University Press.

McAdam, Doug, and Ronnelle Paulsen. 1993. "Specifying the Relationship between Social Ties and Activism." *American Journal of Sociology* 99 (3): 640–67.

McAdam, Doug, Sidney G. Tarrow, and Charles Tilly. 2001. *Dynamics of Contention*. New York: Cambridge University Press.

McCammon, Holly J., Courtney Sanders Muse, Harmony D. Newman, and Teresa M. Terrell. 2007. "Movement Framing and Discursive Opportunity Structures: The Political Successes of the U.S. Women's Jury Movements." *American Sociological Review* 72 (5): 725–49.

McCarthy, John D., and Mayer N. Zald. 1973. *The Trend of Social Movements*. Morristown, NJ: General Learning.

———. 1977. "Resource Mobilization and Social Movements: A Partial Theory." *American Journal of Sociology* 82 (6): 1212–41.

McFarland, Daniel A., and Reuben J. Thomas. 2006. "Bowling Young: How Youth Voluntary Associations Influence Adult Political Participation." *American Sociological Review* 71 (3): 401–25.

McKnight, John. 1995. *The Careless Society: Community and Its Counterfeits*. New York: Basic Books.

McQuarrie, Michael. 2013. "No Contest: Participatory Technologies and the Transformation of Urban Authority." *Public Culture* 25 (1): 143–75.

McRoberts, Omar. 2003. *Streets of Glory: Church and Community in a Black Urban Neighborhood*. Chicago: University of Chicago Press.

Mele, Christopher. 2000. *Selling the Lower East Side: Culture, Real Estate, and Resistance in New York City*. Minneapolis: University of Minnesota Press.

Melucci, Alberto. 1988. "Getting Involved: Identity and Mobilization in Social Movements." In *International Social Movement Research*, edited by Bert Klandermans, Hanspeter Kriesi, and Sidney Tarrow, 1:329–48. Greenwich, CT: JAI Press.

———. 1989. *Nomads of the Present*. Philadelphia: Temple University Press.

Miller, Gale, and James A. Holstein, eds. 1993. *Constructionist Controversies: Issues in Social Problems Theory*. New York: Transaction Publishers.

Minkoff, Debra C. 2002. "The Emergence of Hybrid Organizational Forms: Combining Identity-Based Service Provision and Political Action." *Nonprofit and Voluntary Sector Quarterly* 31 (3): 377–401.

Mische, Ann. 2003. "Cross-Talk in Movements: Reconceiving the Culture-Network Link." In *Social Movements and Networks: Relational Approaches to Collective Action*, edited by Mario Diani and Doug McAdam, 258–80. New York: Oxford University Press.

———. 2008. *Partisan Publics: Communication and Contention across Brazilian Youth Activist Networks*. Princeton, NJ: Princeton University Press.

———. 2009. "Projects and Possibilities: Researching Futures in Action." *Sociological Forum* 24 (3): 694–704.

———. 2011. "Relational Sociology, Culture, and Agency." In *The SAGE Handbook of Social Network Analysis*, edited by John Scott and Peter J. Carrington, 80–97. Thousand Oaks, CA: Sage Publications.

———. Forthcoming. *Futures in Contention: Public Scenarios and Transformative Politics in the Global Arena*.

Morris, Alton D., and Carol McClurg Mueller, eds. 1992. *Frontiers in Social Movement Theory*. New Haven, CT: Yale University Press.

Moseley, Jennifer. 2012. "Keeping the Lights On: How Government Funding Concerns Drive the Advocacy Agenda of Nonprofit Homeless Service Providers." *Journal of Public Administration Research and Theory* 22 (4): 841–66.

Mukhija, Vinit, Lara Regus, Sara Slovin, and Ashok Das. 2010. "Can Inclusionary Zoning Be an Effective and Efficient Housing Policy?: Evidence from Los Angeles and Orange Counties." *Journal of Urban Affairs* 32 (2): 229–52.

Munkres, Susan. 2003. "Activists for Others?: How Privileged People Build Alliance Movements." PhD diss., University of Wisconsin at Madison.

Novotny, Patrick. 2000. *Where We Live, Work, and Play: The Environmental Justice Movement and the Struggle for a New Environmentalism*. Westport, CT: Praeger Publishers.

Noy, Darren. 2009. "When Framing Fails: Ideas, Influence, and Resources in San Francisco's Homeless Policy Field." *Social Problems* 56 (2): 223–42.

Obach, Brian K. 2004. *Labor and the Environmental Movement: The Quest for Common Ground*. Cambridge, MA: MIT Press.

Oliver, Pamela, and Hank Johnston. 2000. "What a Good Idea!: Ideologies and Frames in Social Movement Research." *Mobilization* 5 (1): 37–54.

Pacewicz, Josh. 2015. "Playing the Neoliberal Game: Why Community Leaders Left Party Politics to Partisan Activists." *American Journal of Sociology* 121 (3): 826–81.

Parkin, Frank. 1968. *Middle-Class Radicalism: The Social Bases of the British Campaign for Nuclear Disarmament*. New York: Manchester University Press.

Pascale, Celine-Marie. 2005. "There's No Place Like Home: The Discursive Creation of Homelessness." *Cultural Studies ↔ Critical Methodologies* 5 (2): 250–68.

Pattillo-McCoy, Mary. 1998. "Church Culture as a Strategy of Action in the Black Community." *American Sociological Review* 63 (6): 767–784.

Peirce, Charles S. (1868) 1992. "Some Consequences of Four Incapacities." In *The Essential Peirce: Selected Philosophical Writings*, edited by Nathan Houser and Christian Kloesel, 1:28–55. Bloomington: Indiana University Press.

———. (1877) 1992. "The Fixation of Belief." In *The Essential Peirce: Selected Philosophical Writings*, edited by Nathan Houser and Christian Kloesel, 1:109–23. Bloomington: Indiana University Press.

Perez, Gina. 2004. "Gentrification, Intrametropolitan Migration, and the Politics of Place." In *The Gentrification Debates*, edited by Japonica Brown-Saracino, 319–30. New York: Routledge.

Pettinicchio, David. 2012. "Institutional Activism: Reconsidering the Insider/Outsider Dichotomy." *Sociology Compass* 6 (6): 499–510.

———. 2019. *Politics of Empowerment: Disability Rights and the Cycle of American Policy*. Stanford, CA: Stanford University Press.

Piven, Frances Fox, and Richard A. Cloward. 1979. *Poor People's Movements: Why They Succeed, How They Fail*. New York: Vintage Books.

Polletta, Francesca. 2002. *Freedom Is an Endless Meeting*. Chicago: University of Chicago Press.

———. 2006. *It Was Like a Fever: Storytelling in Protest and Politics*. Chicago: University of Chicago Press.

Polletta, Francesca, and M. Kai Ho. 2006. "Frames and Their Consequences." In *The Oxford Handbook of Contextual Political Analysis*, edited by Robert E. Goodin and Charles Tilly, 189–209. New York: Oxford University Press.

Polletta, Francesca, and James M. Jasper. 2001. "Collective Identity and Social Movements." *Annual Review of Sociology* 27 (1): 283–305.

Poppendieck, Janet. 1999. *Emergency Food and the End of Entitlement*. New York: Penguin Books.

Purcell, Mark. 2000. "The Decline of the Political Consensus for Urban Growth: Evidence from Los Angeles." *Journal of Urban Affairs* 22 (1): 85–100.

Putnam, Robert D. 1995. "Bowling Alone: America's Declining Social Capital." *Journal of Democracy* 6:65–78.

———. 1996. "Strange Disappearance of Civic America." *American Prospect* 7, no. 24 (December 1).

———. 2000. *Bowling Alone: The Collapse and Revival of American Community*. New York: Simon and Schuster.

Putnam, Robert D., and Lewis Feldstein. 2003. *Better Together: Restoring the American Community*. New York: Simon and Schuster.

Quillian, Lincoln, and Devah Pager. 2001. "Black Neighbors, Higher Crime?: The Role of Racial Stereotypes in Evaluations of Neighborhood Crime." *American Journal of Sociology* 107 (3): 717–67.

Ragin, Charles, and Howard Becker, eds. 1992. *What Is a Case?: Exploring the Foundations of Social Inquiry*. New York: Cambridge University Press.

Ray, Raka. 1999. *Fields of Protest: Women's Movements in India*. Minneapolis: University of Minnesota Press.

Reed, Adolph L. 1986. *The Jesse Jackson Phenomenon: The Crisis of Purpose in Afro-American Politics*. New Haven, CT: Yale University Press.

Reed, Isaac. 2011. *Interpretation and Social Knowledge: On the Use of Theory in the Human Sciences*. Chicago: University of Chicago Press.

Reed, Isaac, and Paul Lichterman. 2017. "Towards a Pragmatist Sociological History." Paper presented at the conference Sociology and Pragmatism: Renewing the Conversation, Radcliffe Institute for Advanced Study, Harvard University, June.

Reed, Isaac, and Paul Lichterman. Forthcoming. "Pragmatist Comparative-Historical Sociology." In *Agency, Inquiry, and Democracy: The New Pragmatist Social Science*, edited by Isaac Reed, Christopher Winship, and Neil Gross.

Rochon, Thomas R., and David S. Meyer, eds. 1997. *Coalitions and Political Movements: The Lessons of the Nuclear Freeze*. Boulder, CO: Lynne Rienner.

Rose, Fred. 2000. *Coalitions across the Class Divide: Lessons from the Labor, Peace, and Environmental Movements*. Ithaca, NY: Cornell University Press.

Roth, Benita. 2010. "'Organizing One's Own' as Good Politics: Second Wave Feminists and the Meaning of Coalition." In *Strategic Alliances: Coalition Building and Social Movements*, edited by Nella Van Dyke and Holly J. McCammon, 99–118. Minneapolis: University of Minnesota Press.

Rucht, Dieter. 2004. "Movement Allies, Adversaries, and Third Parties." In *The Blackwell Companion to Social Movements*, edited by David Snow, Sarah Soule, and Hanspeter Kriesi, 197–216. Malden, MA: Blackwell.

Rudrappa, Sharmila. 2004. *Ethnic Routes to Becoming American: Indian Immigrants and the Cultures of Citizenship*. New Brunswick, NJ: Rutgers University Press.

Saegert, Susan, J. Phillip Thompson, and Mark R. Warren. 2001. *Social Capital and Poor Communities*. New York: Russell Sage Foundation.

Saito, Leland T. 2012. "How Low-Income Residents Can Benefit from Urban Development: The LA Live Community Benefits Agreement." *City and Community* 11 (2): 129–50.

Saito, Leland. 2019. "Urban Development and the Growth with Equity Framework: The National Football League Stadium in Downtown Los Angeles." *Urban Affairs Review* 55 (5): 1370–1401.

Sampson, Robert J. 1999. "What 'Community' Supplies." In *Urban Problems and Community Development*, edited by Ronald F. Ferguson and William T. Dickens, 241–92. Washington, DC: Brookings Institution Press.

———. 2012. *Great American City: Chicago and the Enduring Neighborhood Effect*. Chicago: University of Chicago Press.

Sampson, Robert J., Doug McAdam, Heather MacIndoe, and Simón Weffer-Elizondo. 2005. "Civil Society Reconsidered: The Durable Nature and Community Structure of Collective Civic Action." *American Journal of Sociology* 111 (3): 673–714.

Sampson, Robert J., Jeffrey Morenoff, and Felton Earls. 1999. "Beyond Social Capital: Spatial Dynamics of Collective Efficacy for Children." *American Journal of Sociology* 64 (5): 633–60.

Schlozman, Kay Lehman, Sidney Verba, and Henry E. Brady. 2013. *The Unheavenly Chorus: Unequal Political Voice and the Broken Promise of American Democracy*. Princeton, NJ: Princeton University Press.

Schudson, Michael. 1998. *The Good Citizen: A History of American Civic Life*. New York: Simon and Schuster.

Scott, James C. 1998. *Seeing Like a State: How Certain Schemes to Improve the Human Condition Have Failed*. New Haven, CT: Yale University Press.

Sewell, William H., Jr. 1992. "A Theory of Structure: Duality, Agency, and Transformation." *American Journal of Sociology*, 1–29.

Silver, Daniel, and Terry Clark. 2016. *Scenescapes: How Qualities of Place Shape Social Life*. Chicago: University of Chicago Press.

Sirianni, Carmen, and Lewis A. Friedland. 2001. *Civic Innovation in America: Community Empowerment, Public Policy, and the Movement for Civic Renewal*. Berkeley: University of California Press.

Skocpol, Theda. 1999. "How Americans Became Civic." In *Civic Engagement in American Democracy*, edited by Theda Skocpol and Morris P. Fiorina, 27–80. Washington, DC: Brookings Institution Press.

Skocpol, Theda. 2002. "United States: From Membership to Advocacy." In *Democracies in Flux: The Evolution of Social Capital in Contemporary Society*, edited by Robert D. Putnam, 103–36. New York: Oxford University Press.

Skocpol, Theda, and Morris P. Fiorina, eds. 1999. *Civic Engagement in American Democracy*. Washington, DC: Brookings Institution Press.

Small, Mario. 2004. *Villa Victoria: The Transformation of Social Capital in a Boston Barrio*. Chicago: University of Chicago Press.

Smelser, Neil. 1962. *Theory of Collective Behavior*. New York: Free Press.

Smilde, David, and Daniel Hellinger, eds. 2011. *Venezuela's Bolivarian Democracy: Participation, Politics, and Culture under Chávez*. Durham, NC: Duke University Press.

Smith, Andrea. 2007. "Introduction: The Revolution Will Not Be Funded." In *The Revolution Will Not Be Funded*, edited by INCITE!, 1–18. Cambridge, MA: South End Press.

Smith, Christian. 1996. *Resisting Reagan: The U.S. Central America Peace Movement*. Chicago: University of Chicago Press.

———. 2016. "The Conceptual Incoherence of 'Culture' in American Sociology." *American Sociologist* 47 (4): 388–415.

Smith, Neil. 1996. *The New Urban Frontier: Gentrification and the Revanchist City*. New York: Routledge.

———. 2002. "New Globalism, New Urbanism: Gentrification as Global Urban Strategy." *Antipode* 34 (3): 427–50.

Smith, Philip, ed. 1998. *The New American Cultural Sociology*. New York: Cambridge University Press.

Smith, Steven R., and Michael Lipsky. 1993. *Nonprofits for Hire: The Welfare State in the Age of Contracting*. Cambridge, MA: Harvard University Press.

Snow, David. 2004. "Framing Processes, Ideology, and Discursive Fields." In *The Blackwell Companion to Social Movements*, edited by David Snow, Sarah Soule, and Hanspeter Kriesi, 380–412. Malden, MA: Blackwell Publishing.

———. 2008. "Elaborating the Discursive Contexts of Framing: Discursive Fields and Spaces." *Studies in Symbolic Interaction* 30:3–28.

Snow, David, and Robert Benford. 1988. "Ideology, Frame Resonance, and Participant Mobilization." *International Social Movement Research* 1 (1): 197–217.

Snow, David, Robert Benford, Holly McCammon, Lyndi Hewitt, and Scott Fitzgerald. 2014. "The Emergence, Development, and Future of the Framing Perspective: 25+ Years since 'Frame Alignment.'" *Mobilization* 19 (1): 23–46.

Snow, David, E. Burke Rochford, Steven Worden, and Robert Benford. 1986. "Frame Alignment Processes, Micromobilization, and Movement Participation." *American Sociological Review* 51 (4): 464.

Snow, David A., Sarah Soule, and Hanspeter Kriesi, eds. 2004. *The Blackwell Companion to Social Movements*. Malden, MA: Blackwell.

Somers, Margaret. 2005. "Beware Trojan Horses Bearing Social Capital: How Privatization Turned Solidarity into a Bowling Team." In *The Politics of Method in the Human Sciences*, edited by George Steinmetz, 233–74. Durham, NC: Duke University Press.

Spillman, Lyn. 1995. "Culture, Social Structures, and Discursive Fields." *Current Perspectives in Social Theory* 15 (1): 129–54.

———. 1997. *Nation and Commemoration: Creating National Identities in the United States and Australia*. New York: Cambridge University Press.

———. 2012. *Solidarity in Strategy: Making Business Meaningful in American Trade Associations*. Chicago: University of Chicago Press.

Staggenborg, Suzanne. 1986. "Coalition Work in the Pro-Choice Movement: Organizational and Environmental Opportunities and Obstacles." *Social Problems* 33 (5): 374–90.

Stall, Susan, and Randy Stoecker. 1998. "Community Organizing or Organizing Community: Gender and the Crafts of Empowerment." *Gender and Society* 12 (6): 729–56.

Stavo-Debauge, Joan, and Danny Trom. 2004. "Le pragmatisme et son public à l'épreuve du terrain. Penser avec Dewey contre Dewey." In *La croyance et l'enquête. Aux sources du pragmatism*, edited by Bruno Karsenti and Louis Quéré, 195–226. Paris: Raisons Pratiques.

Stebbins, Robert A. 1996. "Volunteering: A Serious Leisure Perspective." *Nonprofit and Voluntary Sector Quarterly* 25 (2): 211–24.

Steckler, Beth, and Adam Garcia. 2008. *Affordability Matters: A Look at Housing Construction and Affordability in Los Angeles*. Los Angeles: Livable Places.

Steinberg, Marc. 1998. "Tilting the Frame: Considerations on Collective Action Framing from a Discursive Turn." *Theory and Society* 27 (6): 845–72.

———. 1999. "The Talk and Back Talk of Collective Action: A Dialogic Analysis of Repertoires of Discourse among Nineteenth-Century English Cotton Spinners." *American Journal of Sociology* 105 (3): 736–80.

———. 2002. "Toward a More Dialogic Analysis of Social Movement Culture." In *Social Movements: Identity, Culture, and the State*, edited by David S. Meyer, Nancy Whittier, and Belinda Robnett, 208–25. New York: Oxford University Press.

Steinberg, Walter, and W. Powell Richard, eds. 2006. *The Nonprofit Sector: A Research Handbook*. New Haven, CT: Yale University Press.

Strauss, Anselm. 1987. *Qualitative Analysis for Social Scientists*. New York: Cambridge University Press.

Strauss, Anselm, and Juliet Corbin. 1991. *Basics of Qualitative Research: Techniques and Procedures for Developing Grounded Theory*. Newbury Park, CA: Sage.

Stuart, Forrest. 2011. "Constructing Police Abuse after Rodney King: How Skid Row Residents and the Los Angeles Police Department Contest Video Evidence." *Law and Social Inquiry* 36 (2): 327–53.

Swedberg, Richard. 2014. *The Art of Social Theory*. Princeton, NJ: Princeton University Press.

Swidler, Ann. 1986. "Culture in Action: Symbols and Strategies." *American Sociological Review* 51 (2): 273–286.

———. 2001. *Talk of Love: How Culture Matters*. Chicago: University of Chicago Press.

Tajfel, Henri, and John Turner. 1986. "The Social Identity Theory of Intergroup Behavior." In *Psychology of Intergroup Relations*, edited by Stephen Worchel and William G. Austin, 7–24. Chicago: Nelson Hall.

Talpin, Julien. 2017. "The Americanization of French Social Movements?: Community Organizing and Its Discontents in the *banlieues*." *Metropolitics*, June 29. https://www.metropolitiques.eu/The-Americanization-of-French.html.

Tarrow, Sidney. 1994. *Power in Movement: Social Movements, Collective Action, and Politics*. New York: Cambridge University Press.

Tavory, Iddo, and Nina Eliasoph. 2013. "Coordinating Futures: Toward a Theory of Anticipation." *American Journal of Sociology* 118 (4): 908–42.

Taylor, Charles. 1993. "To Follow a Rule." In *Bourdieu: Critical Perspectives*, edited by Craig Calhoun, Edward LiPuma, and Moishe Postone, 45–60. Chicago: University of Chicago Press.

———. 1994. "The Politics of Recognition." In *Multiculturalism: Examining the Politics of Recognition*, edited by Amy Gutmann, 25–74. Princeton, NJ: Princeton University Press.

Taylor, Verta, and Nancy Whittier. 1992. "Collective Identity in Social Movement." In *Frontiers in Social Movement Theory*, edited by Aldon D. Morris and Carol McClurg Mueller, 104–30. New Haven, CT: Yale University Press.

Taylor, Verta, and Nicole Raeburn. 1995. "Identity Politics as High-Risk Activism: Career Consequences for Lesbian, Gay, and Bisexual Sociologists." *Social Problems* 42 (2): 252–73.

Thévenot, Laurent. 2006. *L'action au pluriel: sociologie des régimes d'engagement*. Paris: Éditions La Découverte.

Thompson, James D. 1967. *Organizations in Action: Social Science Bases of Administrative Theory*. New York: McGraw-Hill.

Timmermans, Stefan, and Iddo Tavory. 2012. "Theory Construction in Qualitative Research: From Grounded Theory to Abductive Analysis." *Sociological Theory* 30 (3): 167–86.

Tocqueville, Alexis de. (1835) 1969. *Democracy in America*. New York: Harper Perennial Modern Classics.

Trumpy, Alexa J. 2016. "'I Hate It, but It Still Sounds Good': Collective Identity and the Evaluation of Oppositional Frame Resonance." *Social Movement Studies* 15 (2): 164–79.

United States Interagency Council on Homelessness (USICH). 2015. *Opening Doors: Federal Strategic Plan to Prevent and End Homelessness*. Washington, DC: United States Interagency Council on Homelessness.

Van Dyke, Nella. 2003. "Crossing Movement Boundaries: Factors That Facilitate Coalition Protest by American College Students, 1930–1990." *Social Problems* 50 (2): 226–50.

Van Dyke, Nella, and Holly J. McCammon, eds. 2010. *Strategic Alliances: Coalition Building and Social Movements*. Minneapolis: University of Minnesota Press.

Verba, Sidney, Kay Lehman Schlozman, and Henry E. Brady. 1995. *Voice and Equality: Civic Voluntarism in American Politics*. Cambridge, MA: Harvard University Press.

Verhoeven, Imrat, and Evelien Tonkens. 2013. "Talking Active Citizenship: Framing Welfare State Reform in England and the Netherlands." *Social Policy and Society* 12 (3): 415–26.

von Hoffman, Alexander. 2000. "A Study in Contradictions: The Origins and Legacy of the Housing Act of 1949." *Housing Policy Debate* 11 (2): 299–326.

Walgrave, Stefaan, Jonas Lefevere, and Anke Tresch. 2012. "The Associative Dimension of Issue Ownership." *Public Opinion Quarterly* 76 (4): 771–82.

Walker, Edward T. 2014. *Grassroots for Hire: Public Affairs Consultants in American Democracy.* New York: Cambridge University Press.

Walzer, Michael. 1992. "The Civil Society Argument." In *Dimensions of Radical Democracy*, edited by Chantal Mouffe, 89–107. London: Verso.

Wardrip, Keith. 2009. *Housing Affordability: Trends for Working Households.* Washington, DC: Center for Housing Policy.

Warren, Mark R. 2001. *Dry Bones Rattling: Community Building to Revitalize American Democracy.* Princeton, NJ: Princeton University Press.

Weare, Christopher, Nicole Esparza, and Paul Lichterman. 2011. "Collaboration and Culture: Organizational Style as a Cause and Consequence of Collaborative Networks." Paper presented at the Fourth Annual Political Networks Conference, Ann Arbor, MI, June.

Weare, Christopher, Paul Lichterman, and Nicole Esparza. 2014. "Collaboration and Culture: Organizational Culture and the Dynamics of Collaborative Policy Networks." *Policy Studies Journal* 42 (4): 590–619.

Whalen, Jack, and Richard Flacks. 1989. *Beyond the Barricades: The Sixties Generation Grows Up.* Philadelphia: Temple University Press.

Wherry, Frederick. 2011. *The Philadelphia Barrio: The Arts, Branding, and Neighborhood Transformation.* Chicago: University of Chicago Press.

Whitford, Josh. 2002. "Pragmatism and the Untenable Dualism of Means and Ends: Why Rational Choice Theory Does Not Deserve Paradigmatic Privilege." *Theory and Society* 31:325–63.

Whittier, Nancy. 2009. *The Politics of Child Sexual Abuse: Emotion, Social Movements, and the State.* New York: Oxford University Press.

Williams, Rhys. 1995. "Constructing the Public Good: Social Movements and Cultural Resources." *Social Problems* 42 (1): 124–44.

———. 2004. "The Cultural Contexts of Collective Action: Constraints, Opportunities, and the Symbolic Life of Social Movements." In *The Blackwell Companion to Social Movements*, edited by David Snow, Sarah Soule, and Hanspeter Kriesi, 91–115. Malden, MA: Blackwell Publishing.

Williams, Rhys, and Robert Benford. 2000. "Two Faces of Collective Action Frames: A Theoretical Consideration." *Research in Social Movements, Conflict, and Change* 20:127–51.

Wilson, John, and Marc Musick. 1999. "The Effects of Volunteering on the Volunteer." *Law and Contemporary Problems* 62 (4): 141–168.

Wolfe, Alan. 1989. *Whose Keeper?: Social Science and Moral Obligation.* Berkeley: University of California Press.

Wolf-Powers, Laura. 2010. "Community Benefits Agreements and Local Government: A Review of Recent Evidence." *Journal of the American Planning Association* 76 (2): 141–59.

Wood, Richard L. 2002. *Faith in Action: Religion, Race, and Democratic Organizing in America.* Chicago: University of Chicago Press.

Wood, Richard L., Mariah Davis, and Amelia Rouse. 2004. "Diving into Quicksand: Program Implementation and Police Subcultures." In *Community Policing: Can It Work?*, edited by Wesley G. Skogan, 136–61. Belmont, CA: Wadsworth.

Wu, Daniel. 2012. "Reimagining and Restructuring the Figueroa Corridor, 1990–2005: Growth Politics, Policy, and Displacement." *Race, Gender, and Class* 19 (1–2): 244–65.

Wuthnow, Robert. 1989. *Communities of Discourse: Ideology and Social Structure in the Reformation, the Enlightenment, and European Socialism.* Cambridge, MA: Harvard University Press.

———. 1991a. *Acts of Compassion: Caring for Others and Helping Ourselves.* Princeton, NJ: Princeton University Press.

———, ed. 1991b. *Between States and Markets: The Voluntary Sector in Comparative Perspectives.* Princeton, NJ: Princeton University Press.

———. 1998a. *Loose Connections: Joining Together in America's Fragmented Communities.* Cambridge, MA: Harvard University Press.

———. 1998b. *Poor Richard's Principle: Recovering the American Dream through the Moral Dimension of Work, Business, and Money.* Princeton, NJ: Princeton University Press.

———. 2002. "Bridging the Privileged and the Marginalized?" In *Democracies in Flux: The Evolution of Social Capital in Contemporary Society*, edited by Robert D. Putnam, 59–102. Oxford: Oxford University Press.

Wyly, Elvin K., and Daniel J. Hammel. 2004. "Gentrification, Segregation, and Discrimination in the American Urban System." *Environment and Planning A* 36 (7): 1215–41.

Xu, Bin. 2017. *The Politics of Compassion: The Sichuan Earthquake and Civic Engagement in China.* Stanford, CA: Stanford University Press.

Young, Iris Marion. 1990. *Justice and the Politics of Difference.* Princeton, NJ: Princeton University Press.

Zhou, Mujun. 2018. "Fissures between Human Rights Advocates and NGO Practitioners in China's Civil Society: A Case Study of the Equal Education Campaign, 2009–2013." *China Quarterly* 234:486–505.

Zubrzycki, Genevive. 2001. "'We, the Polish Nation': Ethnic and Civic Visions of Nationhood in Post-Communist Constitutional Debates." *Theory and Society* 30 (5): 629–68.

Zukin, Sharon. 1995. *The Cultures of Cities.* New York: Blackwell.

INDEX

Page numbers with a *t* indicate tables.

A NOTE ON THE TYPE

This book has been composed in Arno, an Old-style serif typeface in the classic Venetian tradition, designed by Robert Slimbach at Adobe.